Six Days in June

ALSO BY ERIC HAMMEL

76 Hours

Chosin

The Root

Ace

Duel for the Golan

Guadalcanal: Starvation Island

Guadalcanal: The Carrier Battles

Guadalcanal: Decision at Sea

Munda Trail

The Jolly Rogers

Khe Sanh

First Across the Rhine

Lima-6

Ambush Valley

Fire in the Streets

Aces Against Japan

Six Days in June

How Israel Won the 1967 Arab-Israeli War

Eric Hammel

Charles Scribner's Sons
NEW YORK
Maxwell Macmillan Canada
TORONTO
Maxwell Macmillan International
NEW YORK   OXFORD   SINGAPORE   SYDNEY

Charles Scribner's Sons	Maxwell Macmillan Canada, Inc.
Macmillan Publishing Company	1200 Eglinton Avenue East
866 Third Avenue	Suite 200
New York, NY 10022	Don Mills, Ontario M3C 3N1

Macmillan Publishing Company is part of the Maxwell Communication
Group of Companies.

Library of Congress Cataloging-in-Publication Data
Hammel, Eric M.
    Six days in June : how Israel won the 1967 Arab-Israeli War / Eric
Hammel.
        p.   cm.
    Includes bibliographical references and index.
    ISBN 0-684-19390-6
    1. Israel-Arab War, 1967—Campaigns.   2. Israel-Arab War, 1967—
Causes.   3. Israel—History, Military.   I. Title.
DS127.H323   1992
956.04'6—dc20   92-4596
                                                                    CIP

Macmillan Books are available at special discounts for bulk
purchases for sales promotions, premiums, fund-raising, or
educational use. For details, contact:

Special Sales Director
Macmillan Publishing Company
866 Third Avenue
New York, NY 10022

10 9 8 7 6 5 4 3 2 1

Printed in the United States of America

In memory of my grandfathers,

MAX HAMMEL

who died at the hands of Nazis, and

SAMUEL LEVE

who helped to build the Promised Land

Contents

Glossary & Guide to Abbreviations

ADM	Admiral
ALOUETTE	French-made two-seat scout helicopter
AML	French-made scout car with 90mm main gun
AMX-13	French-made light tank with 75mm high-velocity main gun
APC	Armored personnel carrier
BAZOOKA	U.S.-made shoulder-fired rocket launcher
BDE	Brigade
BN	Battalion
BIR	Spring (i.e., oasis)
BRIG.	Brigadier
BRIGEN	Brigadier General
CENTURION	British-made main battle tank
COL	Colonel
FATAH	Movement for the National Liberation of Palestine
FOUGA-MAGISTER	French-made jet trainer/attack aircraft
FRENCH SHERMAN	French-modified (M-51) Sherman tank with 75mm high-velocity main gun
GEN	General
GHQ	General Headquarters
GOC	General Officer Commanding

HAGANAH	Jewish pre-Independence self-defense force
HQ	Headquarters
HUNTER	British-made Hawker jet fighter-bomber
IAF	Israeli Air Force
IDF	Israel Defense Force
IL-14	Soviet-made jet transport
IL-28	Soviet-made light twin-jet attack bomber
JS-3	Soviet-made Josef Stalin 122mm artillery tank
JSU-152	Soviet-made Josef Stalin 152mm self-propelled artillery
KINNERET	Sea of Galilee
KNESSET	Israeli parliament
LAAGER	Armored or vehicular defensive deployment
LTCOL	Lieutenant Colonel
LTGEN	Lieutenant General
M-3	U.S.-made halftrack
M-4	U.S.-made Sherman medium tank
M-47/M-48	U.S.-made Patton main battle tank
M-51	French-modified high-velocity 75mm Sherman tank (French Sherman)
M-51HV	Israeli-modified Super Sherman tank with 105mm medium-velocity main gun
MAJGEN	Major General
MIG	Soviet-made jet fighter-interceptor
MIRAGE	French-made jet fighter-interceptor
MUSTANG	U.S.-made P-51 piston fighter
MYSTÈRE	French-made jet fighter-bomber
NCO	Non-commissioned officer
NORATLAS	French-made piston transport aircraft
OURAGAN	French-made jet ground-attack aircraft

P-51	U.S.-made Mustang piston fighter
PALMACH	Jewish pre-Independence "pioneer" shock force
PATTON	U.S.-made M-47 or M-48 main battle tank
PLA	Palestine Liberation Army
PLO	Palestine Liberation Organization
RCN	Reconnaissance
RPG	Soviet-made rocket-propelled grenade
S-55/S-58	U.S.-made medium cargo/transport helicopter
SABRA	Native-born Israeli
SHERMAN	U.S.-made M-4 medium tank and variants
SP	Self-propelled (artillery)
SUPER FRELON	French-made heavy cargo/personnel helicopter
SUPER MYSTÈRE	French-made jet ground-attack aircraft
SUPER SHERMAN	Israeli-modified M-51HV Sherman tank with 105mm medium-velocity main gun
SU-7	Soviet-made jet ground-attack aircraft
SU-100	Soviet-made tracked 100mm gun carrier
T-34	Soviet-made medium tank with 85mm main gun
T-54/T-55	Soviet-made main battle tank with 100mm main gun
TEL	Hill, usually an occupation site
TU-16	Soviet-made jet medium bomber
UGDAH	Israeli divisional task force
UGDOT	Israeli divisional task forces (plural)
U.N.	United Nations
UNEF	United Nations Emergency Force
UNTSO	United Nations Truce Supervision Organization
UZI	Israeli 9mm submachine gun
VAUTOUR	French-made light attack bomber
WADI	Dry stream bed
ZAHAL	Israel Defense Force (*Zvah Haganah L'Yisrael*)

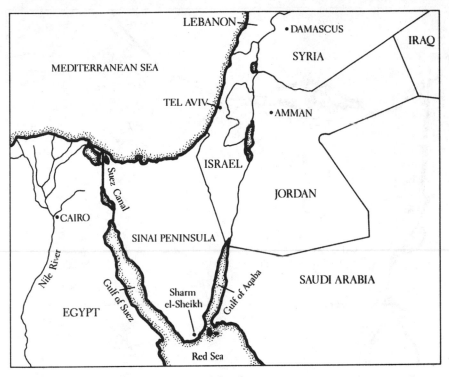

Map 1
THE WAR ZONE

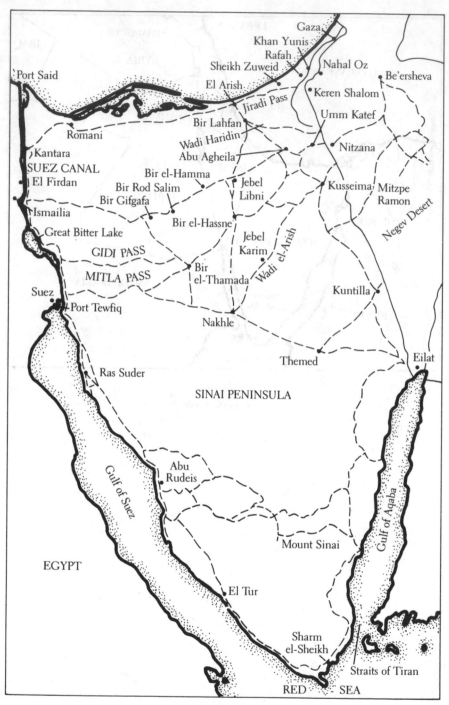

Map 2

SINAI

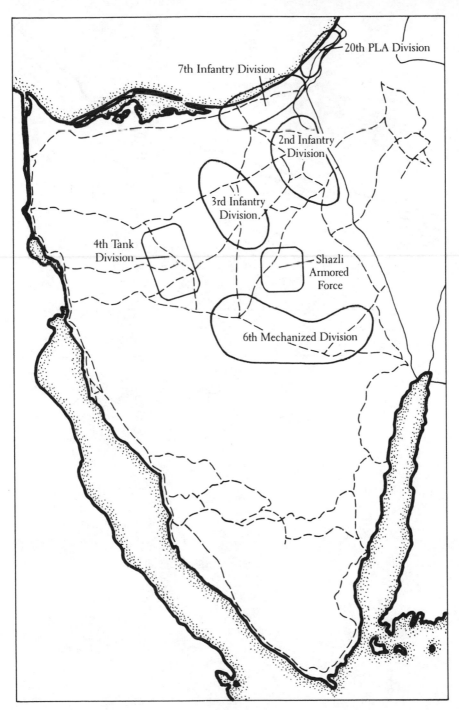

Map 3

INITIAL EGYPTIAN ARMY POSITIONS IN SINAI

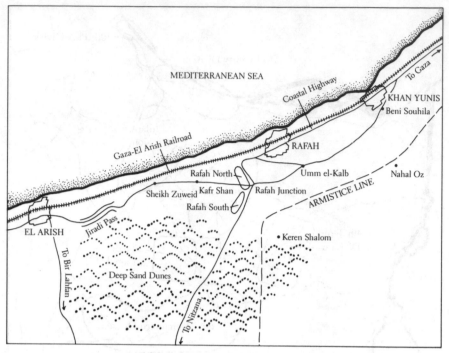

MEDITERRANEAN SEA

Coastal Highway

To Gaza

KHAN YUNIS

Beni Souhila

Gaza-El Arish Railroad

RAFAH

Rafah North

Umm el-Kalb

Nahal Oz

Sheikh Zuweid

Kafr Shan

Rafah Junction

ARMISTICE LINE

Rafah South

EL ARISH

Jiradi Pass

Keren Shalom

To Bir Lahfan

Deep Sand Dunes

To Nitzana

Map 4
THE UGDAH TAL BREAK-IN

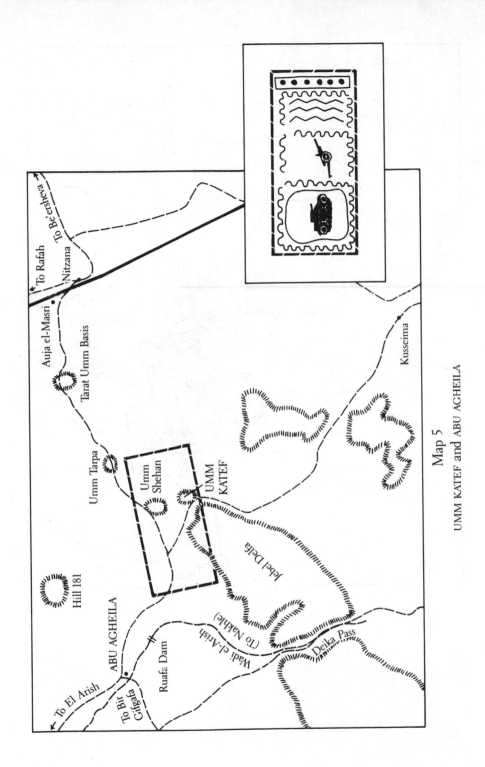

Map 5

UMM KATEF and ABU AGHEILA

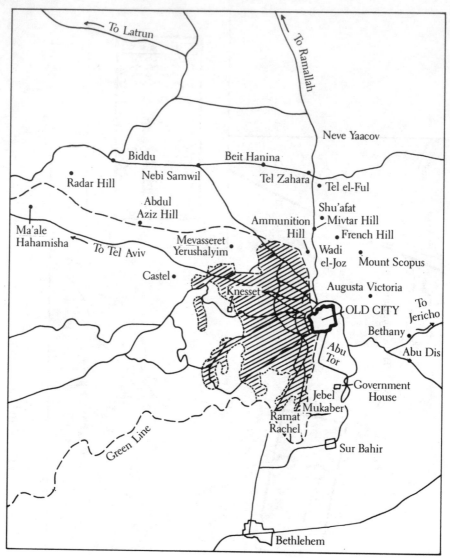

Map 6
JERUSALEM AREA

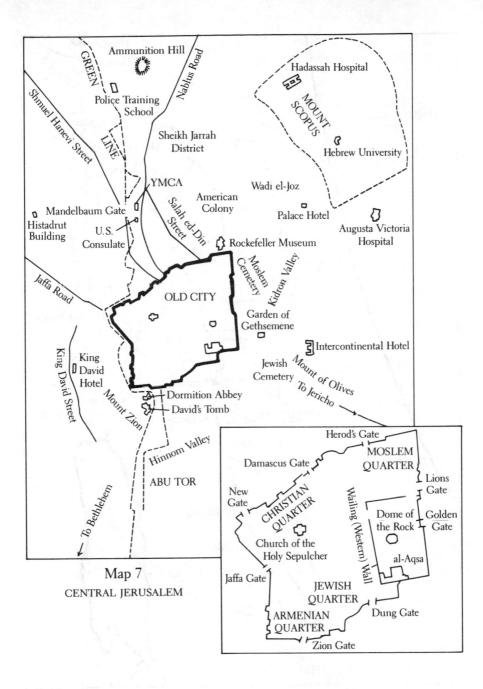

Map 7

CENTRAL JERUSALEM

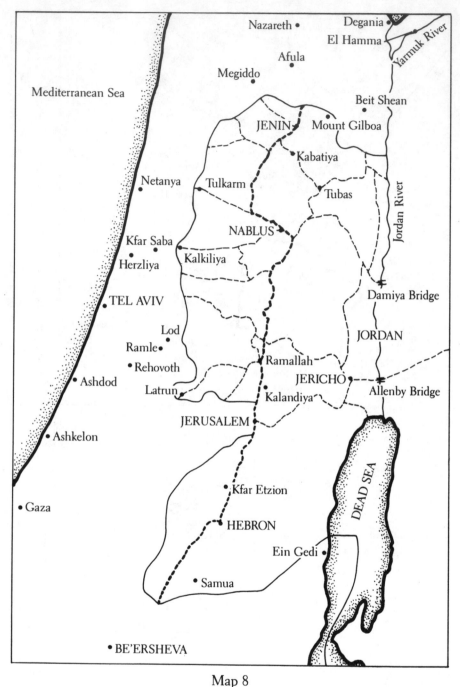

Nazareth •

Degania •

El Hamma •

Yarmuk River

Afula •

Mediterranean Sea

Megiddo •

Beit Shean •

JENIN •

Mount Gilboa •

Kabatiya •

Netanya •

Tulkarm •

Tubas •

Jordan River

NABLUS •

Kfar Saba •

Kalkiliya •

Herzliya •

Damiya Bridge ┿

TEL AVIV •

JORDAN

Lod •

Ramle •

Ramallah ┐

• Rehovoth

JERICHO •

Allenby Bridge ┿

Ashdod •

Latrun •

Kalandiya ┐

JERUSALEM •

DEAD SEA

• Ashkelon

• Kfar Etzion

• Gaza

HEBRON

Ein Gedi •

• Samua

• BE'ERSHEVA

Map 8

THE WEST BANK

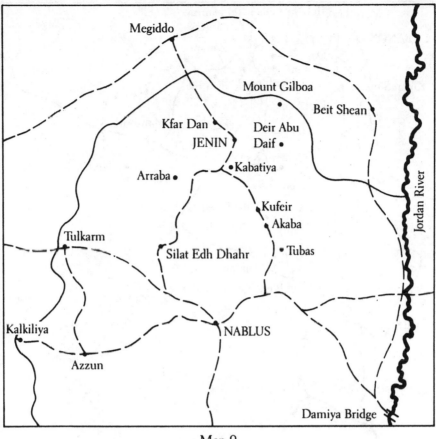

Map 9

NORTHERN SAMARIA

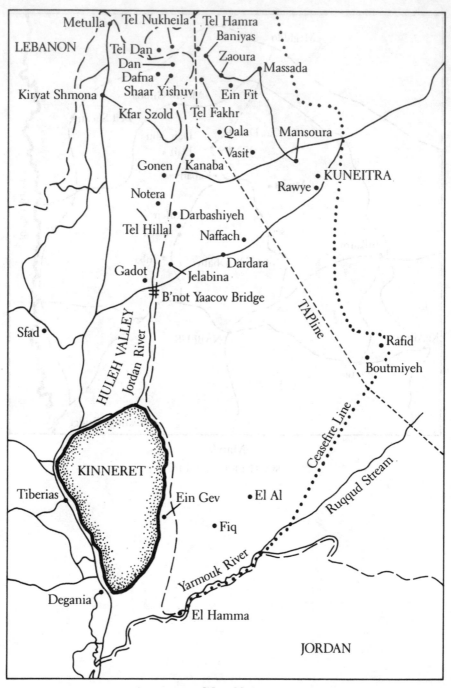

Map 10

THE GOLAN HEIGHTS

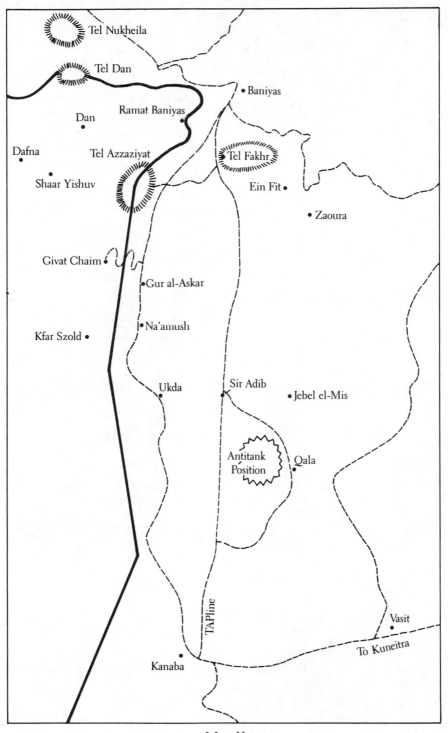

Map 11

THE FAR NORTHERN GOLAN

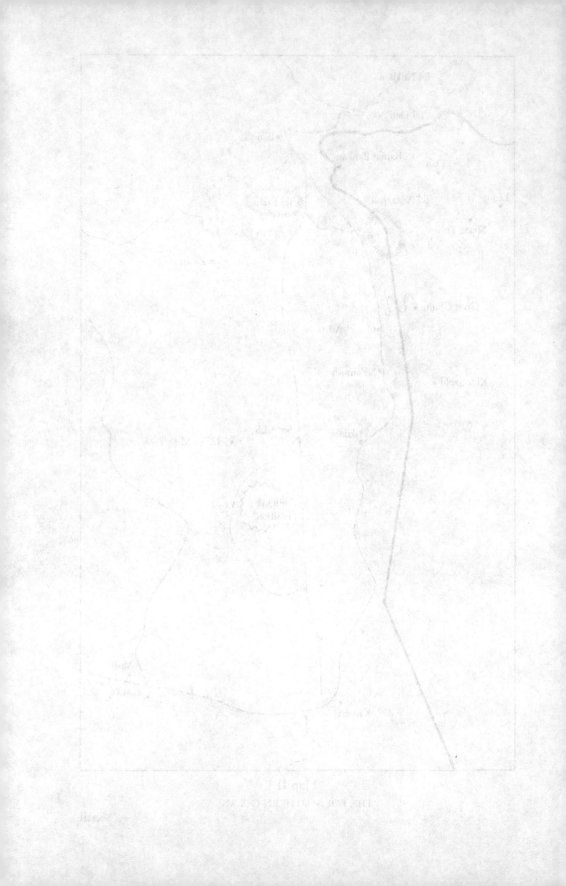

Prologue

"*T'Hiyeh milchamah*—There will be war."

Everywhere you went in Israel that Spring, the people were talking about the war that would be. Of course, in the pastry shops along Tel Aviv's quiet old Ben Yehuda Street, the old men bending over their thick Turkish coffee were speaking of past wars, but at the outdoor cafes and *shwarma* and *felafel* stands along bustling Dizingoff Street, the younger crowd ebbed and flowed amidst incessant discussion of the latest Egyptian or Syrian provocation and speculation as to what Israel would do about it. Out along Tel Aviv's scenic beach, the tourists from America, Europe, and South Africa also discussed the war that would be, wondering aloud if it was yet time to cut short this long-awaited combination vacation and spiritual homecoming. And, through the tiny nation's hinterland, the people speculated endlessly on the brewing hostilities.

At Kibbutz Gevim, a stone's throw from the Gaza Strip, the large field crew that was engaged in the Spring planting gathered each morning in the dining hall and spoke only about the coming war. The young men spoke in forced humor and bonhomie, but their thoughts were more on the new crop of children than the new crops of tomatoes, cotton, and wheat. Most of the young kibbutzniks were paratroopers or tank soldiers, the army's elite; they would be among the first to go to the army, and they would be in the forefront of the upcoming battles. They joked and laughed when they were together, but, like their wives and girlfriends, they wondered how many would be left to attend the pre-dawn coffee klatches after the war had been decided. They wondered who would be left to bring in the vegetables and cotton and plant the sugar beets in the next season. For now, they bent their backs and drove their machinery to the limit, for, if there was even a general call-up—much less a war—the struggling little kibbutz could ill afford to leave so much as an acre of land lying fallow or a container of produce ungathered.

1

When the Gevim men had finished talking and were ready to go to work, each reached under his chair to retrieve his personal submachine gun or automatic rifle. At Gevim these days, with a full division of the Palestine Liberation Army only a few kilometers away, no one who could man a weapon went three steps without actually holding one. Until the army was finally called up and its brigades were in place along the nearby Sinai and Gaza frontiers, Gevim and a double handful of sister kibbutzim in the Shaar HaNegev—Gateway to the Negev—region would be at the forefront of the nation's defense in the event the burgeoning Egyptian Army attacked. It had been thus for nineteen years. But, as everyone knew, the Spring of 1967 was different. This year . . . this year, they all agreed, *t'hiyeh milchamah*.

Part I

The Road to War

Part 1

The Road to War

1

There was no single cause for the war that erupted between Israel and her Arab neighbors in June 1967. There is not even one series of events, logically arranged and logically explained, that can be said to identify all the causes of the war. There are only the sloppy impressions and perceptions of history, working inexorably on the minds, memories, fears, and outlooks of the men destined to be in positions to influence the decision-making processes in their nations and the region.

As good a place as any to begin a countdown toward the Six-Day War was the completion by Israel in July 1964 of its National Water Carrier, an impressive series of canals and aqueducts designed to carry massive quantities of fresh water from the Sea of Galilee—which Israelis call the Kinneret, or "harp"—in the north, to the water-starved Negev Desert, in the south.

When the National Water Carrier project had gotten underway in the 1950s, U.S. President Dwight Eisenhower had expended considerable effort calming Arab fears. A fair distribution of the northern waters—the Jordan River and its sources as well as the Kinneret—was worked out via American auspices. Withal, the Arabs remained fearful that Israel was going to steal all the precious water to support a vast new influx of Jewish settlers from abroad. Thus, in retaliation, the Syrians and the Jordanians created a joint engineering venture to divert much of the Jordan water before it ever reached the river. This joint project, which was begun in desultory fashion before the completion of Israel's National Water Carrier, was designed to carry off the entire flow from the Baniyas, a major source of the Jordan atop the Syrian Golan Heights. Also to be diverted were the Yarmouk River and Ruqqud stream, which, before flowing into the Jordan River, formed the frontier between Jordan and Syria.

At length, as the two antagonists stared back at one another across the expanse of their common border and in the context of their mutual distrust,

5

a rash of border incidents took place. It is not clear if any or all of these incidents were instigated under orders from the Syrian government or merely by soldiers who took the law into their own hands. In any case, invariably, Syrian soldiers atop the Golan escarpment fired down onto Israelis cultivating fields in the shadow of the heights. On November 2, 1964, the Israelis finally sent a company composed of ten battle tanks to the vicinity of Kibbutz Dan, one of the most exposed of the Israeli border settlements in the area.

At noon on November 3, a pair of Syrian tanks set in atop Tel Nukheila, a high hill directly to the north of Dan, opened fire with their machine guns on an Israeli tractor in one of the nearby fields. Several of the Israeli tanks broke cover, advanced toward Tel Nukheila, and returned the Syrian fire. The exchange, which never spread, lasted for several hours, but neither side's tanks was able to hit any of the other's. At length, both sides withdrew.

Next, on the afternoon of November 13, the two Syrian tanks atop Tel Nukheila opened fire with machine guns on a troop-filled halftrack that was routinely patrolling along the border. Israeli tanks waiting in the wings emerged from cover and opened fire on the Syrian tanks, which were emplaced exactly where they had been on November 3. The Israelis, who had closely studied the ineffectual November 3 exchange, advanced boldly toward the Syrian position and took up pre-planned firing positions. In short order, a second Israeli tank platoon entered the fight, and then Syrian positions on nearby hills opened fire on all the Israelis. Next, Syrian heavy mortars opened fire on several of the Israeli border settlements. By the time the Syrian fire abated, three Israeli soldiers were dead and eleven soldiers and civilians had been wounded. In return, at least two Syrian tanks had been destroyed by direct fire from the Israeli tanks.

The November 13, 1964, battle in the north was the biggest confrontation between Syria and Israel in years. Many people on both sides, and elsewhere in the world, feared that it heralded a new round of hostilities that would eventually lead to a general war in the region. Indeed, the Syrians wanted to go to war, but they had been cautioned by their much stronger ally, Egypt, to wait. It was the opinion of the Egyptian government that both nations would be ready for an all-out war with Israel by late in the decade, but not before. So, though several additional border battles were destined to flare in the north over the next few years, it was agreed on the Arab side that there would be no general war for another four or five years.

But the tendency toward war continued to mount despite the cautious plans of the governments hostile to Israel's future. The next big step toward a new war came right on the heels of the Nukheila skirmish. It was the capture and eventual public execution by Syria of the Israeli spy, Elihu Cohen.

Born in Egypt, Eli Cohen emigrated to Israel during the mass expulsion of Jews from Moslem lands in the late 1940s and early 1950s. He eventually was recruited by an Israeli military intelligence organization to infiltrate the higher reaches of Syrian society, with an eye toward ingratiating himself with high-ranking Syrian officers and defense ministry officials.

Masquerading as a Chilean of Syrian descent, Cohen indeed worked his way toward his objectives. By the early 1960s, he was reporting back to his handlers the minutest details of, among other things, the decisions that were being made at the highest reaches of Syria's military establishment. Equally impressive were the photographs, taken by Cohen himself, of the deep Syrian defensive sector along the Golan Heights, the main part of Syria's border with Israel. When Cohen was eventually unmasked at the very beginning of 1965, no doubt with Soviet help, the Syrian government of the day was barely able to cling to power, so damaging and embarrassing were even the carefully circumscribed revelations that reached the Syrian masses.

Eli Cohen was hanged before the masses in Damascus's Martyrs Square on May 19, 1965. On February 23, 1966, the discredited Syrian regime was overthrown in a military coup that was brought on in very large measure by the Cohen affair. It was, of course, incumbent upon the successor government to redress the damage Israel had done to Syria's honor. To do so, the new Syrian military government fronted by Dr. Nur ed-Din Atassi chose an entirely new and strangely enticing tool.

Since the end of the 1956 Sinai Campaign between Egypt on the one hand and Great Britain, France, and Israel on the other, the danger in the Middle East had been far more in the way of inflammatory words than in brave or bloody deeds. There had been blood shed on both sides, to be sure, but it was all blood randomly spilled; there had been, per se, no campaign of terror sponsored by governments on either side. On the part of the Arabs, the bloodletting had been largely symbolic, the acts of frustrated individuals or small groups. If there had been government sponsorship, then it was more in the way of incitement by rhetoric than by serious intent. Since late 1956, virtually all aspects of the perpetual war had been more symbolic than real, an available and readily employed diversion away from the economic or social woes of the moment.

If there was an Arab standard-bearer in the quiescent, largely verbal war against Israel, it was Gamal Abdel Nasser, the Egyptian dictator and the largely self-proclaimed "leader" of the so-called Arab Nation. Nasser's place upon the stage of his region—and in History—was real even if it was not as substantive as he liked to believe. He *had* been the authentic leader of the Arab world's first step away from the old order, the 1952 military coup that overthrew King Farouk. And he was the authentic and largely undisputed leader of his nation. Moreover, on the larger world stage, Nasser was a founding and leading member of the non-aligned group of nations, though by 1966 that sobriquet was a matter of opinion.

There is no one Arab Nation. There never has been. There was nothing for Nasser to be "head" of beyond the nation of Egypt. The Arab world is riven with insoluble class, tribal, regional, factional, and religious disputes. There is not even one Islam; it is a religion as riven by factionalism as the so-called Arab Nation. Nasser, who was a secular moderate, was in constant danger even in Egypt from the religious Right and those who would use the religious Right to achieve secular power. For all that, Nasser's claim to a position of primacy in the Arab Nation had a modest validity, for there was, at least, no Arab or Moslem leader whose prestige on the world stage came close to rivaling Nasser's.

Nasser's position of leadership and moral authority drove the new Syrian nationalistic leadership to distraction. For reasons bound up in the long history of the Syrian peoples, it was felt in Damascus that a Syrian or Syrians should head the Arab Nation. To the degree the Atassi regime had *any* policy beyond simply ruling Syria, the replacement of Nasser as head of the Arab Nation by a Syrian was it.

The method by which the bellicose Syrian rulers chose to steal Nasser's thunder was an active, high-profile, attention-riveting campaign of terror against Israel. And the tool the new Syrian regime chose was a year-old terror organization led by a Palestinian civil engineer who went by the *nom de guerre* Abu Ammar—Yasir Arafat. Arafat's group was the Movement for the National Liberation of Palestine, which was known popularly by one version of its acronym, *Fatah*, or "Victory."

A self-proclaimed "activist" organization, *Fatah* in fact first became active on New Year's Day 1965. A victory communique to the contrary, the *Fatah* commando team on its way to strike the very first blow against Israel was stopped by Lebanese policemen—inside Lebanon!

Notwithstanding the initial humiliation, the very first bomb *Fatah* managed to detonate was set off beneath the Israeli National Water Carrier. There was, however, no damage. Next, during the night of February 28, 1965, a three-man *Fatah* commando team planted a bomb that blew a hole in a grain silo three miles from the Jordanian frontier.

During the first quarter of 1965, *Fatah* commandos were stopped cold several times by Lebanese or Jordanian soldiers and policemen. These interdictions became a source of long-standing bitterness toward the uncooperative governments. Inside Israel, a wide network of night ambushes caught several *Fatah* teams in motion, resulting in death or capture for several terrorists.

Over time, the *Fatah* commandos became more adept both at evading Lebanese and Jordanian border patrols—not to mention Israeli ambushes—and at building explosive devices that indeed exploded. *Fatah*'s "signature" bomb was set off by a timing device after it had been affixed to a structure, usually in some remote place. Always, the raiders were long gone before the timer detonated the bomb.

Over time, the Israelis specifically identified *Fatah* and many of its members. Indeed, by way of its bellicose communiques, *Fatah* usually identified itself by claiming credit for particular incidents. While routinely concerned, the Israeli security forces attached no special significance to the appearance of *Fatah*. Israeli operatives were quick to learn that the militant Palestinian organization boasted fewer than 200 members and apparently enjoyed no official backing from any Arab government. Long after it had ceased to be just another Palestinian debating society, *Fatah* was still only one of many militant Palestinian organizations whose avowed goal was the restoration of the Palestinian state. *Fatah* was noteworthy in that it took a determinedly more activist role than other groups, but it was not the only avowedly activist group and it was by no means considered a serious threat to Israel.

Notwithstanding *Fatah*'s small numbers and relative influence among Palestinian groups, the Israel Defense Force (known in Israel by the Hebrew acronym *Zahal*) decided to nip the terrorist group in the bud. As far as the Israelis could tell, *Fatah* was based solely in Jordan, so it was decided to deliver a message to the Jordanians as well as strike a blow against *Fatah*. (Syria, which was secretly and distantly supporting *Fatah*, would not then allow Arafat's followers to strike directly from inside Syria.) On the night of May 25, 1965, a woman and her two children were injured seriously when their home in Afula was blown in on them. Two nights later, elite Israeli paratroopers crossed into Jordan and destroyed two *Fatah* base camps in the northern part of the West Bank. This was the first reprisal raid to cross into Jordanian territory since the 1956 Sinai Campaign; it thus ended a long period of tacit mutual restraint between the by-then nominally hostile neighbors. The morning after the raid, *Zahal's* chief of staff, Major General Yitzhak Rabin, publicly announced that Israel would take further, similar, action unless Jordan did its part to stop the terrorist raids.

On the night of June 1, 1965, *Fatah* launched its first successful raid from inside Lebanon. This was seen by the commandos and, most importantly, by their Syrian well wishers as a direct challenge to General Rabin's May 28 assertion that *Zahal* had the right to pursue terrorists back to their source. With luck and time, Arafat and the Syrians believed, all of the Arab states bordering Israel could be incited to a state of war.

The raids continued, but overall tension did not increase. Following the February 23, 1966, coup in Syria, it was seen in Damascus that a stronger hand was needed to guide the terrorist effort against Israel. Thus, radically escalating the policy of its predecessors, the new Atassi regime took *Fatah* directly under its wing in March 1966 and gave Arafat permission to mount his campaign of terror from Syrian as well as Jordanian and Lebanese soil. In July 1966, *Fatah* came completely under the control of Syrian military intelligence, whose director was himself a Palestinian. At that point, though no one knew it and hardly anyone could have anticipated it, the slide toward war between Arab and Israeli became virtually inevitable. And, just as Arafat and his followers hoped and prayed, *Fatah* eventually became the prime catalyst for a new war in the Middle East.

Over time, amidst a general backdrop of violent Arab rhetoric backed by decidedly unviolent Arab action, particularly on the part of Arab governments, *Fatah's* expanding record of apparent successes inside Israel began to have an effect in several quarters. Certainly, other Palestinian organizations began to plan for the day when they could rival *Fatah* for attention, not to mention access to modern tools of war. At the same time, Arab governments and institutions whose merely avowed aim was the destruction of Israel began to look puny in comparison to *Fatah*. As Syria's role in abetting *Fatah* became more widely know, this became increasingly true with respect to Nasser and Egypt. Further, of course, Israel also was forced to take increasing notice of *Fatah's* depredations, all to the enhancement of *Fatah's* reputation.

The toll continued to rise. Indeed, it began to rise dramatically and, for

Israel, alarmingly. On April 8, 1966, an Israeli farmer was killed by a *Fatah* mine planted within sight of the Syrian border. A second Israeli farmer was killed and another was injured by yet another bomb in the same area on May 16. Within a 24-hour period on July 12 and 13, *Fatah* commando units moving from inside Syrian territory set four more bombs, which killed two more Israelis and wounded two others. These bombings precipitated the first overt Israeli response against Syria, an air strike against earth-moving equipment that Syria had arrayed on the Golan Heights in order to divert the flow of the Baniyas springs away from the Jordan River.

Syria complained to the United Nations Security Council about the Israeli Air Force's incursion over the Golan Heights, but, to everyone's surprise, the council failed to respond. If anything, an informal poll of the council members revealed, Syria would have to bear equal blame for allowing the precipitating events to be launched from its territory. Alas, thanks to the Soviet Union's support for its client, the Security Council was unable to muster any sort of rebuke against Syria.

Further emboldened by the world body's inability to condemn terrorism, *Fatah* continued to strike targets in Israel, albeit without drawing blood. Israeli jets retaliated once again—though initially with measured restraint—on August 15. This time, the Syrians responded. The brief battle that ensued was composed of exchanges between airplanes, artillery, tanks, and gunboats in and around the Kinneret—the Sea of Galilee. Israel claimed the destruction of two Syrian jets, which is plausible, and the Syrians claimed hits on ten Israeli gunboats, which is wildly exaggerated.

Another bombing incident occurred near the Syrian border on September 6, 1966. On September 7, Israel petitioned the United Nations with a formal complaint. This time, nothing whatever happened. On September 8, an Israeli patrol caught a *Fatah* unit red handed in the upper Galilee, and two commandos were killed in the ensuing gun battle. The very next day, another mine was detonated inside Israel, and this time three Israeli soldiers died in the blast.

Israel publicly blamed Syria for the September 9 bombing, Syria denied involvement, and Israel asked the U.N. to take action. While the U.N. continued to dither, the world waited to see how and when—not *if*—Israel's retaliatory raid was going to unfold. The psychological pressure mounted, but *Zahal* bided its time. Finally, on September 17, 1966, the Syrian foreign minister stated that any form of Israeli "aggression" would be met by a joint

Syrian-Egyptian military response. Indeed, the Syrians announced that they would retaliate against Israeli incursions with incursions of their own against Israeli "bases of aggression."

The U.N. remained utterly passive throughout the period. Arabs in general and *Fatah* in particular took this as a sign of either weakness or indifference.

Fatah struck again on October 8. This time, a total of four Israeli civilians were wounded in three detonations in Israeli West Jerusalem while four other Israeli civilians were hurt in another mine explosion south of the Kinneret.

Rather than waste energy appealing directly and formally to what it saw as an indifferent U.N. Security Council, Israel asked the U.N. Mixed Armistice Commission, the U.N. secretary general, and the president of the U.N. Security Council to get assurances from Syria that it was not, in fact, conducting or sponsoring a formal campaign of terror. Before responding in kind, apparently, Israel wanted to know if it was dealing with Syria or with some sort of rogue entity beyond the control of the Syrian authorities. On October 10, the Syrian prime minister stated at a press conference in Damascus that "We are not sentinels over Israel's security."

Another—surprising—response came from Jordan's King Hussein, who proclaimed that his kingdom's military forces would open a separate front if Israel attacked Syria. Immediately, not to be outdone, Syria's premier announced that Syrian forces would demolish the Jewish state. Israel appealed to the U.N. to restore reason (if not order), but the U.N. made no response.

On October 12, the Soviet Union announced that it had information that Israel was massing troops on the frontier with Syria. Moscow added that it would support Syria if Israel opened hostilities. That same day, Israeli and Jordanian army units suddenly began skirmishing along the common border. Syria announced that it was ready to repel the Israeli aggressors.

What aggressors? Israel had not added to its normal troop concentrations along either the Syrian or Jordanian frontiers. Israel had no intention of invading Syria. Indeed, as unfolding events were to prove, Israel did not even intend to *raid* Syria, even though doing so would have been fully consonant with Israel's long-standing policy of dealing with terrorists and those who would harbor them. The Israeli people simply were not yet prepared—psychologically, at any rate—to take on the Syrian military.

On October 13, 1966, only one day after the Soviet Union's erroneous and inflammatory warning, three Israeli soldiers died in a *Fatah* raid launched from Jordan. Jordan denied involvement, which was probably technically true. Immediately, eleven Arab nations proclaimed solidarity with Syria.

Far from "aggressing," Israel waited for the Security Council to act on earlier complaints. The response, long awaited throughout the region, was handed down on October 14—only one day after three more Israelis died in yet another raid *Fatah* proclaimed as its own. The U.N. decided to take the time necessary to deliberate and reach a decision. That is, the U.N. was going to dither some more, perhaps evermore.

As raids continued through the remainder of October 1966—as more and more Israeli blood was spilled and as Israeli leaders restrained the rising national temper—the U.N. did nothing. Finally, alarmed by hints from Israel that the time for restraint was nearing an end, the United States and Great Britain suggested that the Security Council act on Israel's many requests for support and determine if Syria was, in fact, prepared to assure the world that its intentions were peaceable. (The fact that this entire proceeding was conducted in all seriousness surpasses the surreal.)

Yasir Arafat's tiny activist organization was making an authentic impact on world events! To be sure, *Fatah*'s campaign of terror was having the *desired* effect. For the first time in nearly two decades, the world—to include the Arab world—was waking up and *really* taking notice of the "Palestinian question." Moreover, *Fatah*'s ongoing and growing success was breeding collateral success for other Palestinian activist groups. The Palestine Liberation Army (PLA), the virtually conventional military arm of the Palestine Liberation Organization (PLO)—the Palestinian "government in exile"—was beginning to conduct raids out of Jordan and the Gaza Strip. Even followers of the vociferous but essentially non-activist Grand Mufti of Jerusalem were organizing their own terrorist cells. In time, Israeli intelligence agencies identified sixteen terrorist organizations—all avowedly activist—that were training in or even conducting forays from Syria, Lebanon, Jordan's West Bank, or the Gaza Strip.

On November 4, the U.N. put forth a mild resolution mildly rebuking Syria and merely calling upon "the parties"—in this case, Israel and Syria—to reduce tensions in the area. Ten council members voted for the wording, but even this shallow act was doomed. As promised in advance, the Soviet Union vetoed the measure entirely. On the same day, Syria concluded a mutual-defense pact with the hitherto quiescent Egyptians.

Political avenues for redress—even one as weak as the U.N. Security

Council measure—were demonstrably blocked. As long as the Soviet Union was bent upon currying favor in the Arab world, the U.N. was a dead duck in the realm of actual—or even symbolic—peacemaking. To Israelis, then— and particularly to Israel's professional soldiers—the time for restraining the urge for retaliation against the terrorists and their masters was over. Moreover, the fact that Egypt's Nasser had ended a long period of dormancy with respect to Israel in the form of a military pact with "the crazies" in Syria stripped Israel—most particularly *Zahal*—of an important vestige of psychological security left over from the 1956 victory in Sinai. Until that point, Nasser had banned *Fatah* from establishing bases in or launching raids from Sinai or the Gaza Strip specifically because he wanted to avoid inevitable collateral confrontations between Egyptian and Israeli military forces. Now, with both Jordan and Egypt overtly aligned with *Fatah*'s Syrian sponsors—and, by extension, with *Fatah* itself—it suddenly seemed to Israel's military guardians that a general war was very much in the offing.

It was just as Yasir Arafat and the other *Fatah* leaders had hoped and schemed. The armed struggle for Palestine had achieved its crucial first objective. *Fatah* had backed the Israelis into a corner. Sooner rather than later, the Israelis were bound to react violently and perhaps massively. Maybe just one more bloodletting would do the trick. After its rebuff at the U.N., Israel certainly would react with force. And then the Arab world would react in its turn; Arab armies would crush the Jewish state, and then Palestine would rise from the ashes.

2

It is difficult, and perhaps impossible, for a non-Israeli to conceive of how close-knit Israeli society had become by 1966. There were less than three million Jews living in Israel that year—fewer people than resided in Philadelphia at the time. Given the size of the country and the pervasiveness of its national institutions—for example, *Zahal*, in which all men and many young women served—and a closely integrated national radio system, it is safe to say that every terrorist incident had a *direct* impact on the majority of Israelis; your cousin's boyfriend was hurt in a gun battle with terrorists, or your wife's uncle lived in the farming community whose wheat field was mined, or your comrade from your old paratroop company was killed by a bomb on the way to his office in Jerusalem. Every incident was scrutinized closely, perhaps morbidly, by every Israeli anywhere near a radio for days after the incident; each was discussed ad nauseum for weeks afterwards.

And it wasn't simply a matter of who you knew in the army or in the area most likely to be attacked. Your husband or father or son—or you yourself—was certainly a member of the *Zahal* Reserve, likely to be called to active duty for weeks of routine training or in response to an emergency mobilization. One way or another, each and every terrorist incident directly affected the vast majority of Israelis.

It is at best arguable that all of Israel was in fact the front line, but it is absolute fact that all Israelis *felt* as if they were *on* the front line. This feeling—the palpable fact of it—had the most influence upon Israeli public policy with respect to the terrorists and their backers. Over time, Israelis had ceased to feel safe and secure within the boundaries of their hard-won little state.

Finally, in order to demonstrate to the terrorists and the states that backed them—and to all Israelis!—that Israel was capable of protecting its citizens—and had the will to do so—it was felt by many that a new level of retribution had to be exacted in a war that *Fatah* and like-minded groups of terrorists had brought out of the shadows. It was simply a matter of time before *Zahal* was given the task of making someone pay for *Fatah*'s depredations. And it was only a short time before the government of Israel, through *Zahal*, intentionally *over*reacted to a single terrorist incident, the better to demonstrate to the world that Israel was both capable and ruthlessly willing to protect its territory and its citizens. The government did so to send a message to all terrorists, would-be terrorists, and hostile governments that supported terrorism. But, on a higher plain, to be credible at home, the government also quite simply had to avenge the death of the next brother, cousin, boyfriend, in-law, or army buddy to die in a terrorist bombing. If each individual terrorist-caused death was a personal loss to too many Israelis, then the growing number of deaths Israel had absorbed overall since November 1964 had become a matter of incessant public mourning. Morale was slipping.

During the last quarter of 1966, Syrian artillery dug in along the Golan Heights randomly shelled Israeli fields in the upper Galilee on virtually a daily basis. Israeli artillery responded, of course, but the Syrians had the advantage of position—they were higher and thus could see more. Israel was not willing to use air power, as it had as recently as August 1965, because doing so would have meant mounting incursions over Syrian territory. Israel was not prepared to go to war over vexing but essentially sporadic and not-yet lethal shellings, even shellings as frequent as several days a week. However, it was duly noted that public opinion, particularly in the vulnerable north, was clamoring for a show of force.

The Syrian defensive sector on the Golan Heights represented a particularly restrictive problem to the Israelis. For over ten years, lately with Soviet assistance, the Syrians had developed a formidable defense in depth upon the Golan that frankly intimidated Israeli proponents of the retributive military strike. If Israel chose to strike at Syria by means of the usual night commando raid—a method whose repeated use had quelled an earlier round of terrorist forays from Gaza prior to the 1956 war—then *Zahal* would have to be willing to absorb serious casualties. As the martyred spy, Eli Cohen, had demonstrated conclusively, the Golan was defended stoutly to a depth amounting to kilometers of continuous, permanent military works. Frankly, to attack the Golan in any strength was to risk sparking a general war, which was decidedly *not* Israel's intention. Moreover, no one in Israel had a clue as to what the Soviet Union might do if its nominally socialist client was attacked.

The real moment of truth came when jittery Syria—which expected an Israeli attack imminently—sucked Egypt into the November 4, 1966, mutual-defense pact. If, from the Israeli standpoint, a general war with Syria alone was out of the question, a general war with both Syria *and* Egypt was literally unthinkable. Parenthetically, in addition to scrounging up some credible assistance, the regime in Damascus bought itself a serious dose of legitimacy in the Arab world. Nasser's acquiescence to the mutual-defense pact was taken also as his approval of terrorism as a tool to be used against Israel. (The fact that the second does not logically or even legalistically follow from the first is of no importance; the connection was emotional.)

In sum, then, Syria was too strong at the moment for Israel to attack in anything but a responsive stand-off manner, as in artillery exchanges. Israeli ground troops could not be sent into Syria, period. Indeed, even a mere artillery duel—even one clearly instigated by Syria—might be employed by Syria as a pretext to trigger the implementation of the new Cairo-Damascus mutual-defense pact.

After November 4, 1966, the only possible target against which Israel could retaliate was Jordan. The 55,000-man Royal Jordanian Army was supplied and trained by Western nations—indeed, by Israel's own best allies—but it would be stretching the point to say that Jordan was *backed* by the West. Essentially, Jordan was on its own, a sometimes vocal belligerent, but by no means a player in the new game of escalating violence. That most terrorist raids were mounted from Jordanian territory was a factor of the kingdom's weakness—or, at most, its sentiments—but not its outright complicity. King Hussein had nothing whatever to gain from stirring up the blood lust of Palestinians, for they comprised more than half his subjects and controlled the lion's share of his nation's wealth. If anyone was going to go down beneath an empowered Palestinian people, Hussein could well be among the first.

But Hussein's problems of longevity and control were not Israel's concerns. Israel's ruling Labor government had a serious credibility problem to reconcile. *Something* had to be done to quell domestic criticism. The U.N. and the world community at large had not responded to Israel's plight, so it was left to the Israeli government to send a message all on its own. Syria, which was manifestly at the root of the terrorist problem, was for the moment inviolate. Jordan, which was helplessly at the focus of the same terrorist problem, had no military ties to Egypt or Syria. Indeed, as a relatively weak vestige of the "old order," King Hussein was detested in those two nominally socialist states. Thus, with a small army and no real allies to back its sovereignty, Jordan was vulnerable to Israel's favorite form of public retribution, the night commando raid. A nation that could not stop a handful of terrorists even when its national policy—keep a low profile—was in jeopardy would be about the last nation capable of standing up resolutely against even a small and measured armed incursion by relatively powerful Israel. Israel, which already felt that right was on its side, *knew* in the case of Jordan that might was, too.

The decision to attack a target well inside Jordan was taken; *Zahal* was waiting for a pretext. However, the decision, itself long in coming, had been the signal for a particular wing of the *Zahal* leadership to argue in favor of a far stronger response than anyone in the world dreamed might occur.

The instigators of a stronger-than-usual attack scenario were from among the new breed of Israeli military leaders. Indeed, they were leaders among the new breed of Israelis. From the 1948 War of Independence onward, *Zahal* had been led mainly by officers born in Europe or at least the sons of early European settlers, men whose shared outlook had been formed in some dim, dark past whose lessons no longer seemed to apply. Slowly, as the nation-state endured, the younger *sabras*—as native-born Israelis are known—naturally moved upward into positions of authority. In many cases, the new generation of Israeli military leaders—who by 1966 counted many colonels and most generals among their number—included many ardent Israeli nationalists. That is, they espoused sentiments that flowed from a newer outlook for the Jewish state than had been shared among their European-influenced mentors. Where to the older leaders Israel had remained foremostly a haven for oppressed Jews from around the world, the newer leaders saw their nation first as their nation and only secondarily as a Jewish haven. After all, they were not immigrants; Israel was their country; they had been born there; they had fought for it; it was their home, the home of their children. It follows, then, that the new breed's aspirations for Israel's future differed sharply from the aspirations of their fathers. Their political outlooks, formed over a lifetime of hostility on the part of all their Arab neighbors, was often militant, increasingly far to the Right of the Zionist national leadership.

When the attention of the *Zahal* leadership turned to the question of retaliation against the terrorists, several very highly placed members of the new breed of senior officers argued passionately for making the raid an unequivocal statement of a new sort. Chief among the proponents of stronger action was Brigadier General Ezer Weizman, head of *Zahal's* General Staff Branch, the number-two spot in the armed forces at that time. Weizman was by far the senior member of *Zahal's* young turks. A year earlier, he had concluded a decade-long tour as chief of the Israeli Air Force (IAF), and, of equal or greater importance, he was the nephew of Chaim Weizmann, modern Israel's revered founding father. With Ezer Weizman leading the debate, the nationalist officers argued that they were no longer proud of having to hit back at marauding Arabs by means of hit-and-run pinpricks conducted in the dark of night. They inveighed in favor of a forthright military action, open for the world to see. Weizman later reported in his memoirs that he argued in favor of these sentiments: "In 1966, we can't carry out a 1955-style reprisal raid, going in at night, laying a few pounds of explosives, blowing up a house or a police station, and then clearing off. When a sovereign state decides to strike at its foes, it ought to act differently. We have armor, and we have an air force. Let's go in by day, operating openly and in force."

There it was. The nationalist officers were arguing for a type of response that would tell the world that *Zahal*—and Israel—had come of age. Weizman's hard-edged argument carried the day, and a plan embodying his sentiments was drawn up. The plan was taken by *Zahal's* chief of staff, Major General Yitzhak Rabin, to the so-called War Cabinet. The politicians approved the plan based on Rabin's strong recommendation and in view of the prevailing domestic clamor, the growing regional tensions, and the notable indifference of the world community to Israel's plight.

On November 12, 1966, in the seventieth terrorist incident since January 1965, a truck carrying an Israeli police patrol detonated a terrorist mine near the Jordanian border. Three Israeli border policemen were killed and six others were wounded.

At 0613 on November 13, an Israeli parachute battalion mounted in halftracks and supported by a company of ten light tanks crossed the frontier into the West Bank of Jordan from the vicinity of the Israeli city of Be'ersheva. The Rujem Madfa police station was demolished, presumably with tank fire. Then the Israeli column moved northward down the main road through the area and stopped in Samua, a town of about 5,000 inhabitants located in the far south of the region known as Judea. The nearest large town to the spot at which the Israelis had been killed the previous day, Samua had long been identified as a major jumping-off point for *Fatah* incursions into Israel.

The Israeli paratroopers were armed with a precise plan of action, drawn up in accordance with precise intelligence material collected over a long period of time. Backed by the light tanks, the Israeli paratroopers moved through Samua. Arabic-speaking soldiers equipped with loudspeakers routed the inhabitants of specific buildings into a safe holding area. Then the targeted structures—forty in all—were demolished systematically with high-explosive charges.

At 0730, as the demolition in Samua was proceeding smoothly, a company of the Royal Jordanian Army's Hittin Infantry Brigade burst upon the scene. Unfortunately, due to faulty communications, the approximately 100 Jordanian soldiers, who were aboard approximately twenty trucks, had roared out of their barracks in the Judean capital of Hebron in the belief that the Israelis had struck the town of Yata, which was about 6.5 kilometers beyond Samua. In order to reach Yata from Hebron, the Jordanians had to take the road through Samua.

Both sides were equally surprised when the troop-laden Jordanian trucks ran straight into the Israeli paratroop companies and tank platoons that had established a routine security screen in the direction of Hebron. At least fifteen of the Jordanian trucks were demolished in the initial conflagration, and a dozen or so Jordanian soldiers were killed outright. Nevertheless, the bulk of the Jordanian force recoiled and reorganized, and a brief pitched battle ensued. Several more Jordanians were killed or wounded before the Israelis allowed the survivors to disengage and retire back toward Hebron. Also killed in the melee was the Israeli paratroop commander.

While the ground battle was still underway, a flight of four Royal Jordanian Air Force Hawker Hunter jet fighter-bombers was vectored out to repel the invaders. One Hunter was shot down and one Israeli pilot lost an eye in the brief dogfight. The remaining Hunters withdrew.

The Israelis stayed in Samua for three hours, and then they withdrew in good order. The Israelis claimed to have destroyed only the forty structures on their target list, but other sources—either the Jordanians or, perhaps, U.N. observers—claimed that, in Samua alone, 125 structures were demolished and another twenty-eight were damaged. In addition, these sources claimed, fifteen homes were destroyed and seven more were damaged in a nearby village. Right after the raid, Jordan admitted to losing thirteen killed and thirty-four wounded, possibly including several civilians. However, other sources stated that fifteen soldiers and three civilians were killed and thirty-seven soldiers and seventeen civilians were wounded. In all, the Israelis lost one officer killed and ten soldiers wounded, including the half-blinded pilot.

Militarily, the Samua raid was a mixed success. Certainly, the Israeli force destroyed all the buildings on its hit list, but the confrontation with Jordanian military forces was not supposed to have taken place; the Samua raid was to have been bloodless. Largely because the Jordanian column was reacting to incorrect information, the Israeli success in ambushing the reaction force was decisive. The tank-infantry ambush on the road into Samua was utterly professional in every respect.

But, beyond the military sphere, the Samua raid was a debacle for Israel. It was a first-class political disaster.

In the first place, Israel was perceived by Arabs as being afraid to take on Syria, a perception that strengthened Syria politically and added to the self-perceived stature of the Arab world's most bellicose military dictatorship. It emboldened Syria rather than chastening it with evidence of Israeli audacity and military might—quite the opposite of the desired effect.

Yet more decisive than the effect of the raid upon Syria was the effect upon Egypt. Under long-standing agreements, the Egyptian Air Force was to have come to the immediate aid of Jordanian forces engaged in action with Israeli forces. This did not occur; there was not even an alert issued in Egypt. The failure was employed by the Syrians to goad the thin-skinned Nasser into taking a stand even more threatening than the November mutual-defense pact to which, in part, the Samua action was to have been a warning.

And, of course, even though King Hussein would rather have sat out the rising tide of violence, he now was obliged to erase the blot upon the honor of his army, his nation, and his throne. Israel thus managed to make an active enemy out of a passive one who would have preferred sitting evermore on the sidelines.

Far from intimidating any of the Arab states arrayed on its borders, Israel's first daylight reprisal action bound disparate enemies together and virtually assured that those who had not acted would be certain to act in the future. Even worse, on November 25, 1966, the U.N. Security Council voted to condemn Israel for undertaking the raid. Israeli Prime Minister Levi Eshkol complained that the U.N. measure was one-sided and failed to take into account the precipitating pattern of Arab aggression against Israel. But the world body did not care to listen, a factor that increased Israel's sense of isolation and thus virtually assured recommendations for even stronger measures from the new breed of Israeli hawks.

The great divide had been crossed. Given the effects of scores of misperceptions and cross purposes then pervading the Middle East and the world, a general war became all but inevitable.

3

For six weeks following the Samua raid, the tension between and among the hostile neighbors seemed to ease somewhat. There were no more terror raids launched from within Syria or Jordan, and the Israelis maintained mere vigilance. Clearly, none of the feuding nations was prepared yet to plunge into an abyss deeper than the one in which they already found themselves.

Stung by bitter, hectoring, criticism for not sending its air force to Jordan's aid on November 13, Egypt responded to Samua in a portentous way. In 1960, following a major Israeli retaliatory raid into Syria and fearing that an even larger follow-up incursion was imminent, President Nasser had sent several Egyptian Army divisions into Sinai as a show of force. That strategy had appeared to work because the Israelis had not undertaken a follow-up attack. (There is no evidence that they intended to do so.) Convinced of the deterrent capabilities of his huge military establishment, Nasser in late November 1966 repeated the 1960 gambit; he dispatched four combat divisions to the vicinity of Egypt's Sinai frontier with Israel. When no hostile confrontations ensued for about a month, the Egyptian troops were withdrawn. Nasser was certain that he had shown the Israelis the folly of their ways and filed the plan away for possible use in the future.

There was no movement on the diplomatic front following Israel's rebuff at the U.N. As soon as the region became quiet, its problems disappeared from public view abroad. Inevitably, the raids began anew. Undoubtedly goaded by Soviet support in the U.N. and, no doubt, quiet assurances between friendly foreign ministries and diplomats in Damascus, the bellicose Syrian regime reignited the region in late December 1966.

On December 28, an Israeli patrol discovered a newly planted land mine along a heavily used patrol route in the far upper Galilee. Next day, in the same vicinity, Syrian outposts opened fire on their Israeli counterparts with machine guns. The Israelis responded in kind, and the Syrians raised the ante with mortar fire, to which the Israelis again responded in kind. As the action progressed, tanks exchanged long-range fire, and then Syrian and Israeli artillery began dueling. Every time the Syrians raised the stakes, the Israelis merely responded in kind.

The December 29 action in the upper Galilee was inconclusive; it is doubtful that either side inflicted much damage on the other. Nevertheless, as far as the Syrians were concerned, Israel's position following the Samua debacle appeared weakened; it is virtually assured that the Syrians felt they could incite any sort of border incident without provoking an Israeli overreaction. As far as the Syrians were concerned, the Israelis were afraid to attack Syria. The mid-November raid into Jordan proved it and the December 29 action confirmed it.

Additional border exchanges in early January 1967 garnered the attention of U.N. Secretary General U Thant. He advised the Syrians and Israelis to settle their "border disputes" within the confines of the U.N. Mixed Armistice Commission. There were authentic border disputes stemming from the ceasefire at the conclusion of Israel's War of Independence, which ended with a final armistice in July 1949. These were the putative reasons for the new round of clashes, but invoking them was a smokescreen. In order to remain in the good graces of the U.N., both sides complied with the secretary general's entreaty, but several meetings—in which Syrian and Israeli delegates sat down at the same table—produced no results beyond a no-doubt temporary cessation of direct, overt military clashes.

By February, Jordan was under immense public pressure to get actively involved against Israel. The Palestine Liberation Organization was asking for permission to mount terror raids from Jordanian territory, and the Arab League Defense Council was asking openly that Jordan mount conventional military strikes against Israel. When the Arab League suggested that Iraqi and Saudi troops be stationed in Jordan, King Hussein balked. He feared they would be used to overthrow his dynasty. When the king's prudent decision generated an abusive response directly from Egypt's Nasser, Hussein recalled his ambassador from Cairo on February 22. If tradition won out, healing this broad rift between Jordan and Egypt would require some dramatic gesture by one party or the other.

* * *

Fatah remained unstintingly active throughout the period. By the end of March 1967, ninety border incursions from Syria, Lebanon, and Jordan had been attributed directly to the Arafat organization by Israeli counter-intelligence agencies. Indeed, *Fatah* had claimed responsibility for each successful raid in its own communiques. And other Palestinian organizations were stepping up their own terror campaigns.

Finally, to no one's surprise, Syria pushed Israel one step beyond Israel's ability to contain a defensive reaction. Not surprisingly, the precipitating incident was not from the annals of the Arab-Israeli conflict. As was and is often the case, the energy of domestic violence is often channeled into or blunted by the ongoing war with Israel. In the case of the next major clash between Arab and Jew, the energy that needed redirecting came from a series of religious riots in Syria that had been sparked by an attack on Islam in a Syrian Army newspaper. To coax the public back in line, the regime simply turned on its all-purpose fail-safe trouble emulsifier—it pressed the Israel button.

Early on April 7, 1967, Syrian mortars opened fire from the Golan Heights against Kibbutz Gadot, a farming community that had been struck often down through the years by Syrian fire. As the morning wore on, the rain of mortar shells continued, until finally the Israelis had counted over 200 detonations in and around Gadot. At that point, the Israelis moved tanks into positions from which the Syrian mortars could be interdicted. The Syrians responded in kind. Soon, artillery fire was being exchanged all along the frontier. Finally, at 1330, Israeli Mirage fighter-bombers swept in low over the Golan Heights and bombed and strafed a number of Syrian strong-points and artillery-battery sites. Fifteen minutes later, the Syrian Air Force scrambled a large flight of modern MiG-21 interceptors to challenge the Israeli warplanes. Within minutes, the Mirages had destroyed six MiG-21s in air-to-air combat, and the surviving Syrian interceptors were chased all the way to the outskirts of Damascus. Israeli fighters could be seen plainly from Syria's capital as Syrian fighters fled before them.

The perfectly obvious Israeli victory on April 7 deeply embarrassed the Arab allies. Ignoring the fact that Syrian mortars had fired 200 rounds at an Israeli farming community before the Israelis responded at any level, the Arab propaganda apparatus ginned up a vehement campaign against the Israeli aerial aggression over Syria.

Part of the propaganda campaign was directed against Egypt. Once again, Nasser had failed to send his powerful air force to the aid of brother Arabs suffering at the hands of the Israeli invader. But there had been little Nasser could do. The air clash had erupted and ended within minutes, long before the Egyptians could begin to scramble aircraft. And Nasser was not about to get into a *real* fight with Israel just yet. Since withdrawing his four divisions from Sinai months earlier, he had only his air force with which to fight Israel. Egyptian and Israeli ground forces, including artillery, were not within scores of kilometers of one another, and a U.N. truce force stood between them in any case. Far from launching a strike in the wake of the April 7 action, Nasser did everything in his power to curb the Syrian tendency toward violence. But he failed.

Within the week, the Syrian authorities had fallen under the spell of their own propaganda campaign. They were certain that Israel was poised to take decisive military action against the Golan defensive sector. On April 13, Syria warned the U.N. Security Council that an Israeli invasion was imminent. On April 16, Egypt bowed to rising pressure for a show of solidarity and reestablished formal diplomatic relations with Syria for the first time since the two nations had dissolved their ill-fated United Arab Republic in late 1961. On April 18, the Egyptian premier flew to Damascus to join the commander-in-chief of the Egyptian Air Force, who had arrived there on April 10. On the surface, their brief was to coordinate a stand against Israel. In fact, the Egyptians warned the Syrians of dire consequences if they kept hitting Israel.

The Soviet government jumped into the fray on April 26 with a formal note warning Israel not to provoke the Arabs. A second note, delivered in Moscow by the Soviet deputy foreign minister to Israel's visiting U.N. ambassador, advanced the same dire warning. However, unknown to the Israelis, that very same day the Soviet ambassador to Syria forcefully told the Syrian foreign minister to get his government to curb the *Fatah* raids into Israel.

Syria ignored all would-be mediators. On April 29, *Fatah* commandos blew up a water pipeline in northeastern Israel. Then they destroyed a culvert on May 2. On May 4, they planted a mine that blew up a trailer. On May 5, *Fatah* guerrillas fired a mortar from within Lebanon at an Israeli border kibbutz. A raid that night accounted for an Israeli irrigation pump. On May

7, a command-detonated mine damaged an Israeli army truck on the main highway north of Tiberias.

The Egyptians became so convinced that the Israelis would respond massively that the Egyptian high command met to map out a course of action. For the moment, however it was decided to adopt a wait-and-see policy while keeping military forces at a high state of readiness.

Israel also adopted a waiting game. There was pressure from nationalist activists in *Zahal* to begin planning an offensive war, but Prime Minister Levi Eshkol held firm for a defensive strategy. On May 12, Eshkol issued his sternest public warning to Syria to date. He ended up rambling past his warning and actually watered down the message, but the upshot of the news coverage of his speech was that Israel was prepared to go to war. The May 12 speech added fuel to the fire in that the Soviets were reporting—erroneously—that *Zahal* Chief of Staff Yitzhak Rabin had told a secret May 11 gathering of leading Israeli politicians that *Zahal* was prepared to launch a strike in order to unseat the Damascus regime. Since Syria wanted to foment a war, its government was encouraged by Rabin's alleged statement and Eshkol's apparent dire warning.

The Soviets next told the Syrians that Israel actually was massing its army in the north and preparing for an offensive strike. The Israelis vehemently denied the allegation and even invited the Soviet ambassador in Tev Aviv to tour the region. The Soviet diplomat ignored the invitation and Moscow repeated its warning to Syria several times over the next several weeks. It was patently false. And so was an amplification that warned that the Israeli attack would commence before dawn on May 17.

It is true that there were important Israeli nationalist figures lobbying in favor of an offensive war, but, at the time of the Soviet warning, the Israeli civilian leadership had yet to grapple seriously even with the *question* of an offensive war. Israel officialdom could not have been farther from a decision, much less a date-certain.

The Soviets had much to gain from fomenting trouble in the region. As long as there was instability and intractable hatred afoot between Arab and Jew, there was ample opportunity for the Soviets to strengthen their existing relationships with Arab clients and, indeed, to garner new clients through diplomatic means and the lure of military hardware. Nevertheless, though the Soviets certainly were working hard to keep the pot boiling, it is by no means certain that they actually intended to incite a shooting war.

Soviet and Syrian machinations to the contrary, there would be no war launched from the Arab side without the acquiescence of Gamal Abdel Nasser and the participation of the Egyptian armed forces. In the end, as everyone in the region knew, only Egypt provided a credible threat against Israel. So, into the first half of May 1967, the pressure on Nasser to make a stand intensified. Finally, on May 13, Nasser made up his mind.

4

The course to war was set. From the safety of hindsight, it can be argued with conviction that events large and small were *bound* to lead Israel and her Arab neighbors into a war. If the war did not erupt in 1967, then it would be waged in 1968 or 1969. Any way anyone stacked up the facts, there was going to be a war. Everyone knew it. There was no doubt. And it did not matter how or why it started. All the precipitating factors were in place. There only remained the unfolding of details, minor adjustments in the construction plans for the broad boulevard to war that The Fates had engineered.

It just so happened that the bluff President Gamal Abdel Nasser commenced on May 13, 1967, ensured that the inevitable war would commence sooner rather than later. By the time Nasser decided, and from then on, all the rest was byplay.

The decision Nasser achieved and laid out for his generals on May 13 was essentially a second repeat of his 1960 show-of-force gambit, the one he had used again—successfully, he thought—following the November 1966 Samua raid. He intended to station a vast military force in Sinai and bluff Israel into submission by threatening to use the force in behalf of the interests and honor of his brother Arabs in Jordan and Syria.

It is a virtual certainty that Nasser did not *intend* to go to war. He apparently was *prepared* to do so, but his intentions seem to be reasonably clear: Nasser did not intend to precipitate a war, but he *did* intend to seize back from Syria the moral leadership of the Arab Nation. Perversely, in that place and at that time, in order to achieve his real aims and still delay or deflect an actual shooting war, Nasser had to convince the Arab world that he seriously intended to wage a war of annihilation against Israel.

No wonder war was inevitable! Given the mind sets of at least one set of leaders—the Syrian regime really wanted a war and Egypt's leader wanted to convince everyone that he wanted a war—it is no surprise that things turned out as they did.

The first step in Nasser's plan was to present a credible threat. For years, the Egyptian military garrisons in Sinai had been allowed to dwindle to 30,000 soldiers and airmen in order for Nasser to man his war in Yemen. On May 15, the Egyptian Army and Air Force were put on full nationwide alert.

Nasser had done his planning in advance of the alert, but Israel inadvertently played into the Egyptian leader's hands. As a calming gesture, it withheld tanks and other heavy war equipment from its annual May 15 Independence Day military parade in Jerusalem. The Egyptian press played up the Israeli show of non-force by accusing Israel of massing the missing tanks opposite the Syrian frontier—a play on the ongoing Soviet scare tactics leading to Israel's allegedly upcoming May 17 invasion of Syria.

Next, at 2200 on May 16, in an updated repeat of past gambits, the chief of the Egyptian General Staff sent a note to Major General Indar Jit Rikhye, the Indian commander of the United Nations Emergency Force (UNEF) in Sinai. In the note, Rikhye was ordered to clear virtually his entire 3,400-man international force out of Egyptian territory.

The UNEF commander was flabbergasted by the peremptory order, but he was also an old Middle East hand and knew the sort of people with whom he had to deal. He coolly responded that he had no authority to withdraw all or part of his force from Sinai and that he had to contact U.N. Secretary General U Thant for permission. President Nasser appears to have been delighted with Rikhye's response; he wanted to create a crisis, but he apparently wanted at least part of UNEF to remain in place to prevent a war from actually erupting between Egypt and Israel. (The 3,400 U.N. troops could hardly have stopped either side in fact, but neither side was about to overwhelm it to get to the other side of the line. In that sense, UNEF really was the thin blue line that was keeping the peace between Egypt and Israel.)

Under the February 1957 accord that had handed Sinai back to Egypt following Israel's lightning conquest of the peninsula in late 1956, half of UNEF should have been on the Israeli side of the line. However, Israel steadfastly refused to allow *any* foreign troops to be stationed on its soil. The Israelis wanted it both ways; they preferred the symbolic protection rendered by UNEF's presence, but, for reasons of pride—Israel insisted that she required no foreign protectors on her territory—they insisted that the U.N.

troops remain entirely on the Egyptian side of the line. This ironclad policy placed the initiative concerning UNEF in Nasser's hands.

On May 17, Cairo's demand for the UNEF withdrawal was repeated on Radio Cairo. This ensured that the Arab world and Israel knew of Nasser's serious intent.

Unfortunately, Gamal Abdel Nasser reckoned without knowing the mind of U.N. Secretary General U Thant. Legalistic to a fault, U Thant at first resisted Cairo's order on moral grounds, but he soon conceded that Egypt indeed had the right to demand that UNEF withdraw—in its entirety.

A close reading of the May 16 withdrawal order and several follow-up statements on Radio Cairo revealed that only the UNEF troops in northern Sinai and Gaza had been ordered out. For reasons that became clear in time, the UNEF post at Sharm el-Sheikh, at the southern tip of the Sinai Peninsula, had been left out of the order and follow-up broadcasts. However, U Thant's opinion obliged Nasser to broaden his demand. Though this was not the outcome Nasser had wanted, the Egyptian president requested that UNEF turn *all* of its positions and posts over to the Egyptian Army and depart. For all that, Nasser apparently felt or hoped that U Thant would put up a fight of some sort, that he would argue and thus give Nasser a pretext to allow the secretary general's moral sense to prevail.

But U Thant felt that he had no choice but to accede to Nasser's demand. UNEF was based entirely on Egyptian territory; it was there at Egypt's sufferance. If Nasser wanted the U.N. troops to leave, as he said he did, then U Thant had to comply. Thus, in an announcement that shocked all the parties—Nasser not least—U Thant reported to the U.N. General Assembly on May 19 that he reluctantly had decided to accede to President Nasser's demands. UNEF was ordered officially to depart from Sinai. By then, in a transition that actually had begun with U Thant's permission on May 17, all of UNEF's border posts had been turned over to the Egyptian Army or, in the Gaza Strip, to elements of the Egyptian-supported Palestine Liberation Army (PLA). Shortly after U Thant's General Assembly announcement, the U.N. flag was struck at UNEF headquarters in Gaza City.

U Thant's decision to accede to Nasser's overt demand for UNEF's withdrawal upset the entire balance between Egypt and Israel. By caving in to Nasser's bluff, U Thant inadvertently forced Nasser to back his heroic words with heroic deeds.

By May 19, 1967, events were spinning out of control.

*   *   *

On May 18, in advance of the U.N. General Assembly announcement, the leaders of Israel's ruling coalition reached a consensus at a secret meeting that war was inevitable, and that its onset might be closer at hand than anyone had heretofore realized. It was decided to partially mobilize the *Zahal* Reserve. In Israeli terms, that was roughly as serious as it gets, for the weak national economy would be in jeopardy as long as so many temporary soldiers were away from their civilian jobs.

On May 20, the same day the Israeli Reserve call-up went forward, Egypt called up its own Reserves, and the Iraqi Army was put on a state of alert. Even Lebanese forces were ordered to prepare for war. That day, also, Field Marshal Abdel Hakim Amer, the Egyptian minister of war, made a showy trip to the Gaza Strip to review newly arrived Egyptian and PLA troops as they relieved UNEF posts in the area. All day, farther back, several Egyptian combat divisions poured into Sinai.

By May 21, *Zahal* Chief of Staff Yitzhak Rabin reported to Prime Minister Levi Eshkol that there were 80,000 Egyptian soldiers in Sinai, and many more on the way. Eshkol felt that war was inevitable, but he resisted several attempts by nationalist politicians and military officers to authorize an immediate preemptive strike against Egypt and perhaps Syria. In this he was supported by General Rabin. Eshkol acknowledged that Nasser indeed was making a show of force, but he reasoned that the Egyptian leader's true intentions were as yet unstated.

For the time being, the Israeli prime minister was able to hold the line against the most sanguinary nationalists in *Zahal*—but only if one of the Arab nations confronting Israel did not go farther than even moderate Israelis could tolerate.

There was no end of potential flashpoints. Among them was the Straits of Tiran, an extremely narrow passage connecting the Red Sea to the Gulf of Aqaba. It was the only passage from the Israeli port of Eilat to the wide world. Until the 1956 Suez Campaign, Egypt had blockaded the Straits of Tiran, thus denying passage to ships bound for Eilat. The blockade had been one of the reasons Israel had gone to war in late 1956, and U.N. guarantees to keep the straits open to Israeli shipping had been one of the reasons why Israel had returned Sinai to Egypt in early 1957. By maintaining a post at Sharm el-Sheikh, at the southern tip of the Sinai Peninsula, adjacent to the straits, UNEF had indeed kept the straits open for ships bound for Eilat.

According to Prime Minister Eshkol and those supporting him in favor of working to ease tensions, Nasser's general bombast and even his specific threats could not be taken seriously until or unless Egyptian military forces became actively engaged against Israel—for example, in the event they blockaded the Straits of Tiran. However, even the most ardent doves in Eshkol's cabinet agreed in a private meeting held on May 21 that Egypt's closure of the straits would be tantamount to a declaration of war. Thus, a potential Egyptian blockade of Eilat became, in the minds of Israel's leaders, one of several tripwires for war.

Only one day after the Israeli leaders set out the tripwire, Nasser crossed it. On May 22, the Egyptian leader announced that Egyptian forces newly based at Sharm el-Sheikh were sealing the Straits of Tiran to all Israeli or Israel-bound shipping.

On the surface, Nasser's May 22 decision is difficult to square with earlier hints and announcements. It would appear that, as late as May 20, the Egyptians had no intention of closing the Straits of Tiran. It is most significant that the UNEF post at Sharm el-Sheikh had been tacitly exempted from the original Egyptian withdrawal order delivered to General Rikhye on May 16. Egyptian news reports and propaganda broadcasts through May 19 did not mention the UNEF post at Sharm el-Sheikh along with UNEF posts in Gaza and northern and central Sinai. On his tour of former U.N. posts in Gaza on May 20, the Egyptian war minister, Marshal Amer, told reporters that Egypt had "no intention of closing the Straits of Tiran."

So what happened? Why did Nasser risk war with Israel over one of the very issues that Israeli leaders privately said would lead to war?

From Nasser's standpoint, there was enormous domestic and regional pressure building over the issue of resuming the blockade. As long as there had been U.N. troops occupying Sharm el-Sheikh, Egypt had had no viable access to the narrow Straits of Tiran, all of which was well within the three-mile territorial limit claimed by Egypt. It seems that Sharm el-Sheikh had been exempted purposefully from the initial UNEF withdrawal order so as to keep Nasser's excuse in place. Then, as soon as U Thant inadvertently forced Nasser's hand and the *entire* UNEF had to be asked to leave, Nasser came under serious pressure to renew the blockade. Nasser resisted the mounting pressure for several days, apparently in order to gauge what Israel would do in the event the straits were blockaded.

Eilat's commercial importance to Israel was more symbolic than real. The port was a convenient but not a vital access to markets and goods in East

Africa and Asia. In fact, the commercial rewards to be gleaned from Eilat were so meager that no Israeli-flag vessel had sailed into the port for years. Before 1956—and since—Egypt had given tacit approval for non-Israeli carriers sailing to or from Israel's Mediterranean ports to transit the Suez Canal. So, the issue was less commercial than political.

Israel had always claimed that, notwithstanding Egypt's moderate three-mile territorial limit, the Straits of Tiran constituted an international waterway through which Israeli shipping had a fundamental right of free passage. Many nations agreed with Israel, but few had ever come out publicly in support of Israel's position.

Through two decades of "normal war" with its neighbors, Israel had become extremely prickly over its perquisites as a sovereign nation. In any of its many facets, the issue of free passage on the high seas has long been an issue over which sovereign nations have gone to war. For example, the young United States had fought a war with Great Britain at least in part over the issue of free passage on the high seas—the War of 1812.

Of course, Nasser was far less interested in denying Israel access to its least productive port than he was in scoring points with his Arab constituents—or, at least, in not losing points to his competitors in Syria. But the question remained: Would Israel actually go to war if Egypt blockaded the Straits of Tiran? Nasser waited and waited for a hint. And, finally, Prime Minister Eshkol provided a broad clue.

On the evening of May 21, only hours after the Israeli leadership avowed *in private* that it would go to war over the blockade issue, Eshkol made a speech so conciliatory in tone that Nasser was left with the inescapable impression that the Israeli government was *afraid* to fight under any circumstances. Eshkol did not even mention Sharm el-Sheikh, Eilat, the Straits of Tiran, or the blockade, not even obliquely.

Thus armed, Nasser made his decision. He could score a huge political success with impunity. Eshkol had given him no reason *not* to blockade Eilat. There appeared to be no risk of war. However, if Israel did wind up attacking Egypt because of the blockade, Egypt would be provided with a legal and moral excuse to launch a retaliatory invasion of Israel. But, even after the die had been cast, it is most likely that Nasser remained secure in his belief—perhaps even in his desire—that he could bluff his way to a political victory rather than go to war.

On May 23, the Soviet Union added immeasurably to Nasser's sense of security when it announced that any aggression by Israel upon any Arab state would be viewed as an attack upon the Soviet Union. Prime Minister Eshkol responded indirectly. He announced that, in his opinion, Egypt's closure of the Straits of Tiran amounted to an act of war against Israel and that any Israeli response would be, *de jure,* an act of self-defense.

There was still time for peaceful solutions. On May 24, within hours of the arrival of the advance elements of a Kuwaiti armored brigade at the same airport, Secretary General U Thant landed at Cairo International Airport to meet with President Nasser. Coincidental with U Thant's arrival in the Egyptian capital, Israeli Foreign Minister Abba Eban flew off from Tel Aviv to meet with France's President Charles de Gaulle, who might yet act as a mediator. Eban also hoped to fly on to Washington to seek help from President Lyndon Johnson in averting a war. In the Israeli Cabinet, Prime Minister Eshkol still was defending his position of peace despite increasing pressure from the nationalists in the Knesset (the Israeli parliament) and *Zahal.* But it was obvious to everyone, including Eshkol, that Foreign Minister Eban's mission was the last best hope for peace—unless U Thant talked sense into Nasser. But U Thant had no impact on events; when he left Cairo bound for New York on May 25, he had nothing to show for an exhausting journey. Abba Eban's trip to Paris produced only a haughty lecture from de Gaulle, and the journey on to Washington produced only some misconstruable sounds of support from the American leadership.

On the other hand, Nasser's bold strokes were producing the desired results in the Arab world. While U Thant and Abba Eban were airborne, each on his way home, Algeria and Tunisia proclaimed their support for Egypt. In no time, many Arab and Third World leaders or their high-ranking representatives flew to Cairo to meet with President Nasser.

On May 25, Nasser's war minister, Marshal Amer, arrived in Moscow to receive the Soviet Union's publicly announced support. On the same day, the Egyptian foreign minister trumpeted that rumored Israeli intentions to run the blockade in the Straits of Tiran would be taken by Egypt to be an act of aggression. With that, the United States 6th Fleet, on patrol in the Mediterranean, was put on war alert, and Washington publicly announced the fact to signal its serious concern to all the parties. However, the U.S. move was countered by a Soviet announcement that a unit of the Black Sea Fleet was transiting the Dardanelles to take up station in the Mediterranean.

Some observers and players felt that the looming threat of a Superpower confrontation would force Egypt and Israel to ease tensions, but it was not to be. The very next day, May 26, found Nasser virtually yawning as a peace proposal from President Johnson was read to him by the U.S. ambassador to Egypt. By then, Nasser appeared disinterested in reversing the course that, in only ten days, had restored him to the pinnacle of Arab esteem.

That same day, Great Britain and Canada suggested at the U.N. that an international fleet breach the blockade in the Straits of Tiran. The U.S. immediately supported the proposal. Canada then suggested four-power talks, but the Soviet Union rejected the idea on grounds that Israel could not be reigned in from its aggressive intent. A Security Council meeting on May 27 produced no results. On May 28, Nasser rejected a claim by the U.S. and Great Britain that the Straits of Tiran was an international waterway, not legally subject to an Egyptian blockade.

Nasser's prestige was soaring in the Arab world—and throughout the Third World. It is doubtful that by May 28 he even remembered that the current affair had begun as a bluff aimed at achieving a bloodless *political* victory. On that day, as he did on occasion, Nasser went too far. In this case, at a news conference before hundreds of journalists from around the world, the Egyptian head of state demanded that Israel return Eilat and the Negev Desert border town of Nitzana to Egypt. Further, he announced extemporaneously, "We plan to open a general assault on Israel. This will be total war. Our basic aim is the destruction of Israel." And then he challenged, "If the Jews want war, they are welcome. Let them come."

On May 29, the day after Nasser's intemperate news conference, Soviet Premier Alexei Kosygin pledged that his nation would allow no outside interference. This was an implicit threat to counter in advance any intended U.S. moves in favor of Israel. Also on May 29, Algeria announced that it was sending troops to Egypt to take part in the dismemberment of Israel.

Though incensed that Egypt was stealing its thunder, the Syrian leadership had been going along with Nasser's growing involvement against Israel. No amount of self-delusion could have convinced the Syrian leaders that their army and air force could go up against Israel alone. It was critical to Syrian plans that the huge Egyptian military machine occupy the vast bulk of the Israeli forces. When the war between Egypt and Israel began, Syria would play its role.

But what about Jordan? Even though one of Jordan's two elite armored brigades was sent on May 24 to reinforce the garrison in the West Bank, the Royal Jordanian Army posed no credible threat against Israel. Nevertheless, the Royal Jordanian Army was considered a crack force; if it went to war, Israel would be obliged to attend to it with substantial forces that could best be used against Egypt. So, Jordan was a factor.

But King Hussein had remained out of the fight. Though the monarch was vilified and threatened by his Arab brethren—there were Syrian troops on his border and Syrian saboteurs loose in his kingdom—he remained steadfastly noncommittal with respect to the gathering war. But, as Gamal Abdel Nasser's political offensive against Israel gathered momentum and garnered apparent victories, Hussein began to recalculate the regional balance.

Finally, in a May 25 broadcast, Radio Amman voiced approval of the closing of the Straits of Tiran, and subsequent broadcasts took on an increasingly strident anti-West tone. But, for the time being, the king remained unwilling to commit his forces or his name to Nasser's gambit.

Finally, on May 28, Hussein became convinced that Nasser was going to pull off the political coup of the century—apparently without shedding Arab blood. Eager to get in on the easy spoils and yet more eager to avoid becoming Egypt's or Syria's subsequent victim, the monarch decided to go on record in favor of the winning side. Hussein arranged a face-to-face meeting in Cairo with Nasser. In return for agreeing to receive the king, the Egyptian leader made several heavy demands. Acceding to any of Nasser's demands would have been unthinkable only two weeks earlier, but Hussein agreed to all of them without protest, so eager was he to appease the mighty political and military forces that ultimately might be arrayed against him.

Late in the morning of May 30, King Hussein suddenly appeared in Cairo. There, in what he later described as "taking out a life-insurance policy," the Jordanian monarch openly embraced Nasser, signed aboard the Arab coalition against Israel, and publicly agreed to integrate his forces into the joint Egyptian-Syrian military high command. He even agreed to allow Egyptian and Iraqi troops to be based on Jordanian soil. Sealing the Cairo bazaar of bargains was an arranged rapprochement between Hussein and Ahmed Shukairy, the head of the Palestine Liberation Organization, who for years had been calling for Hussein's overthrow. When Hussein flew home to Amman that afternoon, Shukairy was aboard the plane.

Bitter though Nasser's pill was for the monarch to swallow, the effects were immediate. All the vilification from fellow Arabs ceased, replaced instantaneously with brotherly praise. Even domestic pressures, mainly from Palestinian quarters, evaporated in a twinkling.

* * *

As Egypt and its growing array of allies appeared stronger, Israel appeared considerably weaker. Pretty soon, Israel began to appear ripe for the plucking. By May 30, Nasser had lost sight completely of his original goals; he was engaged actively in plotting Israel's demise through force of arms.

But Israel had not grown weaker. More to the point, Egypt had not grown one iota stronger than it had been on May 13. The addition of Algerian, Iraqi, and even Jordanian forces actually created more military problems than it solved political ones. Indeed, Israel had grown morally stronger in the interim. If Nasser was basking in the illusion that Egypt's stand against Israel was uniting the Arab peoples, the broad spectrum of Israeli opinion was in fact coalescing. As the tiny nation's survival appeared to be increasingly at stake, the diversity of opinion and emotion was clarifying and uniting. The ultimate consensus had not yet been achieved by May 30, but events were leading it forward to an inevitable decision. When the critical moment arrived, the actual most powerful military force in the region would be ready to sweep away everything in its path. Little Israel—successor state to the kingdom of Little David—would rise up and once again slay mighty Goliath.

5

Dire threats and warlike appearances do not in themselves constitute a war. It is known now that Egypt, by far the strongest of the Arab confrontation states, was not ready nor even particularly willing to go to war against Israel. Not just yet. But in late May 1967, Israel's political and military leaders did not know that, and they certainly could not act on such an assumption. It is an ironclad rule of war—the *first* rule of war—that an enemy must be judged on the basis of his capabilities, and not on the basis of his intentions. By June 1, 1967, Syria, Egypt, and even Jordan were *capable* of launching a three-front war against Israel at a moment's notice, so Israel had to assume they would.

Prime Minister Levi Eshkol's so-called War Cabinet had been meeting almost continuously since May 17. Every speech by an Arab leader, every move by an Arab army, every broadcast by an Arab state-run radio station had been dissected and debated in search of every possible nuance, for every hidden meaning. The debate—to go to war or to refrain from war—had been endless, shifting first this way, and then that way. Several of the approximately twenty members of the inner circle had been for war from the start, and several had been against. But the two key players—Prime Minister Levi Eshkol and Chief of Staff Yitzhak Rabin—had adopted wait-and-see attitudes. Yes, Arab intentions had been debated, but everyone in the inner circle, many of them former military professionals, knew the military realities. Over time, though Prime Minister Eshkol earnestly and steadfastly favored peace, the group's sentiment slowly shifted in favor of war. Later than most, the chief of staff finally agreed that war was inevitable. But the prime minister, whose say was final, held out for nearly two weeks, desperately searching for a peaceful middle ground.

It was King Hussein's trip to Cairo that changed Eshkol's outlook.

Whatever Hussein's real motives might have been, his embrace of Nasser dashed Levi Eshkol's last hope for peace.

Major General Yitzhak Rabin had accepted the first news of the Egyptian May 14 moves into Sinai with equanimity. It is possible that the Israeli chief of staff saw the troop movements for what they really were—part of a political bluff. He set long-standing plans for elaborate countermoves into motion and then went about the business of taking part in the May 15 Independence Day ceremonies.

The same was true for Prime Minister Eshkol. Like Rabin, Eshkol had complete confidence in *Zahal's* routine responses to the Egyptian show of force. Based on intelligence analyses of the ongoing long-term development of the Egyptian armed forces, Eshkol was convinced that Egypt would not be capable of waging an offensive war before 1970. So certain was Eshkol that Egypt's Nasser was bluffing that he did not authorize a partial Reserve mobilization—a prudent political countermove—until May 16.

The Israeli political and military leaders remained confident until May 19, when it was at last obvious that UNEF was withdrawing from the Gaza Strip and Sinai. The Israeli leaders retained their belief that Egypt was not ready to go to war, but several members of the Cabinet began worrying that Nasser himself might not realize that central fact, that he might have convinced himself that Egypt could win a war then and there. To allay such fears and signal that Israel was able and willing to defend itself, a larger portion of the *Zahal* Reserve was mobilized.

Israeli confidence in a peaceful outcome slipped dramatically on May 22, when Nasser closed the Straits of Tiran. Until then, a majority in the War Cabinet felt that an elaborate bluff was in progress. But surely Nasser knew that Israel could not and would not tolerate a frontal assault on the very question of her legitimacy as a sovereign state.

For all the vigilance and debate on the part of members of the War Cabinet, Prime Minister Eshkol did not attempt to articulate an official response to the increasingly tense regional situation until after he heard of the blockade on May 22. That day, before the packed Knesset chamber, Eshkol delivered a policy speech so moderate in tone that all who heard it— Arab and Jew alike—took it to be an outright announcement of appeasement.

Emboldened by Eshkol's soft line, President Nasser began dreaming of achieving hitherto unreachable glories. Chilled to the core of their beings, Israel's military leaders began pressuring Chief of Staff Rabin to prepare for a war of national survival. Bolder and more outspokenly nationalistic than most of his colleagues, Brigadier General Ezer Weizman, chief of the General Staff Branch, opened an active campaign to persuade Eshkol to agree to launch an immediate preemptive strike against Egypt and Syria. But it was too soon for Eshkol or even Rabin to consider such dire action; for the moment, both the prime minister and the chief of staff wanted to give peace a chance.

The United States appeared to align itself with Eshkol's hopes for peace by sending word on May 23 that it was considering several options for forcing Egypt to abandon her blockade of the Straits of Tiran. When no immediate American action ensued, Eshkol talked his colleagues into giving the U.S. plan two full days to mature. General Rabin, who by then was beginning to lean toward a military solution, agreed to wait before marshaling his arguments, but he made it clear that he was doing so because he needed roughly two days to complete the mobilization of the *Zahal* Reserve. (Ezer Weizman dissented from Rabin's judgment, perhaps insubordinately; on May 24, he presented a plan directly to Prime Minister Eshkol in which he advocated an immediate strike against the Egyptian forces arrayed in Sinai.)

Since Chief of Staff Rabin still was saying that *Zahal* was not yet ready to fight an offensive war, all arguments to the contrary were moot, and everyone knew it. Most of the hawks in the Cabinet were content to wait because they had been given no choice, but the doves were involved in a whirlwind of peace initiatives at home and abroad. The broad center of the War Cabinet, which had yet to be persuaded in one direction or the other, continued to ponder the issues.

In the meantime, while the last of the *Zahal* Reserve was being mobilized and the doves were seeking peaceful solutions overseas, Israeli politicians active on the far Right-wing fringes of the nation's political spectrum were pressing for creation of a "National Unity" government. The public became involved in the debate by demanding that the ruling Labor coalition admit the ultra-nationalists to the Cabinet. Finally, on May 25, it was announced that, in light of the dire national emergency, the Labor coalition had agreed to relinquish several Cabinet portfolios to representatives of the far Right.

In the midst of debates regarding the composition of the reconciliation cabinet, Foreign Minister Abba Eban returned from his overseas search for political allies. Upon landing at Lod International Airport late in the evening of May 27, Eban went directly to a meeting of the full Cabinet to report. In sum, the foreign minister explained, the U.S. government had urged Israel to sit tight and wait several weeks for a multi-national flotilla to arrive on the scene to break the blockade of Eilat.

Eban convinced even the skeptics that the United States was sincere in its offer to sponsor formation of the flotilla, but it was clear to all that time was not on Israel's side. The Egyptians were sending more troops and tanks to Sinai every day, and more and more Arab nations were sending troops to serve beside the Egyptians. Nasser was growing bolder; it was only a matter of time before he believed that he could launch the all-important first strike. In addition, Israel's economy was unraveling; the nation could not afford to have so many of its otherwise productive citizens—250,000 in all—under arms for even a few more weeks. Finally, the debate turned to casualties. Even if Israel was confident of winning a war Egypt started, every day that passed ensured that the tiny nation would sustain scores and perhaps hundreds of additional deaths.

The night-long debate produced no decision. The full Cabinet of eighteen ministers was evenly divided, and Prime Minister Eshkol abstained from a decision. He sent everyone home at dawn, May 28, to get some rest. When the Cabinet reconvened, he promised, a final vote would be taken.

Before the Cabinet could be called back into session, both the United States and the Soviet Union officially urged Israel to refrain from starting a war. The Soviet Union threatened, but the United States implied that it would help Israel through the crisis. When the full Cabinet heard the news, the debate swung to the doves. It was decided to wait and see.

Immediately following the May 28 Cabinet vote, Prime Minister Eshkol spoke to his pensive countrymen by way of a radio speech. It was imperative that he do so, for the tension in Israel was at the breaking point. Most of the working men had been mobilized and the economy was at a standstill. Most Israelis ruefully expected the prime minister to announce a war policy, but many were hoping against hope that the government could reach some sort of accommodation with the Arabs. Whether war or peace was announced, virtually every Israeli adult desired a break in the tension. The problem was that Levi Eshkol utterly fumbled the opportunity to bring the Israeli people together under his leadership. Aged 72, possessed of a lackluster personality, utterly worn down from lack of sleep and tension, and graced with extremely limited speech-making powers, Eshkol's exhortive abilities were taxed to the hilt. Also, he did not take even a small amount of time to prepare for his milestone presentation. Haltingly, he woodenly mumbled into the live microphone, backtracking often and even questioning aloud the validity of several key passages he was reading aloud. For a nation on the brink of war, a nation literally exhausted by the prospect of war, Eshkol's blundering speech had a shattering impact. Instantly, the national morale fell through the floor.

One key outcome of Eshkol's disastrous May 28 radio address to the nation was a fierce renewal of an old debate regarding Eshkol's fitness to carry on as his own minister of defense. A holdover from the days of Eshkol's predecessor, the fiery David Ben-Gurion, the dual-hatted perquisite clearly was a tradition the nation could no longer afford. Even as Eshkol's fitness to lead the government was being debated openly in the wake of the May 28 debacle, the nation quickly reached a consensus regarding the prime minister's Defense portfolio; it would have to be passed to a competent military man.

There was a short list of candidates on everyone's mind. All were good men—*very* good men—but there was one name that evoked the ultimate emotion every time it came up. Indeed, on May 24, days before the national debate heated up, the man of the hour had been walking alone on an obscure street in the small desert city of Be'ersheva. When his fellow citizens had recognized him, they had begun chanting his name. A public frenzy, rare in Israel, had ensued. At the time, though not encumbered by a modicum of false modesty, Moshe Dayan—a former *Zahal* chief of staff and lionized hero of the 1956 Sinai Campaign—thought that his fellow citizens had lost their minds.

Following horrific machinations that had little to do with any candidate's actual qualifications, politics followed public sentiment and Prime Minister Eshkol grudgingly offered Dayan the Defense portfolio. Dayan was appointed on June 1, 1967, two days after King Hussein embraced President Nasser in Cairo.

Israel's political leaders made little progress in the war debate between the May 28 vote to wait and see and Moshe Dayan's June 1 appointment. By then, events in the region had outpaced the ability of Israel's doves to buy more time to wait and see. The time to wait and see had passed. In the interim, Egypt and Syria had steadily built their military power in Sinai, Gaza, and the Golan Heights, and Jordan suddenly had assumed a threatening military presence on Israel's most vulnerable flank. By then, *Zahal* had achieved full mobilization and was roughly as prepared for war as it was possible to be. Peace initiatives outside the region were no longer relevant.

It was a certainty that there would be war. The only question still to be resolved was who was going to fire the first shot.

On June 2, Minister of Defense Dayan met with Israel's senior generals. Together, these old comrades-in-arms went over the operational plans in detail. Dayan asked questions and listened intently to the answers. Leaving aside the issue of hawks versus doves, Dayan told his generals that the best way to end the two great emergencies—the political threat imposed by the Egyptian blockade of Eilat and the military threat imposed by the huge and growing Egyptian military presence in Sinai—was the same solution: an overwhelming assault to clear the Gaza Strip and all of the Sinai Peninsula of Egyptian forces. Purely on the merits of military arguments—putting aside the simmering nationalistic debate—it was Dayan's opinion that *Zahal* was as ready as it had ever been to erase Egypt as a regional military power. He argued that doing so was a good enough reason in itself to go to war at the earliest opportunity.

Adding immeasurably to Dayan's resolve to strike as soon as possible was late word that the Arabs were massing in even greater strength along virtually Israel's entire border. By then, over 75,000 Syrian troops supported by an estimated 400 tanks were amassed on the Golan Heights; 32,000 Jordanian soldiers and nearly 300 tanks were facing Israel along the meandering Jordanian frontier; and at least 100,000 Egyptians backed by 900 tanks were already deployed in Sinai. Moreover, these were just the Egyptian, Syrian, and Jordanian troops in the forward areas; as Dayan and the generals well knew, Egypt alone had over 100,000 additional combat troops it could deploy on short notice from areas west of the Suez Canal. Altogether, it was estimated that 328,000 Arab soldiers, over 2,300 Arab tanks, and nearly 700 Arab combat aircraft were in proximity to Israel. As a portent of things to come, a Kuwaiti armored brigade already was deployed near Cairo and an Iraqi fighter squadron was in Jordan. In addition, late word indicated that four Iraqi brigades, including 150 tanks, were moving into Jordan and that air, armored, and infantry contingents from several other Arab and North African states also were on the way to get in on what many Arabs were calling "the final battle."

Moshe Dayan spent June 3 firming up *Zahal's* war plan and preparing a presentation. On Sunday morning, June 4, he met with Prime Minister Eshkol and the entire national-unity cabinet. At the outset, Dayan asked for

permission to send *Zahal* to war at a time to be chosen in secret by himself
and Prime Minister Eshkol.

The military briefing preceding the vote lasted for seven hours. Dayan's
basic argument was that Israel could win a war at that moment and that the
state of readiness of *Zahal* was such that there was no reason for Israelis to
feel intimidated in their own country. The optimum moment, Dayan declared, had arrived.

For once, there was no debate, only questions. When Prime Minister
Eshkol finally asked for a show of hands, the vote was unanimous. Shortly
thereafter, in private, Levi Eshkol readily assented to Moshe Dayan's proposal
that Israeli air and ground forces open hostilities in Sinai at 0745, June 5.

So. The moment of truth was only hours in the future. But, for *Zahal*,
it had been years in the making.

Part II

Zahal

6

Israel won her bitter, costly War of Independence in July 1949. Later in the summer, the Israeli Army of Independence was disbanded and the vast majority of 120,000 Army of Independence officers and soldiers were mustered out into the civilian sector. Right away, the newly elected government of Israel decided to develop an entirely new army in response to the numerous special characteristics of Israeli society, population, and geography.

The name of the new army was the Israel Defense Force—*Zvah Haganah L'Yisrael,* or *Zahal,* its acronym in Hebrew. *Zahal's* new chief of staff was newly promoted Major General Yigal Yadin, a brilliant 30-year-old archaeologist who had served as the chief of operations and acting chief of staff of the Army of Independence. Though Yadin personally had never received any formal military training, he was faced with the daunting twin imperatives of developing both a new form for the new army and ensuring that the military force was capable of winning a round of renewed hostilities with Israel's Arab neighbors.

Daunting as the job seemed, Yadin was in many ways blessed with an opportunity to develop his army from the ground up. At the outset, he established two independent study groups, one to study form (structure) and the other to study function (doctrine). Yadin personally headed the committee that looked into the army's organization—issues such as conscription, discipline, and training. The issues of function—operational doctrines—were turned over to another committee.

Yadin's authority to develop an overall form for the new army was immediately challenged. A heated political debate arose from the heavy influence upon the old Army of Independence by Left-wing egalitarian socialists who had achieved a measure of political dominance in pre-Independence Palestine. These Left-wing socialists, most of them members of the kibbutz movement, had backed or been members of the *Palmach* military force, which was transformed in 1948 into the elite "pioneer" shock corps of the Army of Independence. *Palmach* alumni remained highly influential in politics even after David Ben-Gurion's Left-of-Center social-democrat coalition carried the first nationwide elections in January 1949. The result of the far Left's influence was a series of time-consuming debates over such ideas and issues as the propriety of universal conscription; the propriety of appointing formal military leaders; whether subordinates should be required to salute superiors; and whether the Left-wing socialist kibbutz movements should be allowed to sponsor elite, politically motivated "pioneer" units along the lines of the pre-Independence *Palmach*. Each of these issues was considered— and then rejected by Chief of Staff Yadin and Prime Minister Ben-Gurion, who also served as his own defense minister. At the conclusion of the debates, at Ben-Gurion's express insistence, it was firmly fixed in the Israeli national psyche that *Zahal* was to be apolitical in nature and thus completely subordinate to the civilian government.

Largely because the Israel of 1949 was being flooded by refugees from a wide range of social classes and environments, the need for classic forms of military discipline in the largely conscript army became obvious and paramount. Even the most ardent Left-wing ideologues finally conceded that, insofar as *Zahal* was to be an institution whose secondary function was the social leveling of masses of immigrants, traditional military discipline was a necessity. Long after the great immigration influx of 1948–1952 tapered off, *Zahal* remained an instrument of socialization, even among *sabras*— native-born Israelis.

The model for the new Israeli defense forces—army, navy, and air force—in areas of unit organization, rank structure, and military discipline was the British system. It was well recognized in the upper reaches of *Zahal* General Headquarters (GHQ) that the British Army was superb at developing good soldiers from common citizens. Though the U.S. Army was perhaps even better in that regard, the British model was selected because of the decades-long association that had existed between Palestinian Jews and the British Army. More convincingly, despite a distinctly ambivalent relationship between Palestinian Jews and their nominal British overlords, many Palestinian Jews had volunteered for service with the British Army in World War II and were thus more familiar with its ways.

When *Zahal* was formed in 1949, the Israeli population of 600,000 Jews and its weak, immature economy could support a Standing Army of only 37,000.

It was obvious that so small an army would not be able to defend the country successfully in the event of a new Arab invasion, and that there would not be adequate time to train a far larger wartime army after the start of a new military emergency. From 1949 to 1952, Israel's population rose precipitously because Jews were expelled en masse from Arab nations. The Standing Army grew, but, for compelling social and economic reasons, it remained at around 2 percent of the overall population—not nearly enough to stand against the combined weight of the neighboring Arab armies. Fortunately, early on, Chief of Staff Yadin found a way to instantly field a far larger army in wartime than most of the smaller nations of the world, including Israel, could otherwise have supported.

Yadin's solution was to establish a huge Reserve component and to maintain *Zahal* at peak readiness. To accomplish this feat in the shortest time possible, Yadin copied the Swiss model of universal military conscription coupled with a lifelong military Reserve obligation.

Under the Israeli Reserve system, every able-bodied citizen was called up for a fixed period of conscription. Each new conscript was processed, indoctrinated, and trained in the rudiments of military discipline at an army basic-training camp. From basic training, everyone was permanently assigned to a branch of the service—infantry, armor, navy, air force, administration, etc.—and sent to that branch's basic technical school. After attending basic technical school, officer and non-commissioned officer (NCO) candidates were sent on to a service-wide special basic leadership course while all privates were assigned to a standing field unit and trained definitively in fieldcraft and other combat or technical skills. Once assigned, a private male soldier remained on duty with the same unit for the full length of his mandatory service, training steadily while standing ready to conduct emergency wartime military operations.

Upon completion of the fixed term of mandatory conscription, all privates and most officers and NCOs were released to the *Zahal* Reserve and assigned permanently to a Reserve brigade or combat-support unit; only those few selected for Regular career service were retained on active duty. After release from conscript service, every Reserve soldier was liable for a month or so of annual military refresher training, usually with a permanent Reserve unit. At age 39, the Reserve soldier was downgraded to auxiliary status and assigned to a second-line defense unit, usually a local home-defense company or battalion. He remained liable for a month a year on active duty until age 45. (Over the years, the length of mandatory conscript service varied, as did the length of annual Reserve duty, the age at which soldiers were downgraded, and the maximum age at which Reserve obligations ceased.)

In general, the Yadin committee's model of 1949, which became the first iteration of the ever-evolving Defense Service Law, provided that every able-bodied citizen—male and female—be conscripted at age 18 (or up to 29 in the case of new immigrants) and serve on active duty for two years. In practical terms, ultra-Orthodox men were exempted from the service altogether. This concession was partly in consideration of their religious beliefs against bearing arms in a secular struggle but in large measure the policy was simply in response to political demands by their elected representatives in the Knesset. (The ultra-religious parties have formed a bloc that every prime minister since Ben-Gurion has needed to form a coalition government.) For obvious social reasons, married women and mothers have been automatically exempted from their military obligation, but most women who are otherwise subject to conscription are not called up; large numbers of them simply are not needed because the limited number of non-combat billets—usually administrative—that are open to them are first filled by men who are exempted from combat, usually on physical grounds. Non-Jews were also exempted from military conscription, but a small number of Arab volunteers, usually Bedouins, was accepted each year to serve as trackers or scouts. Also, after leaders of the Druze sect had been insisting for years that their young men be conscripted as a matter of course, the conscription law was extended in 1956 to include all able-bodied Druze males.

Only in the complemented areas of officer selection and officer training did Chief of Staff Yadin's recommendations diverge markedly from the British or Swiss models. Most Western armies select officers on the basis of the candidate's formal application and usually coupled with the completion of two or more years of college, following which selected officer candidates are trained within a separate system. Following the recommendations of General Yadin's committee, *Zahal* began inducting all able-bodied conscripts from a given year group in two mass call-ups per year. Since most conscripts entered the service at age 18, a college education could in no way be a factor in officer selection. Only after induction were potential officer candidates selected upon recommendation by their instructors in a process that was based entirely upon performance during the early stages of basic training. Once recommended, potential officer candidates were subjected to an exacting battery of physical, intelligence, psychiatric, and aptitude tests. All Israeli youths who visualized themselves as officer material—and many who did not—started off on an equal footing with all other conscripts in their year group. The system made the selection, and not the individual.

Education or social standing had no bearing whatsoever in the selection process. *Zahal* was on the lookout for *nascent* leaders, not fully formed specimens. In a way, this aspect of *Zahal's* form was a holdover from kibbutz-based egalitarian influences. Far beyond that narrow consideration, however, it started *all* potential leaders off on an equal footing and filtered every potential leader through a screening process that became virtually foolproof. Far from being exclusive, as are the officer-selection processes of most nations, it was the most inclusive process in the world. *Zahal* wanted access to the very best leaders, and the more the better. It used *every one* of its able-bodied youths as a pool.

Before going on to officer training, an officer candidate had to complete basic training in his branch of the service—infantry, armor, supply, manpower, air, navy, etc. Then the candidate had to complete an NCO course, also geared to his service branch. Next, with temporary rank of corporal, the officer candidate had to serve for several months with a standing unit of his or her branch, during which time he actually led other soldiers in the field. Finally, if he got that far, it was on to a *Zahal*-wide junior-officers' course—in fact, an infantry platoon leader's course attended by all army officers regardless of branch, and even by air force pilot candidates and naval officer candidates. From there, if the final course was completed successfully, the newly commissioned second lieutenant was returned to his service branch for the remainder of his mandatory active-duty tour.

In accordance with the Yadin model, *Zahal* selected many of its NCOs on roughly the same basis as it selected commissioned officers. A certain segment of each new conscript year group was bound outright for higher enlisted rank, and was trained accordingly—first in basic training as privates, then in a branch school, and then in the basic leadership course. These NCOs were then assigned to a standing active-duty field unit for the remainder of their mandatory service. Another segment of privates become NCOs over the course of years in the Reserves. However, in *Zahal*, promotion was not ensured merely because time had been served; an NCO candidate of any age or experience always had to be individually selected, tested, and schooled before advancing in rank. Indeed, it was not unusual for late bloomers to be selected to become Reserve officers, though they usually were restricted to technical billets and faced limited prospects for promotion beyond the rank of captain.

The long-term effects of the Yadin model for the selection and training of leaders were to be profoundly positive. However, in the early years, only junior officers and NCOs benefited from the process. Very few of the company- and field-grade officers and only two or three of the generals who were retained in the new post-Independence army had received even a modicum of formal military training—usually during World War II service in the British Army's Jewish Brigade—but the majority of them would not receive any such professional training for years to come. So, while the concept Yadin fostered was excellent, it would take years to effect *Zahal's* performance. The intervening years were destined to be riven by spotty, shoddy, and even disgraceful performance by many *Zahal* officers commanding troops in combat.

Structurally, the Yadin model of 1949 closely paralleled most Western armies. The Army of Independence had fielded twelve infantry brigades by the time the ceasefire was achieved in July 1949, but it had only one complete tank battalion and only a few disparate artillery units. Its air branch was a pitiful collection of fighters and a few bombers literally salvaged from aircraft boneyards throughout the world.

Despite these initial shortcomings—and very few soldiers to begin with—*Zahal* had a ready-made tradition upon which it could build the *esprit* that is necessarily at the heart of every successful army. *Zahal's* lineal predecessor had just won a war against overwhelming odds.

Based upon its own wartime experience, and bolstered somewhat by the British model, *Zahal* was to be governed by a chief of staff—in reality, a Chief of the General Staff—assisted by the heads of four staff branches. Initially, the staff branches were Instruction, General Staff (Operations), Manpower, and Quartermaster. The Instruction Branch was absorbed by the General Staff Branch in 1953, and a new Intelligence Branch was created in 1954 from the Intelligence Section of the General Staff Branch. This later model parallels the British, U.S., and even the old German General Staff system, among others.

In addition to its largest component, the Army, the defense force of 1949 was composed of the Air Force, and the Navy, each under its own General Officer Commanding (GOC). Also, three permanent front headquarters were established, each to oversee forces assigned on a temporary basis to counter a specific regional threat. These were Southern Command (facing Egypt and southern Jordan), Central Command (guarding Jerusalem and facing central Jordan), and Northern Command (facing northern Jordan, Syria, and Lebanon). The branch directors, the Navy and Air Force commanders, and the front commanders all were members of the General Staff, and all reported directly to the chief of staff.

Israeli law made no allowance for a civilian or even a military commander-in-chief, and the line between the minister of defense, a civilian, and the chief of staff, a soldier, was somewhat blurred in that the former was not afforded formal legal authority over the latter. The ultimate national military authority resided in the person of the prime minister, but even he was legally responsible to a committee of the Knesset if he wanted to mobilize the *Zahal* Reserve or open hostilities.

Subordinate to the General Staff were various directorates, inspectorates, and specialized agencies. Among them were inspectorates for the infantry, artillery, armor, engineers, and signals. The directorates included the Woman's Army Corps, a kibbutz-based military agricultural corps, a paramilitary youth movement, the Judge Advocate General Corps, the Army Chief Rabbinate, and numerous others. Most professional officers and soldiers alternated between staff and line jobs every three or four years, and many served outside their own branches at various times in their careers.

The army was divided into a small Standing Army and the preponderant Reserve establishment. Three field brigades—two infantry (later one infantry and one parachute) and one armored—initially formed the backbone of the Standing Army. In the main, the standing brigades were manned by conscripts undergoing their obligatory military service. A cadre of professional Regular officers and NCOs also served in the Standing Army. They were the backbone of the standing brigades, responsible for leadership, training, and technical support. Regulars who manned the permanent cadres of the eight Reserve brigades were responsible for leadership, training, and some technical support. Regulars also oversaw, inspected, and trained several home-guard and territorial defense organizations composed mainly of able-bodied older men no longer subject to annual service in the *Zahal* Reserve. Of course, Regulars held the key staff posts at General Headquarters (GHQ) and the three front commands. Regulars also manned the various schools of the army, oversaw technical inspectorates, and conducted most of the bureaucratic functions of what quickly became one of Israel's largest bureaucracies.

Since there were many more jobs than there were professionals to fill them, *Zahal* relied heavily upon Reserve fillers. Thus, in addition to providing a vast manpower pool for wartime emergencies, the *Zahal* Reserve provided an essential supplement for keeping *Zahal* functioning on a day-to-day basis. Reserve soldiers who were given an opportunity to accomplish productive work in peacetime proved to be more capable in wartime than Reservists in other armies who spent their limited active-duty time merely playing at their wartime jobs. This extremely potent "force multiplier" was one of the qualitative edges *Zahal* had over most of the world's armies.

Given latitude for Israel's specific situation, Yigal Yadin's "new-model" army of 1949 was structurally akin to the British Army—and even the U.S. Army—of the same period. In the realm of form, its most striking characteristic was the way it selected and trained its leaders. However, in the realm of function—mission and doctrine—the *Zahal* of 1949 and beyond had to be an army like no other.

7

An army is not simply a bunch of people, weapons, equipment, and supplies. An army is foremostly an idea, a concept. Structure and operational outlook begin with a definition of mission—a reason for building and maintaining an army, and reasons for that army's being the way it is.

While Chief of Staff Yadin's committee was toiling with developing *Zahal* as an institution, a committee headed by Colonel Chaim Laskov, the head of *Zahal*'s Instruction Branch, was struggling with a list of operational imperatives and necessarily war-winning solutions to them. A veteran of World War II combat service with the British Army and the commander of Israel's only tank battalion during the War of Independence, Laskov was one of the relatively few senior Israeli officers who had opted and been accepted for a full-time military career following Independence.

From the beginning, *Zahal*'s mission was national survival. Everything *Zahal* could be and would become emanated from five basic precepts that were first articulated by the Laskov committee. The five precepts were an amalgam of factors from Israel's own history and geography, and the qualities peculiar to the Arab armed forces *Zahal* was most likely to fight. To remain viable and capable of conducting its mission, *Zahal* had to evolve in response to—often in anticipation of—changes in the situation and in the region of which Israel is a part.

Following careful, brilliantly insightful study, Colonel Laskov's committee established the five bedrock precepts defining *Zahal*'s mission in 1949. It is a glowing testament to the Laskov committee's care and, indeed, its prescience that its look into the future in 1949 proved to be stunningly accurate in 1967—and beyond!

1. *Few Against Many*
There were millions of Arabs who wanted to see Israel destroyed, but

in 1949 there were fewer than 1,000,000 Jews in Israel. Realistically, Israel would be hard pressed to muster as many as 125,000 combat-effective soldiers, including over-age auxiliaries, from so small a population. But no matter how many soldiers Israel squeezed out of its population, virtually any possible combination of Arab armies that went to war against Israel would be sure to outnumber *Zahal*, including the Standing Army, the Reserve, and all of *Zahal*'s static home-defense units.

2. A War of Survival

The Arab states had repeatedly announced that any war they waged against Israel would be rooted in strategies aimed at annihilating the Jewish state and all who lived in it. Even though the Jews had won their War of Independence, there was no assurance that they could win another war, or another, or another. As long as Arabs massively outnumbered Jews—and they always would—Israel stood a good chance of being annihilated.

3. A Strategy of Attrition

In view of Arab aims and numerical superiority, it was in *Zahal*'s interest to wage a war that would—not necessarily kill the maximum number of Arab soldiers but—destroy the maximum amount of Arab weapons and war materiel. It was clearly impossible for Israelis to do to the Arabs what the Arabs said they would do to the Israelis—annihilate them—so *Zahal* would settle for a solution that was possible. If it could not undertake a strategy of annihilation, it would undertake a strategy of attrition. That is, once a war began, *Zahal* would do everything in its power to end that war and put off the next war by crippling Arab war-making ability. A strategy of attrition is not a strategy of mass killing, as is a strategy of annihilation; it is a strategy of mass destruction.

4. Geographic Pressures

At its widest point, an east-to-west line from the southern edge of the Dead Sea to a point along the Negev Desert frontier with Egyptian Sinai, Israel is about 140 kilometers (87 miles) wide. Between the northern edge of the Kinneret and the port of Haifa, Israel is 51 kilometers (32 miles) wide. At its narrowest point, between the West Bank and the coast north of Tel Aviv, it is a little over 14 kilometers (9 miles) wide. All of Israel in 1948 was less than 8,000 square miles. Nearly all of Israel's population lay in the narrow corridor between the West Bank and the Mediterranean. Virtually all of Israel lay on a coastal plain dominated between the Lebanese border and the desert city of Be'ersheva by Arab positions on high ground. Modern Arab artillery pieces emplaced anywhere on the high ground along the West Bank frontier could reach the sea. Israel's most fertile farmland lay within rifle shot of Syrian infantry anywhere along the full length of the Golan escarpment.

In military terms, Israel lacked "strategic depth." That is, *Zahal* could not give up ground to an enemy advance in order to gain any of a number of important strategic advantages, not the least of which was time to marshal a counterforce and launch a counteroffensive. For Israel, there was no space and there was no time.

Zahal not only held the less desirable low ground, it could depend upon no strategic physical barriers—no rivers or mountain passes, for example— at which it could slow or stop an enemy advance across the narrow coastal plain. Israel enjoyed not one advantage arising from terrain. Its only geographic advantage was possession of extremely short lines of supply and communication, but that extremely important plus was more than obviated by a combination of geographical disadvantages.

If Israel was forced into a defensive war, it would have to hold its enemy or enemies at the frontier. To do so, fortified settlements manned by resident home-guard units were intentionally built at key points along the border; they would act as breakwaters against an enemy tide while mobile forces maneuvered against the enemy flank or rear. If Israel fell victim to a surprise attack, whether or not the fortified frontier settlements were breached, *Zahal* would have to launch an immediate counterattack, on the fly, in order to mitigate its geographic disadvantages and then vitiate enemy gains. In that event, overall, Israel's best defense lay in a good offense.

5. A Short War

Israel could not afford to fight a protracted war. As the War of Independence had demonstrated, long wars meant high casualties. Israeli society could not afford losses anywhere near the estimated 4,000 soldiers and 2,000 civilians (amounting to 1 percent of the 1948 population) who had been killed to gain independence. The economy could not sustain that level of loss, nor could the nation's spirit. Not again. Given Israel's physical and political isolation, the relatively small size of its total military force, its struggling economy, a politically inspired paucity of reliable sources for replacement weapons and military supplies, and the relative influence of oil-producing Arab nations in various world forums, the Laskov committee asserted that *Zahal* had to plan for a short, violent war—and that it had to win.

In sum, to avoid the destruction of Israel and the annihilation of the Israelis, *Zahal's* commanders had to build, train, and equip a military force that would wreak maximum destruction upon several numerically superior Arab armies at once—on Arab territory and in the shortest possible time.

As seen by its architects, the only way for *Zahal* to achieve its primary mission was to attain a massive *qualitative* advantage over its more numerous and better positioned adversaries. One way to meet all the conditions identified by the Laskov committee was for *Zahal* to use all its power decisively in the form of a lightning *preemptive* offensive that would immediately take the war into the enemy's land. Tiny Israel's best hope for survival, lay in building the *best* army in the region and using it first.

While Chief of Staff Yadin struggled to provide a defense-force structure, Colonel Laskov's committee began to define the basis of *Zahal's* operational doctrine. In a way, to achieve his goals, Laskov had to ignore the roadblocks Yadin was encountering; he had to plan against an ideal and then hope that he and other professional soldiers would be able to argue successfully for all they needed to implement their plans.

The keystone of the Laskov doctrine, derived from the five precepts, was *an offensive strategy of attrition.* If *Zahal* had the time, it would mount a lightning preemptive strike into enemy territory. If the enemy attacked first, *Zahal* would contain the advance and mount an immediate counteroffensive into enemy territory. In either case, the objective was to win the opening battle and destroy as much enemy military property as possible.

In classic military terms, the strategies Laskov outlined called for several qualities *Zahal* did not possess in 1949, nor for years to come. It required highly mobile forces directed by independent-minded small-unit leaders who could act on the spur of the moment without recourse to time-consuming decisions from higher authority. It required a professional-level world-class officer corps, and it required modern, mobile arms in the hands of superbly trained, highly motivated soldiers. It required a combined-arms approach to warfare—tanks, planes, and soldiers that could operate together fluidly. In short, it required virtually everything that the *Zahal* of 1949 was not. In the short term, it required a consensus among the professional officers and the government. And it required time—years of time—so that the ideal could be achieved.

But Laskov's vision was not a bad thing. Indeed, it was the most important thing of all, for the vision was the blueprint, and, if the blueprint was not the actual army, it was the virtual army. More than once, the actual army that emerged from the Laskov blueprint saved Israel from succumbing to an Arab war of annihilation. And that made Laskov's vision a very good thing, indeed.

8

Leaving to the civilian government the establishment of tripwires—actions the Arab states might take that would trigger an Israeli preemptive attack—the Laskov committee next turned its attention to outlining a force structure and establishing a unified operational scheme based on the five precepts and its resulting offensive strategic doctrine.

The basic maneuver element of the Army of Independence had been the infantry battalion early in the war and the infantry brigade late in the war. Each battalion or brigade had been a single-service organization, infantry only. Supporting-arms units such as air squadrons, artillery batteries, or the lone armored battalion had been doled out by the central command, ostensibly on the basis of need or availability, but sometimes as a result of political factors inimical to the conduct of a rational military operation.

For a time, Colonel Laskov had commanded the only tank battalion in the Army of Independence, and the experience had embittered him. In 1949, he argued forcefully that each of *Zahal's* eleven field brigades really needed to be constituted as a "brigade group." That is, an "independent" self-contained infantry brigade had to include its own administrative, personnel, medical, training, planning, field-intelligence, and supply sections as well as its own permanent "organic" components of artillery, tanks, and other supporting arms. This proposal implied that the brigade was to be capable of conducting sustained independent operations. It was also to be the army's basic administrative and ground-maneuver element. Under the British system adopted by the Yadin committee, the brigade headquarters was to be responsible for supplying its organic subunits and for training its fighters. Also, the basic military organization with which soldiers were to identify—the object of career-long *esprit de corps* (another holdover from the British regimental system)—was to be the brigade.

Given *Zahal's* size and the scope of its mission, the brigades were forced to evolve an ethos of independent action. That is, the commander of the independent brigade—the proverbial man on the scene—had to be imbued with the ability to think for himself, to seize the moment, to maintain the initiative. Over time, as the peculiar nature of Israel's military imperatives became evident and then institutionalized, *Zahal* consciously sought to identify and nurture leaders who could think on the run without recourse to central authority. The selection and advancement of combat officers became geared to identifying and nurturing the leaders who one day would evolve into ideal brigade commanders. The pinnacle of a *Zahal* combat officer's career became command of a brigade. The outcome of this evolution eventually became *Zahal's* most outstanding trait, for along the way to becoming the perfect brigade commander a talented and ambitious combat-arms officer had to become, in succession, a decisive, independent-minded platoon, company, and battalion commander. Over time, the emphasis upon decisive leadership among officers permeated the entire army, down to the level of private soldiers.

Given the size and sophistication of the army of 1949, not to mention the experience of the Army of Independence, Colonel Laskov was not prepared to define formal nor even a standard conditional structure for multi-brigade operations. It was assumed that each of the front headquarters, which were commanded by experienced brigadier generals or senior colonels, would be able to coordinate operations by more than one brigade at a time, and the matter was left at that for the time being.

In 1949, each brigade nominally comprised approximately 6,000 officers and men. Initially, each infantry brigade comprised three identical infantry battalions overseen by a brigade headquarters and supported by a jeep-borne reconnaissance-scout company, an antitank unit, and a 120mm mortar battalion that acted as mobile organic artillery. Later, some brigades incorporated a mobile medium field-gun or howitzer unit. In general, however, field-artillery units were attached from a regionally based artillery brigade directly overseen by a front headquarters. Laskov's plan to assign at least one company of tanks organically to each infantry brigade was obviated by an initial shortage of tanks and was not resurrected for many years.

To facilitate emergency mobilizations, the eight Reserve infantry brigades were regionally based. An unanticipated dividend of the regional system was that Reserve brigades, which were mobilized as complete units during routine annual Reserve training service, became exceedingly close-knit social entities. Also, they often trained in the region from which they were drawn. By doing so over the span of many years, they learned everything there was to know or considered everything there was to consider about attacking and defending upon familiar terrain. Soldiers are more highly motivated when fighting on home ground than when they are sent to strange remote regions. That was a potential benefit, but *Zahal's* Reserve brigades could fight anywhere, and were expected to, depending upon where the actual threat lay. But, even then, there were always one or two Reserve brigades that could get to a particular region faster than brigades from other regions.

The Laskov committee also defined a standard armored brigade, but in 1949 and for years thereafter, there were only enough tanks for a single battalion, so the 7th Armored Brigade began as a *de facto* mechanized brigade that combined *Zahal's* lone tank battalion with one halftrack-mounted ("armored") and one truck-mounted ("motorized") infantry battalions.

Zahal's concept of an offensively oriented combined-arms military machine capable of undertaking a lightning preemptive strike was unattainable at the outset because of overwhelming manpower, training, and equipment deficiencies. Also at this early juncture, the huge influx of poorly educated Jews from Arab lands required that military training take a back seat to mass socialization. Far from training the thousands of newly available conscripts in necessary military skills, *Zahal* became the prime instrument for teaching new immigrants from Arab lands the rudiments of the Hebrew language, not to mention the rudiments of living in the Twentieth Century. (It was only just a little easier to absorb a diverse mix of Bulgarian, French, Rumanian, Russian, American, South American, and who-knew-what-other-kinds of Jews from afar.) Moreover, limited funds that should have gone into weapons procurement and adequate salaries for military professionals were diverted to *Zahal*-run social-welfare programs for the new immigrants. Tens of thousands of foreign-born conscripts passed through *Zahal's* mandatory service, but the gains in overall military preparedness were nil.

One vital aspect of professionalizing *Zahal* that went reasonably well was the upgrading of the officer corps. Personally overseen by Chaim Laskov in his capacity as head of the Instruction Branch was the selection and standardized training of 27,000 junior-grade officers in a period of only eighteen months. To accomplish the task, Laskov established thirty temporary military schools.

He even saw to teaching the rigorously selected candidates English so they could read the best foreign military texts. Laskov next established schools for battalion commanders and senior staff officers (majors and above), many of whom had never received formal military training despite years of continuous service. One offshoot of the senior schools was the ability of *Zahal* to identify its best commanders and staff officers and to put them on career tracks that would assure maximum exploitation of their superior talents and skills. But, though rushed at the outset, the process took years to reach fruition and, until as late as 1953, the officer corps was filled with notorious incompetents.

An important realm over which *Zahal* had little or no control was arms procurement. Even when the Knesset authorized adequate funds, which was rarely, Israeli arms buyers faced hostility or circumspection from potential sellers.

In one notable case, the Canadian Army had thousands of surplus Browning .30-caliber machine guns to sell, but it refused to honor Israel's high bid on the basis that the weapons were offensive in nature and thus counter to the stated desire of the United Nations to demilitarize the Middle East. Similarly, the otherwise supportive United States would not sell to Israel surplus Sherman M-4 medium tanks, which *Zahal* needed at least to replace routine castoffs from among the fifty operational Shermans comprising its lone tank battalion. What the Americans would sell to Israel was scrapped tanks—Shermans that had been partially dismantled and thus were no longer legally considered tanks. Though it meant refurbishing the "demilitarized" Shermans at great cost, the Israeli arms buyers jumped at the opportunity. The Armor Corps was thus able to maintain its one operational tank battalion and, indeed, to grow incrementally.

And so it went. For several years, *Zahal* was unable to issue a standard rifle to all its infantrymen because it could not purchase tens of thousands of a single model—nor even many different service rifles of just one standard caliber.

Though the Israelis recognized that *Zahal* would always be at least partly dependent upon foreign weapons purchases, these early procurement headaches resulted in early moves to develop a domestic arms industry, including weapons-system research and development. (One early and enduring product of the effort was the 9mm Uzi submachine gun, which was first issued in small numbers at the end of 1952.)

*   *   *

For all the brilliant efforts of *Zahal*'s first post-Independence chief of staff, Israel's military nonetheless was considered a barely adequate Third World military force, by no means a standout among the world's armies, nor even among the armies of its own region. This low universal esteem was not in any way the fault of *Zahal*'s leaders. It was more a matter of Israel's grave economic problems and social upheavals—all attending the huge influx of impoverished, largely illiterate new immigrants. Moreover, in the first five years after Independence, *Zahal* simply had not yet had enough time to fully implement and institutionalize all facets of Yadin's and Laskov's comprehensive plan. Indeed, during the tenure of Yadin's successor, *Zahal*'s inadequate budget actually had to be slashed ruthlessly. Of course, that obviated the purchase of modern weapons or even adequate pay to attract talented officers who might otherwise have been retained in the Standing Army. More important, training suffered; at times, Reservists could not be called up for annual training because there were no funds for their pay.

Yigal Yadin finally resigned in November 1952 over a combination of two pressing budgetary issues: adequate pay for career officers and Prime Minister Ben-Gurion's insistence that several Reserve brigades be disbanded as a means for saving money. The new chief of staff, Major General Mordechai Makleff, lasted only eleven months because of budgetary battles with civilian members of the government influential in military affairs. The real problem, it turned out, was that neither Yadin nor Makleff were able to stand their ground against the civilian budget cutters. Fortunately, Makleff's replacement was not someone the civilians could push around.

It was only after Makleff's departure that *Zahal* began to develop toward its true potential. The development process—absolutely relentless in nature—took a dozen years to reach fruition or attain worldwide notice. The development of *Zahal* into a world-class combined-arms military force had its roots in the Yadin-Laskov planning of 1949, but a new age—*Zahal*'s golden age—began on October 6, 1953, with the promotion of the incumbent chief of the General Staff Branch to the post of chief of staff: Moshe Dayan.

9

Moshe Dayan was the first baby born at the first kibbutz founded in Palestine—on May 20, 1915, at Kibbutz Degania. In a way, his birth pre-ordained the birth of a free Jewish state. And Dayan's progress from young-adulthood onward came to symbolize in later years the growth of the ability of the Jews in Palestine and Israel to defend themselves against the increasingly bloody-minded outward signs of Arab hostility.

Early in his youth, Dayan enlisted in *Haganah*, the pre-Independence Jewish self-defense force. He was one of only several Jewish youngsters personally selected by British Army Captain Orde Wingate to receive formal leadership training during the so-called Arab Revolt of the late 1930s. Labeled a terrorist, Dayan was jailed by the British for two years between 1939 and 1941, but he subsequently took part in a Jewish-manned and Jewish-led military operation into pro-Nazi Syria on behalf of the British colonial government that had previously incarcerated him. It was during that 1942 operation that a Vichy French bullet struck Dayan's telescope, an impact that resulted in the loss of his left eye. Early in 1948, Dayan raised an independent jeep-borne commando battalion that served as part of the Israeli armored brigade throughout the War of Independence.

Ending the War of Independence as commander of the embattled Jerusalem District and secure in his position as a political protege of Prime Minister Ben-Gurion, Colonel Moshe Dayan was retained in the post-Independence army. He rose quickly, serving from 1949 through 1951 as GOC, Southern Command, and in 1952 as GOC, Northern Command. When Brigadier General Mordechai Makleff was named to succeed Yigal Yadin as chief of staff, Brigadier General Dayan was named to head *Zahal's* General Staff Branch and act as stand-in chief of staff during Makleff's numerous fact-finding trips out of the country. When Makleff resigned from his post over policy differences with the civilians overseeing *Zahal*, Dayan, then 38 years old, was appointed to replace him. He took over as chief of staff on October 6, 1953.

Dayan was an energetic and creative if notoriously impatient innovator. During his tour as chief of staff—a tour in which his numerous and profound organizational and administrative accomplishments are often overlooked in the shadow of his legendary leadership during the 1956 Sinai Campaign— Dayan was responsible for altering the shape and especially the outlook of *Zahal's* combat arms. In that regard, he had ample assistance from the many talented and vocal leaders he and other senior commanders had nurtured since 1949, but, in the end, it was the stamp of Dayan that most influenced *Zahal's* rise to world-class stature in the years and decades to come.

Beginning with outward appearances, Dayan was able to capitalize on the large and growing base of well-trained Reservists who had been "graduating" from the Yadin-model Standing Army in the years before 1953. During the first three years of Dayan's incumbency, *Zahal's* initial combat force of ten infantry and one armored brigades grew to a combined-arms force structure incorporating thirteen infantry, three armored, and one parachute brigades. This growth was accomplished in large measure with demobilized conscripts, but Dayan also eked out the number of available combatants by awarding contracts to civilian firms for such mundane support services as baking and laundering. Also, he achieved a one-time manpower bonanza by reducing the strength of the approximately 6,000-man combat brigades to 3,500 soldiers in the armored brigades and 4,500 soldiers in the infantry brigades.

Generally, the infantry brigades were organized beneath a headquarters group, small by world military standards, that consisted of a brigade commander, his deputy, an operations officer, an adjutant (personnel officer), a field-intelligence officer, a quartermaster, and the handful of enlisted technicians who manned each staff section. Attached organically to the brigade headquarters were a number of combat-support detachments, including a jeep-borne reconnaissance company, a heavy (120mm) mortar company, a signals platoon, an engineer platoon, and, usually, an antitank platoon. Each brigade also had a medical section with its own doctor.

The main strength of the infantry brigade was provided by three infantry battalions of about 900 soldiers apiece. Designed conceptually as maneuver elements that would almost never stray far from the brigade's administrative or battlefield control, the infantry battalions were extremely lean at the top—

hardly more than a handful of officers, communicators, and medics manned
the command post. Each infantry battalion consisted of three infantry companies and one medium (81mm) mortar platoon.

Zahal's artillery arm had been the army's stepchild before Dayan became
chief of staff, and it would remain so long after he turned the post over to
his successor. There simply were not enough artillery pieces of any type
available, and Israel was pretty much shut out of the lucrative world arms
bazaar. There were enough towed field guns and howitzers of various types
and calibers available to build several 12-gun battalions, but the infantry
brigades had to be trained to rely mainly upon their 120mm heavy-mortar
companies, which in a pinch could be upgraded here and there to battalion
strength. In 1954, the French sold *Zahal* a battalion of 105mm self-propelled
(SP) howitzers grafted to light-tank chasses, but all of these went to the Armor
Corps, which was dying for such weapons. In the same deal, the French also
provided several batteries of towed 155mm medium field guns, the first large-
caliber, long-range weapons to reach *Zahal*.

Artillery support aside, the infantry's greatest weakness was wheeled
transport. There were only several hundred halftracks in Israel going into the
Sinai Campaign, and these were deployed almost exclusively with the by-
then three armored brigades. Standard military vehicles of all types were in
short supply, and most of Israel's military jeeps had been converted for use
as light reconnaissance vehicles. No post–World War II army walked to
war—nor could one afford to do so on the modern battlefield—so a plan to
commandeer civilian vehicles that had been outlined by Dayan's predecessors
was codified under Dayan's leadership. Based on a nationwide survey coordinated with the army's projected needs, the army under Dayan was to take
control of 13,000 civilian vehicles in the event of a general mobilization. It
did not matter what a vehicle looked like; it just needed to be in running
order. Provisions were made to ruggedize and even to repaint civilian vehicles
if there was time, and military accouterments such as machine-gun mounts
could be added in very short order.

The essence of the Dayan-model ground army was a preponderance of
"tooth" over "tail." That is, it was Dayan's wish that the Israeli ground force,
outnumbered almost by definition, work diligently to place the vast bulk of
its available manpower in direct, hostile proximity to the enemy. Non-
combat services were abolished or kept to the absolute minimum, and command echelons were among the leanest in the world. No world-class army

then or now runs its combat brigades, battalions, and companies in combat with fewer headquarters personnel. This ironclad principle was set down by Moshe Dayan in the mid 1950s, and no one has dared to tamper with it.

Another immutable Dayan principle was that professional soldiers leave the Standing Army around the age of 40 and make way for younger men with fresher ideas. Dayan tagged this innovation the "two-career system," and it has influenced the nation as profoundly as it has influenced *Zahal*. By means of obligatory retirement, a fresh crop of vital, disciplined youngish men with a clear concept of service to the nation is turned loose throughout the year every year—to take over companies or even start up new companies, to stand for public office, and generally to do what must be done in the private and public sectors to keep Israel strong or to help Israel grow and prosper. Typically, the retired professional officers whose rank at 40 is usually colonel or brigadier general, remain on Reserve status, subject to annual duty and mobilization. As such, they are conduits for news and innovations from the vital worlds of commerce and finance. Their ongoing contributions to *Zahal*'s growth are at times pivotal to the national survival.

It was an infantryman, Brigadier General Chaim Laskov, who had the most profound impact upon the doctrinal development of the Israeli Air Force (IAF). As the IAF commander for two years between 1951 and 1953, Laskov had ordained that Israel would bypass pure bombers and pure fighters and build an offensive air force composed entirely of fast, sturdy fighter-bombers capable of both defending themselves and delivering precision bombing attacks upon enemy tactical, operational, and strategic targets. The IAF was to be a multi-purpose air force, capable of launching everything from reprisal air raids to strategic air offensives and delivering precision on-call close air support for the ground forces.

Laskov's was a tall order. It was beyond the capabilities of most of the world's air forces, and it remained beyond Israel's reach throughout Laskov's tenure because of budgetary constraints and the old limitations imposed by arms producers unwilling to alienate Arab sentiments in behalf of Israel's survival. However, in addition to identifying the exclusive combat-aircraft type, Laskov had a powerful impact upon the air force's strategic outlook, and even upon tactical doctrine.

It remained to others, notably Laskov's successor, Brigadier General Dan Tolkowsky, to begin to bring Laskov's dream to fruition. From his appointment in late 1953, Tolkowsky, a renowned combat pilot, worked tirelessly to acquire the materiel and to hone the proficiency of his small force of pilots, maintenance technicians, and armorers to world-class standards. Along the way, he achieved a level of autonomy for the IAF that had been unthinkable under his two non-flying predecessors.

Though Tolkowsky and his fellow airmen would have preferred seeing the IAF become a completely autonomous branch of service, as were the air forces of the United States and Great Britain for example, it was one of *Zahal's* inviolate principles that both the air force and the navy operate in clearly subordinate roles to the army. In fact, the IAF is officially styled the "Air Corps," and the official status of its commander is equal to the chief of the Armor Corps or GOC, Southern Command. Indeed, the appointment of infantryman Laskov and his predecessor, also an infantryman, had been made by Chief of Staff Yadin to underscore the air force's subservience to the ground forces. Though many who served in the IAF were volunteers, the army sent conscripts, including pilot candidates, to the air force only after they had completed eight weeks of army basic training—the same as conscripts assigned to the infantry, Armor Corps, or artillery.

The first jet warplanes ordered by Israel, in June 1952, were French Ouragan ground-attack aircraft, a first cousin of the first-generation Soviet and American jet fighter-interceptors that were rewriting aerial history over Korea. However, the first twenty-five Ouragans were not delivered to Israel until October 1954. The arrival of the Ouragans, which were armed with four 20mm cannon and capable of carrying two 250-pound bombs or two rocket pods, allowed the IAF finally to retire its contingent of British-made Spitfire piston-engine fighters. By then, also, the IAF had acquired six twin-engine Meteor jet trainers for evaluation. In 1954, Great Britain sold Israel twenty-five Meteor fighters, but most of these had to be downgraded to jet transition trainers because, by then, aerial combat in Korea had shown the British jets to be far inferior to the MiG-15 fighter-interceptors in the Egyptian arsenal.

An opportunity to purchase a large number of Mystère-II fighters from France in early 1955 led to a dispute between General Tolkowsky and his fighter commander, Colonel Ezer Weizman. Tolkowsky wanted to remain true to the fighter-bomber formula laid down by Chaim Laskov and bypass the Mystère-II fighters in favor of waiting a year longer for the same large number of Mystère-IV fighter-bombers, then still in development. Weizman favored taking the bird in the hand and trying later to order Mystère-IVs. Tolkowsky prevailed. Despite worries that France might renege or at least delay shipment, the first Mystère-IVs were delivered on time in April 1956. Not without considerable forethought, all of the Mystères were specially armed with two 30mm cannon that were as well qualified to disable or destroy the tanks of the day as they were to take on anything that flew. They could also carry beneath their wings 1,000 kilograms of mixed bombs and rockets.

The IAF remained singularly unimpressive in size. By October 1956 its main combat component consisted of eighty-two fighter-bombers, of which fifty-three were jets and twenty-nine were World War II–vintage piston-engine P-51 Mustangs. Inasmuch as the Egyptian Air Force alone deployed several hundred relatively modern warplanes, the IAF had no choice but to make itself felt in the area of quality. As head of the IAF's fighter command, the IAF's operational arm, Ezer Weizman was a bear on pilot selection and training. He was also hell on the maintenance and ordnance crews, for the strength of an air force is not measured in battle by how many planes it carries on its books but by how many armed combatants it can get into the air.

Best efforts aside, the IAF was and remained a third-rate air force at the end of 1956. Its only edge was the desire and bravery of its pilots and the dedication of its ordnance and maintenance crews to keep the warplanes flying. Though there was little they could do to overcome a weak budget or a closed community of arms suppliers, Laskov, Tolkowsky, and Weizman— not to mention approximately 4,500 dedicated subordinates—used the early and mid 1950s to establish the foundation for greater things to come.

The Israeli Navy (or Sea Corps, as it was officially styled) was *Zahal's* weak sister when Moshe Dayan was named chief of staff, and it would remain so long after he left the post. The condition was less the fault of Dayan or any other chief of staff of the era as much as it stemmed from the inability of Israeli arms buyers to buy ships and weapons for ships. In addition to the usual political constraints, Israel had only so much money to invest in warships. Moreover, once acquired, ships are extremely expensive to operate and maintain.

Given Israel's geographic situation and the rather sorry state of the navies of neighboring Arab states, the Sea Corps was the last combat arm in order of urgency that needed to be improved. Until the Egyptian Navy benefited immensely from a huge Czechoslovakian arms shipment in 1955, Israel's two old destroyers, nine torpedo boats, and two large tank landing craft were adequate for her needs—and affordable. After the Egyptian Navy was upgraded in 1955, there was nothing Israel could do for the time being to keep pace.

Zahal's ground and air forces—but not the naval force—were physically streamlined, upgraded, and modernized to the degree possible during the first three years of Moshe Dayan's tour as chief of staff. But, in large measure, such changes were cosmetic. Dayan's greatest contributions to *Zahal*—and upon the survival of his native land—lay in identifying, encouraging, and institutionalizing the innovations of other, younger leaders in the profoundly interconnected doctrines of flexibility and fighting spirit.

10

It was toward the end of Moshe Dayan's eleven-month tenure as director of the General Staff Branch that he began to do his important share in sowing the seeds of *Zahal*'s now-legendary fighting spirit. For, in the years before Dayan's ascension to the post of chief of staff on October 6, 1953, *Zahal*'s primary mission—the defense of Israel against aggression—had been a rather miserable failure.

Fortunately for Israel, social upheavals in the Arab world for years prevented Israel's enemies from mustering a strike, nor even from paying much attention to building offensively oriented armies of their own. Until the mid 1950s, the Arab armies facing Israel were more in the nature of "coup armies," whose orientation was internal rather than external. *Zahal* needed every bit of the time afforded by the fitful unrest in the Arab states to prepare for eventual war, for between 1950 and 1953, Israeli combatants came off second best in several rather tame confrontations with insignificant Arab military threats.

Though the official standing armies of Israel's Arab neighbors undertook no direly threatening moves against Israel for years after the War of Independence, individuals and gangs of raiders, including mere robbers, ardent but incompetent Palestinian guerrilla bands, and officially sanctioned irregular and regular units, conducted cross-border incursions into Israel throughout the period. Often, the raids were merely for purposes of plundering out-of-the-way Jewish border settlements, and many "incidents" involved little more than thieves from East Jerusalem stealing tires off Jewish-owned automobiles and trucks in West Jerusalem. Even a number of land-mine incidents along lonely roads in the Negev Desert could be traced to predatory Bedouin tribesmen whose only motivation was plundering the remains of the automobiles blown up by the mines. But a growing number of incursions over the years were in behalf of political agendas. A growing number of perpetrators were sanctioned officially by hostile Arab governments.

Throughout 1950, Arab raiders of one sort or another killed nineteen and injured thirty-one Israeli civilians, all virtually without effective response from *Zahal*. That year, General Dayan had first-hand experience with *Zahal's* inability to secure Israel's borders. In his capacity as GOC, Southern Command, Dayan witnessed a sorry episode in which the 7th Armored Brigade, incorporating Israel's only tank battalion, was dispatched to the vicinity of Eilat to thwart an effort by the Jordanians to interdict the main road to the city from the northern part of Israel. The Jordanians claimed that the road actually crossed into Jordanian territory, so they had dispatched an army unit to block it. Dayan ordered the commander of the 7th Armored Brigade to clear the road, but, nothing much happened for several days. The Israeli tanks reached the blocked section of the road without a problem, but the brigade commander became indecisive about getting his subordinates deployed to roll forward. In the end, before the threatened Israeli attack commenced, the Jordanians withdrew pretty much of their own accord. Dayan was so angry that he recommended that the 7th Armored Brigade be disbanded and its troops scattered to infantry units.

The next humiliation occurred after Dayan had become head of the General Staff Branch under Chief of Staff Makleff. On Saturday, May 2, 1951, a relatively small band of Syrian irregular fighters apparently supported by regular Syrian Army troops crossed into Israel near the headwaters of the Jordan River and occupied Tel el-Mutilla, a little hill dominating several Jewish settlements at the northern end of the Kinneret. When a call went out to *Zahal*, Northern Command dispatched a battalion of the 1st "Golani" Infantry Brigade, one of *Zahal's* two standing infantry brigades. In a series of ineptly led and desultory attacks, the Israeli battalion, which was composed almost entirely of Yemenite and Bulgarian conscripts, was unable to drive the outnumbered Syrians from Tel el-Mutilla. In three days of sporadic fighting, twenty-seven Israeli soldiers were killed to little or no avail. *Zahal* prevailed only after a battalion of Druze volunteers was thrown into the fray. *Zahal* GHQ considered the Tel el-Mutilla incident to be grave, but nothing was done at that time to mitigate the poor showing.

Overall, in 1951, an estimated 150 Israeli civilians were killed or wounded in clashes *inside Israel*. A combination of lightly armed Israeli Border Policemen and Home Guardsmen, not to mention Standing Army and Reserve units, were unable to stop the rising tide of border incursions, and a high-profile humiliation like the one at Tel el-Mutilla hardly reassured the public at large that its high taxes in behalf of defense and security were being put to good use. Israeli efforts to launch retaliatory strikes against the Arab raiders themselves or reprisal operations against Arab villagers who supported the raiders were all unsuccessful.

The next headline-grabbing incident came in December 1952, when a group of Israeli soldiers was dispatched routinely to carry supplies to the Israeli enclave atop Mount Scopus, in Arab East Jerusalem. When several Jordanian soldiers or civilians merely opened fire, the Israeli soldiers abandoned their laden vehicles on the road and ran back to Israeli West Jerusalem.

In 1952, nearly 150 Israeli civilians were killed or wounded *inside Israel* in a record 1,751 incidents involving Arab infiltrators. That year, Prime Minister David Ben-Gurion officially authorized *Zahal* to conduct retaliatory raids inside Arab borders. Eighty-five such forays were launched, but only fifteen were deemed successful. In one bizarre incident, an Israeli infantry squad sent into the Gaza Strip to conduct a reprisal raid became so completely lost that the humiliated sergeant in command committed suicide with a hand grenade.

Finally, on January 22, 1953, as Moshe Dayan and several other senior officers looked on, a company of infantry was sent into Jordan to attack the hilltop village of Falama in retaliation for an Arab border raid launched from the same general area. Shortly after the Israeli company, which was composed entirely of new immigrants, breached the border fence and crossed the line, rifle fire put out by a mere dozen Jordanian National Guardsmen wounded one Israeli soldier. The attack immediately halted in place. Even the eventual commitment of the entire Israeli battalion was unable to make any headway whatsoever against the twelve Jordanian riflemen. At length, though only six Israelis were wounded, the battalion commander ordered his entire unit to withdraw into Israel. When the commander reported to General Dayan upon clearing the border fence, the livid army operations chief threatened to relieve him on the spot. However, as Dayan's senior colleagues pointed out, the officer was no worse a commander than any other officer commanding any other battalion at that time. Dayan relented for the moment, but it was plain to see that *Zahal's* philosophy of command was in store for some extensive revamping.

Instantly, in view of the poor showing of all-immigrant units at Tel el-Mutilla and Falama, General Dayan ordered that *sabras*—native-born

Israelis—be assigned to all companies of all three standing brigades. More important, Dayan threw open the question of combat leadership, which was dissected, evaluated, and reevaluated with an eye toward placing highly motivated leaders at the head of every combat unit, from squad to brigade. Special renewed emphasis was to be placed on former Chief of Staff Yadin's founding concept regarding the initial selection and subsequent promotion of aggressive junior officers and NCOs and upon fostering aggressive leadership at all levels of training throughout the army. Thereafter, special efforts, beginning with the imposition of universal literacy, were to be made to imbue all troop leaders and their troops with *Zahal*'s special place in Israeli society. Ultimately, the essence of the system that evolved during Moshe Dayan's tenure as chief of staff—at his specific insistence—was that every soldier is a leader and every leader is a soldier. The institutionalization of this core concept was the true beginning of *Zahal*'s legendary performance in years and wars to come and its rise to the ranks of a very few truly world-class armies.

But world-class status was years in the future. For the time being, all a thoroughly frustrated General Dayan could do as chief of operations (and training) was start the ball rolling. He promulgated the extremely harsh peremptory army-wide order that a unit commander could not withdraw from the battlefield before completing his mission unless casualties in his unit amounted to fifty percent killed and wounded. Even by Dayan's own unflagging personal standard, the order was absurd on its face. *Zahal*'s problems were fundamental and systemic. What *Zahal* needed was an ethos of leadership by example. Indeed, despite Dayan's harsh new regime, the toll from cross-border incursions rose in 1953 to a total of 180 Israeli civilian deaths and injuries.

Fortunately, by the time Moshe Dayan became chief of staff, a positive example leading to *Zahal*'s transformation had been discovered and put in motion. The tide began turning when a senior officer suggested that a small special commando unit be established outside of the normal army chain of command in order to undertake "sanitary" reprisal raids against Arab irregular units and their bases. The genius of the suggestion lay in the unit's not appearing on the *Zahal* table of organization and its members receiving no official status. Members of the proposed unit were not even to wear Israeli insignia.

One benefit of such a unit existing outside the army was that its individualistic volunteer members need not accede to the petty rules and restrictions of the organized military. But the more important political reason for the suggestion lay in the fact that Israel's American, British, and French benefactors were at that time attempting to enlist Egypt and Jordan in a regional anti-Soviet coalition. If reprisal raids on Egyptian or Jordanian territory could be linked conclusively to pro-Western Israel, then Egypt and Jordan might be driven into the arms of the Soviets and Israel might lose its Western backing. So, as had their Arab adversaries, it was proposed that Israel establish an irregular unit whose existence could be denied and whose actions could be disowned.

General Dayan objected to the formation of the proposed special unit on the rather idealistic grounds that *every* Israeli combat unit should have been able to undertake the mission that was to be assigned to the new unit. Dayan's senior colleagues agreed that Dayan had identified an ideal situation, but they pointed out that *Zahal* had not reached that qualitative plateau. Meantime, while Dayan strove in that direction, there was a growing emergency to rectify. Accordingly, in August 1953, Chief of Staff Mordechai Makleff authorized the formation of Unit 101.

Selected to command the new unit was Major Ariel "Arik" Sharon, a 25-year-old *sabra* college student who also was commanding officer of a Reserve infantry battalion. Upon accepting the new posting, Sharon quit school and traveled throughout Israel to personally recruit approximately forty of the toughest combat veterans he knew from his service during the War of Independence.

Nearly all of Unit 101's numerous raids occurred in the two-month period in which General Makleff was still chief of staff and General Dayan was still chief of operations. However, on October 14, 1953, only a week after Dayan was appointed chief of staff, Unit 101 attacked the West Bank village of Khibye after an Israeli woman and her two children were gruesomely murdered during an Arab raid against an Israeli village near Lod Airport. The Khibye raid was pure reprisal, as had been many of Unit 101's nocturnal strikes into Arab territory, but it turned out to be both pivotal and seminal in its repercussions.

On the night of October 14, all forty of the Unit 101 commandos crossed into Jordan while sixty-three additional Israelis from *Zahal's* lone paratroop unit, Parachute Battalion 890, waited in support positions just inside the Israeli border. Sharon's commandos were engaged by a large group of defenders as they moved on the village, and the supporting paratroopers were committed to the battle. The Israelis quickly fought their way into Khibye, killing twenty-three armed villagers and Jordanian National Guardsmen in the process. Then, while the paratroopers guarded the approaches to Khibye, the commandos rounded up the villagers and proceeded to destroy forty-nine of 250 houses. Unfortunately, the round-up was rushed and thus incomplete. At least forty villagers—half of them women and children—were killed in the detonations or buried alive in the rubble of their homes. In all, sixty-three Jordanian civilians were killed and an estimated seventy-five were wounded.

Pressure to disown the Khibye raid and disband Unit 101 was intense, but the government decided to overlook the matter and Chief of Staff Dayan decided to absorb the commando unit into Parachute Battalion 890. More importantly, Dayan also decided to use the positive results of the raid—the penetration into the village had been the best-run assault in *Zahal's* post-Independence history—as an example for the rest of *Zahal*. So, Unit 101 was disbanded, but its members became qualified paratroopers and the paratroop battalion in general was held up as an example to the rest of the army. Within the month, underscoring the new chief of staff's brainstorm, Major Sharon was appointed commander of the paratroop battalion, which was redesignated Parachute Battalion 202.

In due course, Parachute Battalion 202 was exhaustively retrained to undertake surgical night operations. All of the officers and men were taught to navigate at night, and they did so in a series of cross-border incursions that were part training exercises and part reprisal raids. After the old Unit 101 irregulars had been spread throughout the battalion, the formerly spic-and-span but undistinguished paratroopers began taking on a raffish but competent air. Pretty soon, the blurred lines between officers and troops that had distinguished Unit 101 came to distinguish Parachute Battalion 202. A new group ethos—an effervescent egalitarian ethos—evolved.

The moment of truth came on the night of March 28, 1954, when Major Sharon led a company of Parachute Battalion 202 against Nahalin, a fortified Jordanian West Bank village. The well-led and highly disciplined paratroopers quickly and easily brushed aside the local Jordanian National Guardsmen. Next, in well-rehearsed stages, the Israelis evacuated specific buildings, which were razed to the ground only after Israelis had checked to see that they were indeed empty. The Israelis withdrew in good order, right on schedule, leaving nine dead and twenty-eight wounded Jordanians, all of whom had been killed or injured resisting the initial attack. The Nahalin raid and eight others by Parachute Battalion 202 that took place in 1954 were perfectly executed.

Though Moshe Dayan had little personal impact upon the actual process that transformed *Zahal* by way of Parachute Battalion 202, it was he who steadfastly injected the trust, unflaggingly contributed the resources, and actively fostered the atmosphere that gave the paratroopers an opportunity to develop. Though Dayan was a man whose place in the history of his nation is assured by endless good works, it was his sponsorship of Parachute Battalion 202 as a leadership and tactical laboratory that yielded *Zahal* and Israel their greatest and most enduring benefits. The fact that Dayan did so at a time when he could not have known how things would unfold says the most for his vision, for he trusted others to take care of the details while he held that vision firmly before himself and the other impatient nation builders at his level.

Parachute Battalion 202's unbroken string of successes was not in the mere completion by its members of a course in jumping out of airplanes. It was a matter of the unit's voluntary discipline—where officers actually and literally *led* their charges into battle as a matter of course and where the troops followed because they chose to. Moreover, in the course of rehearsing each and every night raid, Major Sharon and his officers learned foolproof methods for overcoming defended positions—through the application of information and intellect before the fact, by means of recognizing and improvising better solutions during the attack, and by putting everyone's head together to expand the unit's bag of tricks during post-attack debriefing sessions. The first of Parachute Battalion 202's growing arsenal of secret weapons was consensus; everyone was given a part in the planning and a stake in the outcome; everyone was made to feel that his personal contributions were important and that, through his efforts, he personally could affect events.

Early on, it was Major Sharon himself who made the greatest ultimate impact on Parachute Battalion 202's—and, later, *Zahal*'s—unique fighting doctrine. While recuperating from a wound he sustained in a raid in July 1954, Sharon came up with a tactical concept that set the "accepted wisdom" of Mideast conventional warfare completely on its ear.

Sharon gave enemy soldiers credit for being courageous, disciplined fighters, but he also recognized that in the very discipline of the Arab armies were the seeds of their defeat. Once set into a defended position, even a small

Arab unit was capable of holding its ground against a far larger conventional unit, especially if the attackers held to conventional daytime tactics. This had been proven to *Zahal*'s pure woc on the outskirts of Eilat in 1950, at Tel el-Mutilla in 1951, and at Falama in 1953. But constant nocturnal victories over Arab garrisons suggested to Sharon that even highly disciplined, well-trained, well-equipped, and well-positioned Arab units could not *react* as readily as his relatively free-wheeling paratroopers. Invariably, Sharon's experience indicated, the Arab will to resist collapsed when the pre-arranged Arab defensive plan deteriorated in the face of unanticipated moves on the part of Sharon's attacking paratroopers. Given this central fact, Sharon realized that Parachute Battalion 202 could achieve even better results if it simply incorporated tactical surprise into its standard bag of tricks—if the paratroopers codified tactics they had been using instinctively but without benefit of training or planning. With that, Sharon set himself the task of distilling his comparatively vast tactical experience into a simple battlefield tactic that could be passed on to his present colleagues and, through standardized training, to all new paratroop volunteers.

Since the mid–Nineteenth Century, when massed rapid-fire weapons began to dominate the modern battlefield, infantry tactics had come to be based on the principle of "fire and move." Simply stated, the infantry leapfrogged forward from its line of departure toward the enemy position by alternately firing (from a "base of fire") in support of a sister unit and then moving ahead while the sister unit, in its turn, laid down the base of fire. As machine guns and mortars came to be used in World War I at the level of the infantry company, the effects of the base of fire became more pronounced, more devastating. If there was a basic flaw in the universal "fire-and-move" tactic, it was its predictability; there were few chances to surprise the defender once the pattern of the attack had been established.

Sharon's brainstorm was to do away until the last possible moment with the "fire" portion of the tactic. After isolating the objective by means of a nonpermeable infantry cordon and establishing silent bases of fire, the attack elements were to move silently toward a point or points along the enemy's forward defensive line. If possible, elements of the attack force were even to penetrate silently into the enemy's rear to interdict command-and-control and supporting-arms positions before the shooting started. If wire barriers or other obstacles needed to be breached to allow access to the enemy rear by a large force of attackers, bangalore torpedoes or other types of explosive charges were to be placed appropriately and set off as soon as the shooting started. The action would commence as soon as the enemy discovered the movement and reacted to it, or when all the attack units were in position. In case of discovery by the enemy, all attack elements that were engaged were to run forward instantly, firing from the hip, in order to shock, overwhelm, and breach the enemy firing line. If possible, attack units that were not discovered and taken under fire were to attempt to sneak into the enemy position and swallow up pre-assigned objectives or at least simply sow confusion in the enemy rear.

The tactic Sharon dreamed up and subsequently perfected against live enemy positions was based upon the supreme value of shock. Conceived as a night tactic and used by Sharon exclusively at night, it capitalized upon the apparent universal inability of Arab forces to improvise an adequate defense once their formal, pre-planned defenses had been breached. It also capitalized upon the particular leadership traits Sharon had been cultivating in all members of Parachute Battalion 202. Recognizing that unit leaders could be killed or wounded and that elements of the attack force were apt to go astray or become delayed at night, Sharon insisted that all his men accept responsibility for leading, either to make good the loss of a unit leader or to exploit an unanticipated advantage. At no time is the fog of war less penetrable than it is at night, and at no time is aggressive individual initiative more likely to achieve unexpected dividends. And that it did; as Sharon's paratroopers refined the battalion commander's brainstorm through live use, the reliance upon individual initiative and flexibility in planning—planning on the fly—were seen to pay larger and larger dividends. In very short order, Sharon and his senior subordinates were able to see that broader outlines and shorter plans coupled with better intelligence and training were the wave of the future for Parachute Battalion 202.

As if merely copying the outward trappings of success could impart success itself, parachute training became a virtual fad in *Zahal* throughout 1955. Chief of Staff Dayan earned his silver paratrooper wings that year, and so did most senior officers. Even Colonel Shlomo Goren, the army chief rabbi, mastered jump training (though he broke a leg doing so). But, alas, until the remainder of *Zahal*'s combat units copied and institutionalized the emerging philosophies underpinning Parachute Battalion 202's success, only the lone battalion of paratroopers held the key to reliably defeating the hundreds of thousands of Arab soldiers who could be arrayed to sweep into Israel from three directions.

Fortunately there was nothing especially revolutionary nor hard to grasp in the Sharon tactic; it had been employed in local situations by many armies in wars as far back as anyone could read about. What was new was its standardized application to the ongoing conflict between Israeli and Arab forces. As success followed upon success, Sharon's superiors—not least Chief of Staff Dayan—were able to see that the paratroopers were on to something that could benefit all of *Zahal's* combat units.

Finally, after much deliberation, on November 2, 1955, a battalion of the Golani Infantry Brigade was attached directly to Parachute Battalion 202 for a night dislodging attack against an Egyptian fortified position in Sinai. The attack was an unqualified success. A month later, Golani infantrymen joined the paratroopers in a night attack against Syrian artillery positions on the Golan Heights. Once again, the Golani troops came through with flying colors. Thereafter, once having gained confidence in the paratroop philosophy, the entire Golani Infantry Brigade was trained in short order to Parachute Battalion 202 standards. Shortly, Israel's second standing infantry brigade followed suit. Since the standing infantry brigades were the feeder units for eight reserve infantry brigades, it was only a matter of time before the paratroop philosophy permeated *Zahal's* primary combat arm. In fact, by the end of 1955, Parachute Battalion 202 was considered so reliable and its training and operational procedures were considered so sound that Chief of Staff Dayan insisted that it be upgraded to a complete 3,500-man standing parachute brigade, also numbered 202. And Colonel Arik Sharon was appointed its first commander.

Designed for highly trained, highly motivated, and highly disciplined squads, platoons, and companies, the Sharon tactic—and all that flowed from it—eventually became so concretely embedded in *Zahal* that, by 1967, it was to be employed routinely as well in battalion-and even brigade-size operations. In fact, in 1967, Arik Sharon, who was by then a brigadier general, personally put the Sharon tactic to work in a division-size set-piece night attack on a major Egyptian defensive zone. Even at that divisional level, Sharon's standardized—and by-then institutionalized—techniques were as precise and clear to see as they had been on Parachute Battalion 202's best-executed night raid in 1955.

11

While the paratroopers were inventing and perfecting their tactical philosophy and passing it on to the infantry at large, *Zahal's* 7th Armored Brigade was reaching the same philosophical plateau by its own unique route. As occurred with the paratroop and infantry units, the armored brigade's renaissance began with one man's vision. In this case, the hero was Uri Ben-Ari, the 7th Armored Brigade's deputy commander in 1952.

Born in Berlin in 1925, Ben-Ari (whose family name was Banner) was the son of a German military hero, for the elder Banner had won the Iron Cross while serving with the Kaiser's army in World War I. Nevertheless, the father had died in the Dachau concentration camp, and ninety-three other members of Ben-Ari's family had perished in the Holocaust. Fortunately, Uri had been sent to Palestine in 1939, when he was 14 years old, and he had spent the war years safely ensconced at a kibbutz in northern Israel. He joined the *Palmach*—the elite Jewish "pioneer" shock force—in 1946 and served with distinction as a company commander during the War of Independence. After the war, Ben-Ari had volunteered to remain in *Zahal*, and he had helped form the 7th Armored Brigade.

To make up for his total lack of knowledge about armored warfare, Ben-Ari, who was a major in 1949, became an avid reader of books on the subject. Notable among his sources were the theoretical writings and memoirs of Germany's top panzer leaders. He learned well from his former countrymen, and was not overly squeamish about absorbing lessons taught by men whose regime had all but wiped out his family.

Despite such readings by Major Ben-Ari and like-minded armor officers, the 7th Armored Brigade was extremely slow in absorbing the lessons of past armored practitioners. Though friendly nations such as the United States or Great Britain might have provided training for Israeli tank officers, apparently no one involved in the development of the Israeli armored community thought to ask, or perhaps the issue was too politically sensitive for the potential host armies. Whatever the reason, it was left to Uri Ben-Ari and his comrades to read what they could find and to practice on their own. Classically, the practice sessions with the 7th Armored Brigade's fairly consistent complement of fifty obsolescent Sherman M-4 medium tanks led the Israeli tankers through every wrong turn and up every blind alley German, French, and American experiments of the 1930s had encountered. But, by applying will and intellect to the growing number of problems and emerging possibilities, the Israeli tankers were able to evolve—on their own—more or less the same set of tactics the Germans had hammered into their lightning *blitzkrieg* strategy in time for the outbreak of World War II.

The Israeli tankers recognized that massed armored formations were inherently a combat arm in their own right and that tanks ought not to be parceled out or even tied directly to the infantry. Naturally, in an army in which infantry constituted the preponderant combat force, as was the case in *Zahal*, armored operations needed to be *coordinated* with infantry operations, especially in offensive warfare, but "coordinated with" and "tied to" were seen correctly as being two entirely different animals. The inherent speed, strength, mobility, agility, and fire power of the modern battle tank was seen as a godsend that should not—could not—be wasted. This was especially true where each of those characteristics could work positively upon at least two of the five bedrock precepts guiding Israeli offensive military outlook— "A Strategy of Attrition" and "A Short War." Indeed, if more tanks resulting in larger and more numerous armored formations could be acquired, the entire preemptive strategy arising from the five bedrock precepts could be satisfied in very large part by a mobile—entirely mechanized—army built around a solid core of tanks.

Something else occurred while Uri Ben-Ari and his fellows were reinventing the armor wheel: The armor officers did it themselves, and, in the end, they *knew* they had done it themselves. They *could* have asked for help from knowledgeable outsiders, but they had not. Indeed, along the way, unfettered by the constraints of "conventional wisdom," they unwittingly developed a few unconventional wrinkles that no well-schooled enemy commander could have foreseen, for the wrinkles were not in "the book" used by most of the world's armies for conducting or challenging armored and mechanized operations. Thus, by a very different route, the Israeli tankers invented a uniquely Israeli approach to their professional specialty, an approach that inevitably would diverge increasingly from the world mainstream. Along the way, they also learned the secret of self-sufficiency and the equally important secret of flexible, innovative thought.

It was a long and rocky road to acceptance of the 7th Armored Brigade's doctrine by the infantry-dominated *Zahal* hierarchy. If the infantry was permitted to overcome its notorious humiliations at Tel el-Mutilla and Falama by the reprisal policy of the mid 1950s, it took two consecutive war-game scenarios to pull the 7th Armored Brigade out of the torpor that had engulfed it for several years following its humiliation in 1950 on the road to Eilat.

In the second of *Zahal's* large-scale war games—Maneuver B, in 1952—Lieutenant Colonel Uri Ben-Ari seized the opportunity to put on display the sum of the lessons he and his fellow tankers had learned by trial and error over the preceding three years. The 7th Armored Brigade, of which Ben-Ari was then deputy commander, was part of the Blue Army, commanded by Brigadier General Moshe Dayan, who two years earlier had huffily advocated the brigade's dissolution. Maneuver B was to be a series of careful set-piece maneuvers designed to test the infantry, but Ben-Ari prevailed upon General Dayan and his own brigade commander to allow him to lead an unscheduled armored sweep designed to show Chief of Staff Yigal Yadin and the other *Zahal* commanders that the armored force deserved to be at the forefront of the army's planning and growth. The result was a free-wheeling rout of the opposing infantry force. Chief of Staff Yadin, a rather stolid practitioner of classic infantry tactics who had never been schooled formally in the military arts, was furious with Ben-Ari for upsetting his set-piece war game. Indeed, during the post-exercise commanders' critique, the chief of staff ruled the 7th Armored Brigade's movements null and void. He also made a point of telling the assembled officers that he considered the armored brigade to be an adjunct to the infantry it was supposed to have been supporting. Many, no doubt including the impetuous Lieutenant Colonel Ben-Ari, could not believe that a modern army commander could say such a thing only seven years after the end of World War II. It was easy to understand that *Zahal* had not yet achieved the management expertise required to conduct large-scale combined-arms maneuvers, but Yadin was regressing to a pre–World War II outlook regarding armor. His was exactly the outlook that had seen the vast but fragmented French armored force defeated in a matter of days in May 1940 by the smaller but unfettered German armored force. It was absurd on the face of it.

General Yadin had resigned by the time the 1953 maneuvers were staged, and young Lieutenant Colonel Ben-Ari again prevailed upon his brigade commander to seize the initiative by launching yet another unauthorized armored sweep into the rear of the opposing infantry force. This time, the breathtaking and successful maneuver was not nullified. More important, Prime Minister (and Defense Minister) David Ben-Gurion personally observed the action, and he was singularly impressed.

Impressing Ben-Gurion was not quite enough, however, to catapult *Zahal*'s lone armored brigade to notoriety. Not just yet. Though General Dayan had also been impressed by the 7th Armored Brigade's performance in maneuvers two years running, he was only just a little less stolid in his infantryman's outlook than had been Chief of Staff Yadin. Dayan recognized what an armored breakthrough could mean, but only as it related to enhancing the position of or clearing the way for the infantry. Dayan felt that armor was a useful mobile adjunct to a primarily infantry-based offensive. Indeed, Dayan's experience in the War of Independence as commander of a jeep commando unit convinced him that light wheeled vehicles—jeeps, half-tracks, and armored cars—armed with machine guns and recoilless rifles were best suited for sowing havoc in the enemy's rear. Dayan conceived of tanks as mobile artillery to be used in direct support of the infantry. Despite the example of World War II, Dayan did not perceive that armor was a new type of combat arm that had effectively supplanted the infantry as the queen of the modern battlefield.

Nothing much happened with respect to Israeli armor until 1955. By then, two new Reserve armored brigades had been activated to accept the steady flow of demobilized conscripts from the 7th Armored Brigade, but both were weaker than the 7th Armored Brigade because of equipment shortages. Uri Ben-Ari eventually was promoted to command the 7th Armored Brigade, but no new large-scale maneuvers were conducted, and attention naturally became riveted on the paratroopers and their reprisal raids. Since tanks could not be dropped by parachute, no one gave them much thought.

Changes started occurring when a personality conflict flared up in 1955 between Chief of Staff Dayan and the head of the General Staff Branch, Brigadier General Chaim Laskov. Early in 1956, Dayan evicted Laskov from GHQ and exiled him to head the Armor inspectorate.

Laskov knew a little about tanks; he had commanded Israel's only tank battalion for a time during the War of Independence. He listened to what Colonel Ben-Ari and other armor officers had to say, and he began waging a campaign to upgrade his neglected combat arm.

Fortunately, Laskov had some help from Israel's enemies. In September 1955, the Czech government agreed to sell Egypt approximately 230 obsolescent but potent Soviet-built heavy and medium tanks, 200 armored personnel carriers (APCs), 100 100mm assault-gun carriers, 500 medium howitzers and field guns, 200 light antitank guns, over 100 antiaircraft guns, 1,000 recoilless rifles, countless small arms, and an assortment of scout cars, trucks, and other vehicles. In the same deal, the Egyptian Air Force received fifty twin-engine medium jet bombers, 120 jet fighter-interceptors, and a number of transport planes and helicopters. Also, the Egyptian Navy was increased by two destroyers, fifteen fast minesweepers, several submarines, and several dozen patrol boats.

At one fell swoop, the entire balance of power in the Middle East was upset. Egyptian predominance in armor alone seriously threatened Israel's security. Indeed, in every class of arms, Egypt potentially dominated the region.

Against this—and the weapons already in Arab hands when the Czech deal was struck—Israel's armored force was equipped with an average of fifty surplus American 32-ton Sherman M-4 medium tanks, 100 French-built 14.5-ton AMX-13 light tanks, about 450 surplus American M-3 halftracks, and sixty French-built 105mm SP howitzers. In early 1956, shortly after France learned that Egypt was actively supporting rebels in Algeria, the French Army supplied *Zahal* with sixty M-51 medium tanks, a French-modified Sherman variant that incorporated a powerful 75mm high-velocity main gun. With this addition, amounting to over a battalion, *Zahal's* armored force was able to field an average of 100 Shermans and 100 AMX-13s.

By mid 1956, the 7th Armored Brigade comprised two tank battalions— one each of American Sherman M-4s and French AMX-13s—one *motorized* infantry battalion, a towed artillery battalion, and a variety of company-size combat-support units. The 27th Reserve Armored Brigade was upgraded to field a complete M-51 French Sherman battalion, one AMX-13 company, one 105mm SP artillery battalion, one motorized infantry battalion, and sundry combat-support units. The 37th Reserve Armored Brigade, the last formed, had four independent AMX-13 companies, one armored-infantry battalion mounted in halftracks, one motorized infantry battalion, and a jeep reconnaissance company armed with recoilless rifles.

As if the strange and uneven tables of organization were not enough to drive General Laskov and his brigade commanders to distraction, the 27th Reserve Armored Brigade was tasked with detaching two of its French Sherman companies—twenty-five tanks in all—to a specific Reserve infantry brigade in the event hostilities commenced. Also, if certain contingencies required the use of armored and infantry units together, the armored unit in question was to supply a specific number and types of tanks to specific infantry units, depending on the contingency.

Laskov's contribution to mitigating the extreme confusion and doctrinal chaos besetting the Armor Corps was a rearguard action against Chief of Staff Dayan's outmoded notions regarding the use of armor in combined land operations. Only in September 1956, as Israel was planning to launch a preemptive military campaign against the massively reequipped and threateningly deployed Egyptian Army in Sinai, was Laskov able to even speak to Ben-Gurion (in the latter's capacity as defense minister) about placing the fate of the armored units in the hands of trained armor officers. Because the Egyptians had not had time to evolve an armored-warfare doctrine of their own, their large tank forces in Sinai had been doled out in small parcels to support their large infantry formations, the same as French Army tank units had been on the eve of World War II. Given these findings of *Zahal*'s crack Intelligence Branch, Ben-Gurion saw no reason to create an independent armored strike force, and he backed Dayan against Laskov. But Ben-Gurion also recalled witnessing Uri Ben-Ari's armored tour de force during the 1953 maneuvers, so he agreed to retain the 7th Armored Brigade intact as a special reserve, by which he meant in a subordinate role to the infantry. It was only half a victory, but it provided young Colonel Ben-Ari with a platform from which he would, in only two months' time, change the shape of things to come on the great perpetual Middle East battlefield.

On the very eve of the Sinai Campaign, as a result of an arms deal signed only three weeks before hostilities opened, France hurriedly delivered to Israel an estimated 140 M-51 French Sherman tanks. There was virtually no time to absorb the new tanks into the three armored brigades, but the Israeli tankers did what they could as the clock ran down. Crews were found and makeshift independent "squadrons" of fifteen to twenty French Shermans were formed and doled out to the two Reserve armored brigades or attached directly to several infantry brigades and higher headquarters.

The 27th Reserve Armored Brigade was upgraded by the addition of many of the new French Shermans and a new battery of 105mm SP howitzers, but the brigade was slated to serve as a Southern Command reserve armor pool; it was to be split up and doled out to infantry units and intermediate headquarters (temporary divisional task forces) as needed. The 37th Reserve Armored Brigade, in reality a mechanized infantry brigade, was upgraded by the addition of several independent French Sherman squadrons, but it was to be broken up and doled out for attachment to four separate infantry brigades that were slated to take part in the offensive. The 7th Armored Brigade, which was to form a special reserve, remained unaltered and hopefully would be committed intact. Also, several new independent squadrons of fifteen to twenty French Shermans each were held back from the Sinai table of organization to serve under Central and Northern commands in case Jordan and/or Syria launched attacks to support Egypt.

The expected fragmentation of the 27th and 37th Reserve Armored brigades was extremely hard for the tank soldiers to stomach, but it fulfilled the predominating infantry's perceived need to garner armored support, and there was no use arguing for a change in plans. In the end, this cavalier treatment of the armored force by infantrymen served as a source of additional motivation for the 7th Armored Brigade's strong-willed Colonel Ben-Ari to show his infantry-minded superiors just what massed armor units could do when they were set loose.

The 7th Armored Brigade's mission in the Sinai battle plan was to support a major infantry breakthrough by means of a classic cavalry-type pursuit against broken and fleeing enemy forces. That is, until the Israeli infantry massively and decisively breached the Egyptian main line of resistance in Sinai, the 7th Armored Brigade had no mission beyond being ready to exploit the breach. It was, however, the consensus among Israeli tank officers that the true role of massed armor formations was to achieve their own breakthroughs—break the cohesion of the enemy defensive barrier in several places and then rove freely in the enemy's rear, disrupting lines of supply and communication, and generally tearing down the enemy's will to resist.

So, on the eve of war, with an all-out preemptive offensive poised to take place, the same aggressive tank officer who had engineered and executed back-to-back unauthorized armor sweeps against *friendly* infantry in 1952 and 1953 had retained control over the largest, strongest mobile strike force then poised for battle in the Middle East. All Colonel Uri Ben-Ari needed to do, once the attention of his superiors was riveted on the battle, was find a pretense for slipping the leash and striking out on his own. Once started, he knew, the 7th Armored Brigade would be unstoppable—both by the Egyptian Army and his own Israeli superiors.

12

The Suez-Sinai Campaign of October 29–November 5, 1956, has been seen by many as the last hurrah for British and French colonialist tendencies in the Middle East. Be that as it may, the Sinai Campaign was both *Zahal's* dress rehearsal for the stunning 1967 Six-Day War and an authentic military campaign in its own right. It was in every way *Zahal's* coming-of-age party, and it culminated the first phase of *Zahal's* development.

The seeds of the Suez Crisis were sown on July 23, 1952, when Egyptian Army officers overthrew King Farouk. Emerging at length to head the Egyptian government was the mercurial and charismatic Colonel Gamal Abdel Nasser, a veteran of the Egyptian Army's humiliating defeat inside Israel in 1948. Convinced that he was destined to head the great Arab Nation of millennial myth, Nasser launched simultaneous rhetorical campaigns against Israel, the obvious enemy, and the West, the old colonial bugaboo of the Third World.

Nasser's campaign against Israel—which had less to do with Israel than with providing Nasser with a rallying cry by which he could unite the Arab masses—took the form of state-sponsored terrorism as well as a barrage of vicious radio broadcasts. Nasser was only mildly annoying; he was not seen as a serious threat to Israel until the culmination of the massive 1955 Czech arms deal, which placed Egypt in the preeminent military position in the region.

Backed by his new-found strength, Nasser soon claimed the right to seal the narrow Straits of Tiran against shipping bound for the isolated Israeli port of Eilat, at the head of the Egyptian-dominated Gulf of Aqaba. Further, he closed the air route over the Straits of Tiran to airplanes flying between Israel and East Africa and Asia.

After the United States broke off talks about funding the proposed Aswan Dam across the Nile River, an infuriated Nasser nationalized the Suez Canal on July 27, 1956. Certain that Nasser meant to control the free flow of all Western goods through the canal, Great Britain and France entered into a secret pact that proposed the use of military force to guarantee their rights of passage. This pact tied in nicely with the thought processes prevailing within the Israeli government at the time.

Denied lawful access to markets in Asia and Africa and alarmed by the sudden build-up of the Egyptian armed forces, Israeli leaders were convinced that Nasser intended to launch the oft-promised war of annihilation against the Jewish state. The Israeli government began planning a preemptive strike while trying to purchase arms from nominally friendly Western nations.

On September 1, 1956, the Israeli military attaché in Paris learned of the secret Anglo-French alliance against Egypt. Secret negotiations ensued at high government and military levels, and a deal was struck between Israel, France, and Great Britain on October 21, 1956: While British and French forces parachuted and landed amphibiously to secure the canal itself, *Zahal* would invade the Sinai Peninsula and the Gaza Strip to (a) destroy a large portion of the Egyptian Army's offensive potential, (b) destroy a number of guerrilla bases, and (c) reopen the contested Straits of Tiran.

Israeli planning for the military offensive naturally was placed in the hands of Chief of Staff Moshe Dayan, but its basis was pure Chaim Laskov. Facing a numerically superior and better-equipped Egyptian battle force and expecting the United States and Soviet Union to apply immediate pressure for a cessation of hostilities (albeit for entirely divergent reasons), Dayan and his operations staff outlined a lightning offensive campaign that would achieve all its goals and sow maximum destruction in the shortest possible time.

The Israeli assault against Egypt was to commence on October 29, but the supporting Anglo-French air assault was to begin a day later. This placed enormous political and military pressure on Israel, but that was necessary in order to mitigate extreme political pressures inside Great Britain and France, and the world community at large.

The opening phase of the plan envisaged by Dayan and his planners was a parachute drop far behind Egyptian lines—at Mitla Pass, a bottleneck on two of the three east-west highways that crossed the Sinai Peninsula. There were only enough transport planes in the IAF to drop the bulk of one parachute battalion, 395 men in all. Given the high state of readiness the paratroopers had achieved, not to mention their proven combat prowess, a battalion was thought sufficient to achieve the straightforward goal of creating a confusing and alarming diversion far in the rear of the bulk of the Egyptian forces in Sinai. To ease the isolation of this small force the rest of the parachute brigade was to rush overland to Mitla Pass by way of the southern road, from Kuntilla via Themed and Nakhle. If successful, the paratroop battalion—and, later, the brigade—would be in position to block an important Egyptian line of reinforcement and retreat.

Coupled with the initial parachute drop, one Israeli Reserve infantry brigade was to advance from the Israeli town of Nitzana to seize jump-off positions around the important road junction at the Egyptian town of Kusseima. Behind this advance infantry brigade, two Israeli divisional task forces were to await orders from the government to proceed along the coastal and central east-west axes from Israel to the canal. If the offensive was to proceed—that depended on what Great Britain, France, and Egypt did next— the Israelis were to break through whatever Egyptians they faced on the coast and in the center and advance swiftly across Sinai to within 16 kilometers of the Suez Canal. In a somewhat isolated phase of the campaign, Israeli units were to clean out guerrilla encampments and Egyptian Army bases in the Gaza Strip. Lastly, one Reserve infantry brigade was to advance overland down the east side of the Sinai Peninsula to reopen the Straits of Tiran by overwhelming the Egyptian garrison at Sharm el-Sheikh.

It is interesting to note that, in order to attain both strategic and operational surprise, the Israeli plan was exactly the reverse of any logical or "accepted" military order. The farthest objective—Mitla Pass—was the first objective. Then the general offensive was to open in the isolated center, followed by an attack on the nearest and most vexatious objectives, Gaza and its guerrilla bases. Perversely, Sharm el-Sheikh and the Straits of Tiran, the geostrategic and geopolitical objectives whose control by Egypt had precipitated Israel's decision to go to war, were left for last.

Operationally speaking, the recognition of the strengths of the larger and more powerfully equipped Egyptian forces determined the sequence of the Israeli attacks. Holding or seizing Sinai was largely a matter of holding or seizing Sinai's road network. The Egyptians tended to concentrate their forces at crossroads while often leaving natural obstacles unguarded. The Israeli attack was predictable in that the crossroads had to be seized to gain access to the road net. Therefore, the seeming illogic of the order in which static objectives were to be attacked would, hopefully, keep the Egyptian commanders guessing about where—and when—they should commit their mobile reserves. Also, once a defensive sector close to the Israeli frontier had been reduced or bypassed, long advances into the Egyptian rear could be achieved across unguarded stretches by the relatively more mobile Israeli brigades.

There was considerable concern on the part of French strategists that a force of ten smallish Israeli brigades would be able to master a much larger Egyptian force consisting of two infantry divisions, seven quite large independent infantry brigades, one tank brigade, two independent infantry battalions (at Sharm el-Sheikh), and assorted garrison units. Chief of Staff Dayan had to go out of his way to convince his French colleagues that the Israeli assault force had far greater mobility and agility than the Egyptian force it was facing, and that Israeli leadership, training, morale, and motivation were all far superior to those of the Egyptians. The arguments were tenuous, but Dayan was given the edge when at the last minute the Egyptians moved two infantry divisions and their only tank brigade from eastern Sinai to guard the Suez Canal against a feared Anglo-French assault. At that point, though they enjoyed only a bare advantage in numbers of brigades (but *not* in numbers of troops, tanks, or guns), the Israelis were able to convince their allies that they could achieve their objectives.

In order to keep their intentions cloaked in secrecy as long as possible, the Israelis did not begin to mobilize their Reserve units until the last possible moment, October 26, and then only the two armored-infantry brigades were called up via secret messengers. It was not until October 27, only two days before the initial assault, that the national radio was employed to call up the bulk of Reserve infantry and selected Home Guard units. The delay naturally led to mass confusion. The tanks and halftracks of the two Reserve armored-infantry brigades could not be fully serviced in the time allotted, a factor that led to numerous breakdowns after the war started. Also, many of the 13,000 civilian vehicles that were commandeered could not be readied adequately for combat in under one day. Indeed, most of the Reserve infantrymen themselves could not be readied fully in time. They all reached their unit depots more or less on time, but equipment was not issued or inadvertently left behind. Few Reservists went into battle knowing what they or their units were supposed to accomplish. Nevertheless, the government and GHQ had weighed the risks, and *Zahal's* core of professionals was prepared to make do as never before.

The IAF struck the first blow of the campaign when, late in the afternoon of October 29, four P-51 Mustang fighter-bombers swept in low over Sinai in order to cut many telephone lines with their propellers. This crippled Egyptian command and control. Next, before sunset, 395 paratroopers who jumped into a drop zone just east of Mitla Pass dug into blocking positions in the low hills around the defile's eastern end. During the night, an Israeli Reserve infantry brigade hiked into Sinai from the vicinity of Nitzana and easily secured the Kusseima crossroads. In just three short steps, Israelis severely disrupted Egyptian communications throughout Sinai; blocked a vital line of supply and communication (Mitla Pass); and, from Kusseima, outflanked the bulk of the Egyptian battle force in east-central Sinai.

Shortly, however, Chief of Staff Dayan's carefully orchestrated set-piece plan for an infantry advance in stages across Sinai came unglued. Early in the afternoon of October 30, the GOC, Southern Command, Brigadier General Assaf Simchoni, was informed that a light reconnaissance unit had encountered no Egyptians anywhere near a narrow defile called Deika Pass, through which passed a miserable dirt path, virtually impassable to all but tracked vehicles. The light reconnaissance jeeps had driven from Kusseima almost to the rear of Abu Agheila, the westernmost and largest Egyptian defensive position in east-central Sinai. West of Abu Agheila, Simchoni knew, was virtually nothing that could prevent his brigades from rushing all the way to the Suez Canal city of Ismailia. Leaving Deika Pass unguarded was *the* decisive blunder of the Sinai Campaign, and General Simchoni instantly grasped that it was.

With Kusseima safely under his control, Simchoni was to have advanced one infantry brigade and two armored-infantry combat teams from Nitzana due west to seize Umm Katef. After regrouping at Umm Katef, the infantry and armored-infantry were to launch a frontal assault against Abu Agheila. At this point, before the infantry jumped off, the Fates intervened.

An ad hoc battalion-size task force of 7th Armored Brigade tanks and halftracks had probed along the main road from Kusseima to the southern edge of Abu Agheila without finding a soft spot. This was expected; no one was surprised or disappointed. But the track through Deika Pass was another matter. It was a virtual certainty that the Egyptians would not have built strong defenses in the rear of the Abu Agheila position—and absolutely not if they had not bothered to even outpost Deika Pass.

General Simchoni instinctively recognized that Israel's military and political objectives in Sinai could be achieved in far less time and human cost if he could exploit the Egyptian oversight at Deika Pass by rolling up the Abu Agheila position—and then Umm Katef—from the rear. There was one and only one unit in all of *Zahal* that was equipped almost entirely with tracked vehicles, and most of it just happened to be sitting idle near Nitzana. Without consulting Chief of Staff Dayan, who was roving hither and yon across the entire Southern Command zone of operations, Simchoni, on his own authority, instantly committed the one brigade that he really had no right to commit on his own volition: Colonel Uri Ben-Ari's 7th Armored Brigade.

There is no way to describe the spirit in which Simchoni's unexpected order to advance on Abu Agheila by way of Kusseima and Deika Pass was received at Colonel Ben-Ari's mobile command post. With the skeletal information and instructions provided by General Simchoni, Ben-Ari improvised an assault straight up the rear of the Abu Agheila defensive zone.

When General Dayan discovered at around sun-up on October 31 that the entire 7th Armored Brigade was on the move against Abu Agheila, the chief of staff was on the verge of countermanding Simchoni's attack order. But, by the time Dayan heard the news—just before 0500—the leading elements of Ben-Ari's brigade already were approaching the Egyptian defenses from the rear. Dayan had no choice but to let the battle unfold. Events had overrun planning.

At dawn on October 31, Lieutenant Colonel Avraham "Bren" Adan's tank-infantry task force began its attack into the rear of the Abu Agheila camp. The Egyptians were ready, having noticed hours earlier that an Israeli force of some type was approaching from the south and southwest.

As the halftracks bearing the first armored-infantry company of Bren's force got to within 3 kilometers of the base wire, the Egyptians opened fire with a full battalion of twenty-four 25-pounder field guns and the many antitank and infantry weapons that had been shifted to bear on the attackers. Also, Egyptian soldiers manning the outlying position at Ruefa Dam, on high ground immediately to the south of Abu Agheila, opened fire directly into the right flank of the Israeli assault force. The lead company of Sherman tanks blotted out the fire from Ruefa Dam with its own fire while the infantry-laden Israeli halftracks pressed straight on toward Abu Agheila. Shortly, an Egyptian armored reaction force pressed in from the north along the road from the coastal city of El Arish, but it was countered and defeated by Israeli tanks guarding Bren's left flank. Abu Agheila was held by the equivalent of three Egyptian infantry brigades supported by a battalion of 25-pounders and as many as twenty-three tracked antitank guns. Even though the Egyptians had shifted their defenses to meet the attack of the Israeli armored task force, the vast complex of military camps fell to the equivalent of a battalion of Israeli tanks and armored infantry in only an hour. It was an amazing feat.

After the main base fell, Egyptian artillery continued to fire on Bren's armored task force from another fortified position to the east, and Egyptian tanks continued to move down from the direction of El Arish. However, Bren's tanks and a flock of Israeli fighter-bombers held both threats at bay.

At this point, a second armored task force was to have driven through Bren's to reduce the Ruefa Dam position. Before it could mount out from blocking positions at the head of Deika Pass, news arrived that a large part of Egypt's only tank brigade—two T-34 medium-tank battalions, a company of SU-100 assault guns, and a battalion of mechanized infantry—was moving along the main road from Ismailia toward Abu Agheila.

Immediately, Uri Ben-Ari added his brigade headquarters and a bevy of mobile supporting arms to the second task force and set off hastily down the road to Ismailia. On reaching the major road junction at Jebel Libni, about 25 kilometers west of Abu Agheila, Ben-Ari halted his force and ordered it to dig in to stop the oncoming Egyptian armored force.

The Egyptian force never reached Jebel Libni. Israeli fighter-bombers caught it on the open road about 50 kilometers west of Ben-Ari's ambush and destroyed or disabled many T-34s, SU-100s, and APCs. When Ben-Ari heard that the survivors had begun a bloody withdrawal back toward the canal, he mounted his force out to chase them down. Ben-Ari's armored task force never quite caught up with the retreating Egyptians, but in the course of the chase it advanced to within 16 kilometers of the Suez Canal before it was ordered to stop. Along the way, it easily swept aside several roadblocks the Egyptians had set out to delay it. This advance alone vindicated all of Uri Ben-Ari's arguments in favor of an independent role for armor.

While Ben-Ari's armored task force had been moving west by way of the central east-west route across Sinai, a third 7th Armored Brigade task force also had been moving to the west by a more southerly route. This task force was to have supported Bren's assault on Abu Agheila, but news arrived just before the attack commenced that an Egyptian mechanized force was moving up from the southwest. The third task force was sent to investigate the report and turn back the interlopers. After it had advanced all the way to Bir el-

Hassne without finding any Egyptians, this force was ordered to continue on toward Mitla Pass to bolster the paratroopers.

Meantime, while the other two segments of the 7th Armored Brigade were attacking to the west, Bren's victorious armored task force was ordered on the evening of October 31 to seize the Ruefa Dam defensive position. Bren's tanks and infantry-laden halftracks moved out right at sunset—into the face of nineteen entrenched antitank guns and six 25-pounder artillery pieces. As the Israeli tanks led the way into the Egyptian position, every one of them was struck at least once by antitank rounds, and many were disabled. Bren refused to give in. Even after many of the Shermans ran out of ammunition, the attack bore down on the well-entrenched defenders, running right over them when they did not break and flee. As the halftracks followed the tanks across the Egyptian trenches, the armored infantrymen tossed hand grenades over the sides and sprayed fighting holes with automatic-weapons fire. The defenses cracked and the surviving Egyptians, who had fought bravely, fled or surrendered.

Next, as the Israelis were scouring the abandoned position and taking stock of their own losses, Egyptian artillery from another strongpoint opened fire in support of an infantry counterattack from the Umm Katef position. The Israeli tanks and armored infantrymen easily repulsed the attempt, but Bren's tanks had been rendered virtually ineffective by lack of ammunition and spare parts.

The net effect of splitting the 7th Armored Brigade into three tank-infantry task forces operating over three axes of advance was precisely the prescription that Uri Ben-Ari had been trying to get his superiors to fill since the 1952 war games. The fact that the brigade had been split three ways in response to unanticipated threats made no difference. Indeed, it was precisely the point: Ben-Ari and his subordinates were prepared—literally for any challenge.

On the morning of November 1, General Simchoni reluctantly committed his last Reserve infantry brigade to capturing the powerful Umm Katef defensive sector by direct frontal assault. Simchoni's only purpose in exposing the infantry to the risk of a frontal assault on so powerful a position was the dire necessity of opening a direct line of supply to the three diverging components of the 7th Armored Brigade. Not only had Bren's task force been rendered *hors de combat* by lack of ammunition and maintenance, the two mobile task forces to the west were reporting that increasing numbers of tanks and halftracks were dropping out due to equipment failures. Since Bren was no longer able to fight through from the west, Simchoni was obliged to commit the infantry—the only force he had left—to clearing the Umm Katef bottle-neck from the east.

Two Egyptian outposts between Nitzana and Umm Katef fell to the 10th "Harel" Reserve Infantry Brigade's reconnaissance group almost without bloodshed. However, when the unit was reinforced by an infantry company and sent forward toward Umm Katef itself, the Egyptians issued a bloody repulse. The stunned Harel Brigade commander went more or less to ground for the rest of the day.

Next, as General Simchoni hectored the Harel Brigade to get on with it, two battalions of infantry attempted to deliver a night pincers attack against Umm Katef's northern and southern flanks. Both units went astray in the dark. One of the battalions finally found Umm Katef, but only after sunrise, by which time the Egyptian artillery was able to blow it off the battlefield. The second battalion missed Umm Katef altogether in the dark, but it settled for capturing a small outlying position it literally blundered into.

General Simchoni and General Dayan, who was following the action closely, were not impressed. The Harel Brigade commander was replaced on the spot and two armored-infantry task forces of the 37th Reserve Armored-Infantry Brigade were ordered up from the GHQ Reserve to resume the assault.

The tanks and armored infantrymen attacked Umm Katef frontally. In the course of yet another bloody repulse, the brigade commander was killed while leading a futile last-ditch attack. Though the Israeli survivors pulled back, the Egyptians apparently were impressed with their bravery, or perhaps they were convinced that they were about to be cut off between infantry, tanks, and armored infantry to their front and Bren's armored task force to their rear. Whatever their thinking, most of Umm Katef's defenders slipped away during the night. Next morning, after clearing routes through the Egyptian minefields, the 37th Reserve Armored-Infantry Brigade captured Umm Katef without further loss of life.

On the morning of October 29, at a camp near the Jordanian border, Colonel Arik Sharon had loaded the main body of his 202nd Parachute Brigade aboard a fleet of halftracks and commandeered civilian buses and trucks and sallied deep into the western Negev Desert. Near sunset, the parachute brigade slipped across the frontier near the Egyptian town of Kuntilla, which was located at the eastern end of the southernmost east-west road across Sinai. Supported only by a squadron of thirteen AMX-13 light tanks and accompanied by a towed artillery battery, Sharon's troopers continued their grueling road journey of 300 kilometers to link up with the parachute battalion holding the eastern end of Mitla Pass. To get there, the brigade first had to clear Egyptian outposts and defensive sectors at the three way stations— Kuntilla, Themed, and Nakhle.

At Kuntilla, the brigade reconnaissance company circled around to the west and attacked from out of the setting sun. Only a few shots were fired before the outpost's defenders fled for their lives and the main body of the brigade streamed past.

Along the way to Themed, ten of the thirteen light tanks fell victim to maintenance problems, and numerous other vehicles had to drop out for the same reason. Nevertheless, the parachute brigade was able to attack the objective from right out of the rising sun. It was a classic use of the Sharon night tactic on a broader scale than had ever been attempted. The dazzled and surprised defenders were able to hold out for only 40 minutes.

After clearing Themed, the Israeli column rushed headlong to engage the reinforced Egyptian battalion standing athwart the crossroads at Nakhle. This time, the defenders had air support, but Sharon would not allow even this potentially decisive advantage to stop or even to slow his men. The Egyptian jets were driven off by ground fire. Following brief preparatory fires by the Israeli artillery battery, the paratroopers jumped off at 1700—and fell into the vacuum created by the fleeing defenders.

The main body of Sharon's 202nd Parachute Brigade completed its dash to Mitla Pass at 2230 on October 29, a mere 28 hours after crossing the frontier near Kuntilla. Once joined with the paratroop battalion guarding the eastern end of the pass, Sharon's brigade was to have sat still and merely guarded the pass. This it did for one day. Then, after asking Chief of Staff Dayan for permission to reconnoiter the western end of the pass, Sharon mounted a completely unnecessary and totally unauthorized offensive clearing operation. In a full day of bitter fighting that eventually drew in the bulk of his brigade, Sharon lost 38 paratroopers killed and 120 wounded. It is true that at least 200 Egyptian soldiers also died and that an Egyptian battalion was driven from its defensive positions, but no gain worth all those deaths and injuries had been—or even could be—accomplished.

It is easy to understand why Dayan chose to overlook General Simchoni's unauthorized premature use of the 7th Armored Brigade—it was successful and, indeed, decisive—but Dayan subsequently made no effort whatsoever to discipline nor even admonish the bloody-minded Colonel Sharon. That is extremely hard to justify in light of the heavy losses and useless results emanating from Sharon's subterfuge and insubordination.

While the fighting in the center was raging, an Israeli divisional task force commanded by Brigadier General Chaim Laskov and consisting of the 1st "Golani" Infantry Brigade and the 27th Reserve Armored-Infantry Brigade opened an attack through Rafah to seal off the southwestern end of the Gaza Strip. Launched just after midnight on November 1, the meticulously planned attack by four infantry and one armored-infantry battalions quickly ran afoul of Egyptian minefields, but the commanders were able to improvise responses that quickly carried ad hoc assaults into and through the Egyptian defensive zone. By dawn, Laskov's main body was in the clear on the coastal highway, bound for the main Egyptian headquarters center of El Arish. However, the Laskov force was held for a time that afternoon at Jiradi Pass by a strong Egyptian defensive position. By the time the Israelis overran Jiradi Pass, it was late in the day and General Dayan had become a bit unnerved by reports that the Egyptians were holding El Arish in considerable strength. The chief of staff did not want to risk heavy casualties that late in the game, so he ordered Laskov to stop 4 or 5 kilometers east of El Arish and spend the night preparing to deliver a major assault.

When the attack was renewed at 0600 on November 2, the 27th Reserve Armored-Infantry Brigade spearhead entered the city virtually without a fight. From there, the Laskov force raced almost all the way to the Suez Canal, rolling up retreating Egyptians all along the way.

At the same time the 27th Reserve Armored-Infantry Brigade was rolling into El Arish—0600 on November 2—two Reserve infantry brigades supported by a task force of the 37th Reserve Armored-Infantry Brigade were launching their attack on the city of Gaza. While 120mm mortars and tank guns dropped shells on the stoutly defended ridges that dominated the sprawling city, an armored-infantry battalion and a squadron of tanks broke through the Egyptian main line of defense. Thereafter, an infantry battalion entered the city on foot to mop up Egyptian defenders, most of whom were quite eager to surrender. At noon, the city's Egyptian governor surrendered and, thereafter, the bulk of the Egyptian garrison followed suit.

Only at Khan Yunis did the attackers meet resolute resistance. There, a brigade of the Palestine Liberation Army (PLA) refused to bow to reality—Israelis held all of the Gaza Strip to the north, south, and east of them—and so it took until the afternoon of November 3 for an Israeli Reserve infantry brigade and an armored combat team to secure the town.

By prior arrangement, Israel had already accepted a disingenuous October 30 Anglo-French ultimatum that battling Egyptian and Israeli forces remain clear of a *cordon sanitaire* extending 16 kilometers on either side of the Suez Canal. While British and French forces occupied the "demilitarized" zone, Israeli brigades advancing along the coastal and central highways hounded the disintegrating Egyptian Army all the way across Sinai. The Israelis halted on November 3 on a line precisely 16 kilometers from the Suez Canal. Thereafter, a pincers consisting of the 202nd Parachute Brigade advancing down the west side of Sinai and a fresh Reserve infantry brigade advancing down the east side closed on Sharm el-Sheikh. Following a huge air strike on November 4, the two Israeli brigades advanced into Sharm el-Sheikh and thus reopened the Straits of Tiran to Israeli shipping and overflights by Israeli commercial aircraft. The last Egyptian holdouts in Sinai and Gaza surrendered or withdrew on November 5.

13

The Sinai Campaign of 1956 was a turning point in the modern Israeli military experience. Beginning virtually the hour the guns went silent, the campaign was transmuted into a huge retrospective experiment whose results and ramifications were analyzed and debated over the next decade and beyond. By 1967, there was nothing about the Sinai Campaign that had not been scrutinized closely by Israel's professional officers and, likely, not one lesson that eluded the Israelis. Without Sinai in late 1956, there could have been no Six-Day War as it was waged in mid 1967.

There is a caveat shared among military commentators that describes the age-old tendency of military strategists to fall into the trap of planning for the last war. Given the fact that Egypt was the odds-on favorite to engage Israel in the *next* regional war, this tendency was a very real threat to Israeli military policies for the post-Sinai years. Fortunately, *Zahal* was filled with original thinkers unwilling to accept the past as a template. Unlike their counterparts in other military establishments of the world, *Zahal* planners gave short shrift to the things their forces had done right in Sinai and began a relentless pursuit of every error that their forces and soldiers had made, no matter how minuscule. Once discovered, the error in question was studied relentlessly from every angle. Then it was reassembled in some new and often quite unrecognizable form. It was as if the Israelis were bent upon intentionally overturning the past—the conventional wisdom—simply for the iconoclastic joy of doing so. They might as well have been, for, in the end, they reinvented combined-arms maneuver warfare.

Foremost in the post-1956 analysis was the utter vindication of the first-strike offensive strategy emanating from the five basic precepts first articulated by Colonel Chaim Laskov's doctrinal committee in 1949. If there had been any question whatsoever as to the efficacy of Israel's first-strike offensive strategy going into the Sinai Campaign, then it certainly was erased by the time *Zahal's* portion of the multi-national Sinai-Suez effort ended. Several of the Laskov Committee's postulates needed to be slightly modified on the basis of the actual experience of the war, and several corollaries evolved, but Israel's basic first-strike offensive strategy would remain effectively unchanged over at least the next quarter century.

Also at the strategic end of the spectrum, the Israeli Reserve system was vindicated. The overall performance of Reserve units and individual Reservists thrown into action in the wake of short-notice mobilization orders completely justified the nation's hitherto implicit faith in the Reserve system.

At the opposite end of the spectrum—at the tactical level—the Israeli soldier proved himself to be not only a *far* better fighter than his Egyptian counterpart but the equal as well of his counterparts in at least two of the most highly regarded armies in the West. Indeed, the average Israeli combatant accomplished a great deal more during the campaign—and with a great deal more élan—than his British or French counterparts. Again, some tightening up and buckling down needed to be accomplished with respect to tactics and tactical finesse, but the results in Sinai justified all the changes and hard work that had been undertaken over the years leading up to 1956.

It was in the operational arena—the broad realm between strategy and tactics—that *Zahal* proved to be almost disastrously deficient in 1956. And it was in this operational arena that a decade's worth of concerted Israeli innovation was to place *Zahal* at the forefront of the handful of world-class armies.

At the highest of the operational levels—that occupied by Chief of Staff Dayan and the GHQ staff—Dayan so dominated the scene by his personal presence at the front that the General Staff Branch had little or nothing to do once the campaign plan was written, approved, and promulgated. Always the man of action, Dayan spent the entire war in Sinai, flitting from hotspot to hotspot, sticking his nose into the business of subordinate commanders and staffs all the way down to the battalion level. Fortunately for the chief of staff, Sinai was a small war fought on just one front, and *Zahal* never had more than three or four brigades on the move at once. As such, Dayan's dereliction of his higher responsibilities—seeing to all of Israel's strategic needs on all possible fronts from the confines of a central command post—had few actual ramifications. Indeed, the proximity of the hard-driving and charismatic chief of staff to the battle front might have boosted morale significantly among Israeli combatants. However, Dayan's personal style overlooked the job of the maximum commander, and it certainly rendered the General Staff Branch a moot institution once the shooting got underway in Sinai.

Interestingly, a possibly serendipitous outcome of Dayan's long periods of unavailability—his entire personal staff consisted of one aide and either a driver or a pilot—was the forced reliance of subordinates upon their own powers of decision. GHQ, which did not include the errant chief of staff, was almost never consulted by subordinate field commanders, and Dayan was only a part of the decision loop when he appeared at a hotspot or during those rare occasions when he could be raised via the radio. (And, in that case, he *was* the decision loop!) It is no wonder, then, that Brigadier General Assaf Simchoni, the senior officer overseeing the central prong of the Israeli offensive, committed the 7th Armored Brigade without consulting higher headquarters. Simchoni had voiced his opinion before the war that the 7th Armored Brigade's tanks should be employed en masse, so it is possible that he was predisposed to finding an excuse to override the General Staff's plan for the war. But Dayan's effective absence from the high-level decision loop and the General Staff's moot role in the actual war certainly abetted any prior decision on Simchoni's part to utilize the bulk of the tank brigade as a mobile force in the enemy's rear.

Simchoni's temerity in releasing the 7th Armored Brigade yielded up benefits that actually changed *Zahal* into the modern combined-arms offensive combat force it became by 1967. The successes of the armored-infantry task forces were so profound that, as soon as the war ended, Moshe Dayan completely and unembarrassedly became the ultimate convert to the armored-warfare philosophy Uri Ben-Ari, Assaf Simchoni, and Chaim Laskov had propounded unsuccessfully all through the planning stage.

Organizational considerations aside, Simchoni's decision to send the 7th Armored Brigade into action under the aegis of his own authority drove home to Dayan the 1956 war's ultimate truth: It is inevitable that unforeseen events take place once the war is initiated, and the person with the best chance of overcoming confusion or exploiting an opportunity is *the man on the scene*. From these interrelated insights, which are expressed by Israelis as, "A plan is merely a starting point," *Zahal* eventually developed two uniquely Israeli operational dicta: "Adherence to Mission" and "Optional Control."

* * *

The simplest definition of Adherence to Mission is that higher headquarters establishes a goal in broad terms and the unit charged with achieving the goal may do so by any means at hand. This very definition runs exactly counter to the conventional wisdom pounded between the ears of the soldiers of virtually every military force in the world. Only *Zahal* actively inculcates its leaders—indeed, every single one of its soldiers—with the dictum of Adherence to Mission.

Most wars fought by most modern armies—whether offensive or defensive—begin with a strategic statement from the government that is illuminated with a carefully drawn operational plan. This carefully drawn plan is known as a *sequential* plan, for each phase is dependent upon the successful completion of the previous phase. In the case of a defensive war, the operational plan that is used is usually selected from among a number of contingency plans drawn up in advance and rehearsed under the most realistic conditions possible considering the absence of a real enemy. In the case of a classic offensive plan, the attacking force begins with a goal and is told how to achieve it, usually in the course of several intermediate phases, each one dependent upon the successful completion of the previous phase. Adjustments to the plan may be made—they usually are—but, whether they are promulgated between phases or on the fly, they are almost invariably issued by seniors to juniors.

Though in late October 1956 General Dayan and the General Staff Branch had promulgated a classic and thus carefully controlled sequential war of phases from beginning to end, the reality of the battlefield—the inevitable slide toward chaos—both caused and allowed senior commanders to diverge farther and farther from their operations orders. Very quickly, in the face of such objective reality, all that survived of the Dayan-General Staff master plan were the main strategic objectives and the opening move against the crossroads at Kusseima. The moment Assaf Simchoni released Uri Ben-Ari's 7th Armored Brigade from the Southern Front reserve in order to exploit the unguarded Deika Pass, the detailed campaign plan was knocked into a cocked hat. Because Chief of Staff Dayan never regained control of the entire army—he did not even try—the front-line commanders were effectively on their own for the rest of the war. In the end, Dayan's proposed sequential war had been transformed into a *cumulative* victory in which masses of little events, most of them unforeseen, combined in unanticipated ways to cause the Egyptian Army in Sinai to collapse.

When the basic facts that war is chaos and the fog is most penetrable at the point of contact were recognized, analyzed, and institutionalized in the years after the 1956 war, *Zahal* achieved the ultimate hallmark of its warmaking potential. The Israelis came up with an operational doctrine based upon their own actual experience with cumulative warfare. They would intentionally allow for tactical and operational plans governing movement toward the final objective to be made *on the fly* by the man on the spot: Adherence to Mission.

In all the world's armies—and in virtually every military campaign in recorded history—increasingly detailed orders pass sequentially from higher to lower levels of authority. This is in large part because the senior commander is usually more experienced than his subordinates. Also, because information flows upward from many sources covering an increasingly broad area, the senior is thought to hold a wider view and broader comprehension of the battlefield and other factors than any one of his subordinates. Not so under *Zahal*'s cumulative Adherence to Mission philosophy. While all of the reasons for the old method remain essentially true—senior commanders usually *do* have more experience and higher headquarters usually *do* have access to more information and broader vistas—the Israeli drive for decisive battlefield dominance—and strategic victory in the shortest possible time—cannot tolerate the time lost in passing information up the chain of command and waiting for instructions to come back down the chain. The Israeli subordinate commander is encouraged—indeed, he is virtually forced by the pressures of the command selection process—to act on his own, immediately upon assessing for himself the situation in his immediate zone of action. The Israelis are willing to sacrifice some of the advantages of the broader view for the sake of flexibility and decision at the point of contact, which they consider to be more important than waiting for the broader view to emerge.

Battle is chaos, and the struggle to control the battlefield is in reality a futile war against the effects of unintended consequences—entropy. Carefully drawn and strictly enforced planning is fine before the battle is joined, but the inevitable slide toward entropy that begins with the first shot makes it increasingly difficult for higher headquarters to issue relevant follow-up orders to subordinate units as the violence progresses. If the war in question is a war of movement, then such efforts quickly fall hopelessly behind reality, or movement has to cease while the higher headquarters struggle to sort out and react to what has already happened. Once the shooting starts, there is a tendency for binding intervention by higher headquarters to move farther and farther behind the "power curve"—that is, behind the reality which tactical units are facing on the battlefield. Adherence to Mission obviates the effects of meddling by higher headquarters. It explicitly vests the man on the scene—from individual soldier to fire-team leader and on up the chain of command—with the authority to accomplish his mission based upon what his own senses are telling him in real time.

Far from attempting to control the chaos of the battlefield, Adherence to Mission was the first attempt by any of the world's armies to *accept and exploit* that chaos—virtually to employ chaos as an ally. Israeli soldiers of all ranks are taught that chaos and confusion are inevitable and that their accumulation will definitely lead to opportunities that cannot possibly be foreseen in any sequential plan and might not be noticed by higher authority. The object of Adherence to Mission is to get every soldier at every level to recognize—and then exploit on his own authority—opportunities that are occurring right before his eyes.

There is a sometimes irritating but always essential payment that must be made for the many advantages accruing to the tactical commander from Adherence to Mission. Essentially, in the rush of events, a higher headquarters does not care what a subordinate unit is *going* to do as long as that unit is working to achieve the objective at hand. However, a higher headquarters does need to know, among other things, what the subordinate unit *has* done, what went wrong, and what it learned. Higher headquarters cannot operate in a vacuum, because broad objectives can change as a result of what actually occurs while subordinates are working toward securing lesser objectives. Any single scrap of information can change the entire basis for a war, so seniors must rely upon subordinates to report fully and truthfully. Though the obligation to report does somewhat encumber the subordinate, the payoff is obvious to all once it is made. The fact that the tradeoff results in less meddling by higher authority more than compensates for the extra effort.

To provide higher headquarters with time to collect data from subordinate units and then develop and promulgate updated orders back down the chain of command, the classic sequential offensive plan employed by many of the world's armies calls for pre-set halts at what are commonly known as phase lines—usually terrain features that can be defended in the face of an enemy counterattack. Indeed, the system of scheduled breaks in an offensive are virtually invitations for the enemy to attempt a counterattack. When a unit stops at a phase line so that updated orders can be passed down the chain of command, it is common for the troops to break for rest or meals, to replenish supplies, or to fix or replace broken and worn equipment. Some-times, whole units are replaced by fresh units when a phase line is secured. Inevitably, when the attacking unit stops to regroup, the defending unit also has an opportunity to regroup. The main result of stopping on a phase line is that the attack intentionally bogs down, and sometimes it cannot get going again.

Among its many other advantages, Adherence to Mission cuts out long chains of information reports from the bottom to the top and equally long and extremely complex chains of orders from the top back down to the bottom. By doing so, it cuts down on miscommunication of information to the top, misunderstanding of information at the top, and miscommunication and misunderstanding of orders back down the chain of authority.

Adherence to Mission saves time, rules out some errors, obviates danger-ous and often artificial delays at phase lines, cuts down on the tendency of commanders to interfere with events several levels beneath their responsibil-ity, and fully exploits the eyes and brains of the men on the scene. Adherence to Mission tends to foster a seamless cumulative offensive from line of depar-ture at the start of a conflict to a unit's ultimate war objective.

The most important byproduct of Adherence to Mission is that forces on the move can remain on the move; there is no need to stop and regroup simply because a higher headquarters is groping through a ton of data and senior officers are arguing about what the forces in the field should do next. The result is that the enemy gets no time to rest, no natural breaks that can be exploited to mass troops for counterattacks, move reinforcements, resupply units in contact, or even simply take a breather or collect his wits. Done right—seamless action driven by immediate local decisions made in real time by the commander on the spot—Adherence to Mission affords the enemy no respite and presents the enemy commander with an endless and ultimately overwhelming array of possibilities he cannot possibly factor into his planning without being able to read his counterpart's mind in real time.

Zahal learned to fight with fewer and briefer timeouts.

If Adherence to Mission prevails on the battlefield, what is the purpose and function of higher headquarters in *Zahal*?

The answer to that question derives from the adoption of *Zahal*'s sec-ond—counterbalancing—operational dictum: Optional Control.

While the advantages that are accrued by allowing the man on the spot to run his own battle are manifest, the constant upward flow of information—

and impressions—inevitably allows the more experienced senior commander and his relatively larger staff to mark broader and even nascent trends that are all but impossible to discern at the various subordinate levels. Since the widespread proliferation of tactical radios allows most information to flow upward in *near* real time, higher headquarters are often in a better position than lower headquarters to spot dangers that must be addressed or broader opportunities that can be profitably exploited. Thus, while the man on the scene—however broad that scene might be—is focused on the relatively limited view within that scene, men at higher levels have more experience, perspective, information, and probably even a little more time to fabricate plans or issue warnings that can affect events across broader horizons.

The same marvels of modern communications that facilitate the flow of battlefield information toward the top makes it possible for commanders far from the scene of the action to attempt to control in greater detail actions that are best left to the man on the spot. This tendency manifests itself in battles and battle simulations undertaken by most of the world's armies. For example, it contributed decisively at every level, from strategic to tactical, to America's loss of the Vietnam War. As a result of Israel's Adherence to Mission doctrine, superiors do not get into the business of doing the work their subordinates should be doing. Pride of authorship plays a role, certainly; Israelis have come to understand that the man who must execute the plan will put a lot more into his effort if he is also the man who made the plan. More than that, unless a senior commander is right at the point of contact, it is accepted as a given that he simply cannot be in the best position to direct real-time tactical decisions that will be employed as little as one step closer to the cutting edge. If the man on the scene is a true adherent to the precept of Adherence to Mission, his attention will be riveted solely upon his immediate area of responsibility. Likewise, if the commander one level up is a true adherent to Optional Control, he is focused on the bigger picture across *his* entire area of responsibility (and he is, of course, subject to the optional control of the man at the next higher level). Thus, it as also accepted as a given that a higher headquarters is almost always in a position to direct broader courses of action that will influence the battle across its entire area of responsibility.

The *option* in Optional Control is the senior's. Everyone in the chain of authority knows very well that, to win the war or to achieve some lesser objective, the direction of an attack might need to be changed at a moment's notice, or any of a large number of situations or catastrophes beyond the ken of the local commander might need to be rectified under the aegis of higher authority. That is, while the senior will not interfere in how the subordinate achieves his mission, he may change the mission to which the subordinate must adhere.

None of the advantages of the two operational dicta nullify the subordinate's obligation to obey binding mission orders from above. The aspect of Optional Control that is unique is an implicit compact between commander and subordinate: The subordinate knows that his command prerogatives will not be usurped by a superior who has nothing better to do with his time; the senior will interfere only if he feels there is good and sufficient reason.

In order for Adherence to Mission and Optional Control to work, commanders must have complete faith in the veracity and obedience of their subordinates. In return for the opportunity to lead, subordinate leaders must faithfully adhere to binding orders when they are issued and accept responsibility for their own actions in the absence of direction from above. And they must pay as they go by *reliably* reporting information at all costs—on time and truthfully, no matter what is going on, no matter how bad the news might be, or no matter how bad the light it might cast upon the reporter. Except for indecisiveness, dereliction of duty, and intentionally withholding information, virtually any oversight or misstep can be tolerated and forgiven if it is reported as soon as possible.

Zahal's adoption of its unique Adherence to Mission and Optional Control philosophies directly influenced the selection criteria for leaders and the inculcation of combat standards for soldiers at every level, from private to chief of staff. As exacting as leadership selection criteria had become between 1949 and 1956, they became far stiffer—and training at every level became stiffer—as the two operational dicta and all their emerging ramifications were institutionalized over the course of the succeeding decade. By 1967, *Zahal* was not only guided by unique operational principles, it was, top to bottom, a uniquely trained and uniquely led military force.

In order to exploit the opportunities he sees for himself within his own narrow slice of the battlefield, the Israeli troop leader or unit commander— the terms are virtually interchangeable in *Zahal* up to the post of brigade commander—is expected to be relentless—but *not* reckless—in the pursuit of his objective. *Zahal* wants a leader who can think quickly on his own, who will accept responsibility for his actions, and who is flexible enough of mind and spirit to back off and seek a different course in the event his bold, improvised plan of action comes a cropper. Thus, the adoption and refinement of Adherence to Mission suggested early on that the ideal combat-arms leader be intelligent enough to recognize battlefield opportunities as they occur and sufficiently aggressive, resourceful, and self-assured to exploit them while they still exist. These are the requirements that led to profound changes in the criteria by which leadership candidates were selected from among *Zahal's* annual crop of conscripts.

The relentless search for ideal combat troops has even influenced the assignment of private soldiers. Unlike most military forces the world around, *Zahal* directs its best-educated and smartest conscripts to the combat arms, and not to the technical branches. Assigning smart conscripts to the combat arms translates into a lot of smart people at the point of contact trying to figure out how to defeat the enemy. It provides for a virtually bottomless pool of potential leaders, and it tends to provide combat leaders with plenty of good advice. More to the point, smart soldiers take better care of themselves and their equipment than dumb ones, they are usually better motivated, and they are willing to take on excessive burdens because they are able to recognize the importance of the common goals.

To fully ingrain in its soldiers a sense of community, and to foster a notion that every combatant is a potential leader, it became a policy in *Zahal* that all soldiers are provided with as much information about strategic objectives as there is time to tell them. This gives every Israeli soldier a real stake in the outcome of the war—as if the potential destruction of their homes, families, and nation is not enough of a stake. Also, Israeli soldiers are encouraged and even morally obligated to express a candid opinion about a superior's plan of action. In *Zahal*, it is felt that men whose lives are on the line should be afforded an opportunity, if there is time, to point out flaws in a superior's plan. And, besides, who is to say that a subordinate cannot see a better way to get the job done? So, if there is time, debate is the accepted norm. *Zahal* explicitly recognizes that every Israeli soldier has a moral obliga-tion to object to a stupid or wasteful order, even on a field of battle. Moreover, every Israeli soldier is morally obligated to look after himself and his com-rades. The result: debates, differences of opinion, and, often, screaming arguments became commonplace in *Zahal*, even between leaders and subor-dinates, and sometimes under hostile fire. The unschooled observer might come to believe that *Zahal's* tolerance for debate and the excess of intellect in the ranks would hamper the transmission, acceptance, or execution of cogent orders, but it does not. Smart soldiers know when to shut up and get to work. If they do not, debate ends as soon as the superior cuts it off. At that moment the subordinate's obligation simply to obey is reinstated.

The Israeli concept of leadership—leaders lead from the front—results in abnormally high casualties among leaders. To ensure that the advance does not bog down because everyone who knows the plan has been killed or incapacitated, *everyone* knows the plan. The loss of a tactical or even opcrational leader is no excuse to stop the advance; anyone who can lead or is willing to lead has all the information he needs to keep going. All the emerging leader needs is moral authority and command presence—both of which come from within the individual. The ramifications of this concept add immeasurably to many other of *Zahal's* unique war-fighting abilities.

If a leader is incapacitated and has left no plan, or if the plan has not been shared with the surviving subordinates, then the survivors are encouraged to develop and implement a plan of their own, as long as it is aimed at achieving the last known objective. Likewise, if a combat unit loses touch with higher headquarters but is otherwise capable of operating, the commander or leader of that unit is encouraged to improvise a plan of his own, aimed at achieving the unit's last known objective. In other words, Israeli soldiers who are able to carry on may not use ignorance as an excuse to stop doing anything. If nothing else occurs to anyone, then the unit is obligated to go find an enemy unit to attack, for the enemy's probable confusion in the face of an illogical action might set in motion a chain of events that can change the entire course of a war.

A wide variety of operational corollaries that derive from Adherence to Mission and Optional Planning are taught routinely to Israeli soldiers from their earliest days as conscripts. These corollaries include concepts that can be boiled down to these self-explanatory aphorisms: When your orders have not gotten through, assume what they must be; When in doubt, attack; The battle will never go as planned, so improvise; and, Surprise is your most effective weapon. Above all, Israeli officers and soldiers are taught: Risk, risk, risk.

14

Zahal developed two incredibly good operational ideas after 1956, but it was hobbled with a force structure that was far from being the most effective platform for implementing those better ideas in battle. So, while the doctrinal planners were developing their radical Adherence to Mission and Optional Control dicta, other innovators were more or less simultaneously altering *Zahal's* force structure—just as radically.

One of the vital lessons learned in the course of the Sinai Campaign was that foot infantry simply could not act effectively if left to its own devices to walk to the battle. It is true that the Reserve infantry brigade charged with securing the Kusseima road junction at the outset of the Sinai Campaign had conducted a grueling night march of a dozen kilometers through loose sand, but every other infantry unit on its way to battle had been at least nominally motorized—aboard commandeered two-wheel-drive civilian vehicles if not standard four-wheel-drive military transport. In the decade after 1956, Israeli infantry trained to move to the battlefield solely on wheels or tracks, and special efforts were expended to provide the infantry brigades with wheeled transport. By 1967, many of *Zahal's* infantry brigades were motorized on organic vehicles, but, except for a sprinkling of jeeps and service vehicles, the three parachute-infantry brigades were not.

As the Sinai Campaign was continuously dissected and the development of the Adherence to Mission and Optional Control doctrines continued apace, it became evident that *Zahal* was going to fight its future land battles mainly from tanks and armored support vehicles. So, while for most of the post-Sinai decade the infantry remained the largest of *Zahal's* ground components, *Zahal's* real growth after 1956 took place in the Armor Corps.

The employment of massed tanks and armored infantry in attacking fortified positions and the armored juggernauts across Sinai in pursuit of the fleeing

Egyptian mobile forces made a profound impression upon Chief of Staff Moshe Dayan during the war. Fortunately, Dayan was man enough to recant his earlier philosophy as soon as the war ended. Trained as a light infantryman and hardened in combat in the War of Independence as the commander of a unit of motorized light infantry, Dayan was unable to envision the value of heavy armored forces before he saw Israeli armored task forces in action in Sinai in 1956. Dayan's war plan foresaw breakthroughs along the Egyptian front by tank-supported infantry, followed by a pursuit of fleeing Egyptian units by fast-moving Israeli *motor* columns. By virtue of all his prior experience—and because he utterly missed the point of Uri Ben-Ari's bravura performances during *Zahal's* 1952 and 1953 war games—Dayan had been psychologically and professionally unprepared for what self-contained task forces of tanks and armored infantry actually accomplished in Sinai.

During the remainder of his tenure as chief of staff, Dayan was Israel's most influential—and impatient—proponent of the development of a large armored force. If it had been up to Dayan, and if Israel had had the wherewithal to purchase sufficient arms and equipment, the entire army would have shifted to tanks and modern APCs at a moment's notice. But Israel did not have the funds to buy so many tanks and APCs, and few nations were willing to sell her even what she could afford. Nevertheless, the 7th Armored Brigade received the best battle tanks Israel could procure, and the two Reserve armored-infantry brigades were made over as full armored brigades (two tank battalions plus one armored-infantry battalion, rather than the other way around). Also, several Reserve infantry brigades were selected to become armored-infantry brigades as equipment became available. Thanks to Dayan's initiative and enthusiasm, by mid-1967 *Zahal* fielded an estimated eight armored brigades, three armored-infantry brigades, and several independent tank battalions. Also, nearly all of *Zahal's* infantry brigades, many of which were at least nominally motorized, fielded organic tank companies or squadrons.

Two days after the guns went silent in Sinai, Brigadier General Assaf Simchoni was killed when his light plane became lost in a sandstorm and crashed in Jordan. Simchoni was replaced immediately as GOC, Southern Command, by Chaim Laskov, and Laskov was replaced as head of the Armor Corps by Uri Ben-Ari.

By the end of 1956, Moshe Dayan was at work transforming the Armor Corps into Israel's premier combat arm. Thanks to his new-found enthusiasm, a new crop of extraordinary leaders gravitated to the Armor Corps. One of the first names Dayan lighted on was that of Colonel Yisrael Tal, a 32-year-old infantrymen who had served as a corporal in the British Army's Jewish Brigade (his company commander in Italy had been Major Chaim Laskov). At the moment Dayan called, "Talik" was both commandant of *Zahal's* Officers' School and the newly appointed commander of a Reserve infantry brigade. Though Talik had served as signals officer of the Army of Independence's only armored brigade, his arms-length experience with tanks hardly qualified him for the new post Dayan had in mind for him. Rather, Talik's appeal lay in his extraordinary mechanical aptitude; he was a notorious tinkerer. In Dayan's mind, Talik, who was appointed deputy commander of the Armor Corps on less than a day's notice, was to be the Armor Corps' nuts-and-bolts man behind operational and tactical innovators like Uri Ben-Ari.

It says much for Talik that, as soon as he was appointed to the Armor Corps, he joined a basic class of tank-officer candidates and learned his new trade from the ground up. As did the officer candidates with whom he trained, Talik learned every tank-crew position, from loader to tank commander. He even spent time taking the mechanics' course.

Before Colonel Tal completed his basic armor training, scandal rocked the Armor Corps. After a fairly senior tank officer was caught selling misappropriated government-owned sugar on the black market, an investigation revealed that, while personally innocent of any malfeasance, Colonel Uri Ben-Ari had known of the transactions and had shielded the culprit. Ben-Ari's brilliant professional career was cut short. He was allowed to retain his commission as a colonel, but he had to resign from the Standing Army. Named to succeed Ben-Ari was Brigadier General Chaim Bar-Lev, a professional armor officer who had interrupted his work as head of the Instruction Department of the General Staff Branch to command the 27th Reserve Armored-Infantry Brigade in Sinai. Talik remained as the deputy commander and soon took over responsibility for testing and specifying equipment for the Armor Corps' build-up.

During his two years as Armor Corps deputy commander, Talik looked at all the tanks Israel might be allowed by foreign governments to purchase, but he put off making a decision until he could find out everything there was to know about tank operations in Sinai. When his polling of tank officers was complete, he concluded that the speedy and agile but lightly armored French

AMX-30, which all the Israeli armor professionals preferred, was unsuitable for combat in the Middle East. Tal's rather startling conclusion was that the broad, flat vistas of the Sinai battlefields, plus the heavy concentrations of Egyptian antitank guns encountered around formal defensive positions, rendered the AMX-30 and other lightly-armored battle tanks of the period (including Soviet T-54s and T-55s) too vulnerable. Yes, Tal agreed, the AMX-30 was fast—it could travel 50 miles per hour on the road—but survivability outweighed speed and maneuverability. The AMX-30 did not have enough frontal armor to suit Talik. Though its best road speed was only 20 miles per hour, Talik opted for the heavier 50-ton British Centurion because its thicker frontal armor would be able to survive multiple hits by the antitank guns with which the neighboring Arab armies of the day were equipped. Israel was able to purchase about 250 Centurions. Also, West Germany secretly offered to sell Israel "surplus" American-built M-47 Patton tanks. Talik jumped at the opportunity even though the M-47 was equipped with a gasoline engine because it was the only other modern tank in the world that featured frontal armor comparable to the Centurion's.

Over the years, thanks to Talik, *Zahal* ordnancemen upgraded most of the tanks in the Israeli inventory. They even upgraded the modern Centurions and M-47 Pattons. The standard 20-pounder main gun in each Centurion was replaced with a British-manufactured 105mm high-velocity gyro-stabilized gun. To upgrade and standardize *Zahal*'s various Sherman models—including forty with AMX-13-type turrets that had been captured from the Egyptians in Sinai—Tal hoped to install the same high-velocity 105mm gun that was going into the Centurions. But the aging 32-ton Shermans were too lightly built to absorb the recoil, and the hulls of several of them cracked when the high-velocity 105s were tested. The *Zahal* ordnancemen eventually retrofitted each American and Egyptian Sherman with a new 460-horsepower diesel engine and an Israeli-designed 105mm medium-velocity gyro-stabilized gun capable of penetrating all known Arab armored vehicles. The result was a 39-ton Sherman variant the Israelis called the M-51HV Super Sherman. The conversions were still taking place in 1967, but, by then, all *Zahal* Shermans were either M-51HV Super Shermans with 105mm medium-velocity guns or M-51 French Shermans with 75mm high-velocity guns. Also, all 200 of the West German M-47 Pattons were retrofitted with British-manufactured high-velocity 105mm guns, and their highly flammable gasoline engines were replaced with diesel engines. When West Germany cut off the flow of M-47s in 1964 because of news leaks, the United States direct-shipped a number of M-48 Patton variants that came standard with 105mm guns and diesel engines.

Thanks in very large part to Talik's tinkering, not to mention the heroic efforts of Ministry of Defense arms buyers, *Zahal* was able to field approximately 1,000 reasonably modern battle tanks by the end of May 1967.

As the Shermans and Centurions were upgraded and, later, the Pattons were purchased a few at a time, the Armor Corps expanded apace. As foreseen by Moshe Dayan following the conclusion of the Sinai Campaign, several Reserve infantry brigades became armored-infantry brigades fielding one tank battalion, two halftrack-mounted armored-infantry battalions, and a company of halftrack-mounted 120mm heavy mortars. In time, as *Zahal* acquired more tanks, several of these brigades were further reconfigured with two tank battalions and one armored-infantry battalion apiece, and an SP battery or two.

Talik's study of armor in Sinai also made him a firm believer in the tank soldiers' view that tanks needed to be accompanied by infantry when they went into combat. Even given the broad vistas of the desert, a tank is extremely vulnerable to enemy infantry. Combat in World War II had forged the axiom that tanks could not advance safely against enemy infantry if they were not accompanied by friendly infantry. And tanks could not effectively reduce enemy positions on their own. Infantry units advancing at the same pace as the tanks were essential for clearing enemy soldiers out of trenches and bunkers in positions the tanks helped overrun.

The problem, which was only just being solved in the mid 1950s, was finding a safe, reliable infantry conveyance that could keep pace with tanks. There were good APCs available to Israel in the late 1950s, but none was purchased—not one. Talik would dearly have loved to field masses of APCs to counter the masses of Soviet-built APCs that the Egyptian Army was receiving, but it was not to be. Israel could not *afford* to purchase all the tanks it needed *and* modern APCs besides. For the foreseeable future, the armored infantry would have to make do with the World War II–vintage American-built M-3 halftracks it had on hand at the end of the Sinai Campaign. Maybe someday, but not at the expense of tanks. In fact, Israel purchased no modern APCs before the 1967 war.

The dynamic team of Chaim Bar-Lev and Yisrael Tal worked tirelessly to upgrade every aspect of the Armor Corps, beginning with force structure and equipment tables, and moving on to tactics. The job was far from done, however, when, in 1959, Talik was given command of the 7th Armored Brigade. The new post provided him with fresh vistas, and he continued to have a profound impact upon the development of the Armor Corps.

Talik had heard of massive equipment failures in the tank units during the Sinai Campaign, but it was not until he had taken command of the 7th Armored Brigade—his first protracted experience living among armor troops as one of their own—that he began to realize where the Armor Corps had been going wrong. Over fifty percent of the tanks and other vehicles in some units had suffered mechanical breakdowns—ranging from burned-out engines to damaged optical sights—yet many units had not even taken basic tool kits with them. But the conventional complaint Talik heard around the 7th Armored Brigade was that the equipment wasn't any good. It broke. It was poorly designed. It took too much time to maintain. Talik listened, Talik asked questions, and then Talik read the manuals. And Talik eventually got it into his head that equipment failures were functions of technical ignorance and lax discipline.

After studying all the equipment problems and failures about which his subordinates were complaining, Talik required that every officer in the brigade simply read and master the manual that came with his tank or other vehicle. He did not expect every man in the brigade to know how to fix every type of breakdown, but he did expect his officers and tank commanders to be able to diagnose problems. More profound was his unyielding insistence that the equipment benefit from preventive maintenance, a truly alien concept in the Israeli culture. Yes, he wanted broken equipment fixed when it broke—and fixed by the book—but he especially wanted regular maintenance to be conducted, also by the book. The brigade commander administered iron discipline in this regard, and his imposition of authority was deeply resented. No real progress was made until several years later, until a scrap with Syrian tanks in which lax maintenance and inferior technical knowledge brought about a humiliating comeuppance. Thereafter, attitudes throughout the Armor Corps changed instantly and dramatically.

Since the 7th Armored Brigade was the Armor Corps' training school for young officers and conscripts, Talik's notions of reading the manuals and preventive maintenance slowly spread into the burgeoning Reserve armored and armored-infantry brigades.

No doubt as a result of Talik's focus on simple, direct technical solutions, mobile repair shops were developed to be send forward during an advance in

order to service or repair all manner of wheeled and tracked vehicles and
armaments assigned to armored units. This practice did much to obviate a
repeat of the 1956 situation, in which the extremely large number of tanks
and other vehicles that broke down during the long chase across Sinai had
to be abandoned for lack of spare parts and qualified mechanics. In 1967,
repairs were oftentimes undertaken by mobile ordnance teams in the front
line, sometimes under fire.

Another important innovation arising from Israel's focus on armor-based
lightning warfare was the development of *Zahal*'s dynamic tactical supply
system. The inability of Southern Command in 1956 to resupply any of the
armored task forces of the 7th Armored Brigade once they had passed beyond
Umm Katef was probably the basis of the Israeli innovation. Unless swiftly
moving tanks and other vehicles can be refueled from reliable stocks, or
unless all sorts of munitions and other types of supplies can be moved forward
in a timely manner to the advancing combat forces, there is probably no
advantage in developing a lightning-warfare doctrine.

The supply services of most armies will send needed supplies forward
from rear-area depots upon request. In those armies, tactical units must *pull*
supplies in by sending a request to a depot. Borrowing from an American
innovation worked out in France during World War II, *Zahal* opted to *push*
supplies forward without waiting for requests from ever-more-distant front-
line units. That is, to help keep the front-line units moving forward, the
Israeli supply corps learned to send a steady stream of every type of supply
forward without being asked. If a tactical unit needed something—more rifle
ammunition, for example—it only needed to request it from the supply
section of its own brigade headquarters. As soon as the brigade supply section
dispensed the bullets, it sent a truck back along its former axis of advance
(now its line of supply) to draw a replacement supply of rifle bullets from a
mobile supply depot that had advanced steadily in the wake of the combat
units it was supporting. Meantime, the army supply corps had already sent
more rifle bullets to the mobile depot as a matter of course, and more yet
were on the way without anyone having asked.

In 1961, Brigadier General Chaim Bar-Lev and Colonel Yisrael Tal *both*
interrupted their professional careers to further their educations. Bar-Lev,
who was one of the few *Zahal* officers who had earned a college degree before
attaining the rank of colonel, went to the United States to attend graduate

school. Talik, who had a high-school diploma, went off to study philosophy and political science at the Hebrew University.

Bar-Lev was replaced as GOC, Armor Corps, by newly promoted Brigadier General David Elazar, a distinguished Army of Independence warrior who had commanded an infantry brigade in Gaza in 1956. Dado Elazar had volunteered for the expanding Armor Corps in early 1957, following completion of his tour as commandant of *Zahal's* Infantry School. When Dado completed his basic armor-officer training, he was appointed to command a battalion of the 7th Armored Brigade. Shortly, he assumed command of the entire brigade until 1959, when he succeeded Talik as the Armor Corps deputy commander.

It was during Dado Elazar's tour as GOC, Armor Corps, that many of the new armored and armored-infantry brigades authorized during Chaim Bar-Lev's tenure were actually created. It was Dado, then, who oversaw their training and further development. Also, thanks to his having a far larger force on hand, it was under Dado that many of the Armor Corps' new tactics and standard operating procedures, which had been implemented first under Bar-Lev, were consolidated and refined. And it was Dado who oversaw the application and full development in the armored forces of *Zahal's* emerging Adherence to Mission and Optional Control dicta.

Among the many innovations first undertaken under Bar-Lev and then refined under Elazar was that an Israeli tank commander rode into battle standing tall in his turret. The biggest problem tanks face in battle is the limited vista from within. It is a natural tendency for tankers to want to fight "buttoned up," but then the tank crew is relatively blind and the tank is just that much more vulnerable to enemy countermeasures. Throughout *Zahal*, the status accompanying leadership has its price. In combat that price is usually increased exposure to enemy bullets. In *Zahal*, the tank commander *never* hunkers down in the turret with his hatch pulled down over his head. At first, it was a matter of doctrine. In time, it became a matter of pride.

Dado was appointed GOC, Northern Command, on November 1, 1964, and Talik returned to active duty as a brigadier general to take up the reins as GOC, Armor Corps. At that cusp, with the equipment Talik had earlier selected on line and fully upgraded, and Elazar's consolidation of doctrine complete, the Armor Corps was set to enter its most fruitful period of technical advancement—its last and most important before the 1967 war. Fittingly, it was Talik who set the pace.

* * *

On November 3, 1964, only two days after Talik took command of the Armor Corps and Dado moved up to Northern Command, the 7th Armored Brigade was humiliated in the first Nukheila incident, near Kibbutz Dan, in the very far north of the country. A lengthy gunnery duel between two Syrian tanks and a platoon of Centurions resulted in no hits by the Israelis. Talik was stunned. Years after he had gone to great pains to absorb the complex Centurions into the Armor Corps, the 7th Armored Brigade crews were still blaming their failure on complexity of the British gunsights in particular and the Centurion in general—as if that had anything to do with missing sitting targets upwards of sixty times in a row! Talik and Dado both were livid.

Fresh from nearly three years of thinking rather than reacting, Talik had already formulated a plan of action. He opened his tour as GOC, Armor Corps, with a bang. He called a meeting of senior armor officers and announced that, henceforth, they all had to wear army-issue olive-green work uniforms, the trousers the same color as the blouse. Talik had always been a bear for proper uniforms, but the peremptory announcement was met with incredulity. What did matched uniform parts have to do with the lousy Centurions and crappy British optical sights?

The armor officers began a war of passive aggression. Suffused with the lax outlook toward overt discipline that had taken *Zahal* by storm in the wake of the pre-1956 victories of Arik Sharon's Unit 101 and Parachute Battalion 202, the armor troops considered it to be beneath their dignity to submit to a silly order about the shade of their khaki work uniforms. But Talik knew that the lax outward discipline that had worked so well for the paratroopers was bringing about the degradation of the Armor Corps. So, even if morale suffered in the short term, he insisted upon getting his way. He announced that, in the Armor Corps, orders were to be obeyed simply *because* they were orders; officers and soldiers were no longer free to determine on their own which regulations they were going to obey. And, henceforth, Armor Corps officers and soldiers were to be dressed at all times in regulation uniforms— *neat* regulation uniforms—with their shirts tucked in, shoelaces properly tied, and either the tanker's black beret or a steel helmet on their heads.

Talik was not, as his men believed, a martinet; he was personally disciplined. The point Talik was trying to make—*would* make—was that soldiers entrusted with faithfully maintaining their complex and sensitive equipment first had to accept the notion of looking after themselves, including their appearance, and certainly including their attitude toward discipline. Though reluctant to take Talik's point, the armor troops came around because they had to. Once they did, of course, they took special unit pride in their neat uniforms and the wearing of their black berets. In time, in their minds, their adherence to discipline proved that they were elite—at least as elite as the slouching, red-bereted paratrooper with the tail of his uniform shirt worn down over his belt.

Once he had imposed his will upon the Armor Corps, Talik set about training it up to a new standard. The neatly dressed men who used the equipment were not necessarily obliged to master every technical nuance— that was left to maintenance and engineering specialists—but they were expected to follow an ironclad set of instructions and procedures aimed at keeping the equipment in good running order, whether by rote or technical mastery. Of course, blindly following maintenance and other important procedures to the letter was what blindly adhering to dress codes had been about. It was Talik's belief that the reason the Israeli gunners had missed the Syrian tanks at Nukheila on November 3, 1964—and had not done much better on November 13—was because the gunners had all been zeroing their sights in accordance with their opinions, and not based on rigid directions that came free with the optical-sight manuals. After Nukheila, all Armor Corps optical devices were battle-sight zeroed in the manner the factory manuals said they should be, and no other way. In the next big confrontation with Syria involving tanks, in August 1965, a company of 7th Armored Brigade Centurions scored numerous hits. (Talik himself was lightly wounded in this engagement while serving a stint as a Centurion gunner.)

In the nick of time, when the crunch came in 1967, everything clicked. Israel placed her greatest hopes for salvation in the hands of Yisrael Tal's Armor Corps, and the Armor Corps came through.

15

"Israel's best defense is in the skies over Cairo." This virtual credo of the IAF was the brainchild and pet argument of the tall, gangly *sabra* who directed the IAF's phenomenal growth through eight of the eleven years between the Sinai Campaign and the 1967 war—Brigadier General Ezer Weizman. The chief architect of the IAF's inter-war growth, Weizman headed the IAF's Air Department and served as fighter commander under Brigadier General Dan Tolkowsky. In July 1958, he was promoted to brigadier general to replace Tolkowsky when the latter retired.

Weizman was the nephew and closest male relative of Chaim Weizmann, a revered founder of the modern Jewish state and Israel's first president. Born near Haifa in 1926, he enlisted in the British Army when he was 18 and trained briefly in the Jewish Brigade infantry company commanded by Major Chaim Laskov. He eventually went to flight school in Rhodesia and served in combat in India at the end of World War II as a Royal Air Force Spitfire pilot. In 1948, he led the first Israeli fighters ever to engage in battle—an attack against an Egyptian truck column in the Negev Desert. A short time later, at the controls of a former German fighter, Ezer Weizman was among the first group of IAF fighter pilots ever to shoot at enemy planes in the air. Bullets he fired struck one of the five Egyptian Spitfires. Weizman was an ardent Israeli nationalist who did everything in his power as Air Force commander to bolster Israel against her hostile neighbors. It was Weizman's aggressive maxim—that the best place to defend Israel was in the skies over Cairo—that guided the IAF's growth and improved performance through and beyond the 1967 war.

Of special significance during Weizman's long tenure as IAF chief was the unremitting drive to improve the overall quality of Israel's only truly strategic arm. While all of *Zahal's* other arms were oriented solely toward the tactical and operational levels of fighting, the IAF's most important mission in time of war was the destruction of the strategic war-fighting assets of one or more enemy nations at once—*plus* tactical and operational dominance of the battlefield.

Of all of Israel's combat arms, the IAF possessed the greatest responsibility for undertaking preemptive attacks against the enemy at the outset of a war. The preemptive strategy had evolved quickly from the 1949 findings of the Laskov Committee, but it took Ezer Weizman's blunt articulation of the principle to make a strategic preemptive air strike the IAF's chief mission in life. It had been thus before 1956, but the peculiar nature of Israel's alliance with France and Great Britain during the Suez/Sinai episode had prevented the IAF from utilizing even its rather limited strategic reach to launch preemptive strikes against strategic targets, including air bases, inside Egypt. Rather, the line of demarcation established by Israel's allies 16 kilometers east of the Suez Canal had obliged Israeli pilots to stay clear of Egyptian airfields during the vital early stage of the campaign. Indeed, the Anglo-French prohibition forced the IAF to undertake most of its operational missions in the *wrong direction* during the ground-coverage phase of the war.

Usually, an operational-level direct-air effort in support of ground troops attacks enemy forces first at the enemy's rear and thence toward the enemy's front. Doing so disrupts the enemy's lines of supply, reinforcement, command, and control—and tends to isolate enemy forces on the battlefield by cutting front-line units off from their supports. If the enemy's routes of access to and egress from the battlefield are denied or even severely disrupted, then the operational air plan has been a success and the ensuing close-air tactical phase is usually assured a high degree of success. Adherence to this principle would have obliged the IAF to mount most of its 489 Sinai missions against Egyptian ground targets, especially moving columns or trucks or tanks, from west to east—from the direction of the Suez Canal toward the eastern side of the Sinai Peninsula. However, in 1956, the Anglo-French strictures against Israeli overflights of the Suez Canal and its buffer zone obliged the IAF to attack Egyptian forces from east to west—in the "wrong" direction. The IAF had done well enough in its support mission, but this was largely because Egyptian warplanes avoided direct confrontations with Israel's limited number of modern jet fighter-bombers, and not because of anything the Israelis actually did on their own to fall heirs to regional air superiority. (Once French Air Force fighter-interceptors began operating from Israeli runways, several days into the campaign, Egyptian fighters all but disappeared from the skies over Sinai.)

To Israel's senior aviation commanders, the situation during the Sinai Campaign had been intolerable, even though it was guided by geostrategic considerations. Following Sinai, the hostility of senior IAF officers toward the Sinai strategic and operational aviation scenarios became one of many factors militating against Israel's ever again becoming enmeshed in a strategic alliance with partners whose interests and goals diverged at almost every level from Israel's.

It fell largely to Colonel Ezer Weizman, in his capacity as IAF fighter commander, to oversee an analysis of the use of air power in Sinai and to make recommendations based upon the findings. An inevitable result of the findings was an aviation modernization program in every way as energetic as the equipment-procurement and training programs that engulfed the Israeli armored force. Not coincidentally, it fell to Weizman after his elevation to the post of IAF commander in 1958 to oversee the procurement of new weapons systems.

The backbone of Israel's Sinai air effort had been the piston-engine P-51 Mustang fighter-bomber of World War II vintage. It was plain to see from the air-war analysis that the day of the piston fighter was over and that, to remain competitive, the IAF would have to modernize.

In addition to modernizing, the IAF needed to grow, for it was equally plain to see that the Sinai Campaign had not obviated but only delayed an ultimate day of reckoning between Israel and Egypt. The Egyptian armed forces were certain to expand in the future in an effort to surpass *Zahal*, so there would be more for the IAF to do in a future war.

Israel's choice of airplanes was constrained by the fact that France was the only aircraft-producing nation in the world that was willing to sell modern jet warplanes to Israel. Fortunately, as far as Israeli planners were concerned, French aircraft companies were producing several of the best combat aircraft in the world. By far, the most successful combat airplane employed by either side in Sinai had been the IAF's thirty-six state-of-the-art Mystère-IV fighter-bombers, which had been delivered only a week or two before the war. Though the IAF's very best fighter pilots had been able to amass no more than twenty flight hours apiece in the Mystères, they had bested Egyptian MiG-15s wherever they met them in the air. Moreover, the versatile Mystères had proved to be extremely effective against Egyptian tanks. The twin 30mm cannon and 1,200-round magazines with which they were equipped made them the best air-to-air fighters and aerial tank-killers in the Middle East.

Likewise, the rugged little French Ouragan ground-attack aircraft, of which twenty-four had been delivered to the IAF in 1955, proved to be a superb ground-support airplane, both a stable air-to-ground gunnery platform and extremely survivable in the face of intense enemy ground fire.

More of both the Mystère-IV and Ouragan types were ordered in quantity from France as soon as the results of the Sinai air effort were assessed. Fortunately, France was in a position to help Israel; the French Air Force was in the process of phasing out the Ouragans, so forty-eight—enough to equip four newly created IAF ground-attack squadrons—were immediately available. And the Mystère-IV was still rolling off French assembly lines, so there were enough available in the short term to bring the total number in Israel's arsenal to fifty. Together, the Mystères and Ouragans formed the backbone of the IAF's operational offensive capability well into the 1960s.

In addition to seeking greater numbers of proven Mystères and Ouragans, the IAF found that it needed a modern light attack bomber. Selected was the French Sud Aviation Vautour-IIA single-seat variant of a light attack bomber the French flew in a two-man configuration. This modern all-purpose bomber, which the IAF ordered to be fitted with two 30mm cannon, could carry in its internal bomb bay either 3,000 pounds of bombs or two rocket pods deploying a total of 232 68mm air-to-air missiles. The Vautour-IIA also could carry four removable under-wing rocket pods with nineteen air-to-ground missiles apiece or, as an alternative to an internal bomb load, 4,000 pounds of externally loaded bombs. The Vautour had both the range (a 700-mile combat radius) and payload to become the IAF's first truly effective strategic-type weapon.

France fulfilled another basic IAF requirement with the Air-Fouga CM-170R Magister jet trainer. Not only was the twin-engine Fouga-Magister, as Israelis called it, a superb trainer, a ground-attack role was possible because the extremely agile airplane came standard with mounts for two 7.5mm machine guns, and it could be fitted with air-to-ground rockets and a bomb. Moreover, by the time the Fouga-Magister became available in late 1958, the Israeli Defense Ministry had decided to develop a serious domestic arms industry. The French agreed to license the Fouga-Magister for production in Israel, and an Israeli sports-glider manufacturer upgraded its facilities to assemble the Fougas. Just as the first Israeli-assembled Fouga-Magister was rolling off the new Israeli assembly line in June 1960, the manufacturer changed its name to Israel Aircraft Industries. After a dozen Fouga-Magisters had been assembled in Israel, forty-eight more were produced entirely from domestically manufactured airframes. Thereafter, only engines and armaments were imported from France. In wartime, the Fouga-Magisters were to be turned over to the IAF's only two Reserve squadrons, which were manned by commercial airline pilots.

In 1958, France's Dassault Aviation undertook a general upgrade of the Mystère and came out with the Super Mystère, the first European-designed jet fighter capable of achieving supersonic speeds in level flight. Overall, the Super Mystère was a considerable improvement over the Mystère-IV fighter-bombers then in the hands of the IAF. Its two 30mm cannon came standard, and so did wing pods that each deployed 55 68mm air-to-air missiles. Optional armaments included up to 2,000 pounds of externally loaded bombs. The IAF was able to acquire two Super Mystère squadrons in 1959, and these joined the Mystère-IVs as Israel's first line of aerial defense.

In 1959, Dassault began producing its proven Mach 2.2 Mirage-IIIC for export. By May 1963, the IAF had acquired twenty-seven of the thoroughly modern delta-wing fighters, which, on account of Israeli modifications, were redesignated the Mirage-IIICJ. Over the years leading to 1967, the IAF procured at least seventy-two Mirages in all. The Mirage-IIICJ could attain altitudes of 100,000 feet and, at subsonic speeds with full payloads, fly out to 560 miles at low altitudes or as far as 750 miles at 38,000 feet. Its armament included the signature twin 30mm cannon preferred by the IAF plus a standard package of three air-to-air missiles. In addition, the Mirages could carry a choice of two 1,000-pound centerline bombs or two 1,000-pound wing-mounted bombs plus a centerline air-to-ground missile.

The IAF also expanded its helicopter wing with the purchase in 1960 of twenty-four American-made Sikorsky S-58 medium cargo-transport helicopters to add to the seven Sikorsky S-55s it already had. The S-58s were all procured in secret from West Germany as part of the same deal that netted the Armor Corps its M-47 Patton tanks. (In return, Israel sold numerous Uzi submachine guns to the Germans.) Most of the S-55s and S-58s were dedicated to an assault role in support of the *Zahal* parachute brigades, but all helicopter crews trained to undertake medical evacuations from the front line and, of course, cargo handling.

To take the place of light fixed-wing aircraft employed as artillery spotters and liaison planes in Sinai—four of which had been downed in 1956—the IAF also procured an estimated eight Sud-Aviation Alouette-II light two-place helicopters. A need for heavy cargo helicopters was fulfilled with the purchase of five three-engine Sud-Aviation Super Frelon heavy helicopters, which were all delivered in 1965. The Super Frelons were also capable of carrying thirty fully equipped combat troops, and there was even a way to fit them out to detect submarines. A mixed bag of dedicated military transport aircraft was also pieced together between 1956 and 1967, but the mainstay of this fleet remained the C-47 Dakota transport of World War II fame.

Close support of ground forces by the Air Force, which was based on Chaim Laskov's concept of an air force composed solely of fighter-bombers, was attempted several times in Sinai but not well enough to win any awards. The role of the IAF in Sinai turned out to be operational rather than strategic or tactical. In the years leading up to 1967, the IAF was turned into one of the world's premier ground-support arms. This was accomplished by adopting the American method of posting forward-air-control teams (non-flying pilots accompanied by radiomen) to ground-unit staffs at the battalion, brigade, and higher levels and linking them via reliable radios to their compatriots in the air.

In 1966, Brigadier General Ezer Weizman became the first airman ever to be appointed to head *Zahal*'s General Staff Branch. Before leaving the Air Force, Weizman personally selected his own replacement, an equally skilled pilot and ardent leader named Mordechai Hod.

Motti Hod was a tough-minded 40-year-old *sabra* who had spent the years between World War II and Israeli Independence smuggling Jews from Europe to Palestine. It was during one of the smuggling missions that he became enamored with flight, and he took private flying lessons in Europe between his dangerous missions. In December 1948, Hod smuggled a Spitfire fighter into Israel by flying it all the way from Czechoslovakia. He flew numerous combat missions throughout the War of Independence. As a senior tactical commander in 1956, he flew twelve sorties over Sinai and engaged Egyptian troops on the ground. After attending a senior officers' course in the United States he was appointed to head the IAF's Air Department in 1961, a post he held until he succeeded Ezer Weizman as IAF commander.

Though Motti Hod agreed in principle with every program his predecessor had set in motion, he was even more ardent than Weizman in his shared view that the IAF needed to develop its people to their highest potential. His main task—and outstanding accomplishment—before the 1967 war was to see to it that the IAF achieved the fastest combat turn-around capability in the world. Due to Hod's relentless pursuit of excellence beyond the cockpit,

Israeli ground crews could rearm and refuel a jet fighter-bomber in literally minutes, as against a world-wide standard of as long as several hours.

If the IAF had been a decent regional air force leading up to 1956, it quietly—in fact, secretly—became very nearly the best in the world leading up to 1967. Absolutely nothing was left to chance. Feeling that war with Egypt was inevitable at some unknown future date—or the very next minute—IAF squadrons relentlessly rehearsed the many strategic, operational, and tactical missions they *might* have to undertake at a moment's notice. Wide-ranging and ongoing intelligence operations resulted in plans that were updated almost week by week and which could be altered at a moment's notice, even as individual aircraft were screaming down on their targets. At every minute of every day, a sufficient number of Israeli pilots was on strip alert, sitting in the cockpits of their modern fighter-interceptors, ready to launch into action at the first hint of hostile intent. Indeed, it is likely that never a moment passed when Israeli fighter-bombers were not actually airborne. The entire organization—pilots, maintenance crews, armorers, controllers, everyone who was on duty at a given moment—was keyed up to a war pitch, absolutely prepared to fly straight into an offensive or a defensive fight, just like that.

16

From the close of the Sinai Campaign until he retired from active duty at age 43 to enter politics in 1958, Moshe Dayan remained consumed with erasing all of *Zahal's* past errors and forging for his tiny nation of survivors a military machine that could, hands down, best all the others in the region, and without recourse to outside help. Fittingly, Dayan's successor was Chaim Laskov, who many senior Israelis saw as the real brains behind and chief architect of *Zahal's* growth from infancy in 1949. Indeed, it was Laskov who, under Dayan and during his own tenure, guided virtually all the hard work *Zahal* expended to develop and implement its revolutionary Adherence to Mission and Optional Control dicta.

Laskov's ascension should have been sweetness and light at all levels, but it was not to be. From the beginning, the new chief of staff clashed with a man who should have been his chief ally, Shimon Peres, the newly appointed director general of the Ministry of Defense. Though brilliant, Peres was as prickly as the new chief of staff. Long repressed by his personality conflict with Dayan, Laskov assumed his new office bursting at the seams to advance the many causes he had been propounding for years. As a former Air Force commander, a former Armor Corps commander, a former director of operations, a division commander in Sinai, and most recently GOC, Southern Command, Laskov literally embodied everything that was then transforming *Zahal*. But his energy clashed with the prerogatives of his civilian partners, and he and Shimon Peres descended into an icy relationship. As the top civilian official overseeing defense matters on a day-to-day basis, Peres was bound to win when Laskov finally offered to allow Prime Minister David Ben-Gurion to mediate. And that he did. Unable to operate in the increasingly constrained environment his feud with Peres had created, Major General Chaim Laskov, who was only 41 years old and seemingly far from completing his life's work, abruptly resigned his post in November 1960.

Laskov was replaced by Major General Zvi Zur, a rather pliable 37-year-old technocrat who had commanded an infantry battalion in the War of Independence. Most recently, Zur had taken leave to attend the Sorbonne after serving a brief stint in early 1958 as Dayan's chief of operations. Zur's tenure as chief of staff was a quiet period in which the brainchildren of other men reached maturity.

Zur resigned at the end of 1963, by which time Israel's patriarchal prime minister, David Ben-Gurion, had gone into permanent retirement. To replace Zur, Ben-Gurion's successor, Levi Eshkol, appointed the man who many thought should have been Chaim Laskov's successor. Yitzhak Rabin had been the youngest brigade commander in the Army of Independence and had served as *Zahal's* deputy chief of staff and operations chief from 1959. Many believed that Ben-Gurion had passed over the brilliant if somewhat introverted and colorless Rabin in 1960 because the former *Palmach* officer had slighted the venerable prime minister during a political flap at the very outset of Israel's statehood. No matter; no harm was done during Zvi Zur's brief tenure, and Rabin was indeed the man who led *Zahal* over the last lap to 1967. It was during Rabin's tenure as chief of staff that all the pieces finally fell into place and *Zahal* arguably became the premier combined-arms military force of the age.

It was during Yitzhak Rabin's tenure that the drive to improve *Zahal's* ethos of leadership reached final fruition. The quest, begun under Yigal Yadin, borrowed from many older and better established armies, but the result was purely Israeli.

Ultimately, after all the strategic thinking and operational planning are done, battles and wars are won at the tip of the spear. Your army can have the most insightful strategy, the most brilliant operational plan, and the boldest tactics, but if you cannot motivate the men who must carry them out to close with the enemy, defeat the enemy, and go on to do it again and again, your side cannot win the war.

In modern times—the better part of the Twentieth Century, at any rate—soldiers at the tip of the spear are no longer profoundly patriotic. They might be, of course, but it is more likely that their sense of loyalty extends to the men immediately around them—their crew, squad, section, or platoon. Everyone else is a faceless "them." The men the combat soldier looks up to are—not statesmen or generals, but—the men who stand ready to lead him into battle, men he knows and can see out in front of him when he lifts himself to his feet and charges the enemy trenchworks. The company commander who controls the immediate battle from the rear is too distant a figure in whom to invest loyalty, trust, or pride. If the company commander really wants those feelings to be directed at him, then he must direct his body at the enemy, standing tall and visible at the head of his troops. In *Zahal*, even battalion and brigade commanders must share the risks their subordinates are facing if they are to command the loyalty of those subordinates.

Far from maintaining idealism, Israeli troop leaders, from corporals commanding fire teams to colonels commanding brigades, felt they were being merely practical when they advanced upon the enemy at the forefront of their units. Doing so was dangerous: From the War of Independence onward, 20 percent of Israeli officers have been killed or wounded in battle versus an average of 10 percent in all other armies. But taking the lead is not one iota more dangerous than what the tactical commander in the rear asks the men he commands (rather than leads) to do in his name. So, while the rate of casualties among leaders who lead is quite high, the ratio of success is commensurate with the risks taken by such leaders.

In *Zahal*, leaders who led represented the cultural norm. A leader who did not lead got no results. Indeed, he probably was shunned. The essence of combat in *Zahal* was that brave leaders led and brave soldiers followed. It was practical, it was stirring, and it commanded the only sort of loyalty armies must harness if they are to in fact win battles and wars.

To give meaningful life to their "Follow me" brand of leadership, and to bind it to their philosophy of lightning straight-ahead warfare, the Israelis practiced an especially direct and bloody approach to war on the ground. They developed to the fullest degree the old French concept of élan.

At all levels—strategic, operational, and tactical—and at all times— day or night—the Israeli combat arms were taught to depend upon mobility, maneuver, surprise, psychological shock, and firepower—in that order—to overcome enemy forces and individual enemy soldiers. In the case of the infantry, even parachute infantry, the troops rode as far forward as possible in some sort of mechanical conveyance—airplane, halftrack, truck, jeep, or even bus. While all the other conveyances had to be dismounted in advance of the actual fight, the armored infantry remained within its halftracks if possible even as they drove across the top of enemy positions. Sooner or later, however, someone has to scour an overrun trench or bunker on foot. In the heat of a battle to overrun the enemy position, Israeli armored infantrymen were to attempt to retain their mobility by fighting from within their half-tracks. To do so, a number of the troops riding in the halftrack were designated to drop grenades into the enemy trench as the halftrack advanced across it alongside the tanks. Everyone else was to spray bullets from their machine guns, submachine guns, and rifles in a manner likely to oblige enemy soldiers to keep their heads down. Only as necessary or after the position had been overrun were the armored-infantry troops to dismount to clear all the surviving enemy soldiers from bunkers and trenches.

In daylight, in the case of the foot infantry, or where the armored infantry had to dismount to deliver its attack, the troops were to attack in something called an Opening Wedge formation. The infantrymen formed up in a long, narrow wedge in which the men at the point were exposed to the greatest effects of enemy fire and the men behind the point to successively less fire. The point of the wedge was the place where most formally appointed leaders stationed themselves. Doing so was important for morale purposes, but it also gave the leader a direct feel for the action as it developed. As soon as the leaders at the point of the wedge reached the enemy defensive position, the wedge opened to the left and the right and the ensuing attack developed in the form of a pincers, surrounding the enemy position, bypassing it, or fanning out to clear it.

Since the narrow point of the Opening Wedge was extremely vulnerable to enemy fire during the final approach, the last phase of the attack usually unfolded with telling speed—and thus worked to shock the enemy. If the leaders were killed or wounded by the desperate concentrated enemy fire that often reached out to engulf the point, subordinate leaders instantly took control of the attack. As long as the attacking unit remained effective—capable of achieving its mission—casualties were of no immediate concern. The only criterion for success for an attacking unit was victory.

In battle, *Zahal* was to be a 24-hour-a-day army. The only quarter Israelis gave to the darkness was a modest shift in tactics. The foot-infantry Opening Wedge assault tactic was a daytime version of the Sharon night tactic developed in 1954 for Parachute Battalion 202. At night, the infantry of all three branches—foot, parachute, or armor—followed precisely the example of the pre-Sinai paratroopers.

During the day, the attacking infantry advanced—and, at night, delivered its final assault from close quarters—under cover of one or more bases of fire that provided continuous and continuously advancing covering fire, usually with infantry weapons, machine guns, and bazookas, but also with jeep-mounted recoilless rifles attached out from the brigade reconnaissance company. The troops composing the assault wedge usually did not open fire until they were right on top of the enemy position. At that point, they blasted away indiscriminately from short range, bent upon terrorizing the enemy soldiers as much as killing any of them.

Anathema was an attack that became bogged down. The aphorism, "When in doubt, attack," applied in action at all levels. The army as a whole preferred to keep the situation fluid. Two other aphorisms accrued: "Hesitation is fatal," and "Reluctance is a sin." Some said Israeli soldiers were headstrong and reckless. Israelis felt they were merely relentless in pursuit of victory.

Part III

Countdown to War

17

As the sabers rattled in Cairo, Damascus, and Amman—as Arab rhetoric outstripped Arab self-control—all of Israel quietly went about the deadly serious business of preparing for the ultimate challenge. The best Israeli minds had had a decade to assess the competition, and to tailor an army that was capable of seizing the initiative and achieving a swift victory, destructive and expensive to one, or two, or three of the enemy nations. By the end of May 1967, Israel's was the best all-around military force in the Middle East. In raw numbers it was by no means the largest. It was not even the strongest. But it was the best.

Israel's greatest concern was a war that had to be waged simultaneously on three fronts. But short of that, Israel's least threatening neighbor was Jordan. Though big guns fired from within Jordan could cause the most destruction and the greatest loss of life in Israeli population centers, Jordan was the least likely of Israel's neighbors to precipitate or even become embroiled in a general war. The Royal Jordanian Army, with its British Army traditions, was thought to be very competent, but it was very small and it was not tested in battle. In large measure, it was a palace guard, a predominantly Bedouin force whose real function in life was keeping the Bedouin monarch on his throne in a country filled with nation-craving Palestinians. All around, Jordan was third on Israel's list of priorities.

Next in order of danger was Syria. The Syrian Army was the least effective of the three on Israel's borders. It was not the smallest, but it was the least well trained, the least well equipped, and probably the least motivated. But the Syrians were volatile (Israelis usually referred to them as "the crazies"). They were even more likely than the Egyptians to precipitate a war, although that was widely taken to mean that they might start something the Egyptians would be called upon to finish. The Syrians held the high ground in the north, and they demonstrably were not squeamish about firing down at Jewish settlements nestled beneath the dominating Golan escarpment. Syria was Israel's secondary strategic priority. If a general war broke out, Syria would have to be held off while Egypt was defeated first. If the Syrian Army attacked—if it left its defenses atop the Golan and sallied down to the Huleh Valley, then it would be crushed as soon as it took to the road. No matter what else happened, there would always be enough Israeli brigades in the north to crush an attacking and thus exposed Syrian Army.

Egypt was Israel's main concern. Egyptian guns at the outset of a war would be farthest from Israeli population centers—if Israel had any strategic depth to use, it was in Sinai—but Egypt was the strongest of the Arab confrontation states. It was the most likely to go to war, the most likely to bomb Israeli cities.

Like Israel, Egypt has never released any hard numbers with respect to the overall size of its armed forces on June 4, 1967. Estimates made in the West long after the war range as high as 500,000 Egyptian men under arms overall, including second-and third-line reservists mobilized just before the war. The *average* Egyptian soldier was ill trained and ill motivated, so the gross number, whether it is accurate or not, is meaningless in any comparison with the Israeli force charged with destroying the Egyptian Army in Sinai.

Whatever the true size of the Egyptian armed forces, it appears that no more than 170,000 Egyptian airmen and soldiers were in Sinai on June 4, 1967. Of these, an estimated 100,000 were in first-line combat units deployed in eastern and central Sinai. The remaining 70,000 or so, many of whom were in second-line units or engaged in service jobs, were well to the rear, in far western Sinai. The Egyptian Air Force and Navy aside, many of the remaining 300,000-plus Egyptians under arms at the time were fulfilling security functions throughout Egypt—guarding cities, public buildings, air bases, bridges, or important industrial or strategic sites such as the Aswan Dam.

The components of the Egyptian Army in Sinai were built and trained along the Soviet model. They were largely outfitted with Soviet equipment and their tactics and dispositions were from classic Soviet doctrine. The Egyptian first-line divisions in Sinai were very large and very heavy, and they looked extremely formidable on paper. It is nevertheless incomprehensible how Egyptian and Soviet military professionals came to believe that these heavy divisions filled with ill-trained and unmotivated conscripts—and often commanded by incompetent political sycophants—could be employed in an offensive operation, as had been threatened by President Nasser. It is inconceivable that Nasser, a former military professional and a combat veteran to boot, could delude himself into thinking that his ponderous Soviet-style heavy divisions could undertake a cohesive advance into Israel after defeating the bulk of the Israel's crack mobile ground forces.

A basic Egyptian infantry division was composed of 11,800 troops assigned to three infantry brigades and one organic artillery brigade. The Egyptian artillery brigade, like its Soviet model, was extremely powerful and belies the essentially defensive nature of the divisional makeup. Typically, the infantry-division artillery brigade deployed a battalion of thirty-six 122mm towed medium howitzers, a battalion of twenty-four 160mm towed heavy mortars, a battery of twelve 85mm or 100mm dual-purpose antiaircraft guns (for use against infantry or armor as well as airplanes), a battery of truck-mounted 240mm "Katusha" rockets, a battery of truck-mounted 130mm "Stalin Organ" rockets, and a battalion of assault guns. The assault guns that were available included a very large number of SU-100s (a 100mm flat-trajectory gun mounted in the front of an unturreted T-34 tank chassis), a much smaller number of JS-3 122mm "artillery tanks," and a very small number of JSU-152 152mm heavy assault guns. Except for the JS-3s and JSU-152s, there was no SP artillery per se in the Soviet-supplied Egyptian Army. But to call the JS-3s and JSU-152s "self-propelled artillery" is stretching the definition.

Each infantry brigade was composed of three identical infantry battalions bolstered by a support battalion and an artillery detachment. Most support battalions were equipped with SU-100 assault guns, but many were equipped with T-34 tanks, each equipped with an 85mm main gun. Several infantry battalions in Sinai were supported by Sherman tanks that had been purchased from France before 1956. These were fitted with AMX-13-type turrets mounting 75mm guns. Each infantry brigade deployed its own organic artillery detachment, which in most cases comprised a battalion of eighteen 85mm antitank guns and a battalion of eighteen dual-purpose 57mm antiaircraft guns.

The typical Egyptian infantry battalion was commanded by a lieutenant colonel who oversaw three rifle companies, a weapons company, a machine-gun company, and headquarters medical, signals, supply, engineer, chemical warfare, and reconnaissance platoons. The battalion weapons company deployed six 120mm mortars, six 57mm antitank guns, and six 107mm recoilless rifles. The machine-gun company deployed twelve 12.7mm heavy machine guns and six 37mm dual-purpose antiaircraft cannon. A rifle company's weapons platoon was equipped with three 82mm mortars and three medium machine guns, and even Egyptian rifle platoons included a four-man support section that carried two 82mm recoilless rifles.

The single 11,800-man Egyptian mechanized-infantry division in Sinai deployed one tank brigade, two mechanized-infantry brigades, and one artillery brigade. The tank brigade fielded ninety-nine T-34 medium tanks; the two mechanized-infantry brigades each fielded 150 APCs equipped with light and heavy machine guns and a support company of ten SU-100 assault guns. The divisional artillery brigade fielded a battalion each of twenty-four 122mm field guns and thirty-six 100mm and 85mm dual-purpose antiaircraft guns.

The single Egyptian tank division deployed in Sinai was composed of 11,200 troops organized into one tank brigade, one mechanized-infantry brigade, a heavy support brigade, an artillery brigade, and a reconnaissance battalion. The tank brigade was equipped with ninety-nine T-54 and T-55 battle tanks, each mounting a 100mm gyro-stabilized main gun equipped with infra-red night sights; the heavy support brigade had twenty-five JS-3 122mm artillery tanks and thirty-three SU-100 assault guns; the mechanized-infantry brigade was equipped with 150 APCs and supported by a company of ten SU-100s; and the division reconnaissance battalion was equipped with tracked armored reconnaissance vehicles, each armed with a 76mm main gun, and tracked reconnaissance troop carriers. The tank division's artillery brigade fielded a battalion of twenty-four 122mm towed field guns, a battalion of twelve 240mm Katusha rocket trucks, and a battalion of thirty-four antiaircraft guns.

Several of the Egyptian infantry divisions in Sinai were filled out with one independent tank brigade apiece. These were composed of 100 T-34 tanks; fifty APCs; and an artillery detachment deploying twenty-four 122mm medium howitzers, twenty-four 152mm heavy howitzers, and twelve 130mm long-range guns.

Compared to Israeli combat units of *every* type, the comparable Egyptian unit was much heavier and extremely formidable—on paper, at least. In artillery tubes alone, the Egyptians could theoretically blow the Israelis off the battlefield. This they intended to do. The Egyptians had hundreds more tanks than the Israelis. Further, in antitank guns alone, the Egyptians virtually outnumbered the Israeli tanks deployed opposite the Sinai frontier.

* * *

The Egyptian operational and tactical doctrines in 1967 were straight out of the Soviet rule book. In the defense, which is the only situation that pertained in 1967, the Egyptian infantry battalion was trained to dig in along the forward crest of a ridge or hill. One rifle company was held in reserve on the reverse slope and the other two manned flanking positions. All the antitank guns and most of the machine guns would be heaped in the center. If it was possible to conceal the APCs, then they would be brought forward so their heavy machine guns could cover the flanks or fill in gaps caused by natural breaks in the terrain.

When in the defense, Egyptian tanks and tracked assault guns assigned to the infantry were almost never retained in pools of mobile firepower. They were almost invariably dug in "hull down" on the reverse slope and protected as required by sandbags. They had no mobility. Tank gunners were taught to fire at the enemy's rear rather than pull out of their positions, even if overrun. An Egyptian infantry unit in the defense voluntarily surrendered nearly every aspect of mobility that should have accrued to it from the huge number of tanks, APCs, other vehicles, and artillery tubes with which it was equipped.

On June 4, 1967, the Egyptian Army deployed four infantry divisions, one tank division, one mechanized division, and one division-size task force in Sinai. Also, the 20th Palestine Liberation Army (PLA) light-infantry division was deployed in the Gaza Strip, and an independent Egyptian infantry brigade was holding Sharm el-Sheikh.

The rather top-heavy command structure overseeing this large force was controlled from Egyptian Army Headquarters, in Cairo. The overall commander was the minister of war, Field Marshal Abdel Hakim Amer, who was also the first deputy vice president of Egypt. Also based in Cairo was the commander in chief of the United Arab Command; the Egyptian Armed Forces chief of staff; and the heads of the Egyptian Navy and Egyptian Air Force. The Sinai Front commander was General Abdel Mohsen Morta-gui, whose headquarters was in Ismailia, a port city on the Suez Canal. Next down the chain of command was Lieutenant General Salah ed-Din Mohsen, the Sinai Field Army commander, whose headquarters was at Bir el-Tha-mada, a desert town roughly in the center of the Sinai Peninsula and about a third of the distance south from the Mediterranean coast to Sharm el-

Sheikh. All but one of the division commanders deployed in Sinai reported directly to General Mohsen.

The Arab unit closest to Israeli troops was the 20th PLA Division, which was deployed in the Gaza Strip. This unit, which was commanded by the Egyptian military governor of the Gaza Strip, was supported by an Egyptian tank brigade—an estimated 50 to 100 Sherman tanks—two Egyptian commando battalions, and an Egyptian artillery detachment. Its mission was to launch attacks on a number of Israeli settlements ringing the Gaza Strip and to feint toward the desert city of Be'ersheva. The reinforced 20th PLA Division was considered mediocre and inconsequential by the Israelis.

The 7th Egyptian Infantry Division, which was reinforced by a tank brigade and an artillery brigade, was deployed just to the southwest of the Gaza Strip. Its headquarters was in El Arish, on the Mediterranean coast. The brand-new division, which had been created from two independent infantry brigades and whose headquarters was manned by the commandant of the Egyptian Army Infantry School and members of the school staff, was also considered by *Zahal* to be ineffectual. Its job was to sit on the Sinai coastal highway and deny Israelis access to the fastest, surest route to the Suez Canal.

Southeast of Gaza, on the desert border between Sinai and the Negev Desert was the 2nd Egyptian Infantry Division, plus an attached tank brigade, and two attached artillery brigades. Charged with attacking the Israeli desert town of Nitzana from the Abu Agheila–Kusseima–Umm Katef triangle, the 2nd Egyptian Infantry Division was considered competent and formidable. However, the division's brand new commander, a crony of Field Marshal Amer's, was a political appointee whose military acumen was limited.

South of the 2nd Egyptian Infantry Division zone, centered on Kuntilla, was the 6th Egyptian Mechanized Division, which had been reinforced by the crack 1st Egyptian Tank Brigade and two tiny commando battalions. This force was to punch a hole into the Negev Desert and turn south to seize the Israeli port city of Eilat. Altogether, the reinforced 6th Egyptian Mechanized Division was an excellent, well-trained unit whose commander was held in high regard by knowledgeable Israelis.

The 3rd Egyptian Infantry Division was the Sinai Field Army reserve, and it was based in the region between Jebel Libni and Bir el-Hassne, in central Sinai. The 3rd Egyptian Infantry Division was ideally placed to reinforce sister units on the coast or in the center.

Also in reserve, but southeast of Bir el-Hassne, was an ad hoc light divisional task force—Shazli Force—composed of a tank brigade, a paratroop brigade, and an artillery brigade. This force could support the 6th Egyptian Mechanized Division around Kuntilla or, in a pinch, the 2nd Egyptian Infantry Division around Abu Agheila. Its main task was to exploit the breach made by the 6th Egyptian Mechanized Division and dash across the Negev Desert to the Jordanian border. If needed, it could then assist the 6th Egyptian Mechanized Division in capturing Eilat.

The 4th Egyptian Tank Division was the Egyptian strategic reserve. Though encamped between Bir Gifgafa and Bir el-Thamada, in west-central Sinai, the 4th Egyptian Tank Division was under the direct control of Field Marshal Amer. It was the most mobile and most formidable of all the Egyptian divisions and thus could be employed to assist any other Egyptian unit, across the board. The 4th Egyptian Tank Division was considered to be among the best units in the Egyptian Army, and one of the best led.

Holding Sharm el-Sheikh was an independent infantry brigade manning static defenses. Also, three independent Reserve battalions of very limited competence were manning the strategically vital Gidi and Mitla passes, in western Sinai.

It is estimated that the Sinai Field Army comprised 100,000 troops, approximately 950 tanks and tracked assault guns, as many as 1,100 APCs, and over 1,000 artillery pieces, heavy mortars, and rocket trucks.

The Egyptian deployment and attack plan was *not* the one the Egyptian General Staff had drawn up. There was such a plan, but it had been abrogated by none other than President Gamal Abdel Nasser.

In mid 1966, the Egyptian General Staff had completed work on what its members believed was an extremely realistic plan for the *defense* of Sinai and the destruction of an attacking Israeli army. Operation Kahir was to incorporate a mobile defense in depth aimed at enticing the Israelis deep into the center of the Sinai Peninsula and then launching a series of crushing counterattacks from several directions at once.

To accomplish Kahir's objectives, the main strength of the Sinai Field Army had to be concentrated in several positions near the center of the peninsula, with only light screening forces deployed along the border with Israel. The frontier was to be sacrificed at the outset of an Israeli attack, but such vital positions as El Arish and the Abu Agheila–Umm Katef defensive zone would be held if possible. As soon as the bulk of the Israeli force entered the triangle defined by Jebel Libni, Bir Gifgafa, and Suweitma, the bulk of the Egyptian force in Sinai would strike. Depending upon how the Israeli force was arrayed, it probably would be confronted first by a powerful frontal attack by several divisions and then engulfed in a double envelopment undertaken by several other divisions. No matter how the Israeli forces were arrayed, the Egyptian divisions that were poised for the kill would be able to react. If the Israelis somehow evaded their fate in central Sinai and continued to drive toward the Suez Canal, the entire Sinai Field Army was to fall back to a preestablished defensive line in the hills and across the defiles fronting the Suez Canal. In that case, the surviving Israeli force would be crushed as it contracted its front to pass through the Gidi and Mitla passes.

The sole objective of Operation Kahir was the destruction of the bulk of the Israeli ground forces in Sinai.

Prior to the May 1967, no concrete steps were ever taken to implement Operation Kahir beyond committing the details to paper. The plan was never actually promulgated to division commanders, and no war games were ever conducted. Indeed, no map-table exercise was ever held.

Based as it was on the false but comforting assumption that the heavily motorized Egyptian Army was highly mobile, Kahir was probably doomed to failure. It is doubtful in any case that the complex and bold plan could have been carried off by Egypt's ill-trained army. Nevertheless, when the crisis with Israel reached the saber-rattling stage, the Egyptian General Staff began to deploy the burgeoning Sinai Field Army in accordance with the Kahir plan.

President Nasser had ideas of his own. For obvious political reasons, he was not about to concede Gaza or any other forward position to an attacking Israeli army. Indeed, as Nasser succumbed increasingly to his own fiery rhetoric, he came to believe that it would be he who would do the attacking, and not the weaklings heading Israel's government. Utterly confounding his own army's best-laid plan, Nasser decreed that the abandonment of *any* position in the Gaza Strip or Sinai was unacceptable. In fact, the Egyptian Army in Sinai was to prepare to attack Israel at a time of Nasser's choosing. (Apparently, at no time during the political crisis that preceded the war did Nasser consider the possibility that Israel would attack him!)

In light of Nasser's decree, it is no wonder that the bulk of the Sinai Field Army was deployed en masse right on the frontier with Israel. In complying with Nasser's will, the Egyptian forward divisions were obliged to man temporary static defensive zones. Thus, they sacrificed even the illusion of defensive mobility envisioned in Kahir.

By the time Nasser learned the details of Operation Kahir, a large number of Egyptian Army units were already in position in central and western Sinai. When Nasser issued his no-retreat decree, many of these units had to pack up and abandon their initial positions in order to head for the frontier. The Sinai road net was not up to the overcrowding that resulted, and a very large part of the army became bogged down. Units that evaded the huge traffic jams were obliged to drive as many as hundreds of kilometers out of their way. Quite serious was the added wear and tear the movement inflicted on vital equipment. By the time they received orders to move east, many tank units had sent their vulnerable tank transporters to the rear. Thus, hundreds of tanks and tracked vehicles had to undertake the arduous road march on their own tracks. The result was that hundreds of them were not in peak running order—to put it mildly—when they arrived at the frontier. Then, as many units were engaged in digging in along the frontier, orders from above set them in motion again to claim new positions. For days on end, the Sinai Field Army was jiggered and rejiggered, with the result that many units assigned to many of the temporary frontier defensive zones never had an opportunity to prepare the elaborate defenses decreed by their Soviet doctrine. As late as the evening of June 4, a number of Egyptian units were unable even to reach their new positions.

As if operational problems and dilemmas alone were not enough to place the Sinai Field Army in an ambiguous posture on the eve of war, the general outlook of the troops and their company-grade officers bordered on the disastrous. Very few Egyptians in Sinai believed there would be a war. Many of the Regulars had been in Sinai before—when President Nasser's only objective had been to bluff the Israelis or the United Nations into giving in on some arcane political point. Despite Nasser's recent white-hot rhetoric, his weeks of dithering over an actual decision to go to war hardly infused the field soldiers with a clear sense of mission. And absolutely no specific plans had been promulgated to the brigade level or below. If there was in fact going to be an invasion of Israel, the men who would be called upon to execute it had not been told.

Certain that the entire Sinai Field Army would be withdrawn from Sinai at the end of the unseen political game—or, at least, that their units would move again and again—most soldiers in most units put only a minimum effort into digging defensive positions. In this, they were aided and abetted by their junior officers, who were as far from the information loop as the lowliest private. So, even when the Egyptian combat battalions and companies arrived at their final destinations in Sinai, there was no clue that a battle might erupt, no clue that an invasion of Israel was to take place, no clue that a war might break out at any moment. No training took place, no tactical planning took place, no final effort even to perfect defensive positions took place. In most cases, no one even attempted to rehabilitate the hundreds of tanks and trucks that had been disabled by rough use during the preceding weeks. Mostly, the troops looked around for shaded spots and played endless rounds of backgammon while waiting to be fed.

It is unclear how motivated the average Egyptian soldier would have been even had precise objectives been set out. Despite two decades of anti-Israel rhetoric, the average Egyptian had no coherent concept of a Jewish enemy. The problems most Egyptians faced were more mundane than the presence just over Egypt's border of an alien race of infidel "Westerners." The problems that had motivated most Egyptian soldiers and many junior officers to join the army were not external—they were simply poverty and hunger and a complete paucity of other alternatives. Each year, the Egyptian armed forces turned away many more potential enlistees than they took in—so enhanced were the opportunities of a lowly private over those of an impoverished farmer or a city dweller with absolutely no prospects of employment in Egypt's utterly stagnant economy.

In the main, on many levels, the bulk of the Egyptian Army did not have a clue as to why it was in Sinai. Unlike every single Israeli facing them, most Egyptians in Sinai had no motivation to fight a war, and no motivation at all to die in one.

18

The announcement from Cairo on May 30, 1967, that the Royal Jordanian Army had been linked to the Egyptian and Syrian armies via a joint Arab command was designed to intimidate Israel. However, though the rest of the world trembled, the Israelis knew that it had no basis in reality. Yes, there had been a joint command established by the Arab confrontation states, but it could not possibly be effective in controlling the separate armies of Jordan, Egypt, and Syria, plus whatever contingents more distant nations contributed to the Arab war effort. Arab unity was a myth, the Israelis knew, and the Arab joint command was a sham. Unruffled and certainly unintimidated, the Israelis resolutely stuck to their long-standing plan to defeat Egypt first while holding the Syrian and Jordanian armies in check.

By the time the Israeli mobilization had been completed in late May 1967, *Zahal* stood at a strength of approximately 250,000 men and women under arms. Of these, approximately 50,000 were Regulars and conscripts comprising the Standing Army, and 200,000 were Reservists. Approximately 25,000 Regulars, conscripts, and Reservists were in the IAF and the Navy. Of the 225,000 officers and troops in the ground forces (including women), approximately 70,000 were older men who had been called up to serve in territorial and other second-line defensive units.

Zahal's offensive ground force comprised approximately 155,000 first-line ground troops manning an estimated twenty-five combat brigades and a wide assortment of service and support units and detachments. Initially, eleven ground-combat "field" brigades were tied up in four ad hoc divisional task forces. (One divisional task force is an *ugdah* in Hebrew, and more than one are *ugdot*). Each *ugdah* was commanded by a brigadier general, and its extremely small headquarters staff was manned by officers and enlisted technicians drawn from their regular peacetime duties or called up from the Reserves. Of the four *ugdot*, three were deployed against Egypt as components of Southern Command and one faced Syria and the northern portion of Jordan's West Bank as a component of Northern Command. *Zahal* also deployed at least fourteen independent first-line field brigades and several smaller task forces along the various fronts or in reserve.

The beauty of the Israeli system of divisional task forces was its flexibility. There was no "standard" division in *Zahal*. Rather, brigades were combined on an as-needed or as-available basis to undertake a specific mission. The three *ugdot* serving in Southern Command were widely disparate in their compositions. One was an "armored" division commanded by Brigadier General Yisrael Tal, who in peacetime had been serving as the GOC, Armor Corps. It was composed of two of Israel's three standing brigades, the 7th Armored and 202nd Parachute, and one Reserve armored brigade. A second Southern Command *ugdah* was commanded by Brigadier General Avraham Yoffe, a distinguished 53-year-old infantryman who had been brought out of a three-year retirement to take on this important task. *Ugdah* Yoffe, as it was called, comprised only two Reserve armored brigades. The third Southern Command *ugdah* was an "infantry" division commanded by Brigadier General Ariel Sharon, who had left his post as head of *Zahal's* Instruction Department to take an active combat command. *Ugdah* Sharon was composed of one Reserve armored brigade, one Reserve infantry brigade, and one Reserve parachute brigade, plus an ad hoc artillery brigade composed of six battalions. In addition to the three *ugdot* in its sector, Southern Command oversaw five independent task forces. One was a diversionary force composed of one Reserve armored brigade, and another was a dismounted Reserve armored-infantry brigade tasked with clearing Gaza City. The third command-level task force was a reinforced light reconnaissance tank battalion, the fourth was a Reserve parachute brigade tasked with jumping behind Egyptian lines near the Mediterranean coast, and the last was a two-battalion paratroop task force charged with undertaking an airborne assault into Sharm el-Sheikh.

The combat component of Brigadier General Uzi Narkiss's Central Command was formed in part by the very large 16th "Jerusalem" Infantry Brigade, which was a Reserve unit composed of four first-line and four second-line infantry battalions. Two other Reserve infantry brigades were charged with guarding long sections of the Jordan-Israel frontier. Also stationed in the Central Command region, but really a component of the GHQ Reserve, was the 10th "Harel" Armored-Infantry Brigade. The Harel Armored-Infantry Brigade was the only truly mobile Israeli force in position to deter a thrust by Arab forces from Jordan's West Bank across Israel's narrow waist.

Brigadier General David Elazar's Northern Command oversaw one "armored" *ugdah* composed of two Reserve armored brigades and one Reserve motorized-infantry brigade. The *ugdah* commander was Brigadier General Elad Peled, who regularly served as commandant of an experimental National Security College. *Ugdah* Peled was deployed to counter a threat from Syria by way of the Golan Heights or around the Kinneret, or it could form a barrier across the frontier from the northern part of Jordan's West Bank (Samaria). In addition to *Ugdah* Peled, Northern Command oversaw one Reserve armored-infantry brigade and the Standing Army's mechanized 1st "Golani" Infantry Brigade.

Estimates as to the number of first-line Israeli field brigades are just that, estimates. Long years after the war, Israeli security remains so sensitive that a definitive 1967 order of battle will not be released. It appears that, in addition to the first-line field brigades deployed in the four *ugdot* or as corps troops, there were at least two first-line brigades deployed in proximity to Jordan's West Bank as elements of the GHQ Reserve. These were the Harel Armored-Infantry Brigade and a Reserve motorized infantry brigade bivouacked near Beit Shean, which was just west of the Jordan River just north of Jordan's West Bank. Four other first-line Reserve infantry brigades were apparently deployed under GHQ control to undertake unspecified duties during the build-up and the war itself. It is conceivable that these comprised a secret strategic reserve, or that one or two of them were deployed in proximity to the Lebanese frontier. Lebanon was seen as no threat at all, but it is not credible that *Zahal* would have left the rugged border with this nominal confrontation state unattended. Perhaps one or two of the brigades were deployed in reserve near the northern centers of Israel's large and generally passive Arab population. If so, however, no word of such a security role has ever surfaced. Also, no specific accounting has been made of Israel's various second-line units. It is certain that all that were mobilized were manning static defensive positions in proximity to either the frontier or major population centers. Undoubtedly, a number of second-line units undertook security missions in and around Israeli strategic sites, such as the nuclear plant at Dimona, or around isolated Eilat. Some of the second-line units that were composed of relatively younger men who had recently been mustered out of first-line Reserve units might have had a more active contingency role than units composed of men at the highest end of the mobilization age curve.

The *ugdot*, corps-level, and GHQ Reserve units in the Northern and Central commands were to remain passive at the outset of the war. No one knew for a certainty that King Hussein would actually honor his elaborately delivered pledge to go to war beside Egypt and Syria. If Jordan did go to war, Israel's initial inclination was to contain the damage with the limited force on hand in Central and Northern commands and then deal appropriately with Jordan after Egypt had been defeated. Similarly, Syria was not to be seriously molested until after Egypt had been defeated. It was dead certain that the Syrian armed forces would become involved in the war at some level—at least by way of shelling or perhaps bombing Israeli villages and towns—but Syria was not seen in Israel as a life-threatening power. There were more than enough troops arrayed in Northern Command to deal with anything the bellicose Syrians did or attempted to do.

Typical of the Israelis, and down to the very last minute, all the top-level plans were, by definition, contingent upon real-time events. Nothing was graven in stone save that the Egyptian Army presented the most serious threat to Israel and that, if nothing else was accomplished, President Nasser's heaviest bargaining chip—his army—was going to be removed from the board. By the time Israel decided to fight, on June 4, it had been determined that, no matter what, the Egyptian Army in Sinai was going to be forcibly dismantled. Israel could no longer tolerate the uses to which President Nasser had become increasingly willing to put it.

19

The Israelis had planned well. They had planned ceaselessly. They had made over the entire concept of mobile warfare. They were ready. They were so ready that for a decade Israeli reconnaissance teams had been infiltrating into the West Bank and Sinai—and even into the impenetrable Golan Heights—to map out Egyptian, Syrian, and Jordanian military positions; every track and hill and valley; every wrinkle and fold in the ground; and every shifting sand dune. As the data mounted, as the tactical maps filled in, a generation of Israeli officers and NCOs memorized the topography of the enemy's home ground, and countless discussions had woven miles of plans, which then were constantly updated to account for every shift in every sort of wind. In classrooms and command posts for eleven years, officers who might be charged with seizing Sinai or the West Bank or the Golan Plateau had relentlessly debated, perfected, and memorized their plans.

Zahal was ready. All the generals needed to know was *when* and *where* the government wanted it to strike. The world might wait with bated breath to see who would emerge on top of a new Middle East war, but, in Israel, there was no doubt—none whatsoever. Israel would win. There was no doubt. None.

Even before Moshe Dayan assumed the mantle as minister of defense on June 1, 1967, he knew the details of several strategic contingency plans that *Zahal* had developed over the years for the conduct of a war against Egypt. Dayan knew this because, ambitious politician that he was, he had several weeks earlier exploited his position as a former chief of staff to review the current war plans.

Late the first night of his tour as minister of defense, Dayan called Chief of Staff Yitzhak Rabin and Brigadier General Yeshayahu Gavish, the GOC, Southern Command, to present the plan they thought should be implemented against Egypt. Dayan did not know at the time that the two senior generals had each come up with a plan that differed sharply from the other's. Dayan also did not know and would not learn until later that Rabin had ordered Gavish to keep silent about his own plan.

Rabin's plan, which the chief of staff had first formulated as a theoretical offering in 1963, was the simpler, more conservative, and limited of the two. Southern Command would merely fight its way into the Gaza Strip and Israel would hold the territory and its people hostage until Egypt negotiated their return for a guarantee of free access by Israeli shipping through the disputed Straits of Tiran. Gavish's far more comprehensive plan was aimed at destroying whatever forces Egypt had deployed in Sinai. It did not call specifically for the complete occupation of the Sinai Peninsula, but only for the destruction of the Egyptian forces deployed there—and elsewhere within reach of the Israeli Air Force. Without its air force and army, Egypt was nothing to Israel. Indeed, without its army and air force, Egypt would slip from its leadership role in the Arab world. The objective of the broader Israeli plan was a secure foreseeable future without the specter of a strong Egyptian Army to contend with again in a year or two.

At the moment of truth, Dayan asked the generals to explain their plan. When Rabin ordered Gavish to make the presentation, Gavish asked Rabin (presumably in all innocence), "Which plan?" To Gavish's amazement, Rabin replied, "The second," meaning Gavish's plan.

Without a qualm and hardly a question, Dayan approved Gavish's plan. However, he did caution Rabin and would caution the Cabinet against mounting a simultaneous offensive against an aroused Syria. And, as soon as he could, Dayan begged the diplomats in the government to seek a *modus vivendi* with Jordan's King Hussein despite the monarch's May 30 Cairo summit with President Nasser.

Brigadier General Yeshayahu Gavish was called "Shaike" by his friends and associates. He was a 42-year-old *sabra*, tall, athletically built, but with a limp from an old war wound. Shaike's smile was broad, warm, and authentic, and the man was possessed of a friendly yet authoritative air. After graduating from an agricultural high school in 1944, young Gavish had enlisted in the *Palmach*. Completing his officer training course too late to participate in World War II, he opted to become a full-time soldier and took command of a *Palmach* company in the infantry battalion commanded by Chaim Bar-Lev. Shaike was wounded seriously in the leg by a mortar round in May

1948. After recuperating from his wounds, which resulted in his life-long limp, he became a battalion operations officer under Assaf Simchoni. Shaike later commanded the battalion and then served as a deputy brigade commander under Simchoni. After the War of Independence, as a lieutenant colonel, Shaike was appointed deputy commander of the 7th Armored Brigade. Later, he helped oversee the *Zahal* Reserve system. Eventually, at the beginning of 1956, Colonel Gavish was appointed Director of Operations on the General Staff, a post he held during the 1956 Sinai Campaign. During that General Staff tour, Shaike played a vital role in dotting the *i*'s and crossing the *t*'s in *Zahal's* comprehensive contingency war plans—plans he would in part personally oversee a decade later. Shaike was posted to France's *École de Guerre* in 1958. There, for the first time, he formally learned many of the things he had been doing for his entire adult life. He returned to Israel in 1960 to serve as commandant of *Zahal's* Command and Staff College. In 1962, he returned to the General Staff as assistant to the Director of Operations. Shaike was promoted brigadier general in 1963 and given charge of the General Staff Instruction Department—the head of training for all of *Zahal*. He was appointed GOC, Southern Command, on January 1, 1965, and it was in this capacity that Shaike oversaw the first two major reprisal raids undertaken by Southern Command since 1956. (The second of the forays was the Samua Raid.)

In late 1964, while still head of the Instruction Department, Shaike had planned a series of combined-arms maneuvers in the Negev Desert, the largest of their kind ever undertaken by *Zahal*. Fortuitously, as GOC, Southern Command, Shaike also directly *ran* the Negev maneuvers, which approximated a deep strike by Israeli mobile forces into the heart of the Sinai Peninsula. In other words, one of Israel's best trained, most experienced, and most competent field generals personally implemented what in retrospect would be a chillingly accurate simulation of both the plan he had helped draw up in 1957 and the breathtaking mobile campaign he would actually oversee in 1967. Withal, the 1965 maneuvers—Israel's largest armor exercise until then—pitted a mere 180 *Zahal* tanks against an Israeli-manned representation of a modern Soviet-style defensive zone.

Of all Israel's senior soldiers, Shaike was *the* one who had the most to do after May 15, 1967, with preparing his nation for a war with Egypt. The saber-rattling in Cairo affected Shaike and his subordinates the most, and the earliest. As a necessary first step, even as many thousands of mobilized

Reservists were pouring in and vying for his attention with a million requests and complaints, Shaike set about imposing upon his burgeoning command the moral will to win. *Zahal* had not fought a war in over ten years; no one *really* knew if all the changes that had been wrought would see it through to victory against an Egyptian Army that was vastly superior in raw numbers and combat strength to what it had been in 1956 and what *Zahal* had become since 1956. In whatever time he had before the war started—be it a day or ten days—Shaike's first priority was instilling in his subordinate commanders the absolute conviction that Southern Command could and would defeat the larger Egyptian Sinai Field Army. This Gavish accomplished through sheer force of will, by communicating in words and even body language his own calm but deeply held conviction that Israel's was the better army and that Israelis were the better soldiers. Who could know better? For it was Shaike who had trained many of the senior officers at the Staff and Command College and, indeed, many of the troops during his tenure as head of the Instruction Department. And it was Shaike who had drawn up much of the basic offensive battle plan, and who had tested it in the Negev in 1965.

Shaike's protests aside, the situation in Southern Command was never rosy after May 15. The Egyptians built a far vaster army in Sinai and Gaza than Israel could possibly build on her side of the line. Faced with just one enemy, the Egyptian Army could mass virtually all its tanks—and certainly all its best soldiers—on the front opposite Southern Command. And the Egyptian Air Force had nothing better to do than attack Israel en masse, at a time of its own choosing.

While the old men in Jerusalem haggled among themselves about *if* there would be a war, and then *when* there would be a war, and then who would oversee the conduct of the war, Shaike and his subordinates felt the initiative slip between their fingers like the sand from a broken hourglass. After a certain point, the confidence Shaike had so painstakingly nurtured within his command began to deteriorate as international news reports about the capabilities of the Egyptian bomber fleet caused the soldiers to turn their concerns to the loved ones they had left at home. Moreover, many businesses were on the verge of failing because their owners and workers were at the front, sitting on their packs, doing nothing. In time, the entire Israeli economy was in danger of failing, and this affected the spirit and outlook of the entire armed forces.

But Shaike's chief concern during the period of protracted waiting was what the Egyptians would do while Israel's political leaders blathered on and on in their closed councils. Southern Command was ready to strike. It was at its peak. And now, as the first days of June were frittered away in more needless debate, the danger signs were becoming evident everywhere. By June 3, Shaike knew for a certainty that in only a day or two his army was going to begin to lose its incredibly sharp edge.

As the two armies touched and felt one another—measuring the opposition in a number of vital ways—there were incidents, and there was shooting, but the pressure to do something was never relieved. Indeed, it was exacerbated.

On May 27, an Israeli halftrack touched off a mine planted by Egyptian infiltrators on the Israeli side of the frontier in the dangerous corner formed by Israeli's boundary with the Gaza Strip and Sinai. Several Israelis were injured, and the patrol was pinned by gunfire from nearby Egyptian or Palestinian positions. News of the incident was flashed to Brigadier General Yisrael Tal's divisional command post, as was a request to allow a more powerful Israeli force to blot out the Egyptian fire so the men in the patrol could extricate themselves. Talik sent down orders for the patrol to take care of its wounded and remain where it was. Other units were to withhold their fire. Talik wanted to get the wounded men to safety, of course, but he was under strict orders from above to avoid being drawn into a general battle. Talik stood ready to send help if the Egyptians actually attacked the stranded patrol, but he would do nothing else. So, the patrol hung on, returning fire in its own behalf but receiving no outside assistance. After three hours, the Egyptians simply withdrew.

At 1235 on May 29, a foot patrol led by the commander of *Ugdah* Tal's 202nd Parachute Brigade was waylaid by an even larger Egyptian patrol near Kibbutz Be'eri, a short distance to the southeast of the Gaza Strip frontier. The paratroop colonel sent a runner to Talik's headquarters to request artillery support, but Talik refused even though the Egyptians were inside Israel. Shortly, Talik received word from the brigade commander that Egyptian artillery rounds were striking Kibbutz Be'eri and other border settlements. But he stood firm, refusing to be drawn into an exchange. In time, the Israeli patrol extricated itself from its predicament and the Egyptian artillery ceased firing.

These little incidents, and a rising toll of others like them, were beginning to wear down nerves. Sooner or later, morale was going to suffer—or someone was going to take matters into his own hands, with who knew what consequences?

The mere news that Moshe Dayan had been appointed defense minister on June 1 blew a fresh breeze across Southern Command's stale battlements. The older soldiers recalled the fiery Dayan from their service days a decade earlier, and even the younger men knew exactly what his appointment had to mean. For a day or two, the men stood taller and a freshly aggressive spirit pervaded Southern Command. But then, once again, nothing much seemed to be happening. Once again, morale seemed to be slipping toward the brink of a deep abyss.

Little did the troops know that from the first moment of his incumbency, Dayan had been battling mightily to overcome the inertia of his colleagues in government. One of his first tasks was to poll high-ranking Zahal commanders regarding Israel's readiness to go to war. As soon as he had spoken with all of Zahal's senior field commanders—particularly a visibly concerned Shaike—Dayan put it to his colleagues in the Cabinet that it was time to step up to the plate and play ball. This the new national-unity government finally agreed to do on the morning of Sunday, June 4, and this Dayan communicated immediately to Chief of Staff Yitzhak Rabin and his field commanders.

Late in the evening of June 4, Southern Command was revitalized. In secret communiques passed down from the government via GHQ and Southern Command, the news filtered to the troops: Next morning, upon the order "Red Sheet," the attack against Egypt was to be executed.

In typical Israeli style, it was left to Shaike to determine how the destruction of the Egyptian Army in Sinai was to be accomplished. For his part, Shaike had already determined how he was going to employ the largest Israeli field force ever assembled to that time under a single command.

Shaike's plan for the war against Egypt was based in very large part upon the Israeli interpretation of the Egyptian preparations for the war against Israel. Amazing to the Israelis was the fact that, though President Nasser was filling the airwaves with screeches and bellows promising that his army was ready to invade Israel, the burgeoning Egyptian force in Sinai was deployed predominantly in a defensive posture. Nevertheless, until the government in Jerusalem got around to deciding in favor of launching a preemptive strike against Egypt, Shaike was faced with the problem of planning to kick off an offensive with an army that was obliged by the possibility of an Egyptian first strike to maintain a defensive posture of its own. That is, the three *ugdot* comprising the main body of Southern Command had to depart directly into the offensive from defensive zones set fairly far inside Israel.

But the defensive imperative prior to June 4 was only one reason for the *ugdot* to have been deployed relatively far from the frontier. Certainly, if the Egyptians attacked first, the Israeli mobile brigades had to be able to develop defensive operations to cut off the Egyptian spearheads before they did much damage inside Israel. Offensively speaking, however—for the sake of strategic secrecy and operational security—all but *Ugdah* Tal and a diversionary brigade screening Eilat had to remain well out of range of Egyptian patrols and aerial reconnaissance. Retaining the element of offensive surprise and keeping the Egyptians guessing meant placing *Ugdah* Sharon and *Ugdah* Yoffe well back from the frontier. And, though its presence was apparent to the Egyptians, *Ugdah* Tal had to appear as if its three field brigades were merely guarding the main axis of advance from Sinai through Gaza and on up the coastal highway toward Tel Aviv. Indeed, *Ugdah* Tal's position hard against the Gaza Strip obliged the Egyptian commanders to guard against the lesser Israeli strategic option—a first strike by the Israelis merely to seize Gaza and hold it hostage against a settlement over Sharm el-Sheikh. Guarding against that meant that there would be fewer Egyptians deployed down along the Sinai-Negev frontier.

To keep the Egyptian reserve divisions deployed in central Sinai off guard and guessing, Shaike openly deployed his diversionary armored brigade just across the border from Kuntilla. This was the area from which, in 1956, the main body of Arik Sharon's road-bound parachute brigade had begun its epic march to the Mitla Pass. When the diversionary brigade arrived opposite Kuntilla in late May, its preparations were conspicuous to a fault. After extensive defensive positions had been developed, most of the brigade withdrew in one night, but it left enough troops and vehicles behind to dupe the Egyptians into believing that the position was still fully manned. Several days later, the bulk of the brigade reemerged in a different place and openly dug in there. As a result of all the new activity, the Egyptian screening forces around Kuntilla believed they were facing an Israeli division. Also, throughout the period, Israeli reconnaissance planes and helicopters were extremely active around Kuntilla, further implying that a major attack would be launched there. The ruse kept the 6th Egyptian Mechanized Division in place behind Kuntilla, ready to defend the area if necessary or to storm a long stretch of apparently heavily defended border land that was in reality only lightly defended and which could have been breached by a much smaller force.

Immediately following the first phase of a massive preemptive strategic strike against the Egyptian Air Force by the IAF, the main Israeli ground attack was going to fall against the northern one-third of the Sinai-Negev frontier, between the Gaza Strip and Kusseima. In the first of three ground-combat phases foreseen by Shaike, *Ugdah* Tal was to break into the Gaza Strip opposite Khan Yunis, turn southwest toward Rafah, and advance toward El Arish along the Sinai coastal highway. Simultaneously, *Ugdah* Sharon was to cross the frontier near Nitzana and isolate the Umm Katef–Abu Agheila hedgehog. Then, during the first night of the war, *Ugdah* Sharon was to systematically engulf and reduce its objective and, in so doing, destroy the main body of the reinforced 2nd Egyptian Infantry Division. In the second phase, *Ugdah* Yoffe was to advance from well inside Israel and open a new axis of advance between the Tal and Sharon *ugdot*. *Ugdah* Yoffe was to cut off any reinforcements from the Egyptian reserve as they attempted to counterattack Talik's or Sharon's flanks. Then, once that danger was past, *Ugdah* Yoffe was to attack into the Jebel Libni area, in central Sinai, which the Israelis believed was the anchor point of an Egyptian second line of defense. In the third and possibly final phase, the armored units of all three *ugdot* were to clear the triangle formed by the Mitla Pass, Nakhle, and Bir Gifgafa.

All aspects of the Israeli offensive, with the exception of the opening moves of the opening phase, were conditional. Shaike and all his senior subordinates were extremely deft operational planners; they were capable of fabricating and implementing incredibly complex brigade-, division-, and even corps-level maneuvers on the fly.

Several subsidiary and follow-on operations were also scheduled. Once *Ugdah* Tal's initial penetrations had been accomplished around Khan Yunis and Rafah, in the Gaza Strip, an armored-infantry brigade was to occupy Gaza City. Also, as *Ugdah* Sharon opened its attack from around Nitzana, the diversionary brigade was to initiate a series of threatening moves toward Kuntilla. On the first night of the war, in support of *Ugdah* Tal, a Reserve parachute brigade was to conduct a full-scale night combat jump ahead of friendly armor units to seize or at least cordon off El Arish airfield from the rear (west). Finally, a task force composed of two parachute battalions was to wait on the sidelines until it was ordered to seize Sharm el-Sheikh by means of an airborne assault.

By the evening of June 4, all Southern Command required was the government's permission to attack.

Part IV

Sinai

20

It was 0700 Israeli time,* three hours after dawn on Monday, June 5, 1967. The summer season's daily thick morning mist was just lifting from the coastal areas, across the breadth of the humid Nile Delta, and along the Suez Canal. The air was calm. The angle of the sun rendered visibility throughout the coastal region as good as it was going to be all day.

Right on time, forty Israeli combat jets took off from their Negev Desert base as they did each and every morning. And, as it did each and every morning, the Israeli formation swept to the west, out across the neutral Mediterranean Sea. To the southwest, Egyptian radar operators noted the regular morning flight and thought nothing of it. It was not their job to think. Even with the war in danger of breaking out at any moment, there simply was no need to concern higher headquarters with news of what for two full years had been a routine so unvarying that it was possible to set clocks by it throughout the troubled region. In due course, precisely on time, the Israeli jets would dive to wave-top height and turn for home. In a short time, the skies over the southeastern corner of the Med, where Africa touched Asia, would be clear.

Along the Egyptian shore and inland, at all eighteen of the Egyptian military air bases scattered throughout upper Egypt and across the uneasy Sinai Peninsula, Egyptian pilots and ground crews were eating breakfast. There had been a dawn alert—there was a dawn alert every day—but no Israeli attack had materialized despite the extremely tense situation along the Egyptian-Israeli frontier in Sinai. Everyone thought the war would have started by now, but it had not. For one more day, the feared Israeli preemptive

---

*All times will be given as Israeli time. Egyptian time is one hour later, so 0700 in Tel Aviv is 0800 in Cairo.

dawn strike had not materialized, as common wisdom said it must. So, after all, the day's normal routine had to be played out.

The Egyptian Air Force was ready. Before dawn, dozens of Egyptian combat fighter pilots had been in the cockpits of their jet interceptors, sitting at the ends of the various runways, all on five-minute strip alert. From 0400 until 0735, pairs of Egyptian MiG-17 and MiG-21 fighter-interceptors had been flying a succession of half-hour combat air patrols along the Egyptian-Israeli frontier in Sinai. But the last patrol fighters had landed, and nearly all the pilots were eating breakfast. At 0740, nearly every pilot in the Egyptian Air Force was eating breakfast.

Elsewhere in Egypt, top military commanders and government leaders were on their way to work; most of them would be unavailable to receive information or make decisions until 0800. The only Egyptian commanders who were focusing specifically on what the Israelis might be doing at that moment were Field Marshal Abdel Hakim Amer, the Egyptian minister of war, and General Mohammed Sidki Mahmoud, the Egyptian Air Force chief of staff. Together with the Soviet brigadier general who was then serving as senior liaison to the Egyptian Air Force, Amer and Sidki were aloft in a Soviet-built twin-engine Ilyushin Il-14 transport fitted out as a flying command post. Sidki had spent the past hour monitoring transmissions from the combat air patrols along the frontier, but he and Marshal Amer decided to head home at 0740, five minutes after the last patrolling MiG fighters had touched down. As the Il-14 turned toward Kabrit air base, near Cairo, the ground controller reported that there was no traffic anywhere near Sinai, except for the daily Israeli mission over the Med.

At 0745, precisely on schedule, the Israeli jets dived and disappeared below the horizons of all the radar in the area—Egyptian, American, and Soviet. The daily event was duly noted. At the same moment, precisely, the pilot of the Il-14 flying command post reported to General Sidki that, following a brief burst of voices, radio contact with Kabrit had gone dead.

It was at that precise moment that the bombs began to fall.

As General Sidki stared at a dark cloud expanding from the ground upward over the huge Cairo West airport, nine of the eighteen Egyptian front-line airfields—from mid-Sinai to west of Cairo—each were struck by four Israeli jet fighter-bombers flying in two pairs per flight. Minutes later, a tenth Egyptian runway, at Fayid, also was struck.

Each quartet of Israeli strike aircraft arrived low over its target precisely on time, at the exact moment detailed in the plan the Israeli Air Force had been formulating for years. They had taken off from their home bases at precise intervals and had adhered to precise navigational and air-speed criteria even though they were all flying at extremely low altitudes. So as not to alert the enemy, the routes of all ten flights in the leading wave had been circuitous, away from all manner of prying eyes and eavesdropping electronics.

The precautions worked. As a result, the runways at nine Egyptian air bases were disabled by Israeli bombs at precisely the same instant, and Fayid was disabled minutes later, also right on schedule. Each and every bomb exploded, and each one did so precisely on cue.

Many of the Israeli bombs were French-manufactured 1,200-pound concrete busters equipped with small rockets designed to retard forward momentum and drive the bomb straight downward into and even through a concrete runway surface. A time-delay fuse prevented the bomb from going off until it was as deep as it could go—the better to inflict lasting damage, to blow deeper, less easily repairable holes. Young Israeli pilots—their average age was 23—whose fighter-bombers were rigged out with standard 500- and 1,000-pound high-explosive "iron" bombs enhanced the penetration characteristics of the payloads their airplanes were carrying by swooping up and then steeply down at the last moment so they actually could dive-bomb the runways. Most of the bombs in the initial delivery detonated within a heartbeat, but a number of the bomb fuses were set to explode at varying times, some long hours after the Israeli raiders had departed. This would prevent maintenance crews from safely filling craters—or wanting to.

As the initial flights of Israeli fighter-bombers recovered from their bombing runs, they turned back and, still at very low altitude, launched French-built air-to-ground missiles and sprayed 30mm cannon shells at every Egyptian airplane upon which the pilots could lay their sights. The employment of the air-to-ground missiles on strafing passes was particularly diabolical in that the missile's infra-red heat-seeking system was especially effective against quick-reacting Egyptian pilots who were just starting engines when the missiles were fired. The missiles were designed to home in on jet-engine heat signatures.

If there were no unsmitten Egyptian aircraft within reach, the Israeli strafers shot up vehicles and buildings. Each Israeli fighter-bomber made two strafing passes—or maybe three, if there was time. By dint of unbelievably accurate intelligence and unbelievably detailed briefings, the Israeli pilots—

though they were streaking in at hundreds of miles per hour—left untouched virtually all of the many dummy aircraft the Egyptians had placed in many airfield revetments.

As the first wave of Israeli jets was arriving over their targets—right on the deck, well below Egyptian radar horizons and nearly 4,000 feet lower than the effective altitude of Soviet-supplied antiaircraft missiles—the second fighter-bomber wave was halfway to its targets, and the third wave was just getting airborne. By the time the third wave reached Sinai and Egypt, the breadth of the attack would have expanded to encompass several additional Egyptian airfields.

The only Egyptian aircraft in the air at the moment the IAF was unleashed were General Sidki's Il-14 and four unarmed jet trainers—an instructor shepherding three student pilots. The Il-14 evaded the Israeli fighter-bombers, but the trainers all were downed, almost as an afterthought. The first flight of four Israeli Mirage delta-wing fighter-bombers to reach the air base at Abu Sueir bagged four MiG-21s that apparently just happened to be taxiing routinely toward the end of the runway.

The first Israeli jets to strike Cairo West and nearby Beni Sueif air bases dropped their bombs and then returned specifically to destroy the thirty huge Tupelov Tu-16 twin-jet medium bombers comprising the two squadrons of the Egyptian Air Force's Strategic Bombing Regiment. The eight Israeli Mirages cratered all the runways at both bases and then accounted for sixteen of the medium bombers with their 30mm cannon. They thus cut the heart out of the strategic bombing threat against Israeli cities. Three minutes later, a second relay of eight Israeli Mirages bombed the runways again and then destroyed all the remaining Tu-16s, also with 30mm cannon fire.

Egyptian air bases west of the Suez Canal that were attacked by the first wave of Mirage and Super Mystère fighter-bombers were Cairo West, Kabrit, Abu Sueir, Beni Sueif, Fayid, and Inchas. Simultaneously, Israeli Ouragan ground-attack jets and Mystère fighter-bombers attacked all four of the Egyptian forward air bases in Sinai—El Arish, Jebel Libni, Bir el-Thamada, and Bir Gifgafa. In fact, the Sinai attack developed so quickly that two MiG-17 ready fighters at Jebel Libni were incinerated by the second pair of Israeli Mystères before the Egyptian pilots in the cockpits could even start engines.

Meantime, the lead pair of Mystères over Jebel Libni dropped their bombs on the runway and then went around to destroy many of the thirteen remaining MiG-17s and MiG-19s parked in the base's revetments. The four Mystères destroyed every Egyptian fighter at Jebel Libni with cannon fire before they turned for home. Not by accident, the carefully briefed, exhaustively practiced Mystère pilots cratered only half of Jebel Libni's 7,000-foot runway. The 3,500 feet of the runway they intentionally left intact was just enough to support operations by Israeli transport planes after the projected capture of the base by Israeli ground forces. A strike at dusk by Mystères and Ouragans was to sow small delayed-action anti-personnel bombs all across Jebel Libni to slow or prevent altogether Egyptian efforts to repair the cratered half of the runway.

The six MiG-17s lined up in revetments at the Sinai coastal air base at El Arish were destroyed by precision rocket fire from four Super Mystère fighter-bombers in order to prevent serious damage to the facilities. The runway at El Arish was spared entirely from bombing because Israeli ground forces planned to overrun it in only one day. Then the base was slated to become Southern Command's forward medical air-evacuation depot.

The runways at the two remaining Sinai air bases—Bir Gifgafa and Bir el-Thamada—were routinely cratered. All of the transports and a few helicopters at these two bases were destroyed with 30mm cannon fire by the attacking Mystères.

The initial Israeli attack wave departed from the target area after only seven minutes. The average return flight to air bases in Israel was twenty minutes. Once the fighter-bombers were on the ground, waiting ground crews were able to rearm them with bombs and cannon ammunition—even refuel them—in a world-record eight minutes. Thus, within about an hour after launching for the first strike, the initial attackers were ready to launch again. Each Israeli fighter-bomber was capable of flying eight sorties per day, a stunning accomplishment to which no other air force in the world came close.

Each wave of Israeli fighter-bombers arrived precisely ten minutes after the arrival of the preceding wave. The Israeli pilots were restricted to just seven minutes over their targets—barely enough time to drop bombs and carry out two or three strafing runs. The only opportunity the surviving Egyptian aircraft had to get airborne was during the three-minute lulls the Israeli planners had factored in for navigational errors. Over the course of the first eighty minutes of the war, only eight pairs of Egyptian interceptors attempted to scramble aloft despite falling bombs and runway damage. Israeli jets streaking in to bomb or strafe the air bases destroyed every one of them. Indeed, not one Egyptian jet survived the ordeal of taxiing as far as the end of its runway.

Twelve MiG-21s and eight MiG-19s had been redeployed a few days earlier to the Hurghada air base, in southern Sinai, following a number of feints by Israeli jets in that direction. This potentially formidable force of first-line fighter-interceptors was launched as soon as news of the Israeli strike reached its base. After waiting over Hurghada in vain for a while, it was vectored north to relieve the carnage over the Suez Canal. At about 0830, as the twenty newly arrived MiGs curiously overflew the ruined and silent Abu Sueir air base, they were bounced by the sixteen Israeli Mirage fighters charged with guarding the next attack wave. The aggressive Egyptian pilots put up a ferocious struggle, but four of the MiGs were shot down in short order by cannon fire and heat-seeking air-to-air missiles. By then, the remaining MiGs were critically low on fuel, so they disengaged and eluded the Mirages. Only then did the Egyptian pilots learn that Israeli bombs had disabled every one of the runways within range. None of the MiGs had enough fuel to return to Hurghada, so the Egyptians scattered and tried to set down wherever they could. Most of the MiGs barreled into runway craters and were destroyed or seriously disabled.

Launched from the Negev Desert's Hatzerim air base at the same time as the first attack wave, fifteen twin-engine Israeli Vautour attack bombers were obliged to fly a circuitous route to the Egyptian air bases at Ras Banas and Luxor, the most distant targets of the day. After skirting the Saudi Arabian coast and flying most of the length of the Red Sea on the deck, the Vautor squadron turned west and split up after making landfall over Egypt. Their objectives were the runways from which the Egyptian Air Force had been bombing the Yemeni Royalist forces with impunity for several years. After the runway at Ras Banas was put out of commission by 500-pound high-explosive bombs, the sixteen Il-28 light bombers parked in neat ranks there all were destroyed by 30mm cannon fire from only two of the Vautours. At Luxor, however, heavy antiaircraft fire rose to challenge the Vautours as they turned back after bombing to strafe the MiG-17 squadron parked there. One of the Vautours lurched to the side and lost altitude after being hit, but the pilot intentionally flew his crippled jet into a covey of four parked MiGs, which erupted in a huge fireball. The remaining Vautours used up their 30mm ammunition on the remaining MiGs and the base facilities and then returned to Hatzerim at high altitude.

During the morning's second 80-minute strike sequence, the Egyptians managed to get eight MiGs airborne, mostly from Abu Sueir. Two Israeli Mystères were downed as they arrived to carry out follow-on attacks, but all of the Egyptian planes were shot down by members of the Mirage squadron responsible for providing top cover. The Israelis all used their 30mm cannon, which they preferred to the French-built air-to-air missiles with which their fighters were also equipped.

The only Egyptian plane to land safely during this time frame was General Sidki's. The Il-14 command post finally set down at Cairo International Airport at 0945, after being turned away from a dozen unserviceable runways throughout the expanding battle zone. In the two hours Sidki's plane had been flying from pillar to post in search of a safe haven, Sidki's guest, Field Marshal Amer, the Egyptian war minister, had been out of effective touch with his field commanders—an unexpected touch the Israeli planners of so much mayhem would have taken great satisfaction and joy from knowing at the time.

By the time the second strike sequence ended at 1035, at least thirteen of the eighteen Egyptian air bases in Sinai and upper Egypt were non-operational, and five outlying or minor airfields—none of which housed combat aircraft that day—were due for destruction by midnight. The only front-line air base in the region that would be left unscathed by the following morning—intentionally, at that—was El Arish.

Over 250 Egyptian aircraft had been destroyed or severely damaged. In addition, twenty-three radar installations and antiaircraft-missile sites had been destroyed or incapacitated. Approximately 100 of Egypt's 350 qualified air-combat pilots were dead, and many more had been injured, mostly in strafing attacks. Thus, by 1035, June 5, 1967, the Egyptian Air Force was no longer a factor in the war that by then was embroiling that pivotal corner of the Middle East.

Balanced against the Egyptian Air Force's horrific demise, the IAF lost just nineteen bombers and fighter-bombers during the course of the June 5 morning air assault. However, only one Vautour was shot down by ground fire and two Mystères were downed in air-to-air combat. The rest were operational losses.

A number of attacks still remained to be launched against the Egyptian Air Force, mainly missile sites and several outlying air bases. However, after 1035, June 5, 1967, the bulk of the Israeli Air Force was free to destroy the Jordanian, Syrian, and Iraqi air forces and to engage directly in the destruction of Egyptian armored formations in the Gaza Strip and across Sinai.

21

"*Sadin Adom*," the tactical radios blared—"Red Sheet."

As the first waves of IAF fighter-bombers streaked across the surface of the Mediterranean to launch the war deep inside Egypt, the headquarters caravans of the three Southern Command *ugdot* and all the brigades and task forces arrayed opposite Egypt's Sinai Field Army became suffused with action as officers shouted to make themselves heard above the instant cross-currents of orders and questions and whoops of relief.

In the 7th Armored Brigade's command caravan, a thickset, dark-bespectacled colonel named Shmuel Gonen—"Shmulik"—turned to his deputy, Lieutenant Colonel Baruch Harel—"Pinko"—and ordered him to form an ad hoc secondary command group. Neither officer needed to go into details; Pinko, who was to oversee the brigade reserve anyway, knew that Shmulik intended to personally lead the 7th Armored Brigade into action and that the colonel's chances of surviving the first clash with the Egyptian Army were limited. Pinko snapped out a hearty "Yes, sir," indulged in a rare salute, and left.

Shmulik, a 37-year-old professional soldier who always wore tinted or darkened glasses with black horn rims, was a Lithuanian by birth, the scion of a deeply religious family. He had attended a religious school until he was 16, but he had since become a devout atheist. He had been taken by his parents to Palestine when he was only three years old, but he had only recently Hebraicized his last name, Gorodisch. He had joined a religious paramilitary unit in Jerusalem when he was only 13 and had fought as a sergeant in the War of Independence. Army life had suited him; he had stayed in, earned a commission, and had commanded one of the 7th Armored Brigade's tank companies in 1956, the first to link up with the Anglo-French forces east of the Suez Canal. He was considered to be one of the Armor Corps' sternest disciplinarians, an unyielding perfectionist who by far exceeded Talik in his zeal to get things just so. Many thought that, after Talik, Shmulik had the best mind in the Armor Corps and that one day he would be chief of staff.

Now that the die was about to be cast, Shmulik was sternly snapping out orders to his radiomen, who needed to tell the battalion commanders to begin moving their units toward the frontier—and beyond. This war—Shmulik's third—the 7th Armored Brigade was to be the first of all *Zahal*'s brigades to begin moving.

At his commanders' conference on the evening of June 4, Brigadier General Yisrael Tal had capsulized his feelings—and theirs—in some sober expressions: "If we are to win the war, we must win the first battle. The battle must be fought with no retreats. Every objective must be taken—no matter what the cost in casualties. We must succeed or die."

No matter what the cost said it all. Though *Zahal* and Israel felt the war against Egypt was theirs to win, all the men and the few women in *Ugdah* Tal knew very well that it was not a war they or their nation could afford to lose. The mood was one of "do or die." There would be no second chances. The will of the Egyptian Army in Sinai had to be cracked at the first encounter, or *Zahal*'s will might go down in flames.

The initial break-in by the 7th Armored Brigade spearhead would begin from behind Kibbutz Nahal Oz and proceed directly toward the Gaza Strip town of Khan Yunis. Leading the attack would be the main body of Major Ehud Elad's Tank Battalion 77, which was equipped with M-48 Patton tanks. The 7th Armored Brigade's second tank unit, Tank Battalion 82, was equipped with Centurions; it and one armored-infantry company would be the backup. Three companies and the headquarters of the 7th Armored Brigade's Armored-Infantry Battalion 75 had been detached to form the divisional reserve, and one Patton company from Tank Battalion 77 had been attached to the 202nd Parachute Brigade.

Talik's plan for the opening phase of the war had been carefully considered. As they had been in 1956, the sprawling Rafah military camps were the real initial objective of the northern Israeli *ugdah*. But Talik reasoned that the coastal highway through Khan Yunis would not be mined or zeroed in for heavy artillery interdiction because it was used daily by many Egyptian Army vehicles plying between Gaza City, to the northeast, and Rafah, to the southeast. As soon as the 7th Armored Brigade spearhead companies reached the coast highway, they were to pivot to the left, sweep through Khan Yunis without pausing, and attack the Rafah complex from the northeast in support of a direct assault by another brigade of *Ugdah* Tal. In fact, the 7th Armored Brigade was to attempt to drive through Rafah if it could and attack straight through to the preliminary divisional objective, the city of El Arish, which was approximately 60 road kilometers from Khan Yunis.

Once the Khan Yunis attack began against what was expected to be a reinforced infantry battalion of the 20th PLA Division, *Ugdah* Tal's other two brigades were to strike into the zone of the 7th Egyptian Infantry Division. Two battalions and the headquarters of Colonel Rafael Eitan's 202nd Parachute Brigade were poised to strike north toward Rafah from the vicinity of Kibbutz Keren Shalom, at the point where Sinai and the Gaza Strip joined. For this mission, the paratroopers were mounted in halftracks stripped from the armored-infantry brigade that was to seize Gaza City. Bolstering Eitan's brigade was a company of Pattons from the 7th Armored Brigade and the Armor School Tank Battalion, another Patton unit.

Ugdah Tal's third brigade, Colonel Menachem "Men" Aviram's armored brigade, was to stand by initially in the event it was needed to help reduce Rafah. If not, Men was to exploit the breaches completed by Talik's other two brigades.

Not directly associated with *Ugdah* Tal but dependent upon the successful reduction of the Khan Yunis garrison was the Gaza Task Force. This dismounted armored-infantry brigade was to attack Gaza City from the direction of Khan Yunis.

So, the words *"Sadin Adom"* passed from GHQ to Southern Command to *Ugdah Tal* to the 7th Armored Brigade, and on down to the battalions and companies that had been charged with breaking into the Gaza Strip and driving portions of the reinforced 20th PLA and 7th Egyptian Infantry divisions from the field. The tanks and other vehicles had been idling for hours, and fuel had just been topped off in anticipation of the order to attack. When the order arrived, everyone was ready to go.

At the head of the entire break-in force was the Patton tank commanded by Lieutenant Avigdor Kahalani, a 23-year-old professional soldier who had been born in Yemen and raised in Israel, a dark-skinned young man with a mop of curly hair and a shy toothy smile. Right behind Kahalani's command tank, mixed in with the lead Patton company, was the Tank Battalion 77 command group, overseen by Major Ehud Elad, the battalion commander.

Elad was a 31-year-old *sabra* who had been elevated to command Tank Battalion 77 over the heads of several senior majors and lieutenant colonels. Many of his contemporaries and not a few of his superiors were certain that he would be a general some day.

Right behind Kahalani's lead company and Elad's command group was Shmulik's personal command Patton. Shmulik was not aboard the antenna-festooned tank, but his antenna-festooned command halftrack was only a short distance to the rear, with the rear element of Tank Battalion 77 and the half-dozen jeeps and trucks comprising the 7th Armored Brigade mobile command post.

Lieutenant Kahalani's tank left the Battalion 77 laager at 0815 and turned toward the frontier. At 0830, while the Pattons waited behind Kibbutz Nahal Oz, a large flight of IAF Fouga-Magisters passed overhead on their way to strike targets and sow confusion around the vital Rafah road junction. At 0840, while the tanks remained in position and the crews nervously conducted last-minute checks, several Palestinian National Guard 25-pounder light artillery pieces emplaced near Khan Yunis opened a desultory fire in the direction of Nahal Oz. It was unclear if the fire was aimed at the tanks or if it was just a routine morning harassment mission. It was known at the brigade level and higher that the 20th PLA and 7th Egyptian Infantry divisions were for all intents leaderless. The commanders of all the Egyptian divisions were at Sinai Field Army headquarters for a major briefing.

The Palestinian artillery fire remained light, but it began getting closer and closer to the waiting tanks. Shmulik reported this news to Talik, and Talik ordered his two 105mm SP artillery battalions into action at 0837. Directed by an artillery forward observer riding in a halftrack with the armored-infantry company attached to Tank Battalion 77, Israeli rounds began landing among the enemy battery emplacements. The Palestinian artillery fire, which had never heated up, became noticeably lighter. The danger dissipated, but, by then, Talik had decided to get on with it. H-Hour was set for 0900, but it was only 0847 when he ordered Shmulik to breach the border fence.

The word flashed down the 7th Armored Brigade communications net. Almost instantly, Avigdor Kahalani's lead Patton revved up and lurched forward. To Kahalani's far right, so did a pair of reconnaissance Pattons that had been detailed to screen the brigade's open right flank. Smoothly—swiftly—the Pattons nosed out beyond the cluster of buildings defining the Nahal Oz settlement and then entered the buffer zone of Israeli fields and orchards beyond. Precisely at 0848, Lieutenant Kahalani's Patton crashed across the border fence and turned up the narrow lane bifurcating a minuscule Arab farming village. Immediately, the lead Patton slowed to accommodate its bulk to the twisting lane. It was a tight fit. To the rear, several other tanks turned out into neighboring sand dunes or between high-walled family farm plots in quest of a clear path.

Shortly, as the lead Pattons backed and turned to spin through a series of tight turns defined by the walls of cultivated fields, the 7th Armored Brigade suffered its first war casualty. Shmulik's personal tank backed up too far and crushed one of the headquarters jeeps. The tiny vehicle burst into flames and the driver, who had been crushed and thus might have been dead by then anyway, could not be extricated from the burning jeep, atop which the tank had stalled. There was a rush of men toward the fire, and fire extinguishers were emptied into the blaze, at least to keep the fire from spreading to the tank. In a minute, the tank driver restarted the engine and pulled ahead. The jeep driver was obviously beyond help; his crushed and charred body was lifted from the wreckage and the jeep was ruthlessly shoved aside to make way for the vehicles trapped in the jam, including Shmulik's command halftrack. By then, in any case, most Tank Battalion 77 drivers had found other ways through and around the clutter of buildings and narrow country lanes.

It was just 6 kilometers from the breach to Khan Yunis. The way was mostly open, a mix of walled postage-stamp fields and stretches of loose sand that tended to channelize the Israeli tank columns. Defending the route were the Palestinian 25-pounders and a cluster of Palestinian-manned antitank guns rounded out by a few infantry positions. As soon as the border fence had been breached, a section of the 7th Armored Brigade reconnaissance company—the two Pattons and several reconnaissance halftracks commanded by Lieutenant Yosef Algamis—had surged ahead on the far right to take the measure of the defenders. Meantime, Major Ben-Zion Carmeli's Patton company of Tank Battalion 77 moved forward to Beni Souhila, a township on a bit of high ground overlooking Khan Yunis. Carmeli's company was to cover the main attack, which was to strike Khan Yunis from the northeast in order to avoid a possible minefield belt that apparently had been sown to the east and southeast.

The Palestinian National Guard troops—nearly a brigade, and not the expected battalion of them—had done a creditable job of defending the direct route to Khan Yunis. The main east-west road through the area had been pitted with a series of antitank ditches, each dug halfway across the road, first from one side and then from the other. Had the Israeli tanks gone straight up the road, they would have been obliged to slow down and turn sharply, first to the left and then to the right, and then to the left and right again. Opposite the antitank obstacles were concrete pillboxes and concrete-lined trenches from which the Palestinian Guardsmen could fire machine guns, rifles, and RPGs. Here and there near the road, a dug-in and camouflaged T-34 tank lay hull-down behind a hummock or in a stand of trees. Also, the local Palestinian 25-pounder battalion had the area fairly well zeroed in.

Though the Israelis had failed to grasp the size of the defending force, they knew a great deal about the Palestinian defensive system centered on the main road, so they avoided the direct route altogether. But, though less likely to draw hostile fire, the job of traveling cross-country in the overpopulated Gaza Strip was tedious and not without its pitfalls. Israeli tank units became hung up in the impossibly narrow lanes that separated the tiny walled fields favored by the local Arab farmers. A number of Pattons even became trapped when they tried to squeeze between ancient stone walls that were too stoutly built even for the tanks to shoulder aside. And other Pattons bogged down in loose sand at the fringes of obvious and therefore defended routes. Here and there, desperately lost tank platoons blundered into enemy fire zones, and thus flared brief pitched battles that usually were resolved in favor of the surprised but overwhelmingly more powerful tank crews. In many cases, unit integrity foundered as impatient individual tank commanders followed their training and surged off from the slowed main body to test their own solutions.

It turned out that the Beni Souhila ridge was defended in considerably more strength than had been anticipated. As the other two companies of Tank Battalion 77—such as they were by then—drove on in hopes of joining up at the Khan Yunis railway station, Major Carmeli's Patton company ran headlong into renewed fire from the Palestinian 25-pounder battalion and an unexpected strongpoint defended by massed antitank guns. The first antitank volley obliterated the Israeli halftrack that had the artillery forward observer aboard, and that sort of stopped Carmeli's company cold.

Compounding the surprise and shock that overtook Carmeli's Patton company was the loss of the two Pattons accompanying Lieutenant Yosef Algamis's reconnaissance detachment. They became hopelessly stranded in a narrow side street as they attempted to find a way around the antitank guns.

When Algamis learned that the reconnaissance Pattons were bogged down, he attempted to lead Carmeli's company around them by way of another side street. However, Algamis's halftrack was itself stopped by a machine gun set in a water tower overlooking the street. When Algamis tried to duel the Palestinian machine gun, he was mortally wounded by a bullet in the head.

Carmeli's Patton company attempted to sideslip the antitank sector, but without guidance from the reconnaissance detachment the tanks quickly became bogged down again. They were neither able to support the main attack on Khan Yunis nor extricate themselves from the enemy antitank defenses. Several of the Pattons were hit and disabled, and a number of crewmen were killed or wounded. Major Carmeli was so severely wounded in the face that one of his eyes eventually had to be removed.

The plan to sweep the Khan Yunis defenses aside and race toward Rafah was coming unhinged in a plethora of unanticipated pitfalls. Right at the crucial outset, Israel's vaunted intelligence services had failed. There was supposed to be only a second-rate Palestinian battalion holding the entire Khan Yunis area, but nearly a full brigade appeared to be present. Goaded by higher headquarters—even Southern Command was demanding a solution—a thoroughly frustrated Shmulik fell back on years of training and improvised a workable solution to the 7th Armored Brigade's manifold problems.

The forces Shmulik had available were the three Patton companies of Tank Battalion 77, two Centurion companies and the headquarters of Tank Battalion 82, and two more Tank Battalion 82 Centurion companies comprising the brigade reserve under Lieutenant Colonel Pinko Harel, the deputy brigade commander. One Patton company, Carmeli's, was engaged to the hilt on the east side of Beni Souhila, and at least half of its Pattons had been damaged by antitank fire. The other two Patton companies were to the north or northeast, more or less intact but still making slow progress through the cluttered terrain. So were all the Centurions, which were farther back.

Shmulik ordered the two Tank Battalion 77 Patton companies to push straight through to the northeast end of Khan Yunis and form up on the right side of the Gaza-Rafah highway, which ran through the middle of the town. He next ordered the commander of Tank Battalion 82, Lieutenant Colonel Gavriel "Gabi" Amir, to move with the two Centurion companies under his direct command to the left side of the highway. Then the main bodies of both tank battalions were to attack side-by-side through Khan Yunis.

As ordered, but only after a considerable additional period of pushing through narrow places, the main body of Major Ehud Elad's Tank Battalion 77—with the 7th Armored Brigade command group in tow—penetrated nearly to the coast and turned left into the northeastern outskirts of Khan Yunis. Shortly, the main body of Gabi Amir's Tank Battalion 82 drew up on Elad's left flank. And then both tank battalions lurched forward into the town. Though Khan Yunis was held in considerable strength by Palestinian National Guardsmen, the twin Israeli battle columns apparently unnerved the majority of the defenders, and the streets were soon filled with uniformed but unarmed Palestinians fleeing in all directions. Barely a shot was fired at the Israeli tank columns even though the Tank Battalion 82 Centurions quickly became bogged down in narrow, twisting side streets. Presently, windowsills as far as the eye could see were draped with white headdresses, bedsheets, and towels.

As the Tank Battalion 77 Pattons finally broke free and left Khan Yunis at about 1000, elements of a seventy-two-gun Egyptian 122mm howitzer brigade emplaced near Rafah opened fire at them. Shmulik complained to Talik, who agreed to blot out the Egyptian guns with the *ugdah*'s SP artillery and to call a Fouga strike—all of which was laid on in short order. On the far side of the town, the Pattons were joined by the armored-infantry company from Armored-Infantry Battalion 75. Quickly, this force passed from the scene in the direction of Rafah, pulling the brigade command group and the main body of the brigade reconnaissance company in its wake. However, the main body of Tank Battalion 82 lagged behind in Khan Yunis in order to intimidate the populace.

The Palestinian National Guardsmen in Beni Souhila who had stood up so well in the face of a frontal attack by Major Carmeli's reinforced Patton company ran for their lives when the Khan Yunis defenses began to crumble. After they did, and Beni Souhila had been mopped up, the remnants of Carmeli's company raced down the coast highway to catch up with the main body of Tank Battalion 77.

In all, the clever plan to "sweep through" Khan Yunis cost the 7th Armored Brigade seven tanks and a handful of halftracks and jeeps destroyed or disabled. Twelve Israeli soldiers died in the effort, and fifteen were wounded.

22

Ugdah Tal's first objective of the war was the Rafah Junction. This strategically vital crossroads lay just to the south of the sprawling Rafah military camps, a complex whose foundations had been set by the British Army in World War I.

Though the El Arish–based 7th Egyptian Infantry Division had resumed control of the Rafah area only in mid to late May, Israeli intelligence had been able to report on short notice that there appeared to be two main defensive sectors, both set into dunes or rolling terrain immediately to the west of the camps, on the west side of the road junction. Activity in the area seemed to indicate that the defensive sectors—Rafah North, which was north of the Rafah –El Arish highway, and Rafah South, which was south of the highway—were manned by two Egyptian infantry brigades, one Palestinian infantry battalion, at least one Egyptian 122mm howitzer brigade, a 100mm gun battalion, at least a battalion of T-34 medium tanks, a battalion of JS-3 122mm artillery tanks, and numerous SU-100 assault guns. It was unclear exactly how the troops, guns, and tanks were deployed in the two defensive sectors, nor exactly where all the Egyptian and Palestinian emplacements had been constructed.

Following its breaching operation opposite Kibbutz Nahal Oz and its sweep through Khan Yunis, the main body of the 7th Armored Brigade was to reduce the Rafah North position and advance toward El Arish on and north of the Rafah–El Arish highway. To do so, the Israeli brigade would have to defeat the massively reinforced 11th Egyptian Infantry Brigade, whose two infantry, one JS-3, and two artillery battalions were dug in to a depth of several kilometers north and west of the Rafah Junction.

The second act in the 7th Armored Brigade zone of operations began shortly before 1015, when the main body of Major Ehud Elad's Tank Battalion 77 began arriving near the town of Rafah from the direction of Khan Yunis.

Elad's immediate concern was the reduction of Egyptian defenses astride the 7th Armored Brigade's route through the area in the direction of El Arish.

The first opposition Elad's column of Pattons encountered was some extremely spotty rifle fire along the highway through Rafah. This the tankers all but ignored, but Major Elad ordered the commander of the accompanying armored-infantry company to drop out of the column to run the armed Egyptians or Palestinians out of the town. The garrison turned out to be so far out of the picture that the Israelis came upon a number of Egyptian soldiers whose entire attention was devoted to the backgammon games they were playing. At this stage of events, the Israeli troops could not afford to become encumbered with prisoners. They simply scared the Egyptians to their feet and allowed them to run away.

Meantime, the Pattons, followed by the brigade mobile command post, turned north off the main highway and followed a low ridgeline that led away to the west. A short distance along the ridgeline, Elad sent one Patton company ahead under the command of his deputy and stopped the other company where it was. Both companies could overlook the town in the event fire from their guns was needed, or they could continue to the west above the highway and the railway.

After Elad's Pattons stopped along the ridgeline north of the highway, the brigade mobile command post returned to the highway and drove due west until the roadway turned sharply to due south. Just beyond the turn, the command vehicles pulled off to the east side of the road and parked beside a huge water tower. From there, Shmulik wanted to oversee the reorganization of the various elements of his two tank battalions for the planned move against and through the Rafah Junction, which was 4 kilometers south of the water tower.

Through much of the latter stages of the bitter fighting in Beni Souhila, overlooking Khan Yunis, the 7th Armored Brigade reserve squadron of eighteen Centurions under Lieutenant Colonel Pinko Harel, the deputy brigade commander, had been sitting on the open road between Khan Yunis and Rafah, awaiting orders that never came. As it turned out, Pinko was utterly unsuited to his passive role. He vividly imagined that he and his tanks were needed, that the brigade objectives could not be achieved without them. When Pinko heard that Lieutenant Colonel Gabi Amir and the main body of Tank Battalion 82 were hung up in Khan Yunis, he decided to act on his own authority.

Without orders, nor even a map of the area, Pinko simply left his stand-by position and led his two Centurion companies down the main highway to Rafah. He radioed the brigade operations officer to say that he was doing so, but that is as far as he went to make his self-imposed mission official.

Only a little beyond the spot at which Tank Battalion 77 had veered off the main highway, the reserve Centurion squadron arrived before Umm el-Kalb, a tiny highway village in which Egyptian National Guardsmen had set up a tiny roadblock. At Pinko's order, all eighteen Centurions traversed their long 105mm main guns to the right side and, without ever leaving the road, lined up opposite Umm el-Kalb. As soon as the Israeli turret machine guns began firing, the Egyptian Guardsmen in the village fled from the scene. The Centurions rolled on a bit farther, and then Pinko ordered them to disperse in a roadside orchard until he could find out what was going on elsewhere in the brigade zone. In fact, Pinko was lost and without a clue as to where other Israeli units were.

After a few minutes, Pinko was able to raise Shmulik on the brigade command net. Shmulik helped Pinko figure out where he was, and he agreed to send a reconnaissance detachment back to help Pinko's Centurion squadron find its way from Umm el-Kalb. However, Pinko again became impatient to join in the action, so he ordered the two Centurion companies to follow his command halftrack farther along the highway.

Only a short distance farther on, Pinko's squadron ran into another small defended zone—this one centered on the level crossing that carried the main highway at an oblique angle across the railroad tracks. There were concrete tetrahedrons ahead that impinged the roadway to a single lane that was too narrow for the Centurions. Pinko solved the problem by ordering several of the best Centurion gunners to fire their main guns at the tetrahedrons. The obstructions were cleared in a matter of minutes and Pinko led the way west along the highway.

At this point, about 1025, the 7th Armored Brigade was fragmented into seven groups. The main body of Elad's Tank Battalion 77 was deployed in two one-company sections. The first, which was with Elad, was on the low ridgeline to the northeast of the Rafah North defensive zone, north of the railroad tracks and the main highway. The second Patton company, which was with Major "Chaim," the Tank Battalion 77 deputy commander, was west of Elad's position, also on the high ground. Pinko's Centurion squadron was rolling along the main highway, slightly to the east of Elad's position.

Lieutenant Colonel Gabi Amir's half of Tank Battalion 82, which was finally through Khan Yunis, was well to the east but closing rapidly along the main highway. A fifth Israeli unit, the main body of the 7th Armored Brigade reconnaissance company, was ahead of Pinko, slightly to the east of the spot at which the main highway turned south. The sixth brigade element, the armored-infantry company, was in Rafah, scaring the hell out of numerous Egyptian soldiers but not rounding any of them up. And the last element of the brigade, the shattered Patton company formerly commanded by Major Ben-Zion Carmeli, was somewhere behind the main body of Tank Battalion 82.

For the moment Shmulik's small command group was the closest Israeli unit to the objective—the stoutly manned Rafah Junction. However, as soon as Shmulik realized that most of his brigade's tanks and reconnaissance vehicles were on the scene or nearing it, he began rattling off orders aimed at effecting the seizure of the brigade objective.

The first brigade unit Gonen set to moving on the brigade objective was the main body of the reconnaissance company. The halftracks and jeeps, led by two Patton tanks, quickly drove forward and turned left toward the Rafah Junction. The reconnaissance vehicles paused briefly at the water tower while Captain "Ori," the company commander, conferred with Shmulik. A small reconnaissance detachment was sent back to find Pinko, and then, at just about 1030, the reconnaissance company advanced down the highway at full speed.

Minutes later, and only 100 meters north of the Rafah Junction, the reconnaissance vehicles came under intense fire from a well-camouflaged bunker complex none of the Israelis had been able to see until that very moment. The Egyptian positions were set in low to the ground on a little height to the west (right) of the roadway, behind a thick belt of mines.

As soon as the shooting started, an antitank round hit the engineers' halftrack that was accompanying the reconnaissance company. The wreck came to rest at an angle that blocked the roadway. The reconnaissance jeep platoon pulled out of the column and gingerly led the way around the wreck. At that point, heavy Egyptian artillery fire fell all around the Israeli vehicles. As the heavy rounds were striking on the road, two JS-3 artillery tanks emerged from the bunker complex to the west. These were easily disabled by one of the Pattons at a range of 200 meters, but volleys of antitank fire from many other hitherto unseen Egyptian positions to the west of the roadway reached out at the roadbound Israeli vehicles.

There was nowhere for the reconnaissance company to go. The road ahead and behind was covered by long lines of Egyptian bunkers and there were minefields all around, beginning at the edge of the roadway and continuing right up to the firing embrasures of the Egyptian pillboxes. Advancing was as dangerous as falling back; there was no telling how deeply the reconnaissance force was embedded in a perfectly executed ambush. The Israelis could not withdraw to the east side of the roadway, which appeared to be undefended, because running up that ridge would have exposed the vehicles to fire from the rear. To Captain Ori, the *only* way out of the trap seemed to be *through* the Egyptian lines. Besides, wasn't one of his prime tactical tenets, "When in doubt, attack?"

Ori ordered all the vehicles to turn to the right and charge the nearest bunker complex. This the Israelis did, with never a backward glance. The attack up the mine-sown slope was hideously expensive, but the sheer audacity of the Israeli charge shook the Egyptian soldiers manning the nearest trenchline and bunkers from their firing positions. One Patton, two half-tracks, and two jeeps were knocked out on the way up to the Egyptian positions. And, after that sector was quelled in hand-to-hand fighting, the other Patton and several additional jeeps and halftracks touched off mines or were disabled by artillery fire on the way back to the road. By the time the brave little attack was over, the main body of the 7th Armored Brigade reconnaissance company was reduced to a few jeeps, a few halftracks, and about half its original complement of officers and men. Captain Ori led the survivors back up the road to rejoin Shmulik's command group.

Though Ori's reconnaissance company had failed to reach the Rafah Junction, its brief battle had forced the Egyptians in the area to reveal much about the outline, strength, and composition of their Rafah North defensive zone. And that information was all Shmulik needed to plot Rafah North's demise.

The next Israeli combat unit to reach the scene was Pinko's Centurion squadron, which had been joined by the reconnaissance detachment Shmulik had sent back moments earlier. The Centurions were already nearing the water tower at full speed when Pinko first heard the Egyptian guns open fire on Ori's company.

The reconnaissance company's battle had only just begun when Shmulik ordered Pinko to push the entire Centurion squadron across to the west side of the highway and turn south to advance along the low, rolling dunes just to the west of the roadway. The idea was to advance Pinko's force off the zeroed-in highway but without allowing it to become bogged down or lost in the firm but undulating country beyond—or blown to bits in the continuous mine belt between the Egyptian line and the highway.

Pinko snapped out orders to the two Centurion company commanders and jumped back into his command halftrack to follow the tanks. The lead company, commanded by Captain "Aharon," crossed the highway, turned south all of 50 meters, and ran straight into a massed volley from at least five Egyptian antitank guns. The three Centurions at the head of Aharon's company breasted the intense fire, but the fourth tank was set aflame by a direct hit from a dug-in T-34. A halftrack that came forward to rescue the wounded crewmen was also struck by the antitank guns. At least two Israeli tank crewmen died.

At this juncture, as most of Pinko's Centurions bulled their way southward at right angles to and right on top of the Egyptian defensive zone, Shmulik ordered Pinko to return to the brigade command post. There, Shmulik pointed out the details of the Egyptian defenses, which were fully ablaze in opposition to the Centurions. The two agreed that they had reached the critical juncture—perhaps of the war. The 7th Armored Brigade was behind schedule, and now it was faced with a truly formidable obstacle. If it could not breast the Rafah North defenses, it would fail in its bid to win its part of the war. "No matter what the cost," Talik had admonished, but until that moment, Shmulik and Pinko had not realized precisely what their commander had meant.

No matter what the cost. Pinko had to reach the Rafah Junction—no matter what the cost. And the 7th Armored Brigade had to overcome Rafah North—no matter what the cost. Pinko favored an attack straight through, but Shmulik was more realistic. If the 7th Armored Brigade merely breached the Egyptian defenses and then left the scene, someone else would have to fight these same Egyptians later on. No, Shmulik decided, the 7th Armored Brigade would have to *defeat* these Egyptians—defeat them and disperse them, once and for all.

Shmulik rattled off a series of orders. Pinko did not have a map, so Shmulik had to point to each of the intermediate objectives. Then the two tank officers parted. Pinko wanted to rejoin the Centurions and Shmulik wanted to move his halftrack farther south so he could see what was going on.

It was moments before 1100 hours when Pinko left Shmulik. As soon as the deputy commander's halftrack was gone, Shmulik moved, too. He ordered Major Ehud Elad's two Patton companies to attack the northern end of the Rafah North defenses. Moments later, as Colonel Shmulik Gonen glanced over his shoulder at the ridgeline to the north, he saw a single Patton appear momentarily as it crossed the skyline from the rear to the forward slope. Already, there was the flash of gunfire, followed a moment later by the *crack-crack-crack* of the Egyptian tank or antitank guns.

At just 1100, Ehud Elad rattled off his version of Shmulik's orders over his battalion command net, but he received no acknowledgements. It was impossible to know if his deputy, Major Chaim, or the two company commanders had received the order, and there was no time to find out. Elad ordered his driver to break cover and make for the nearest Egyptian position at the northern shoulder of the Rafah North defenses.

No other Patton moved. The tank commanders all assumed that Elad was making a reconnaissance run. As the tank commanders watched, five Egyptian antitank guns fired at Elad's Patton. The best the Egyptian gunners could do was put one round through the bustle rack at the rear of Elad's turret. The shell carried away the crew's belongings and set fire to the camouflage net. Splinters hit Elad in the face and the palm of one hand, but none of the wounds was serious enough to merit attention. More seriously hurt, but not badly enough to seek relief, was the battalion operations officer, who was serving as Elad's gunner.

So far, none of the other Israeli Pattons had moved. Elad yelled for his driver to reverse back over the crest of the coastal ridgeline and for his radioman to break out the spare radio. He tried once again to tell the other Pattons to advance, but he was not heard this time, either. Nevertheless, when Elad once again ordered his driver to advance, the other Patton commanders got the message, and the entire Israeli tank company boiled up out of the ground, making directly for the Egyptian antitank guns.

Three Pattons were hit as the Israeli company neared the Egyptian bunkers, but just then the company led by Major Chaim attacked the antitank locale from the rear. Chaim had found a covered approach from the west, and no one knew he was inside the Egyptian position until the guns of his Pattons thundered and bellowed their announcement. Nine Egyptian T-34s were destroyed from the rear, and, suddenly, fleeing Egyptian soldiers were running every which way. The Israeli tank crews raked the Egyptians with their machine guns, shooting individual Egyptian soldiers who had failed to throw away their weapons. Several more T-34s and a number of antitank guns were blown to bits by the Pattons' main guns, but a score of trucks, APCs, and other soft vehicles were set ablaze by machine-gun bullets after Major Elad cautioned his gunners to conserve their cannon rounds.

In one fell swoop, the northern end of Rafah North was overwhelmed and one wing of the 11th Egyptian Infantry Brigade was defeated. As the shooting died down, Elad led what was left of his two Patton companies west along the hills fronting the coast. Elad's next objective was the Jiradi Pass.

About 3 kilometers due south of Elad's killing zone, Pinko's Centurion squadron was also making progress on firm ground, albeit at a more deliberate pace. The two Centurions companies, which had suffered several losses breaking into the Egyptian defenses, were advancing abreast along the low ridgeline—Captain Aharon's company on the right and Major Shamai Kaplan's company on the left.

For Shamai Kaplan, the battle inside the Rafah North position was an opportunity to make amends for a shoddy performance he—and many other Israeli tank officers—believed he had turned in on November 3, 1964, in the battle against Syrian tanks at Tel Nukheila. Then, before Talik had had an opportunity to impose his will upon the Centurion crews and gunners, Shamai's company had been the one that had fired nearly sixty 105mm rounds at two stationary Syrian tanks without scoring a single hit. Despite Talik's protests at the time, Shamai Kaplan had been made the butt of the lesson. It had taken an enormous effort by Talik himself to rebuild Shamai's confidence. For the past two years, Shamai had been working at the Armor School, where, fittingly, he had been overseeing the Centurion specialization course offered to Armor Corps officer cadets. Shamai knew as much about *Zahal's* Centurions as any man alive, but was his confidence restored? The June 5 attack into Rafah North was the acid test.

Shamai was a godsend to his crews on June 5. Standing extra tall in the turret of his command Centurion, he calmly called out targets, designated gunners, and observed results. If a gunner became rattled, Shamai calmed him down with a word of advice or a compliment. All the way along the Egyptian trenchline, as the Centurions blasted one position or dug-in SU-100 or T-34 after another, Shamai fairly exuded confidence and power and authority. Even after he was wounded painfully in both hands by a near miss, Shamai held his company firmly and confidently in his grip. Talik's hard work to rehabilitate Shamai Kaplan paid off in ways neither could have dreamed. At this critical moment of the war, Shamai was the sparkplug that drove the *Zahal* engine.

As the Centurions ground inexorably forward, driving hundreds of Egyptians before them, Pinko radioed Shmulik and pleaded to be allowed to turn up the Rafah–El Arish highway to storm forward to the brigade's next intermediate objective, the town of Sheikh Zuweid. By then, at least one of *Ugdah* Tal's 105mm SP artillery battalions was butchering the fleeing Egyptians, and Rafah North was obviously a shambles. After a moment of silence, Shmulik came back up on the net: "Deputy, this is [Shmulik]. Move now." But, except for his own command halftrack, Pinko had nothing to move *with*.

Just then, three of Shamai Kaplan's Centurions appeared on the skyline. They turned toward Pinko's waiting halftrack. A fourth Centurion, also one of Shamai's, appeared next, but it was stopped cold and set afire by a direct hit from an antitank gun. Then a fifth Centurion from Shamai's company appeared. The commander, who was standing tall in the turret hatch, was shot dead, and the tank nearly collided with the one that had been set ablaze seconds earlier. The gunner took control in the nick of time, but he had no idea what to do next. None of the tankers did. Even Shamai, whose tank appeared next, was without a clue.

Pinko rolled up in his command halftrack and, over the din of the waning battle, issued a piercing whistle that drew everyone's attention. The 7th Armored Brigade deputy commander simply pointed west, up the Rafah–El Arish highway. Shamai nodded at Pinko and bellowed into his command radio, "Follow me in column. Move out!" Moments later, word arrived by radio that Lieutenant Colonel Gabi Amir's main body of Tank Battalion 82 had caught up and was closing on Shamai's company from the rear.

No one else knew it, but the bulk of Captain Aharon's Centurion company was already ahead of Pinko and Gabi. Through a mix-up in orders and Aharon's own zealous nature, Aharon's company had turned west while it was still inside the Rafah North position, and it had paralleled the highway on its north side, on firm, rolling ground. Farther on, while Pinko was still waiting on Shmulik's approval, Aharon had cut onto the highway itself. In two separated sections, the company was sailing smoothly westward by the time Pinko's and Gabi's Centurions rolled through the Rafah Junction.

So far, neither section of Aharon's company had met opposition. The way to the west appeared to be open.

The defeat of the 11th Egyptian Infantry Brigade in the Rafah North position and the seizure of the Rafah Junction had cost the 7th Armored Brigade twenty-six officers and men killed and twenty officers and men wounded. In any other army, these would have been seen as "light" casualties in return for a stupendous victory. However, even in a battle waged "no matter what the cost," the nation of Israel viewed these losses as a tragedy of the first magnitude.

And there were even heavier casualties to be endured in the 202nd Parachute Brigade's merciless three-hour-old battle to reduce the Rafah South position.

23

Colonel Rafael Eitan, the 38-year-old commander of the 202nd Parachute Brigade, was one of Israel's toughest and most blooded warriors. His paratroopers called him "the greatest fighter of us all," but he had not intended to be a soldier. Short and wiry—the perfect paratrooper's physique—"Raful" was a *sabra* who had served in the War of Independence as a sergeant in the company commanded by Dado Elazar. He had mustered out as a lieutenant after the war and gone back to his farm. In 1953, while serving out his annual month on active duty, Captain Eitan had been asked to replace a Regular paratroop company commander who had lost a foot when he stepped on a mine. Eitan had accepted the assignment on what he insisted was a temporary basis, but he never left the army to return to his farming. In 1955, Raful was severely wounded in the chest during a raid into Syria, but he recovered just in time to lead 394 other paratroopers in the jump into Mitla Pass at the start of the Sinai Campaign. After Sinai, Lieutenant Colonel Eitan attended the *Zahal* Command and Staff College, and then he was sent to the United States for advanced leadership training. He subsequently served on the operations staff at GHQ and was among the first graduates of the National Defense College, after which he assumed command of the 202nd Parachute Brigade. It is said of many brilliant soldiers that this one is a future general and that one is a future chief of staff. In Raful's case both prognostications were commonplace—if he managed to survive his renowned penchant for killing his enemies eye to eye.

When Raful heard the "Red Sheet" broadcast come in over his command radio that first morning of the war, he leaned out the door of his command caravan and simply waved a sheet he had had dyed a bright red.

The 202nd Parachute Brigade's initial war objective was the Rafah Junction. Before the planning was very far advanced, Raful had to give up one of his paratroop battalions to a special task force that was being formed to drop into Sharm el-Sheikh. This he did with reluctance even though a Patton company from the 7th Armored Brigade was attached to his brigade as partial compensation. Later, an ad hoc Patton battalion known as Baron Force was also attached to Raful's command. In early June, Raful's brigade was equipped with halftracks that had been taken from the armored-infantry brigade that was to secure Gaza City. Without anyone really meaning to, then, the 202nd Parachute Brigade was transformed by parts into what appeared to be an armored-infantry brigade. Indeed, it was seen as being an *elite* armored-infantry brigade, for the main body of Baron Force was the Armor School Tank Battalion, a professional fighting unit composed of the Armor School staff and such of their students as were needed to round out crews for the Patton tanks. Also serving as part of Baron Force was a company of AMX-13 light tanks, also crewed by tank-reconnaissance instructors and some of their students. The commander of the tanks was Colonel Uri Baron, the commandant of the Armor School.

The Rafah operation was planned by Lieutenant Colonel Kalman Magen, the *Ugdah* Tal operations officer and, in peacetime, the Armor Corps operations officer. Magen had many initial objectives to consider in his initial divisional area of operations, and many unknowns to ponder. His combat force was the largest *Zahal* had been able to assemble for the war, and two of his brigades were composed of full-time soldiers.

Since it was necessary for *Ugdah* Tal to open a route into the central Gaza Strip so Gaza City could be attacked from the unexpected southwesterly direction, Magen had to devote one brigade to sweeping Khan Yunis. Only then could that brigade participate in helping to seize Rafah Junction. Magen and Talik naturally chose the 7th Armored Brigade because it was entirely mobile—it could clear Khan Yunis by main force and then *quickly* make an appearance near Rafah. The armored-warfare experts also decided to hold *Ugdah* Tal's second armored brigade, commanded by Colonel Men Aviram, near Keren Shalom. There, in textbook compliance with Israeli armored doctrine, it would be in position to exploit a breach and range far into the enemy's rear—or, if it came down to that kind of a contest, to assist in the breaching operation itself. That more or less left the initial assault on Rafah Junction to 202nd Parachute Brigade.

To hold the Rafah garrison in place, and to cover the 7th Armored Brigade's approach and assault from the direction of Khan Yunis, Raful's

transformed 202nd Parachute Brigade was to launch a *limited* assault westward out of Keren Shalom and then north in the direction of Rafah Junction
along the disused Rafah-Nitzana road. If it could, the brigade was encouraged
to secure Rafah Junction from the south after reducing the Rafah South
defenses, but it need not cross the Rafah–El Arish highway, because the 7th
Armored Brigade was expected to seize that axis well before noon. Indeed,
Raful's main objective was preventing the reinforced 16th Egyptian Mechanized Brigade, holding Rafah South, from going to the aid of Rafah North
when the 7th Armored Brigade arrived on the scene and overwhelmed the
11th Egyptian Infantry Brigade. Raful's role would be diversionary at the
outset, and then his brigade was to mop up in the wake of the 7th Armored
Brigade.

Raful's force of paratroopers and tanks moved out of covered positions behind
Keren Shalom at 0855 and crossed the frontier in a due westerly direction at
a point about 6 kilometers south of the kibbutz. As the vanguard tank company turned north to probe toward the Rafah-Nitzana road, the Baron Force
AMX-13 company and the 202nd Brigade jeep-reconnaissance company
surged up the line and turned south to establish blocking positions and a
screening line across Raful's southern flank.

Raful's first concern was reaching the old, disused Rafah-Nitzana road.
There, the lead Patton company was to turn north and advance along the rear
of the Rafah South defensive zone. One of the halftrack-mounted paratroop
battalions was to follow the Patton company and help clear the zone.

There is much to be said for selecting aggressive leaders and training
them to fend for themselves, but there are limits that must be imposed by
means of rigorous training if too much of a good thing is not to get in the
way of achieving objectives. The company of Tank Battalion 77 and the
Armor School Battalion were superb tank formations, ably led by the best
company-grade officers in the Armor Corps. And there were no units in
Zahal as aggressive as the paratroop battalions serving under Raful. On paper,
the transformed 202nd Parachute Brigade looked perfect. But it was not.
Though the tankers and the paratroopers had been training together for over
a week, the halftracks had arrived only a few days earlier, and the paratroopers
had not had an opportunity to learn much about armored-infantry tactics or
trade secrets from the drivers or the tankers. It was no accident that Israeli
armored infantrymen were members of the Armor Corps, for the principles
by which they fought had to be the principles by which the tankers fought.

History had made that much clear. The paratroopers rolling out of Israel to envelop Rafah South did not appreciate the role of armored infantrymen, and the tankers did not realize that paratroopers mounted in halftracks were not, ipso facto, armored infantrymen.

Captain Amnon Giladi's Patton company of Tank Battalion 77 got ahead of the paratroop battalion with which it was supposed to be traveling, and then it ran into an Egyptian antitank complex that was much farther south than any Egyptian defenses were known to be. At 0910, Egyptian JS-3s dug into the dunes to the southwest opened fire, and one of the first 122mm rounds burst inside the turret of Captain Giladi's tank. The company commander was killed and his Patton was set on fire. The rest of Giladi's company, which was strung out in single file behind the dunes, simply stopped where it was. It apparently had lost heart at the first volley.

When Giladi's company failed to move forward, Colonel Uri Baron, the Armor School Battalion commander, ordered his nearest company to lead the paratroop battalion forward. Baron told the commander of this Patton company, Lieutenant "Ein-Gil," to probe around the Egyptian main line of defense, but, rather than gingerly feeling out the defenses, Ein-Gil barreled straight into them. And then he cut right through them. He thus lost sight of the paratrooper-laden halftracks because of intervening sand dunes, and the paratroopers lost sight of the Pattons.

Once into the dunes north of the JS-3s, Ein-Gil deployed one of his platoons in firing positions overlooking Giladi's stalled, strung-out company. Then, with his six remaining tanks, he penetrated farther into the dunes to try to outflank the JS-3s from the north and west. The dunes ran in the wrong direction, however, and Ein-Gil's Pattons had to expose themselves to the JS-3s in order to fire at all. At this juncture, mysteriously, Ein-Gil received orders via radio to break contact with the JS-3s and advance to the west. The order was meant to get the deputy commander of *Giladi's* stalled company moving again toward the Rafah-Nitzana road, but Lieutenant Ein-Gil was certain it was meant for him. He disengaged from the JS-3s and ended up striking deep into the enemy's rear with his entire company.

Ein-Gil's departure temporarily confused his countrymen, but the confusion it caused the Egyptians was more or less permanent, for in the ensuing hours Ein-Gil's company cut a swath of destruction through outlying Egyptian defensive posts many kilometers in the Egyptian rear. Operating alone and out of touch with higher authority, Lieutenant Ein-Gil and his nine

Pattons roved the area south of the Rafah–El Arish highway and far to the west of Rafah Junction. The Pattons shot up whatever Egyptian positions or vehicles they could find and generally deepened the Egyptian sector commander's considerable angst. It was a textbook response to Adherence to Mission—Ein-Gil's last order was to run to the west—and to a lack of orders from above: "When in doubt, find someone to attack."

As soon as Ein-Gil's company left the battalion communications net, Colonel Baron ordered a thirteen-tank Patton company commanded by Captain "Amos" to lead the second paratroop battalion around to the south of the pocket of Egyptian JS-3s. This Amos did with alacrity and skill, and the paratroop column kept up without a hint of trouble.

Once across the Rafah-Nitzana road, Amos turned northeast and headed directly toward the town of Kafr Shan, a way station on the Rafah–El Arish highway. Once there, Amos and the paratroop battalion were to turn east and attack the Rafah Junction from the rear. But it would take hours for the long column of tanks and slow-moving halftracks to traverse the kilometers of unstable dunes and stretches of broken hardpan separating them from their objective.

After Ein-Gil's departure from the scene and Amos's run around the JS-3 strongpoint, Raful was still faced with advancing his lead paratroop battalion to the Rafah-Nitzana roadway and advancing north up the long axis of the Rafah South defensive zone. He asked Colonel Baron to make yet another tank company available to accompany the paratroop battalion. The only one Baron had left was the nine-tank Patton company commanded by Captain "Danny."

While the Giladi Patton company crawled forward and blotted out the fire from the JS-3 strongpoint to the southwest, Danny's tanks left their covered position and turned sharply northward, right onto the trace of crumbling asphalt that had been the Rafah-Nitzana road. The halftracks bearing the paratroopers surged to keep up with the Pattons.

The Pattons had run only a short distance along the roadway when they found themselves intermingled with what seemed to be hundreds of Egyptian soldiers, wheeled and tracked vehicles of every description, and many towed antitank guns. Apparently, Danny's company had run smack into an Egyptian motorized infantry battalion that either had just arrived on the scene or was in the process of changing positions. The Israeli tanks opened fire at whatever they could reach and then spread out to find more targets—especially any antitank guns that had gotten away. In short order, the main body of the tank company lost sight of the roadway—and the paratroop battalion—and there was no finding either one again. Danny decided to head north and maybe seize Rafah Junction on his own.

Danny was sure the paratroopers would follow his tanks if they could. But they could not. The halftracks could not advance up the road, which was blanketed by Egyptian antitank guns, nor make it through the loose sand as surely as the Pattons could. Momentarily, the Egyptians, who had been on the run, were able to knit together a defense that eventually stopped and finally surrounded the Israeli halftracks.

Danny's nine Pattons and a small reconnaissance detachment of paratroopers were temporarily adrift in a sea of sand, but Danny was sure that he was heading north, so he stayed on course—another perfect example of Adherence to Mission. Everything else was going wrong, but Captain Danny was pushing forward in the proper direction.

Shortly after reaching level ground—he knew not where—Danny saw two T-34s and an SU-100 at a range of about a kilometer. A moment later, he saw movement that resolved itself into a pair of antitank guns traversing in his direction.

Danny laid his Patton's gun from the tank commander's cupola, and the gunner fired and traversed on the second antitank gun. Both antitank guns were hit and many of the crewmen seemed to be down. By then, the bulk of the Patton company was drawing abreast Danny's command tank, firing as it came at the enemy armor. The enemy force was growing—APCs were appearing atop the dunes, and there seemed to be more SU-100s. The Israeli gunners were picking them off at ranges of 800 to 1,000 meters—superb shooting by trained professionals.

Two of the Israeli tank platoons surged ahead. Danny tried to keep up, but his Patton's engine quit. As the driver tried to restart the balky engine, the paratroop reconnaissance commander radioed from his halftrack that Egyptian JS-3s were closing in from the rear. When Danny turned to look, he saw two burning Pattons. A third Patton lay motionless and still. Danny yelled at his driver to restart the engine, but it took long moments to do so. Meantime, Danny ordered the platoons that had charged ahead to reverse direction and head for cover in the dunes. When his Patton's engine started, he did the same.

Danny's six remaining Pattons regrouped in a tiny valley between the dunes, and then crept out of the valley to snipe at Egyptian tanks and antitank guns in other isolated little sand valleys. Four of the Pattons covering the rear of the position ambushed five of the ponderous JS-3s as the heavies waddled through the undulating terrain, but there were plenty more JS-3s coming on, and several of them found firing positions that dominated the Israeli laager. Then Egyptian heavy-mortar shells began to fall on the Israelis.

In the midst of the Egyptian attack, one of Danny's Pattons was disabled by a glancing hit on the turret that damaged the gun's traverse and elevation mechanisms. On the other hand, four survivors from the three tanks that had been knocked out earlier arrived in the company laager with their personal weapons, one of the damaged tanks (its turret was blown), and five dead crewmen.

The duel intensified—and the prospects of survival for Danny's company waned. Following a long radio blackout, Danny was finally able to reach Colonel Uri Baron on the battalion command net. By then, Baron was in his command tank, heading north to join Captain Amos's company and the paratroop battalion Amos was escorting over the trackless route to Kafr Shan. He told Danny that as soon as Kafr Shan was safely in the hands of the paratroopers, he would join up with Amos's Patton company and move east to relieve Danny's company. At Baron's order, Danny's tankers launched several colored smoke grenades, which allowed the Armor School Battalion commander to locate the besieged company. Danny's position was just short of the Rafah–El Arish highway, just to the west of the Rafah Junction.

Colonel Baron fully intended to rush to the aid of Danny's company, but he couldn't do a thing until he caught up with Amos and the paratroopers and helped secure Kafr Shan. Thus stranded, Danny was forced to fight a standoff battle against a vastly superior and seemingly inexhaustible Egyptian armor force. What Danny's company lacked in numbers its gunners made up for in accuracy, but even their rather large supplies of ammunition (sixty-four rounds per Patton versus twenty-eight per JS-3) were far from infinite.

Amos's Armor School Patton company and the halftrack-mounted paratroop battalion it was escorting crawled across the dunes west and northwest of the Rafah-Nitzana road. On the way, one of Amos's thirteen Pattons was disabled when it ran over a mine, and then Amos's own command tank was disabled by a hydraulic leak.

At about 1130 and just a kilometer short of Kafr Shan, the tanks ran smack into a defensive position held by an estimated two Egyptian infantry companies and bolstered by many antitank guns. But the surprise of the Israeli force's laborious, hours-long end run paid off; the Egyptians were all facing east and northeast, away toward the Rafah–El Arish highway.

The Israeli tank company never faltered; Amos led his Pattons straight into the Egyptian position, all guns blazing. The defenders were routed, the antitank guns were disabled, and then the tanks arrowed straight toward Kafr Shan with the paratroop battalion in tow.

A few minutes after noon, as soon as the tanks and paratroop-filled halftracks entered the twisting alleys of Kafr Shan, the 213th Egyptian Tank Battalion, an independent divisional unit consisting of seventeen T-34s, entered the town from the opposite side, bent upon cutting off the intruders before they could cut across the vital Rafah–El Arish highway. The 213th Egyptian Tank Battalion was the 7th Egyptian Infantry Division's "sword" force, which in Soviet doctrine was a mobile tank force that was to cut off an attacking enemy force from its supports and annihilate it with the aid of artillery and such other weapons and units as became available. In this case, the Egyptian sword was unleashed too early, for Amos's lone Patton company was hardly the worst threat facing the embattled 7th Egyptian Infantry Division.

As soon as the Egyptian tanks appeared, the gunner of Captain Amos's Patton fired at the lead T-34, which erupted in flames. At the same instant, another T-34 fired an 85mm round into a halftrack full of paratroopers. Among the dead was Captain Giora Eitan, Raful's nephew. Amos, whose tank was right next to the stricken halftrack, spotted the second T-34. His tank and the T-34 fired at one another at the same instant. Both tanks scored direct hits, and both were set aflame. Amos and his crewmen all leaped out of their burning Patton, but the T-34 crew did not. Amos's clothing was on fire, but he rolled around in the dirt and doused the flames. Then he climbed aboard another Patton and resumed the battle.

At that moment, Colonel Uri Baron was approaching Kafr Shan over the route Amos and the paratroopers had followed. He was aboard his command Patton and had two or three other Pattons with him. It was not much of a reinforcement, but every gun would count in overcoming the aggressive T-34 battalion.

Suddenly, a column of battle-damaged Israeli Centurions appeared from the direction of the Rafah Junction. This was the remnant of Captain Shamai Kaplan's company of Tank Battalion 82, under the command of Lieutenant

Colonel Pinko Harel. Pinko's 7th Armored Brigade Centurions skirted the northern edge of the battle around Kafr Shan, but they had no impact on it. Pinko had his mission to perform and the Egyptian T-34 battalion had its; neither tank force paid any attention to the other, and the T-34s continued to hold off the Armor School Battalion command group, Captain Amos's Patton company, and the halftrack-mounted paratroop battalion (which stayed well clear of the tank duel).

Fleetingly, the pincers formed by the attacks of the 7th Armored and 202nd Parachute brigades closed at Kafr Shan. Momentarily, the 7th Egyptian Infantry Division's access to Rafah and the Gaza Strip was severed and blocked. But, then, Pinko went his way, and the pincers opened again in a new direction.

The 213th Egyptian Tank Battalion T-34 crews were stubborn, resourceful foes. Uri Baron was eager to help Danny's beleaguered company, but the fight to secure Kafr Shan could not be abandoned—not even to save Danny and his men.

The halftrack-mounted paratroop battalion that Giladi's, Ein-Gil's, and Danny's Patton companies were all, in their turns, supposed to have escorted northward up the Rafah-Nitzana road had not been able to follow any of the Patton units. In the end, the sudden onset of Danny's moving battle in the dunes had turned the paratroop-laden halftracks off the road into the dunes and, like Danny, they were unable to find the roadway again.

The rolling ground north of the Rafah–El Arish highway was firm enough to support tanks and halftracks, but the dunes south of the highway were sandy and loose. The paratrooper-laden halftracks were unable to make much progress. As a result, after Danny's tanks had passed from the scene, the Israeli paratroopers were left to face the bulk of the reinforced 16th Egyptian Mechanized Brigade on their own. The Egyptian brigade commander had fled in fear before Danny's tanks, but his operations officer, an extremely brave and resourceful major, was able to rally many of his soldiers. These Egyptians succeeded in cutting off and virtually surrounding nearly the entire paratroop battalion.

Many Egyptian antitank guns were turned to face the struggling troop-laden halftracks. One after another, the halftracks were reduced to shattered hulks. Slowly, however, paratroopers on foot engulfed the hastily established Egyptian gun emplacements, one after another. Progress was extremely slow, but the brave, stubborn Egyptians were driven inexorably from their defensive emplacements. Finally, at 1135, the paratroop battalion commander radioed Raful that the Egyptians had been overcome.

Raful radioed Talik at 1136 that the 202nd Parachute Brigade was about to begin its final advance on the Rafah Junction. By then, Talik knew that the 7th Armored Brigade had reached the Rafah Junction. At 1157, Talik released the Aviram Armored Brigade from its holding position west of Kibbutz Keren Shalom and ordered it to proceed by an off-road route to secure the vital Jiradi Pass from the "impassable" inland flank. At 1207, Talik's headquarters contacted Southern Command and informed Brigadier General Shaike Gavish that "two enemy brigades in [*Ugdah* Tal's] operational area are about to be finished off."

At 1210, only three minutes after Talik's command post gave Southern Command the good news, a radio message from Colonel Uri Baron, the Armor School Tank Battalion commander, set the division commander's spirits back. There was, Baron revealed, a battle raging around Kafr Shan; it appeared that a mixed paratroop-tank force had met its match beyond the range of assistance. Talik got in immediate contact with Colonel Shmulik Gonen and ordered him to send 7th Armored Brigade tanks to help take Kafr Shan. Shmulik diverted the main body of Major Ehud Elad's Tank Battalion 77 from its overland dash toward Sheikh Zuweid, but, minutes later, Elad's Pattons were again directed toward Sheikh Zuweid when Uri Baron informed Talik that the Egyptian T-34s appeared to be pulling out of Kafr Shan.

As soon as the shifting scene west of the Rafah Junction crystallized, Talik released the main body of the 7th Armored Brigade's Armored-Infantry Battalion 75 from his division reserve and ordered it into Rafah to clear the town and take into custody as many Egyptian and Palestinian soldiers as it could. When the armored-infantry battalion pulled out of its bivouac near Keren Shalom a few minutes later, it was accompanied by the bulk of *Ugdah* Tal's engineering force, which was charged with clearing mines and repairing the highway all the way from Khan Yunis to the Rafah Junction. As soon as the engineers had their situation in hand, *Ugdah* Tal could begin pushing supplies and fuel forward to the advancing combat units.

A great deal of progress was made in the Rafah South sector, but at 1251 Raful informed Talik that the resistance there had suddenly stiffened and coalesced. When Talik heard the sound of an Uzi submachine gun being fired beside the open mike of Raful's radio handset—Raful himself was doing the firing as he spoke—the division commander needed no convincing that

Raful's previous control of the battlefield had been undermined. As it turned out, a large part of the 16th Egyptian Mechanized Brigade had eluded capture and, under the sterling leadership of its operations officer, had once again managed to cobble together a viable defense. In fact, as Talik listened, Egyptian infantrymen counterattacked the Israeli paratroopers in the dunes.

Talik decided to concentrate all available forces at the Rafah Junction and press the feisty 16th Egyptian Mechanized Brigade out of Rafah South simultaneously from north, south, and west. He ordered Shmulik to dispatch Tank Battalion 77 from Sheikh Zuweid, and Armored-Infantry Battalion 75 was ordered west from Rafah. Lastly, Talik ordered Colonel Men Aviram to send his armored-infantry battalion to the Rafah Junction.

At 1340, long before the many-faceted attack on the Rafah Junction was able to crystallize, Colonel Uri Baron informed Lieutenant Colonel Kalman Magen, the *Ugdah* Tal operations officer, that all the Armor School Pattons that had survived the fighting around Kafr Shan were finally on the road toward the Rafah Junction to assist Captain Danny's company. Captain Amos's company rushed ahead of the Armor School Battalion command group and, guided by Danny, struck at the rear of a force of JS-3s that Danny had been unable to engage on his own. Then Amos joined up with Danny's company, saw to the wounded, and streamed off with Danny's five operable Pattons to help the parachute battalion that was struggling to clear Rafah South.

The final attack on the Rafah Junction opened at 1436. The Aviram Armored Brigade's armored-infantry battalion had been unable to return from the west, but Raful had at his disposal one parachute battalion and about two dozen Patton tanks.

At Raful's order, following a heavy close-air-support mission provided by IAF Fouga-Magisters, fifteen Armor School Pattons under Colonel Uri Baron (the battalion command group plus Amos's and Danny's companies) led the halftrack-mounted paratroopers out of the dunes west and south of the junction. The Israeli force swept through the last defended sector of the Rafah South defensive zone, and then repeated the maneuver from east and north. The second armored sweep, which was also supported by low-flying Fougas, broke the back of the defenses. At 1445, Major Ehud Elad's Tank Battalion 77 was once again returned to the control of the 7th Armored Brigade without being employed by Raful. However, over three additional hours passed before Raful was satisfied that his carefully probing tanks and paratroopers had utterly quelled the opposition and rounded up the last significant batches of prisoners. Among the hundreds of Egyptians taken prisoner was the 16th Egyptian Mechanized Brigade's operations officer, the brave, resourceful major who had masterminded the time-consuming, schedule-destroying defensive struggle.

The perilous break-in battle for the Rafah Junction was the most significant action of the Six-Day War. Had either the 7th Armored or 202nd Parachute brigades been deterred, history would have been altered. Sinai might not have fallen and Israel would never have gone to war against Jordan or Syria.

24

For the leading elements of the 7th Armored Brigade, the third act of the first day of Israel's third war began with the approach of Captain Aharon's seven-tank Centurion company on the roadside town of Sheikh Zuweid. Aharon's position in the lead of the entire 7th Armored Brigade was a direct outgrowth of *Zahal*'s principle of Adherence to Mission. Aharon had lost touch with higher authority during the hard fight down the length of the Rafah North position, but, like all Israeli sub-unit commanders, he had been fully briefed on his brigade's intermediate and long-range objectives. So, without a clue that he was in the lead, and in the absence of fresher orders, he simply turned his Centurions toward Sheikh Zuweid because he knew that in the town was the 7th Egyptian Infantry Division's forward supply depot. In fact, Aharon's company turned west in two separate elements, for four of the Centurions led by the deputy company commander had become separated from Aharon's three tanks. The deputy also knew that Sheikh Zuweid was the next brigade objective. After reporting to Aharon on the company tactical net, the lieutenant also turned west in the hope of meeting up with other friendly units.

After running beyond the Rafah North zone, Aharon's two company elements cut left separately to the main highway and sped toward Sheikh Zuweid. The deputy's four Centurions arrived first—only a few minutes after noon—and quickly bested a covey of heavy machine guns that caused some damage to the tanks and wounded one of the tank commanders. These Centurions also flushed a pair of T-34s and destroyed them with gunfire. They narrowly avoided opening fire on Aharon when he arrived with his company's three remaining tanks.

No sooner had the two elements of the company joined than an Egyptian truck convoy entered the town from the west. To save ammunition, the tank commanders opened fire on the trucks with their machine guns, which were set to fire single shots. An Egyptian fuel tanker was set ablaze, and then two trucks filled with ammunition were blown up by .50-caliber tracer rounds. Any Egyptian soldiers who had remained in the town hid out.

A short time after Aharon's tanks ambushed the Egyptian supply convoy, the main body of Tank Battalion 82 deployed to attack the town under the direction of the 7th Armored Brigade deputy commander, Lieutenant Colonel Pinko Harel. However, on the final approach, the Centurion commanders witnessed a scene of utter chaos. Fleeing Egyptians filled the rolling landscape, and many approached the startled tank crews with their hands raised. At the last minute, in the only display of resistance, a company of ten T-34s counterattacked in the direction of the Centurion battalion's main body. All of the Egyptian tanks were destroyed.

Shortly, as the tankers shepherded scores of shocked and embarrassingly meek Egyptian soldiers toward the town square, the main body of Tank Battalion 77 and the brigade command group arrived. Shmulik called a commanders' meeting, heard casualty reports, and went over the brigade's options. So far, including one man killed at Sheikh Zuweid, the 7th Armored Brigade had lost thirty-nine soldiers killed. The figure for wounded was put at thirty-six, but that did not include the wounded men who were still manning the tanks, of which there were many.

At 1332, as the senior officers were planning the brigade assault on the next objective, Jiradi Pass, Talik radioed Shmulik with an update on Raful's ongoing fight at the Rafah Junction. When ordered to contribute one of his battalions to assist Raful, Shmulik selected Major Ehud Elad's Tank Battalion 77 and elected to accompany it because the 7th Armored Brigade's Armored-Infantry Battalion 75 was also slated to be fully engaged around Rafah. Shmulik placed Pinko in command of Tank Battalion 82 and the severely reduced brigade reconnaissance company. Pinko was to leave one complete Centurion company to guard the highway through Sheikh Zuweid and probe ahead toward Jiradi Pass with the remaining Centurions and the reconnaissance company.

Jiradi Pass was *not* an objective of the 7th Armored Brigade. The brigade was to secure only the highway leading to the pass, but the pass itself was slated to fall to an enveloping attack conducted by Colonel Men Aviram's entire armored brigade, which, as far as Shmulik knew, was proceeding at that moment to jump-off positions via a trackless route through the shifting dunes south of the Rafah–El Arish highway.

Unbeknown to Shmulik, the main body of the Aviram Armored Brigade had been redirected by Talik to seize the El Arish airfield by way of its inland route. As far as Shmulik still knew, the airfield was to be seized in a night parachute jump by the 55th Reserve Parachute Brigade, and the entire Aviram Armored Brigade was still assigned to attack Jiradi Pass from the south. However, the IAF's quick seizure of air supremacy over Sinai allowed for a deep penetration by the Aviram Armored Brigade without fear of aerial interdiction. So, following Jordan's entry into the war before noon, the 55th Parachute Brigade was reassigned to the Jerusalem sector and the main body of the Aviram Armored Brigade was ordered to lengthen its end run and seize El Arish airfield. Shmulik was inadvertently excluded from the decision loop, so this is one time when *Zahal*'s flexibility of command threatened to undo a major combat unit's hard-won operational advantages.

In his parting comments to Pinko, Shmulik enjoined his deputy to go easy—to advance only if resistance was light. He also promised to rejoin Pinko as soon as possible at the *east* end of the pass. By that time, he expected to have with him Elad's Pattons and the brigade's fuel tankers and ammunition trucks.

Moments after Shmulik left Sheikh Zuweid with Elad's battalion, as Pinko was preparing to advance west with his force, there appeared to the south of the town an intact company of Patton tanks with Israeli markings. There was no raising the Pattons on the radio, so no one could imagine whose tanks they were until they stopped in the town itself. Pinko made his way to the commander's tank and found that this was Lieutenant Ein-Gil's long-lost company of the Armor School Battalion. Ein-Gil had been out of contact with other Israeli units for most of the day, but he had nevertheless led his company westward more or less parallel to the Rafah–El Arish highway, shooting up whatever Egyptian vehicles and installations his tanks happened to encounter. Ein-Gil had no idea what was going on elsewhere in the *Ugdah* Tal zone; he had simply been following his instincts.

Pinko enthusiastically welcomed Ein-Gil and offered him and his ten Pattons a role with Tank Battalion 82. Ein-Gil, however, was exhausted and a little overwhelmed. Now that he was back among friends and, indeed, confronted once again with the army's command structure, he suddenly felt the need to regain contact with his own battalion's chain of authority. He demurred at Pinko's offer to join the 7th Armored Brigade and explained with uncharacteristic meekness that he had no orders to do so. With that, the fiery Pinko huffily left Ein-Gil's company to guard the town and proceeded on his way with his own force of three Centurion companies, reconnaissance jeeps and halftracks, and two reconnaissance company Pattons, which had been salvaged from the minefield fronting Rafah North.

Pinko's column of seventeen Centurions, two Pattons, and a dozen reconnaissance jeeps and halftracks took Jiradi Pass by storm. The Egyptians manning the pass's static defenses in brigade-plus strength had no idea that there were Israelis so close to their position. Despite the morning's many shocks, the bulk of the Egyptian Army was hearing on the radio that Egyptian units were advancing up Israel's coastal plain toward Tel Aviv, and that the Egyptian Air Force's absence from the skies over Sinai was the result of massive airstrikes against Israeli cities. So, when Major Shamai Kaplan's Centurion company of Tank Battalion 82 appeared on the open road just to the east of the mouth of the narrow pass, the Egyptian defenders simply sat and watched them come on. Nothing could be farther from the minds of the defenders than the possibility that Israeli tanks were advancing 30 kilometers that side of Egypt's frontier with Israel. True to his word to halt if he ran into any but light opposition, Pinko continued his advance against no opposition whatsoever.

The narrow Jiradi defile was 14 kilometers long. Late Israeli intelligence reports had it that the mouth of the pass was held by an Egyptian infantry battalion emplaced in bunkers, bolstered by antitank guns and tanks, and covered by mortars and artillery pieces. This report was incorrect by half. The entire 112th Egyptian Infantry Brigade—two infantry battalions and two Sherman tank battalions—was manning a triple defensive line in conjunction with a complete field-artillery brigade bolstered by a heavy coast-artillery detachment. Despite the massive strength of this force, however, not a shot was fired at Shamai's company as it passed completely through the outer ring of the defenses at the rather sluggish top speed of the Centurions. On his way through, Shamai took note of the strength of the defenses, and he was impressed. The Egyptian Shermans were all dug in, and their French high-velocity 75mm guns could cover the entire roadway as far as the eye could see. There were also numerous towed antitank guns, which were emplaced in stout bunkers. And infantry positions covering the roadway were too numerous to count from the moving command Centurion.

As Shamai's company was streaming between the defensive works, Pinko ordered all weapons to open fire. This was done, and the lassitude of hundreds of watching Egyptian soldiers was turned to shock and fear. Israelis who could see outside the tanks and other vehicles were awed when every Egyptian in sight simply dived away from view. The Israelis steeled themselves for a deadly response, but no Egyptian guns were fired. When nothing happened, Pinko ordered all his guns shut off in order to conserve ammunition. As he passed the silent Egyptian Shermans, Pinko thought of directing his tanks to torch them with their main guns, but he thought better of it. As far as the 7th Armored Brigade deputy commander could tell, the Shermans had been abandoned. If so, then better to leave them intact so they could be taken over and put to use by *Zahal*. Pinko's was a snap decision made rational by *Zahal*'s decades of facing equipment shortages, but it was to have tragic results.

All of Shamai's Centurions, Pinko's command halftrack, and Lieutenant Colonel Gabi Amir's command group made it past the Egyptian outer defenses without incident. So did the leading elements of Captain Ori's reconnaissance company and a second Centurion company. But one of Ori's two Pattons was not so fortunate. A very small number of Egyptian tank gunners finally recovered from their initial shock in time to open fire at it. One of the Egyptian rounds struck the Patton's turret as the tank topped the first hill east of the pass's mouth. The tank reversed, and a second Sherman round meant for it destroyed a reconnaissance jeep and killed both occupants. A reconnaissance halftrack that topped the hill right behind the jeep was also blown up, but its crew of six was able to escape. Next up, six of Captain Aharon's seven Centurions breasted the fire unscathed, but Aharon's tank, which was the very last vehicle in the Israeli column, took a 75mm round straight through its turret. The radioman was killed, the turret was set ablaze, machine-gun ammunition began cooking off, and communications were knocked out. The tank was brought under control with great effort, and in the midst of an intense duel between two other Centurions and nearby Egyptian emplacements, Aharon and his surviving crewmen brought the fire under control, after which the three Centurions raced to catch up with the tail of the receding Israeli column.

Within a half-hour, Pinko's force had advanced without further incident down the entire length of the Jiradi defile—all the way to the outskirts of El Arish. As far as Pinko was concerned, he still had not met serious opposition, and he was thus well within the letter of Shmulik's last directive. When Pinko reported to the division command post by radio at around 1500, Talik and his senior staff officers refused to believe that the 7th Armored Brigade's deputy commander was anywhere near where he said he was.

The next Israelis to reach the mouth of Jiradi Pass were Shmulik and the driver of his radio jeep. This was at about 1630, two hours after the dramatic advance of the 7th Armored Brigade's forward elements through the Egyptian killing zone.

As the solitary Israeli jeep neared the top of the last rise east of the pass, moments before it would have entered the killing zone, a solitary figure stood up. The man ran between streams of machine-gun bullets toward the roadway, waving his arms to attract the attention of the radio jeep's occupants. Without knowing who the man was, Shmulik's jeep driver stood on his brakes just as the vehicle topped the rise, and then he reversed back down the slope, out of danger.

The running man turned out to be Sergeant "Shuval," the leader of the six-man reconnaissance team that had been blown out of its halftrack at the mouth of the pass two hours earlier. Shuval and his troopers had been holed up in the broken ground fronting the pass ever since, doing what little they could to monitor the Egyptians while preserving life and limb. Throughout the wait, the Egyptians had fired mortars at the six Israelis, but they had never come forward to capture or kill them.

Shuval outlined Pinko's advance through the pass and advised Shmulik to wait where he was until tanks arrived to overcome the formidable Egyptian defensive sector. Shmulik radioed Major Ehud Elad to get forward as quickly as possible with the main body of Tank Battalion 77. When Elad replied that he was only 20 or 30 minutes away, Shmulik used the time to brief Talik by radio.

Talik was dumbstruck by Shmulik's update. By then, in the absence of better information, Talik had convinced himself that Pinko and Tank Battalion 82 were indeed west of Jiradi Pass, on the outskirts of El Arish, and thus blocking access to the pass from the 7th Egyptian Infantry Division's rear area. Talik had further assumed that the pass was completely open to the 7th Armored Brigade's rear elements and that *Ugdah* Tal was roughly a half day ahead of schedule. Talik also knew—and Shmulik still did not—that the Aviram Armored Brigade was no longer slated to attack the pass from the trackless inland flank. However, far from thrusting on to secure the El Arish airfield, as they were supposed to be doing, Men's battalions were making extremely slow progress through the wastes, and no one knew when they might arrive in supporting range of Pinko's force. Far from being on top of the situation and ahead of schedule, *Ugdah* Tal suddenly appeared to be in danger of losing control of the situation in its zone of action.

The key was Jiradi Pass. If it could be opened and its garrison overcome or dispersed, then the fall of El Arish would be assured and all the hard, bloody work of the day would be validated. However, Shmulik estimated that so many Egyptians were so firmly entrenched at the mouth of the pass—and beyond, presumably—that it would take a coordinated assault by two Israeli brigades to clear the defile. Talik concurred with his man on the spot and contacted Colonel Men Aviram with new orders. Men's battalion of M-51HV Super Sherman tanks was to advance to bolster Pinko's force near El Arish to help take the airport, if possible. Men himself was to retrace his route to a point south of Jiradi Pass with his armored-infantry and AMX-13 battalions. (Men's armored-infantry battalion was by then nominally on the return route to help clear the Rafah Junction, but it was in fact still making extremely slow progress through the trackless, sandy wastes *west* of Jiradi Pass.) Once in position with his brigade's main body, Men was to drive northward out of the dunes and take the Egyptian defenses from their flank—a flank the Egyptians considered impassable and thus had not defended.

Talik's revised plan sounded reasonable to Men, who had the farthest to travel and the most to do once the main body of his brigade reached the pass, but it did not sound very good to Shmulik. There was still the matter of Pinko's force to consider. Though Men's Super Sherman battalion was advancing slowly toward El Arish, it had no fuel or ammunition to spare for Pinko's force—even assuming the two could link up. Pinko had already explained that he was hampered by a lack of fuel and ammunition, so Shmulik decided to thrust through the pass with Tank Battalion 77 and as many supply vehicles as he could get forward. He also arranged with Talik to release Armored-Infantry Battalion 75 back to 7th Armored Brigade control as soon as possible, and he ordered his rear command post to send a large supply convoy forward with the armored infantrymen.

All the improvisational planning was more than reasonable, but, alas, it was doomed from the start. Talik could indeed release Armored-Infantry Battalion 75, but he could not guaranty the timely passage of Men's battalions through the dunes south of the pass. Men told Talik straight out that he was mired in the sand, unable to advance or retrace his steps with any useful speed, but Talik simply hoped for the best and remained firm in his life-long conviction that Israeli soldiers could perform miracles if they knew the stakes. Besides, it would be several hours, at least, before the 7th Armored Brigade's armored infantrymen and supply convoy could get through to Shmulik's position east of the pass. So, when Elad's Tank Battalion 77—by then only fourteen serviceable Pattons—arrived at Shmulik's position only twenty minutes behind the command jeep, Shmulik decided to force the pass and link up with Pinko right away.

The first Pattons to reach Shmulik's position were Lieutenant Avigdor Kahalani's company. When Shmulik approached Kahalani's tank in search of someone in authority, Kahalani flashed his characteristic smile and motioned with his hands toward Major Elad's tank, which was just to the rear. Then, as Shmulik and Elad conversed, Major Chaim, the battalion deputy commander, drove up with the second reduced Patton company. Word was that Lieutenant Ein-Gil's Armor School Patton company was also on its way forward from Sheikh Zuweid, a welcome and important reinforcement.

Shmulik told Elad everything he knew about the layout and strength of the Egyptian forward defenses, and then he left it to Elad to plan his battalion's advance. Elad divided his meager force into two parts. He would advance with Kahalani's company on the south side of the roadway—nine tanks in all—and Chaim would take the second company ahead on the north side. If Ein-Gil's company arrived in time, it would be used as required.

Without further ado, Kahalani led his company off the road to the left, into soft dunes that immediately obliged his driver to downshift to low gear. As Kahalani's Patton crawled over the top of the rise facing the mouth of the pass, mortar rounds, antitank rounds, assault-gun rounds, and Egyptian Sherman rounds blew up or burrowed into the sand all around it. Moments later, the other two Pattons of Kahalani's lead platoon joined the company commander on the crest—and the incoming fire doubled.

True to his doctrine, Lieutenant Kahalani ordered his driver to stop the lead Patton as soon as it reached a spot from which the entire Egyptian position south of the roadway could be observed. It was Kahalani's job to direct pinpoint fire by each of his gunners, but an Egyptian antitank gunner was quicker. As the Israeli lieutenant swept the Egyptian line with his field glasses, an antitank round scored a direct hit, severed a fuel line, and set the command Patton ablaze. Kahalani was engulfed instantly in towering flames, and he was barely able to climb out of his cupola and drop into the sand.

The rest of the crew also scrambled to safety. Kahalani rolled in the sand to douse the flames that were consuming his clothing, and then he got to his feet and ran back up the hill to signal the rest of his company to stop where it was, before the rear Pattons ran into the wall of gunfire the Egyptians were putting out.

Though burned over much of his body, Kahalani climbed aboard the Patton commanded by his deputy, Lieutenant "Ilan," and attempted to resume control of his unit. Seconds later, however, the smoldering fire in his clothing reignited, and it was all Ilan could do to put it out again. Ilan ordered the company headquarters halftrack forward, saw to Kahalani's safe evacuation, and assumed command of the company.

By then, one of the two Pattons that had followed Kahalani's tank over the crest of the hill was a mass of flames, and two of Major Chaim's Pattons that had unwittingly advanced into a minefield on the right side of the road had been disabled. The crew of one of the latter Pattons stayed inside the tank and sniped at Egyptian antitank guns, but, including Kahalani's tank, three Pattons had been put out of action in a matter of moments. Shortly, the disabled Patton that continued to fire was itself fired on. The tank commander's hand was severed by a direct hit on the turret, and the crew bailed out.

As Lieutenant Ilan was seeing to Avigdor Kahalani's evacuation, Major Ehud Elad ordered the driver of his antenna-studded command tank to drive across the top of the hill on the left side of the road. The Egyptian fire forced the tank to edge farther to the left, away from the road, until Elad finally sensed that he might be nearing the left extremity of the defended zone. He stood straight up in the commander's cupola and swept the front with his binoculars, undoubtedly searching for a way around the massed Egyptian antitank guns. Beside Elad, to his left, the battalion operations officer, who was acting as Elad's gunner, was helping the battalion signals technician load the main gun. The lieutenant heard Elad yell, "Driver, faster," in the intercom, and then he felt the battalion commander fall out of the cupola. When the lieutenant looked down, Ehud Elad's headless corpse was sprawled on the tank's deck.

A beloved commander's sudden death can wreak havoc upon a combat unit in the face of the enemy. The operations officer kept his mouth shut and calmly ordered the driver to reverse the command tank out of the fight. He first told Shmulik of Elad's death, face-to-face, and a short time later whispered the news directly to Major Chaim. By then, Tank Battalion 77 was about used up. Its ten operable Pattons were simply unable to advance against the Jiradi forward defenses. Virtually the last of Tank Battalion 77's will was expended pulling several of the Pattons out of the loose sand in which they had become mired.

As Major Chaim worked to rejigger the surviving Pattons, Lieutenant Ein-Gil arrived with his ten Armor School Pattons. The appearance of a fresh company of virtually unscathed Pattons put the spine back in the survivors of Tank Battalion 77. Shmulik issued a simple command, and, a little after 1700, Ein-Gil led his company and Major Chaim's survivors straight up the road, all guns blazing.

The shock of Ein-Gil's vigorous attack carried the Pattons straight through the Egyptian forward defenses. Only one of the Israeli tanks was disabled. After driving into some dead ground behind the mouth of the pass, Major Chaim radioed Shmulik with an offer to clear the Egyptian defenses from the rear. It was a very sound idea, but Shmulik's concern was with Pinko's "trapped" force of Centurions and reconnaissance vehicles. He reckoned that the Egyptians between his position and Chaim's would cut and run, so he ordered Chaim to proceed to the west at top speed. This Chaim did. A short time later, when Shmulik attempted to follow with the brigade's and Tank Battalion 77's mobile command posts, the roadway was still blocked by numerous Egyptian defensive positions. It was all Shmulik and the other Israelis could do to back down to the east again without losing their lives in the deadly crossfires.

The surviving Pattons of Tank Battalion 77, plus Ein-Gil's complete Armor School Patton company, joined Pinko's force east of El Arish without further incident. There was not enough fuel or ammunition left in any of the tanks to allow Pinko to take any decisive action, but he was able to seal the highway against the advance of Egyptian reinforcements from El Arish to Jiradi Pass. At the least, this would allow Shmulik and Talik to come up with some way of clearing the pass once and for all.

Talik and Shmulik were working hard to do just that. Though every available infantry unit was sorely needed to help clear thousands of armed Egyptians out of the Khan Yunis, Rafah, and the Rafah North and Rafah South defensive zones, it appeared increasingly likely that Talik would have to release Armored-Infantry Battalion 75 from divisional control and send it forward to clear Jiradi Pass. Talik continued to hope that the main body of the Aviram Armored Brigade could attack the pass from the south, but that hope grew fainter with each passing minute. Finally, at 1930, Men radioed Talik with the depressing news that his brigade's AMX-13 and armored-infantry battalions were hopelessly bogged down and without fuel in the sandy wastes west and south of the objective. Men's armored infantrymen made a game attempt to hike to the pass, but before long that effort proved to be futile. The loose sand was too much for laden men on foot. If Jiradi Pass was to be cleared that night, Shmulik would have to do it with Armored-Infantry Battalion 75 alone.

The situation facing Shmulik's troops in front of Jiradi Pass and across the 7th Armored Brigade zone of action points up both the blessing and the curse of *Zahal's* relentlessly aggressive fighting doctrine. The 7th Armored Brigade had twice done the most that was expected of Israeli units in the attack. Pinko had breached the Jiradi forward defenses almost without a shot being fired, and he had proceeded pell-mell to the *divisional* objective. And Shmulik had advanced all the Pattons on the same account. But neither felt they could take the time or trouble to save the next guy the headache and horror of breaching the same defenses again at who-knew-what cost. It is true that Pinko's and then Chaim's arrival on the outskirts of El Arish denied the 7th Egyptian Infantry Division the option of *easily* advancing reinforcements or mounting a counterattack to the east, but the presence of so many Israelis deep behind Egyptian lines exerted undue pressures upon the men running *Ugdah* Tal's entire break-in battle. It forced Talik to discard the prudent plans he and staff had arranged—the Aviram Armored Brigade's attack on El Arish airfield and the systematic clearing operation from Khan Yunis to the Rafah Junction. The sum of events in the 7th Armored Brigade zone actually had the division's overall situation teetering on the edge of a deep abyss; it even threatened to undo Southern Command's entire plan for the prosecution of the war against Egypt. For one thing was clear: No Israeli senior officer could or would stop at anything short of linking up with Pinko's force.

The blessing was that Pinko was at El Arish. The curse was that Talik had to drop everything and send infantrymen who were desperately needed elsewhere to bail him out.

Amidst scenes of incredible chaos—thousands of armed Egyptians and Palestinians were running around loose in *Ugdah* Tal's rear—Lieutenant Colonel "Maxie," the commander of Armored-Infantry Battalion 75, prepared to lead his unit and the 7th Armored Brigade supply train from Rafah directly to Jiradi Pass. Maxie's orders were to drop the supply trucks off at Sheikh Zuweid, pick up the Centurion company that Pinko had left behind to picket the road through the town, and join Shmulik at the head of the pass to undertake a final clearing operation.

The highway west of Rafah was bedlam, and Maxie's battalion and the supply train immediately came unglued in the ebb and flow of lurching traffic and sporadic gun duels. Maxie reported the delays directly to Talik, and Talik dispatched his chief of staff, Colonel Herzl Shafir, to personally clear a path for Maxie's convoy through scores of stalled commandeered civilian vehicles. This project took a great deal of yelling, screaming, and carrying on—and finally the use of a bulldozer to intimidate drivers of two-wheel-drive vehicles who would not otherwise leave the firm roadway. Finally, the terribly confused and separated elements of the 7th Armored Brigade convoy were able to pull off the road and reorganize beside Talik's command post. Once the convoy was back on the road, it was smooth sailing all the way to Sheikh Zuweid and on west to the spot at which Shmulik was waiting. By then, it was midnight and the rear Centurion company of Tank Battalion 82 had engaged the forward Egyptian defenses, taking advantage of the darkness to screen its final approach and gingerly advance.

While IAF Fougas and Ouragans attacked the Egyptian defenses, Armored-Infantry Battalion 75 halftracks advanced straight into the fight beneath the continual glow of Egyptian flares and illumination rounds. After penetrating into the Egyptian defensive zone with the aid of the close air support, the armored infantrymen dismounted and directly engaged the defenders on foot while machine gunners left in the halftracks doused enemy positions with fire from their .50-and .30-caliber machine guns. The essence of the clearing operation was the reduction of each Egyptian bunker, trench, pillbox, or tank, and the death, demoralization, or the capture of each and every Egyptian soldier. In time, under relentless pressure from attacking warplanes and the Israeli armored infantrymen, the 112th Egyptian Infantry Brigade collapsed. Hundreds of Egyptian soldiers who simply lost heart surrendered in droves.

The initial clearing operation consumed four hours that began in tension and ended in elation. In that time, the Egyptian units defending the pass were utterly broken—all their troops were dead, running for their lives into the desert, or trying to find an Israeli soldier to take them prisoner. At 0130, June 6, after calling the brigade supply train forward from Sheikh Zuweid,

Shmulik left Maxie's battalion and the Centurion company to hold the mouth of the pass and mop up outlying defensive positions while he advanced with a small group of headquarters halftracks and jeeps toward El Arish.

Shmulik and the 7th Armored Brigade command group joined with Pinko and Tank Battalions 77 and 82 at about 0200, June 6. Thereafter, as teams of tanks penetrated into the city, a short distance west along the El Arish–Kantara coastal highway, and south along the El Arish–Bir Lahfan road, relays of Centurions and Pattons made their way to the rear to replenish fuel and ammunition supplies and undertake field-expedient repairs. The tank crews ate and slept if they could during their brief respites, and then they returned to the clearing operation.

Talik arrived at the eastern edge of El Arish at 0420, and his command group set up a new temporary field headquarters while a thoroughly exhausted and emotionally drained Shmulik reported. At 0600, Major Chaim led seven of Lieutenant Ein-Gil's Armor School Pattons out to clear the El Arish airfield, and this mission was accomplished by 0730.

At dawn, a pair of Egyptian Air Force Sukhoi Su-7 ground-attack jets that had evaded destruction the previous morning attempted to attack the vulnerable 7th Armored Brigade supply trains. Before the Sukhois could begin their firing runs, however, they were shot out of the sky by a pair of IAF Mirages.

The abortive dawn air attack was the last attempt the Egyptians made to stop the 7th Armored Brigade. Though not by any means in accordance with the brilliant plans advanced by the *Ugdah* Tal commander or his operations staff, El Arish had fallen to the northern Israeli division in roughly the time allotted. In the course of reaching El Arish, *Ugdah* Tal had utterly destroyed the reinforced Egyptian 7th Infantry Division and had even overcome a brigade of the 20th PLA Division. *Ugdah* Tal had lost approximately 100 soldiers killed and about 200 wounded and evacuated. In all, thirty-five of Talik's tank commanders had been killed or wounded in action—an amazingly high percentage of the overall casualties—and thirty-four tanks were destroyed or at least required extensive repairs. Virtually every 7th Armored Brigade or Armor School tank that was not listed as destroyed or disabled was in some way damaged by enemy fire. And dozens—perhaps scores—of tankers, paratroopers, and armored infantrymen who had been wounded (including one tank lieutenant who lost an eye!) did not turn themselves in for treatment for fear of being relieved of their duties and sent to the rear.

Egyptian losses along the 60 kilometers of roadway between Khan Yunis and El Arish were placed by the Israelis at 1,500 killed. No effort was made at the time to even begin to estimate how many thousands of would-be prisoners were wandering untended in *Ugdah* Tal's rear, because there were nowhere near enough Israeli soldiers to take them into custody.

The decisive break-in battle in the northern Sinai had been an unqualified Israeli victory, but the war with Egypt was far from over. Victory would be proclaimed by Israel only when the Egyptian Army was no longer capable of waging an offensive war.

25

As soon as the 7th Armored Brigade had left Khan Yunis in the first hours of the war, a dismounted battalion from the Reshef Armored-Infantry Brigade entered the town to open the main highway north to Gaza City. It was the armored infantrymen's intention to quickly clear a reinforced battalion of the 20th PLA Division out of Khan Ynis and then to advance northeast in brigade strength upon the populous city of Gaza.

The resistance in and around Khan Yunis was stubborn at the outset. The lead battalion of the Reshef Armored-Infantry Brigade quickly became bogged down in running street fights with scores of armed defenders. Many of the fighters were uniformed members of the PLA and even Egyptian soldiers, but a significant proportion appeared to be armed civilians—an ad hoc militia, perhaps. Most threatening was the very large number of RPGs that were in the hands of both the uniformed and irregular fighters, and the very large number of antitank mines that had been sown along the routes to Gaza City from Khan Yunis. Also, a number of Egyptian Sherman tanks and antitank guns up to 100mm had survived the brush with the 7th Armored Brigade, and these were employed to the decided advantage of the defenders. While lithe and speedy, the Reshef Armored-Infantry Brigade's AMX-13 light tanks were no match for the Palestinian and Egyptian firepower if it was accurate, and several of the AMX-13s had their bottoms blown out when they ran over antitank mines. (By nightfall, after a total of eight AMX-13s had been destroyed and many crewmen had been killed or maimed by mines around Khan Yunis and Gaza City, Shaike Gavish ordered the light-tank battalion out of the fight.)

While the lead armored-infantry battalion attempted to break into Khan Yunis, the bulk of the AMX-13 battalion and the remainder of the brigade bypassed the town and advanced by several routes toward Gaza City. The brigade's initial objective was the Ali Muntar ridge, which dominated the

216

east side of the sprawling city. The ridge's fall to the Israelis in 1956 had been decisive.

The Israeli force veered off the highway well short of the city and marched overland to approach the Ali Muntar ridge in such a way as to strike the defenses from the rear. Under ample air and artillery support, the Israeli infantry attack proceeded, and the defenders fled or surrendered in short order, at about 1800. The ridgeline was firmly in Israeli hands by dusk and, thus, Gaza lay at the Israeli brigade's feet.

Khan Yunis was still firmly in the hands of determined Egyptian soldiers and Palestinian soldiers and irregulars. It was obvious by nightfall on June 5 that there had not been sufficient Israeli troops assigned to subdue the entire Gaza Strip. Plans needed to be altered.

After Shaike had heard reports from all his front-line commanders, he decided to commit Colonel Raful Eitan's 202nd Parachute Brigade to the mopping-up operation in Gaza. There was no way the Israelis were going to let hundreds of armed Arabs run riot in the rear of their receding army— and so close to relatively unguarded Israeli border settlements—but Raful's brigade was the only combat unit in proximity that could be spared from missions elsewhere.

Accompanied by a light reconnaissance force, Raful's 202nd Parachute Brigade was to have stormed westward from El Arish to the Suez Canal by way of the coast highway. However, its rough handling in the Rafah South defenses had delayed its departure for the second phase of its mission in Sinai. Its need to stop and reorganize itself around the Rafah Junction on the evening of June 5 made it fair game in Shaike's eyes for use in clearing Khan Yunis, Gaza, and other hotspots in the Gaza Strip.

Raful was disappointed when Shaike told him that his brigade was being detached temporarily from *Ugdah* Tal, but he entered the planning phase with his usual enthusiasm. In the end, one of Raful's paratroop battalions had to be held back at Rafah to mop up the camps and the town, and the bulk of the Armor School Battalion had to be withdrawn to its base in Israel to reorganize and reequip. That left Raful with one parachute battalion and the Patton company that was still on loan from Tank Battalion 77.

At dawn, June 6, Palestinian and Egyptian defensive emplacements throughout Gaza City were struck by IAF Fougas and Ouragans. Then, as Israeli artillery and heavy mortars fired at pinpoint military targets, one dismounted armored-infantry battalion, Raful's halftrack-mounted paratroop battalion, and the Patton company pitched straight into the fight from several directions at once. The only untoward incident of the day was the inadvertent bombing of a building housing United Nations soldiers who were awaiting a flight out of the Middle East. Fourteen UNEF troops were killed and twenty-five were wounded.

A large part of Gaza was in Israeli hands by 1700, and at that point Lieutenant General Mohammed Abdel Moneim Husseini, the Egyptian military governor of the Gaza Strip, succumbed to pleas by the Israelis that he surrender immediately in order to avoid heavy civilian casualties. Husseini ordered an immediate ceasefire throughout the Gaza Strip and agreed to sign a formal surrender document the following morning.

The Egyptian and Palestinian troops in Gaza City did indeed lay down their arms after General Husseini signed the official surrender document at 1020 on June 7, and Husseini even rode through the city in an Israeli weapons carrier to show the populace that he had indeed surrendered. Nevertheless, the garrison in Khan Yunis continued its defiant resistance.

Raful's lead paratroop battalion was dispatched to Khan Yunis on the afternoon of June 6, after General Husseini agreed to surrender, but a late-afternoon attack failed to budge the defenders. The paratroopers withdrew to the beach north of the town and were joined there during the night by the paratroop battalion that had been clearing Rafah. Before dawn, the paratroop battalions and one of the armored-infantry battalions moved into attack positions all around Khan Yunis.

A stiff dawn assault on June 7 hit the town from several directions at once and swiftly broke through the outer defenses. Fierce fighting through the rabbit's warren of narrow, twisting lanes carried the Israelis to the town square by 0900. Many of the defenders surrendered at that point, but heavy fighting ensued into the early afternoon. Beyond that, it took days of tense house-by-house searches to root out the last sniper.

Raful and one of his paratroop battalions, accompanied by the 7th Armored Brigade's Patton company, left the waning fight in Khan Yunis at noon on June 7, and raced west to catch up with the Israeli force that was advancing swiftly down the Sinai coastal highway.

26

In 1967, Brigadier General Avraham Yoffe was 53 years old. Though technically still subject to call-ups, he thought he had been fully retired from military life for three years. Not so. After leaving the army, the robust and rotund general had taken a job heading Israel's Nature Conservancy and had long since adjusted to a new life and a new role in service to the nation. During the early days of the 1967 mobilization, Yoffe had been invited to Southern Command Headquarters by Shaike Gavish. He had willingly complied to what he thought was merely a courtesy stemming from his service as GOC, Southern Command from 1958 to 1962. He assumed Gavish wanted to ask him a few questions or simply show him around. When Yoffe arrived dressed in civilian clothing, Shaike wondered aloud why the former general was not attired in a suitable uniform. After an exchange that embarrassed both men, it was finally revealed that Shaike's invitation had been meant as a mobilization order; Shaike wanted Yoffe to assume command of an *ugdah* composed of two Reserve armored brigades. While an aide rushed to Yoffe's home to pick up the general's uniforms, Yoffe got straight to work. He did not return home once until the war was over.

In 1956, Colonel Yoffe had commanded a Reserve infantry brigade on a grueling overland march to Sharm el-Sheikh down the east side of the Sinai Peninsula. The brigade's long march had been over terrain the Egyptians and many others thought to be impassable. There is much to suggest that, in 1967, Shaike specifically selected the retired Yoffe to command an *ugdah* because many believed that Yoffe himself had been the key to his brigade's success in 1956. Yoffe was less sanguine; he was already on record in sharing credit with his Reserve soldiers, whom he believed to be the match of the world's best Regulars. So, there is the second reason for mobilizing Yoffe to command an all-Reserve *ugdah*; no Israeli general had more faith in the Reserve system than Avraham Yoffe.

No matter the precise manner in which *Ugdah* Yoffe wound up being employed—toward *Ugdah* Tal's zone to the north or toward *Ugdah* Sharon's zone to the south—it first would be faced with traversing a vast area that all the Egyptian generals and all their Soviet advisors considered to be impassable. Indeed, the defensive concepts of the 7th and 2nd Egyptian Infantry divisions were anchored in the belief that the sandy wastes between the divisions were impassable to men on foot, wheeled vehicles, halftracks, and even large formations of tanks.

It was Yoffe's job between his arrival at Southern Command Headquarters and the morning of June 5 to find a way to prove all the experts wrong. This he did.

Once El Arish was in the hands of *Ugdah* Tal, the pivot point in the extreme northern part of central Sinai became the road junction at Bir Lahfan. Located 20 kilometers south of El Arish at the crown point of an equilateral triangle of roads whose base points were Jebel Libni and Abu Agheila, Bir Lahfan was critical to the Southern Command's war strategy because a strong Egyptian force traveling through it could either turn into Israeli units advancing through El Arish or pitch into the flank of the Israeli units slated to advance toward the Mitla Pass from Nitzana by way of Umm Katef and Abu Agheila. On the other hand, if the Israelis could seize and firmly hold Bir Lahfan, they would be in a position to block access between Jebel Libni and the northern highway and, if required, to themselves pitch into the northern flank of any reinforcements the Egyptians sent directly from Jebel Libni or via the Mitla Pass to Abu Agheila and Umm Katef, the primary objectives of *Ugdah* Sharon's attack out of Nitzana.

Bir Lahfan was so critical to Israeli needs that Southern Command decided to seize it in an extremely novel operation—one only Israelis would dare. At about 0900, June 5, just as *Ugdah* Sharon opened its attack on the Umm Katef–Abu Agheila defensive zone from the vicinity of Nitzana, Colonel Isaachar "Yiska" Shadmi's armored brigade crossed the frontier just north of Nitzana and angled toward the northwest by way of the Wadi Haridin, a bone-dry streambed that cut nearly 50 kilometers through the desert almost precisely to Bir Lahfan.

Yiska's brigade was considered the best Reserve armored brigade in the army. It was composed of two Centurion battalions and one armored-infantry battalion, plus support units, that were manned almost entirely by young soldiers who had been released from the Standing Army in very recent years. Yiska himself was a 49-year-old Reserve officer who had recently taken a job managing Israel's tallest highrise, following a successful full-time military career. His balding, studious appearance and easy manner belied the heart and spirit of a tiger.

While the Sela Armored Brigade, *Ugdah* Yoffe's other component, waited behind Nitzana for further orders, the vanguard elements of Yiska's lead Centurion battalion ran right over the frontier fence and immediately engaged a small Egyptian reconnaissance force. Several Egyptian vehicles were destroyed by gunfire, but several others escaped. There was no telling who knew that Yiska's brigade was on the move.

The Wadi Haridin provided a straight shot to Bir Lahfan, but by no means an easy one. Loose sand, beds of dust, and no end of larger obstructions stood in the way all along the otherwise trackless waste between the coastal highway and the Umm Katef–Ismailia road. The Egyptians did not even have patrols out along the wadi, but they had mined it in places, and that certainly slowed Yiska's advance. Furthermore, the tanks and accompanying vehicles were obliged to traverse the entire 50 kilometers in low gear, so it took until 1400 for Lieutenant Colonel Avraham Bar-Am's lead Centurion battalion to arrive at an outlying position manned by an Egyptian National Guard company supported by several antitank guns.

Bar-Am's tanks, of which for some reason there were only twenty-four, deployed out of sight of the Egyptians and attacked the infantry position in a loose formation. Four of the 50-ton Centurions became mired in loose sand, but the objective was overrun without the loss of any Israeli lives. Most of the Egyptians fled into the desert on foot. As soon as Bar-Am's two lead companies reformed—the third one stayed back to tow the mired tanks out of the loose sand—the advance continued. Bir Lahfan was about 16 kilometers farther on.

The first of Bar-Am's Centurions rolled up onto the Abu Agheila–Bir Lahfan roadway at 1600, but it took two hours for the rear company to catch up. Additional maneuvering was required, so it was not until about 1845 that the attack on the Bir Lahfan road junction commenced. By then, Bar-Am's battalion and an armored-infantry company had circled out to the rear of the objective, a radar station on a hill that was manned by another Egyptian National Guard infantry company and protected by a battery each of light antiaircraft guns and antitank guns. Three kilometers to the north, but not yet directly threatened by the Israelis, was a major Egyptian blocking position manned by the main body of one Egyptian National Guard infantry brigade and an artillery detachment.

As the Israelis moved in the failing light against the radar station, the Egyptian artillery opened with inaccurate fire, but the large Egyptian infantry force at the roadblock never moved. The Israeli tanks, which could not surmount the hill, provided cover for the armored infantrymen, who could The radar site was overrun in short order. It was by then too dark to engage the Egyptians manning the Bir Lahfan roadblock, so Bar-Am's Centurion battalion moved to cover the three routes leading to the road junction and waited for the rest of the Shadmi Armored Brigade to close up on it. The Israelis ignored the Egyptian artillery, and the Egyptian artillery ignored the Israelis.

In as neat an indirect maneuver as *Zahal* had ever executed, a crack Israeli brigade stood at the pivot point of Southern Command's first-day war plan. El Arish, which was in imminent danger of falling to the 7th Armored Brigade, was less than 20 kilometers—under an hour away—to the north, and Yiska's brigade was actually in supporting range of *Ugdah* Sharon's attack on Umm Katef and Abu Agheila.

At 2200 hours, June 5, shortly after the Shadmi Armored Brigade closed up on Bir Lahfan and set in, there arrived in its position a jeep manned by Colonel Avraham "Bren" Adan, General Yoffe's chief of staff. Bren was a distinguished armor officer whose accomplishments at Abu Agheila in 1956 were already legendary; he had been assigned to guide infantrymen Yoffe through the intricacies of running an armored division. Bren spoke at length with Yiska, and then the two turned in around midnight. Before Bren fell asleep, however, General Yoffe radioed a change in plans.

Ugdah Sharon's attack was meeting strong opposition at Umm Katef, and its schedule was coming unglued. In the last few hours, Sharon's problems had been multiplying, and it seemed like a good idea for Bren to attack Abu Agheila from the rear at the head of one of Yiska's Centurion battalions. Bren was elated, for he had not only seized Abu Agheila in 1956, he had done so as a young company commander in 1948.

As soon as Bren finished speaking with Yoffe, he woke Yiska to tell him the news. Yiska was upset. Naturally, he did not want to give up a battalion, even to Bren. Besides, his job was to prevent the powerful 4th Egyptian Tank Division—the Sinai Field Army's "sword"—from falling on El Arish or Abu

Agheila, or both—by way of Bir Lahfan. He asked Bren how he was supposed to stand against a whole tank division if the Egyptians sent their 4th in his direction. Bren was scornful of the Egyptians, and he reminded Yiska that the order had come from on high. Yiska relented—but only because he had no choice. Bren then released another tidbit of news that he had heard from Yoffe: "Oh, by the way," Bren cautioned, "two Egyptian brigades are moving in your direction to make a counterattack. One is definitely a tank brigade."

Bren left Bir Lahfan with Lieutenant Colonel "Fedele's" Centurion battalion at 2300 hours, June 5. By then, Yiska had advanced several kilometers in the direction of Jebel Libni with one of Bar-Am's Centurion companies. It was Yiska's hope that the lone Centurion company would delay the Egyptian brigade long enough on the darkened roadway for the armored-infantry battalion and remaining Centurions to fashion an impenetrable hedgehog position on the high ground around the road junction.

After speaking with Bren, Yoffe released Colonel Elchanan Sela's armored brigade—two Centurion battalions and an armored-infantry battalion—from its holding position behind Nitzana. Shortly after Sela's brigade left its cantonment, it skirted the Umm Katef–Abu Agheila area to the north—even though a battle royal was raging there between *Ugdah* Sharon and the 2nd Egyptian Infantry Division. Once past the battlefield, Sela struck for the Abu Agheila–Bir Lahfan road, but even then his vanguard could not possibly arrive at Bir Lahfan before mid morning. So, even with Sela in motion, Shadmi was on his own.

One Egyptian tank brigade and one Egyptian mechanized brigade were rushing along the Jebel Libni–Bir Lahfan road, bound for El Arish to turn back the 7th Armored Brigade. They had left Jebel Libni after sunset and thus had not been molested by any of the several pairs of IAF fighter-bombers that had been roving across central Sinai all afternoon. The Egyptian commanders had no idea that the road junction just ahead was in Israeli hands, so all the T-55 tanks and other vehicles had their headlights on to help maintain their rapid progress along the roadway.

Yiska let them come on until the lead company of Egyptian tanks had arrived within point-blank range of the advance Centurion company. At Yiska's order, the Centurion platoon nearest the T-55s opened fire, one round apiece, and all three of the lead T-55s burst into flames.

All lights along the Egyptian column were doused in a heartbeat. There was a brief pause as each side waited to see what the other could do. Then the Centurion company commander lit his tank's coaxial searchlight to fix the Egyptian tanks in the sights of his gunners. A T-55 immediately fired at the command Centurion, and the company commander was mortally wounded by shell splinters. By then, both sides were exchanging intense fire. One Israeli round torched an Egyptian fuel tanker, and the roadway and its verges were lighted brighter than day. Firing as they went, the Egyptian tanks moved backwards out of the harsh glare. With that, the firing died down and dwindled to silence. The only sign of the battle was the burning fuel from the fuel tanker and the flickering corpses of nine T-55s.

Yiska withdrew to the road junction with the lead Centurion company. By then, the remainder of the Centurions and the armored-infantry battalion were set in to repel the attack everyone was certain would fall upon the brigade position.

The commanders of the Egyptian tank brigades were mighty confused. They had heard that there were Israelis in El Arish—but Bir Lahfan? Certainly, there was a handful of Israeli tanks ahead, but were there more? What lay ahead? The Egyptian brigade commanders were unwilling to find out in the dark, so they withdrew to a position about 3 kilometers southwest of the road junction and ordered their tanks to form a protective laager. The only Egyptians who molested the main body of the Shadmi Armored Brigade that night were the artillerymen in the blocking position to the north. They fired light harassment-and-interdiction missions starting at 0400, June 6, but they had no observers out, so the fall of the shells was ineffectual.

The Centurions were running low on fuel, and that threatened to close down Yiska's stand. The tanks needed to keep their engines running to traverse their turrets and fire their guns. They need not move if it came to that, but they needed fuel to fight. Following some frantic negotiations on the radio between Yiska and Southern Command, the brigade supply officer established a fuel point 2 kilometers east of the junction, well away from the Egyptians. While other classes of supplies were dropped by fixed-wing transports, IAF helicopters laden with fuel bladders sneaked in and quickly unharnessed their loads. The Centurions crept out of their defensive positions in platoon relays, topped off, and scuttled back to the defensive line while the next platoon filled up. Everyone's heart was in his mouth during the vulnerable procedure, but there was no danger whatsoever beyond the chance of the Egyptian gunners to the north blowing up the fueling point with a really lucky hit.

* * *

The T-55s remained in their laagers until dawn. Then, at 0600, as they began stirring to form up and probe toward the road junction, four IAF Mystères rigged out as ground-support aircraft rolled in from out of the sun and laid waste to four tanks and numerous APCs and soft-skinned trucks with their 30mm cannon, rockets, and bombs. One of the Mystères was hit by ground fire and left the scene trailing smoke. The pilot, who had to eject from the crippled airplane, came down within several hundred meters of Yiska's armored infantrymen. Meanwhile, even under incessant attack by additional flights of Mystères and Ouragans, sixty-five of the crack Egyptian tank crews—two battalions—formed up and advanced toward the Israeli-held road junction. Pussycats in the dark, they had become tigers in full daylight even though they had to pass the guttering ruins of the nine T-55s that had been destroyed in the night meeting engagement.

But the airstrikes proved to be overwhelming. Relatively few of the first wave of T-55s made it into the killing zones established by Bar-Am's Centurion battalion. As increasingly stronger and more accurate Egyptian artillery fire felt its way toward the Israeli positions from southwest and north, the Israeli tank gunners opened fire from ranges between 3,000 and 4,000 meters shortly after 0600. The superbly trained Centurion gunners exacted a terrifying toll—against no losses of their own—but the T-55s continued to edge forward.

A very long hour into the battle, the vanguard company of Lieutenant Colonel Fedele's Centurion battalion arrived from the direction of Abu Agheila to catch the Egyptian tank formations in the flank. Hours earlier, Bren had been within 3 kilometers of leading his third attack into Abu Agheila when an urgent communication from General Yoffe had turned him in his tracks. Yoffe had just received a report from Yiska detailing the approach of the two Egyptian brigades on Bir Lahfan and the progress of the initial meeting engagement. Yoffe reacted instantly to the news by calling off Fedele's impending attack on Abu Agheila. Now, Fedele's Centurions had arrived at the critical moment. Bar-Am's small battalion and the IAF fighter-bombers were doing a beautiful job holding off the T-55 battalions, but they were outnumbered and outgunned; they stood a good chance of being overwhelmed without help.

Despite Fedele's flank attack, the T-55 crews would not quit the field. Those that needed to turned to take on Fedele's Centurions, and those that could ground slowly forward against Bar-Am's. To the rear of the Egyptian formations, IAF Mystères and Ouragans inexorably chewed away at APCs and soft vehicles.

It was a wild and ultimately purposeless fight. The Egyptian tank crews—the very best their nation had ever produced—were killed for nothing. It was coming up 1000 when their commanders finally acceded to reality and ordered their combat units to disengage and withdraw. Even then, the IAF formations continued to exact a toll. Twenty-eight T-55s were destroyed or disabled in the killing zone in front of Bar-Am's Centurion battalion, and many others were set ablaze as they pulled back by the swooping, cannon-firing Super Mystères.

Shortly after the Egyptian T-55s withdrew back toward Jebel Libni, the main body of the 7th Armored Brigade fought its way into the Egyptian blocking position across the El Arish–Bir Lahfan road. There, beginning after 0800, while the refueled and once-again mobile Aviram Armored Brigade mopped up in and around El Arish, the Pattons of Major Chaim's Tank Battalion 77 had attacked the reduced Egyptian National Guard brigade that, with fourteen tanks, was holding the block. Once the attack by the Pattons was well developed, Shmulik won permission to add the weight of Tank Battalion 82's refueled and rearmed Centurions. The Egyptian defenses cracked swiftly under the weight of the Israeli armored attack, and the majority of the defenders fled toward Bir Lahfan at just about the time the Shadmi Armored Brigade was standing down in its defensive positions following the repulse of the 4th Egyptian Tank Division's T-55s. Yiska's Centurion and halftrack crews destroyed many of the oncoming Egyptian vehicles with machine-gun fire, and most of the Egyptian National Guardsmen who survived the turkey shoot fled into the desert wastes on foot. When last seen, many of them had just pulled off their shoes and boots to do so.

Shortly after noon, the Pattons and Centurions of the 7th Armored Brigade linked up with the Centurions of the Shadmi Armored Brigade near the Bir Lahfan road junction. A short time later, General Yoffe ordered Yiska to pursue the fleeing Egyptian tank and mechanized brigades. And shortly after that, Talik ordered Shmulik to attend a divisional orders group at the El Arish airfield. The 7th Armored Brigade was to rest and replenish while the Aviram Armored Brigade took up the drive toward the Suez Canal. The Egyptian Army in northern Sinai was on the ropes or on the run, and the pursuit phase in the sectors of *Ugdah* Tal and *Ugdah* Yoffe was about to begin.

* * *

Bir Lahfan was a major victory for the Shadmi Armored Brigade, which lost just one man killed in thirty hours of often bitter fighting. In the end, Bir Lahfan proved to be one of the several *decisive* battles waged by Southern Command formations during the first twenty-four hours of the war. It broke the back of the Egyptian Army's strategic reserve in Sinai, the incomparable 4th Egyptian Tank Division. Egypt had no better tank crews than the ones she lost at Bir Lahfan.

27

The Sinai Campaign had been fought in late October and early November of 1956. By late November, many of *Zahal's* leading tacticians were at hard work trying to solve the puzzle of Umm Katef, which had not fallen to Israeli troops before it had been abandoned by its Egyptian defenders. The rebuff administered to the Israeli force charged with securing Umm Katef frontally in 1956 had been treated ad nauseam ever since to detailed planning sessions under the auspices of the Instruction Department of *Zahal's* General Staff Branch. There was nothing about this prospective battlefield that was not known in intimate detail by *Zahal*, and no eventuality that had not been considered.

For over a year prior to the outbreak of war in 1967, the head of the Instruction Department—the man in whose care the many papers on Umm Katef had been placed—was Brigadier General Arik Sharon. Sharon's focus on Umm Katef became complete when in mid May 1967 he was assigned to command the southern Sinai *ugdah*, into whose area of operations Umm Katef and Abu Agheila fell.

Sharon's conception for an operation against Umm Katef was breathtaking. Viewed by military scholars solely in its context as a plan brings forth comments that tend to center on Sharon's gall, and not his military acumen. Viewed in hindsight, with full knowledge of the outcome, the informed critic still tends to focus on Sharon's sheer gall.

The objective of Sharon's plan was simply overcoming the Egyptian defensive zone in order to secure passage along the Sinai Peninsula's central highway all the way from the former U.N. border post at El Auja, opposite Nitzana, to the Mitla Pass. To do this, *Ugdah* Sharon had been concentrated behind the Israeli town of Shivta, a lonely desert community east of Nitzana, about 25 kilometers from the frontier. To get from there to the Mitla Pass, the three *Zahal* Reserve brigades comprising *Ugdah* Sharon—one armored, one infantry, and one parachute—had to either bypass or reduce all three of the Egyptian fortified positions at Kusseima, Umm Katef, and Abu Agheila.

There was no viable route around Umm Katef. If there had been, Sharon would have taken it. So would Moshe Dayan have taken it in 1956. The Umm Katef position stood firmly astride the main highway through the area, and it was surrounded by impassable ground to the north and the south. Or so the Egyptians believed.

Beyond Umm Katef was a second strong defensive position at Abu Agheila, and far beyond Abu Agheila were the Egyptian Army base camps at Jebel Libni and Bir el-Thamada. It was Southern Command's hope to concentrate elements of all three of its *ugdot* at Jebel Libni to fight what Shaike Gavish hoped would be the decisive battle of the war. It was thus imperative for *Ugdah* Sharon to overcome Umm Katef and Abu Agheila and join Tal's and Yoffe's *ugdot* in time to take on the main body of the Sinai Field Army—the 3rd Infantry and 4th Tank divisions and Shazli Force.

Umm Katef itself is an 80-foot-high mesa just to the south of the main highway. Nearly adjacent on the south side is a second low mesa, Umm Shihan. Long before the 1956 Sinai Campaign, the two mesas had been linked by British-built fortifications to form a powerful position designed to be held by a large infantry force supported by artillery. After 1956, and particularly following the arrival of massive Soviet assistance in 1964 and 1965, the position had been strengthened to form one of the most formidable defensive zones in the Middle East. Screened by several sentinel positions to the east and northeast, the Umm Katef position itself began with a thickly sown belt of mines extending in places to a depth of 200 meters. Behind the mine belt, in classic Soviet style, were three solid ribbons of infantry trenches, each sufficient to emplace a reinforced infantry battalion. In 1956, there had been British-built trenches *atop* each of three 17-meter-high man-made "ridges," but since then the Egyptian Army's Soviet advisors had ordered the British trenches filled in and replaced by new ones in the low ground *between* the man-made ridges. Each of the concrete-lined Soviet trenches was 4 kilometers long, and defended by concrete pillboxes, bunkers, and antitank and assault-gun emplacements. However, each trenchline was protected by only a single strand of barbed wire, and not the thick belt of concertina wire that other armies would have set out.

Behind the infantry trenches was the artillery position, which could accommodate a reinforced artillery brigade. Finally, in accordance with the Soviet "sword" doctrine, a tank park for a complete Soviet-style tank brigade had been established to the rear of the artillery position. The entire main Umm Katef position was nearly 13 kilometers deep, from east to west, and over 4 kilometers wide, from north to south.

Until June 3, the main Umm Katef position had been held by only one reinforced infantry battalion. However, on that day the main body of the 2nd Egyptian Infantry Division suddenly emerged from the chaos of Sinai's hopelessly snarled road network. The 12th Egyptian Infantry Brigade took up residence in Umm Katef itself, with an infantry battalion in each of the three concrete-lined infantry trenches. The division's organic artillery brigade of seventy-two 122mm field guns and the 12th Egyptian Infantry Brigade's somewhat lighter organic artillery detachment were ensconced within the artillery sector directly behind the infantry. The 2nd Egyptian Infantry Division's "sword" force—reportedly two tank battalions amounting to sixty-six T-34s and a battalion of twenty-two SU-100 assault guns—occupied the tank park. The divisional headquarters was set up near the tank park.

Approximately 10 kilometers along a roadway winding west from the main Umm Katef position was Abu Agheila. Here, the main body of the second of the 2nd Egyptian Infantry Division's three infantry brigades and at least one T-34 battalion occupied an extensive self-contained defensive position. In the midst of the Abu Agheila position was a vitally important road junction. The main El Auja–Ismailia highway ran to the east, and the Abu Agheila–Bir Lahfan road branched off to the northwest.

The Israelis assumed—correctly, as it turned out—that the Egyptian tank-infantry force at Abu Agheila would be held there in reserve until after *Ugdah* Sharon had shown its hand. Thus, the overland push and evening arrival at Bir Lahfan by *Ugdah* Yoffe's Shadmi Armored Brigade was timed to inflict operational uncertainty upon the 2nd Egyptian Infantry Division staff at the precise moment the Egyptians were confronted with a decision to commit or withhold their Abu Agheila reserves to the battle for Umm Katef. One of the Shadmi Armored Brigade's many jobs was to keep the Abu Agheila force at Abu Agheila while Sharon's main attack went in at Umm Katef. In any case, at least part of the Abu Agheila force would be obliged to hold in place to prevent a repeat of the 7th Armored Brigade's unforeseen 1956 attack into their position by way of the unguarded Deika Pass. In the decade since, the crude Deika Pass track that had carried Israeli tanks to and beyond Abu

Agheila had been allowed to deteriorate, and in 1967 it was covered with sand drifts. Also in the interim, the Egyptians had gained the good sense to keep a weather eye on that potential threat—albeit to the detriment of the Abu Agheila garrison's maneuverability.

Outlying posts around Umm Katef included Tarat Umm Basis, which was about 3 kilometers from the Israeli frontier, directly opposite Nitzana. It was Umm Katef's best-placed lookout post. About 4 kilometers west of Tarat Umm Basis was Umm Tarpa, a tiny mesa just to the north of the main highway and directly overlooking a barely motorable camel track that skirted the Umm Katef position about 2 kilometers to the north. Though conventional wisdom argued vehemently against an Israeli flanking maneuver across the impassable sand sea to the north of the Umm Katef position or the broken hilly country to the south (the Jebel Delfa), the Egyptians had taken precautions. The sandy rise topping Umm Tarpa—Hill 181—had been outposted in the two days since June 3 by one infantry company and a squadron of twenty T-34 tanks. The outpost was static, but it provided a necessary vista toward a vulnerable flank and might serve as a breakwater in the unlikely event the unpredictable Israelis launched a feint or a spoiling attack from that direction.

Kusseima, which after June 3 was held by the third, somewhat reduced, infantry brigade of the 2nd Egyptian Infantry Division, was a little out of the way of the main route, but common wisdom held that it had to be secured by the Israelis in order to prevent its garrison from pitching into the southern flank of an Israeli force advancing frontally toward or beyond Umm Katef, to which Kusseima was linked by a good road. The Sharon plan all but ignored Kusseima. Even after Kusseima was occupied by the Egyptian brigade on June 3, Sharon reckoned that he had barely enough resources to reduce Umm Katef and Abu Agheila, and he could not afford to commit the brigade or more that would be required to attack Kusseima. Sharon prudently planned to dispatch his divisional AMX-13 reconnaissance battalion to cover and monitor Kusseima, but he had no plans to attack it. If the Kusseima garrison attacked him, he would deal with it. But, if not, he would give it no more thought.

Ugdah Sharon was to open its advance across the frontier from Nitzana at about 0830 on June 5, more or less in conjunction with *Ugdah* Tal's attack into the Gaza Strip. However, the main attack upon Umm Katef itself was not slated to begin until dusk. That gave Arik Sharon, Israel's consummate night warrior, a long summer day to play around with the minds of his adversaries.

Sharon's superiors were openly dubious that so complex a plan as Sharon contemplated could be carried off, and some, including Shaike Gavish, argued passionately to dissuade him from executing it. However, after all the haggling, the actual operation by which *Ugdah* Sharon took on the Umm Katef–Abu Agheila–Kusseima hedgehog was virtually identical to the plan Sharon had cooked up in the first place. In fact, the execution phase came as close to coinciding with the written plan as ever a military operation has done.

The reduction of Umm Katef took place in five acts.

In the first phase of Act I, IAF Fouga-Magisters swept down upon the artillery position inside the Umm Katef position and Israeli artillery near Nitzana pummeled the outposts fronting Umm Katef and the main Egyptian defensive positions inside Umm Katef itself. The object of the air strike and bombardment, which began simultaneously at 0815 on June 5, was to cover an advance across the "impassable" open ground to the north by Lieutenant Colonel Natan "Natke" Nir's Centurion tank battalion of Colonel Mordechai "Motke" Zippori's armored brigade.

Natke's Centurions were accompanied by one armored-infantry company, a battery of four 120mm heavy mortars mounted in halftracks, and a platoon of engineers, also in halftracks. The Centurions and halftracks crashed across the border fence north of Tarat Umm Basis at 0840 and, covered by direct artillery fire, bypassed the deserted former U.N. observation post at El Auja. Egyptian infantrymen and antitank gunners on Tarat Umm Basis immediately opened fire on the vanguard Centurions, but the Israelis bypassed the Egyptian outpost, because they did not want to waste time grappling with the minefield fronting the elevated position. Israeli artillery— of which Sharon had amassed six sixteen-gun battalions of 155mm SPs, 105mm SPs, and towed 25-pounders—continued to pound the outpost until Natke's entire force had traversed the area. As it did, a company of Motke's Super Sherman tank battalion—which was armed with 105mm gyro-stabilized guns—rolled across the border and opened fire on Tarat Umm Basis from a distance. Later, shortly before noon, the main body of Motke's armored-infantry battalion assaulted the hill and quickly took possession of this Egyptian outpost and three others to the east of Umm Katef.

After bypassing Tarat Umm Basis, Natke's Centurion battalion swung onto the main highway in order to secure Umm Tarpa and Hill 181 by direct assault. In short order, the battalion vanguard encountered a huge crater that the Egyptians had blown in the roadway, and this obliged the Israeli tanks to leave the highway. They exited on the north side of the crater. Before the lead Centurions could proceed with the attack, however, seven of them had been destroyed or damaged by Egyptian antitank fire or in the extensive Egyptian minefield. One company commander and three platoon commanders were killed and both of the other Centurion company commanders were wounded in the explosive clash. Natke ordered the entire battalion to cover or assist in recovering the damaged tanks, and then he ordered the battalion to withdraw and reorganize while he rethought his approach on the objective. Umm Tarpa was far from being Natke's ultimate goal and it was not worth the losses his battalion already had suffered. At that stage of the war, however, Israeli combat units were under orders to advance at all costs. Natke decided to rush Umm Tarpa from the north, and he allocated his two rear Centurions companies and the armored-infantry company to attack across the minefield—regardless of losses.

After a divisional staff officer overflew the battlefield in Sharon's personal helicopter, Natke was directed along a route that purportedly skirted the main Egyptian mine belt. Even so, the Israeli armored vehicles lined up in several columns and proceeded into the attack, one behind the other. The idea was that the lead tank would advance until it touched off a mine and then the rest of the column, which had been advancing in its track, would cut around it until the succeeding lead tank touched off another mine—and so forth until all the tanks were gone or the objective had been overrun. That everyone agreed to this is a testament to training and the consensus about doctrine.

True to his calling, Natke directed his own tank to the lead-off position and heralded the attack by shouting "Follow me! Advance!" into his radio microphone. In the next breath, Natke ordered hovering Fougas and Ouragans to deliver an air strike aimed at getting the defenders' heads down. The Israeli ground-attack pilots gamely swooped almost to ground level, but they lost sight of the target in a swirling dust storm and pulled off without delivering their bullets, rockets, or bombs. However, the hurtling jets must have had some effect upon the defenders, for Natke's tanks and halftracks advanced through light fire, surmounted the slope, and crushed the defenders. There was no problem with mines. All of the T-34s that had been occupying static positions on Hill 181 were torched, and the few Egyptian soldiers who did not flee were rounded up and sent toward the Israeli rear under their own power, because there was no one available to escort them.

As Natke's task force was sorting itself out atop Umm Tarpa, Egyptian 122mm guns in the Umm Katef position opened fire on the hill, and that obliged the Israelis to leave rather more quickly than they had planned. Natke called his reserve company forward to replace the company that had been rendered ineffective in the minefield, and then he started moving his tanks and halftracks unhindered toward the Abu Agheila crossroads by way of the camel track that ran north of Umm Katef. The Egyptian artillery tried to range in on the Israeli tanks, but the undulating dunes through which Natke's battalion was advancing screened the Centurions and halftracks from effective observation.

Late in the afternoon, Natke radioed Motke to report that he was quite close to the Abu Agheila road junction, at which the main highway and the Abu Agheila–Bir Lahfan road diverged. Though it was still earlier than detailed in Sharon's plan, Motke told Natke that he could attack then and there if he wanted to. Natke did just that, but the Egyptians holding Abu Agheila were prepared to meet the onslaught. The premature frontal attack was repulsed, and Natke withdrew to safe positions in the dunes. He would return, per Sharon's plan, after sunset.

While Natke's task force was inching through the dunes north of Umm Katef, Motke's Super Shermans battalion closed on the minefield fronting Umm Katef. From behind handy cover, the tanks sniped away at pinpoint targets along the Egyptian trenchlines. Next, late in the afternoon, all six of Sharon's artillery battalions crossed the frontier and set up battery sites in the broken ground from Tarat Umm Basis to just behind the Super Sherman battalion. Every one of the ninety-six Israeli artillery pieces was well within range of the much longer ranged Egyptian 122mm field guns in Umm Katef, but being there is what it took to complete their part in Sharon's master plan. The Israeli guns fired registration rounds on a selection of targets, but, once registered, they all fell silent. The Super Shermans continued to snipe at Egyptian targets of opportunity, but, even though Egyptian 122mm rounds continued to fall sporadically, the Israeli guns remained silent and their crews remained under cover.

Also during the afternoon of May 5, a motley array of civilian vehicles out of Shivta brought forward Colonel Yekutiel "Kutty" Adam's Reserve infantry brigade. Daubed with mud to, in Sharon's words, "make them look more military," the two-wheel-drive buses, trucks, and automobiles drove to within 12 kilometers of Umm Katef. They could advance no closer to the objective without being observed by the Egyptians, so Kutty's infantrymen donned their packs, lifted their heavy loads of ammunition and other necessities, and began the arduous trudge through soft sand toward their battalion lines of departure. Lacking air support of any type, having lost all the observation posts east of Umm Katef, and with their attention riveted on the Israeli Super Shermans and silent Israeli artillery battalions to their front, the Egyptians in Umm Katef utterly failed to note the arrival of Kutty's brigade nor the singular fact that it was slowly walking around Umm Katef's northern flank.

The arrival of Kutty's infantry brigade and the arm's-length stand-off battle between Umm Katef's entrenched infantry and the Israeli Super Shermans comprised separate scenes in Act II of Arik Sharon's unfolding battle plan.

Shaike arrived at Sharon's headquarters a little before dusk. Though Gavish was the busiest man in Southern Command, he felt he had to be with Sharon during the most complex military operation in Israel's history. As soon as Shaike arrived at Sharon's mobile command post on the front side of Tarat Umm Basis, Yitzhak Rabin radioed to ask Gavish and Sharon to postpone the attack so the IAF could soften Umm Katef for a full day. Shaike shot back, "No," but thought the better of it because he had not asked Sharon to speak. But Sharon said, "No," too, and that is the answer Rabin accepted. Minutes later, Shaike discovered that radio contact with the outside world had been lost. A freak atmospheric disturbance simply rendered his and Sharon's command radios inoperative, and it would be hours before Shaike could regain contact with his own headquarters.

Act III began shortly after 1900, a few minutes after the sun set. A pair of IAF Alouette light observation helicopters flitted across the frontier at extremely low altitude and landed several kilometers due north of the Umm Katef artillery position. When the helicopter crews were certain they were in the right place, they lit off several flares and stood by while a flight of six Super Frelon and Sikorsky S-58 helicopters arrived to deliver a total of fifty paratroopers from Colonel Dani Matt's 31st Parachute Brigade. Very quickly, the transport helicopters disgorged their human cargoes and returned to Israel to collect more paratroopers. The Egyptians, however, heard the clatter and probed the area with their artillery. No Israelis were hurt, but one of the 122mm rounds struck a marker panel that had been set out to guide the returning transport helicopters. This accurate fire forced the first lift of troops to go to ground, and the next lift was landed farther to the north, as was a third lift.

There were supposed to have been a dozen helicopters made available to transport a total of 300 paratroopers to the vicinity of Umm Tarpa, but the need to resupply the Shadmi Armored Brigade at Bir Lahfan had drawn off half the squadron. Also, the landing operation took longer than antici-pated, and more time was lost reassembling the dispersed components of the three lifts. Colonel Matt, who had commanded a parachute battalion under Sharon in 1956, decided to conduct the mission with just the 150 men who had arrived in the three initial lifts. For all that, Matt had to break the news to Arik Sharon that the four half-strength paratroop commando groups were 30 minutes behind schedule. Sharon had no choice but to agree to postpone his final attack on Umm Katef for a half hour.

Minor irritants aside, the pieces of Sharon's plan were coming together as nicely as anyone could have dared to hope. The attention of the 12th Egyptian Infantry Brigade and its supports was riveted to the east, where Motke's Super Sherman battalion continued to snipe at the Egyptian trenchline. Certainly, the Egyptians knew that there were Israeli Centurions northwest of Umm Katef, but Natke's afternoon rebuff in front of the Abu Agheila crossroads probably lulled the Egyptian commanders into a secure feeling.

Great care had been taken to prevent the Egyptians from learning of the existence, much less the whereabouts, of Kutty Adam's infantry brigade. After leaving its gypsy caravan of commandeered civilian vehicles north of Tarat Umm Basis, Kutty and his troops had spent the entire afternoon struggling through loose sand. Just before sunset, they all reached their jump-off positions due north of the triple trenchline that was the heart of the Umm Katef defensive zone.

As far as the Egyptians inside Umm Katef knew, the Israelis had ad-vanced one armored brigade and a lot of artillery to the environs east of Umm Katef. It seemed likely that they were simply going to isolate the base with artillery fire and armored patrols, or, at most, that they would attempt to seize the Abu Agheila crossroads with the Centurion battalion. The Egyptians knew nothing of Kutty's infantry or the make-up of the paratroop force, and they certainly did not expect a frontal attack to be made against Umm Katef by only part of an armored brigade.

Sharon was cutting it close. His entire divisional reserve consisted of the main body of the 31st Parachute Brigade (Matt's third paratroop battalion had been detached to help form the Sharm el-Sheikh Task Force) and the main body of the armored-infantry battalion from the Zippori Armored Brigade. However, these battalions were initially too far from Umm Katef to be of much use if Sharon's plan came a cropper.

Minutes before a scheduled air strike was to engulf Umm Katef, Shaike had to inform Sharon that it was off. Jordan's entry into the war that morning had drawn off the IAF's reserve, and there were not enough warplanes covering Sinai to deal with a number of emergencies and the night strike against Umm Katef. Fortunately, that was about as far as Sharon's plan unraveled.

Act IV began at 2230, when Sharon ordered his six artillery battalions to open fire on preregistered targets inside the Umm Katef position. Sharon's exact words were, "Let everything tremble." Then, as all ninety-six artillery pieces let loose and the ground indeed trembled, Sharon smiled at his artillery commander and exclaimed, "Such a barrage I have never seen."

For twenty explosive minutes, while the Egyptians in ground zero had their heads down against the impact of 6,000 Israeli artillery rounds, Kutty's three infantry battalions broke from the cover of the dunes just to the north of the trench system and, in three battalion columns of companies, advanced to their lines of departure. According to Sharon's plan, each infantry battalion was to advance straight down along one of the man-made ridges overlooking the Egyptian trenchlines, overcoming the Egyptian infantry by fire as it went.

Kutty was to report to Sharon when all three battalions were in position, and then wait while the artillery delivered a resounding 10-minute crescendo before shifting fires from the trenchlines to other targets. But Kutty was eager to begin. He reported to Sharon and asked that the artillery fires be shifted at that moment so he could get on with his attack before there was an accident or his battalions were discovered. Sharon agreed. At 2250, the three infantry companies leading the attack broke from cover in the classic formations whose use had been pioneered in 1955 by Arik Sharon himself.

There was an added twist. Each infantry battalion had been equipped with fifty flashlights with colored lens filters. One battalion had all red filters, another had all green, and the third had all yellow. It was possible for an observer directly to the east of the man-made ridges to monitor the progress of the battalions along each of the three trenchlines. In this case, the primary observers were the tank commanders and gunners of Motke's Super Sherman battalion. As the infantry advanced, firing down into the trenches, each Super Sherman company followed a particular set of colored lights from right to left (north to south) and laid fire just ahead of the leftmost lights. The tank gunners could not see any details of the fighting, but the system remained foolproof as long as the lead infantrymen kept their flashlights illuminated. Meantime, Kutty and his artillery liaison officer had direct control over as much of the artillery as they needed or wanted. This was used mainly to pound the trenchlines farther to the south of the areas the tanks were covering—down to ranges of only 50 meters ahead of the advancing infantry.

As Kutty's infantry attack unfolded, the Egyptians in the trenches called their own supporting artillery and requested that prearranged final protective fires be unleashed. By then, however, the Egyptian artillerymen were beset with life-or-death confusion in their sector.

Under cover of the preliminary Israeli artillery barrage, the four groups of Israeli paratroopers had infiltrated into the northern edge of the Egyptian artillery sector, a task that was made much easier by the lack of an all-around protected trenchline. As the battle for the trenchlines began, one group of Israeli paratroopers was detected, and an intense little fire fight got underway. Several paratroopers were killed or wounded, but, firing their Uzi submachine guns from the hip, the remainder rushed 200 meters into the nearest gun pits and shot or chased away all the crewmen. Then they overran another Egyptian battery position. However, as they reached out toward a third battery site, the Israelis were driven back with additional casualties, and the commander decided to withdraw to save the wounded. As this tiny group of paratroopers neared the highway, a column of Egyptian trucks passed right in front of it, and the Israelis shot all the drivers to death at close range. However, artillery ammunition aboard one of the trucks was set off, and two paratroopers were killed and six were wounded in the blast. This group withdrew with its dead and wounded, but shortly thereafter a second group of paratroopers ambushed a second convoy of Egyptian trucks. The resulting fuel fires brought down an intense reaction, and the paratroopers were forced to take cover in nearby bunkers. An intense fire fight raged without let-up on one side of the artillery sector until 0200, when the paratroopers began clearing out of Umm Katef in order to make way for the next surprise on Sharon's agenda.

The paratroopers' infiltration plan fell apart almost as soon as it got underway, but the confusion and terror that was sown among the crews of the Egyptian big guns helped slow the rate of fire even though the guns themselves were not silenced.

Act V was the final step in Sharon's carefully orchestrated set-piece attack. The unplanned afternoon attack on the Abu Agheila crossroads by Natke's Centurion battalion had been an authentic effort to seize the junction, but Natke's real goal was the tank park in the western one-third of the Umm Katef position. If the 2nd Egyptian Infantry Division possessed one asset with which it could blot out the Israeli successes, it was the "sword" force of sixty-six T-34s and twenty-two SU-100s backing the "shield" force of Egyptian infantrymen and artillery.

At 0100, June 6, Natke left small detachments of Centurions and armored infantrymen to block the road from Abu Agheila to Umm Katef and pitched straight *through* the Abu Agheila position. The Centurions shot up what they could while running at full speed and then swept on down the highway straight into the rear of the Umm Katef tank park. As the break-in attack at Umm Katef was unfolding, there were several minutes of sheer terror for Natke and his crews when scores of tanks and other vehicles skirted Umm Katef just to the north, from east to west. Natke and his crews didn't know what to think, and they were on the verge of turning to face the new challenge when word came over the command radio that *Ugdah* Yoffe's Sela Armored Brigade was advancing across the open desert toward the Abu Agheila–Bir Lahfan road so it could bolster the embattled Shadmi Armored Brigade at Bir Lahfan. As soon as this news spread, Natke and his tankers forgot about the scare and bored in up the rear of the Egyptian tank park.

While Natke's main body was attacking the Egyptian tank park from the rear, the Super Sherman battalion advanced to the edge of the Egyptian minefield fronting Umm Katef and prepared to advance toward the tank park by way of the main highway. At 0200, while the rear Super Shermans continued to lay direct fire ahead of the advancing Israeli infantrymen, the lead Super Shermans cut onto the highway. However, as Natke's Centurion crews had discovered earlier, the Egyptians had effectively blocked the route by blasting a huge crater in the roadway. The Super Shermans gingerly felt their way into the sand. Four made it around the crater, but the fifth was disabled by a mine. This brought the Super Sherman battalion to a dead stop.

Ugdah Sharon included a complete engineer battalion, the largest such unit assembled to that time by *Zahal*. The engineers had been at work clearing mines since sunset, and they knew what they were doing. A large supply of bangalore torpedoes was rushed forward to the head of the Super Sherman column, but the engineer battalion commander objected to using them to clear mines because of the danger of triggering uncontrollable sympathetic detonations elsewhere in the minefield. Two mine-clearing flail tanks had been left back at Tarat Umm Basis. These were called forward, but it would be hours before they could breast the long line of resupply and transport vehicles that was clogging the roadway between the frontier and the verges of Umm Katef. Once that had been determined, volunteers from the engineer battalion and even tank crewmen and armored infantrymen probed out into the sand and began clearing mines by hand—an extremely dangerous proposition even in daylight. Within the hour, by 0400, a path had been cleared around the crater, and the Super Shermans were able to advance at top speed toward the embattled Egyptian tank park.

Unfortunately, the sudden appearance of Super Shermans in the tank park shortly after 0400 inhibited Natke's Centurion gunners, who had been doing remarkably well to that point. Despite numerous fires that were consuming a score or more of the T-34s and SU-100s, there was not enough light to tell friend from foe. There was a real danger and a real fear that Centurions might fire on Super Shermans that were attacking straight toward them, and vice versa. After only a few moments of indecision, however, Motke arranged to fall back on an old training trick. He ordered the Super Shermans to cease firing in order to find out if the Centurions were being fired on by friend or foe. The Centurions continued to receive fire from ranges as close as 10 meters, but they fired back, assured that they were engaging enemy tanks. By then, the Super Shermans had resumed firing at the tanks they encountered along their front.

Just before the Super Shermans went into the attack after 0400, Kutty informed Sharon that all three of his infantry battalions had returned to the main highway north of Umm Katef and that each commander had reported that his unit's trenchline had been cleared. According to Kutty, twelve Israelis had been killed and forty-five had been wounded against claims of over 300 Egyptians killed and over 100 taken prisoner. Unbeknownst to Kutty, however, hundreds of Egyptian infantryman had bolted into living bunkers and had not been molested thereafter as the rapidly moving Israeli infantry columns proceeded down along the high ground overlooking the low-lying trenches. As the tank battle spread throughout the Umm Katef position, many of the Egyptian infantrymen emerged from their boltholes and attacked the Israeli Centurions and Super Shermans with RPGs and machine guns. Sharon ordered Kutty's brigade to clear the area by sweeping along *inside* the trenches themselves. As the tank battle died down, Centurions, Super Shermans, and armored infantrymen fought up the highway toward Abu Agheila, chasing Egyptian soldiers, tanks, and other vehicles as they went.

Arik Sharon's minutely planned multi-prong attack on Umm Katef was a complete success. By 0800, June 6, the Israelis were mopping up the last holdouts in the Egyptian trenchline, artillery sector, and tank park. Dozens of 122mm and other artillery pieces fell into Israeli hands—enough to form several new Israeli artillery battalions, in fact. Though Lieutenant Colonel Natke Nir was severely wounded in both legs during the night battle and a total of nineteen Centurions and Super Shermans were destroyed or disabled, the Israeli tankers accounted for over forty T-34s and SU-100s, and the remainder of the Egyptian "sword" force fled into the desert. Motke's armored brigade opened a final advance on Abu Agheila and nearby Ruefa Dam at 0600, but both positions had been abandoned. Sharon later reported that Umm Katef and Abu Agheila fell at a cost of 40 Israelis killed and 120 wounded, as against Egyptian losses amounting to an estimated 1,000 killed and many, many more wounded or captured.

The Egyptian infantry brigade holding Kusseima never stirred during the long night battles at Umm Katef. Screened and monitored by the main body of Colonel Dani Matt's 31st Parachute Brigade and reconnaissance units, the utterly passive Kusseima garrison was left to rot on the vine. During the second night of the war, the Kusseima garrison buried its weapons and stole out into the desert, every man for himself.

An utterly victorious *Ugdah* Sharon spent the morning of June 6 regrouping. One of Kutty's infantry battalions was left to finish mopping up Umm Katef while the main body drove up to Bir Lahfan aboard captured Egyptian military vehicles. Kutty's troops spent the rest of the war mopping up Umm Katef, El Arish, Jiradi Pass, and Sheikh Zuweid. Dani Matt's parachute brigade, which did not have adequate transport to take part in the pursuit, was initially left to cover Kusseima. After the Kusseima garrison evaporated,

Matt's paratroopers mopped up in and around the Umm Katef–Abu Agheila–Kusseima hedgehog. One of Matt's battalions also fought in Syria.

That left Motke's armored brigade and several battalions of SP artillery. At 1700 on June 6, after first threatening Kusseima, this force and Arik Sharon's mobile headquarters opened a laborious overland advance along the Wadi el-Arish from Abu Agheila southwest toward Nakhle. There Sharon's force was to link up with Colonel Avraham "Albert" Mendler's independent armored brigade, which was to begin a slow advance from east of Kuntilla when the Zippori Armored Brigade arrived in Nakhle. The Zippori and Mendler Armored brigades were slated to trap the Shazli Force and the 6th Egyptian Mechanized Division in a pincers attack that was to join at Kuraiya Pass, between Nakhle and Themed.

28

By noon on Tuesday, June 6, 1967, Brigadier General Shaike Gavish's Southern Command had fulfilled its strategic obligations under two of *Zahal's* five bedrock precepts—"Few Against Many" and "Geographic Pressures." The IAF had nearly annihilated the far larger Egyptian Air Force and Israeli ground forces had defeated larger Egyptian ground forces in little more than a full day of battle. The entire war so far had been waged in the enemy's land, farther and farther away from Israel. Moreover, it appeared that, in the south at least, a third bedrock precept, "A War of Survival" was on the brink of being fulfilled, for every step Southern Command took to the west from the frontier with Egypt was a step away from the potential annihilation of the Jewish state by its strongest enemy. There remained a danger that the thus-far unmolested 6th Egyptian Mechanized Division and Shazli Force might invade the Negev region and cut off Eilat, but that eventuality grew increasingly remote as Israeli victories piled up in northern and central Sinai.

The two precepts remaining to be fulfilled by Southern Command in its area of responsibility were "A War of Attrition" and "Time is of the Essence." Unbeknown to the Israelis until after noon on the war's second day, the key to their fulfillment—indeed, the concrete fulfillment of all five of the bedrock precepts—was handed to Southern Command at a single stroke by the psychological collapse of just one individual.

Field Marshal Abdel Hakim Amer, the Egyptian minister of war and commander in chief of the armed forces, lost his nerve early on, by the late morning of June 5, in fact. Amer, who had been caught aloft in the Air Force commander's airplane during the entire IAF preemptive strike, had learned of the Israeli ground attack in the Gaza Strip and Sinai shortly after returning to his headquarters in Cairo, and it appears that he had been kept more or less honestly apprised of ongoing calamities by his subordinates.

This is something Amer initially had over President Gamal Abdel Nasser, whom Amer himself kept in the dark about the death of the Egyptian Air Force and the progress of Israeli armored spearheads until after 1600 on June 5. Then, late in the afternoon of that first day, after isolating himself from his staff, Amer fell apart. He perceived the Israeli breakthroughs as utterly and irretrievably calamitous, even though the scrapped Kahir Plan, which Amer himself had helped create, had foreseen the shape of the Israeli thrusts of June 5 with stark prescience. The Egyptian war minister began in the late afternoon of that first day to contact division and even brigade commanders direct with a stream of orders that became confusing and even conflicting. In the meantime, Amer assured President Nasser that Egypt had launched the war, that the Egyptian Air Force had achieved air supremacy over Israel, and that the Egyptian Army was advancing deep into Israel on all fronts. Late in the day, however, when Amer finally described the day's true events to Nasser, the two managed to convince themselves that British and American warplanes had had a hand in the destruction of the Egyptian Air Force and that an Anglo-American amphibious invasion of the Suez Canal was imminent.

Amer is reputed to have been an alcoholic and heavy drug user, and it is said that he kept himself in an alcoholic or drug-induced stupor from the time he landed in the Air Force command plane on the morning of June 5 until the end of the war. Be that as it may, the avalanche of bad news that reached Amer throughout June 5 and long into the night finally caused the war minister to order the entire Sinai Field Army to quit its positions throughout Sinai. On the morning of June 6, in identical telegraph messages to the Sinai Front commander in chief, the Sinai Field Army commander, and the commanders of all divisions and independent brigades serving in Sinai, Amer ordered all units to fall back across the Suez Canal and thus—hopefully— save themselves. In sending out his withdrawal order—without even consulting President Nasser or any of his senior subordinates—Amer handed *Zahal* and Israel a strategic gift they had not quite earned as yet on their own.

Despite the virtual death of the 7th and 2nd Egyptian Infantry divisions and the costly repulse of two-thirds of the crack 4th Egyptian Tank Division at Bir Lahfan, the vast bulk of the Sinai Field Army was not only intact and unscathed, it was in possession of an overall deployment scheme that Israel's Southern Command would have been hardpressed to overcome as easily as it had overcome the incomplete forward defenses around Rafah and even

Umm Katef. Farther south, for example, the quite powerful 6th Egyptian Mechanized Division remained unmolested in its deep zone from Kuntilla all the way back to Nakhle, and the only slightly less powerful Shazli Force was likewise intact and unmolested—even from the air. In fact, if they had been ordered to do so, both the 6th Egyptian Mechanized Division and Shazli Force could have advanced deep into Israel's Negev Desert—precisely as it had been intended they do when Field Marshal Amer and President Nasser had boasted that Egypt could and would start the war wherever and whenever it chose. Farther back, in general compliance with the Kahir Plan for the deep defense of Sinai, the entire 3rd Egyptian Infantry Division and a large part of the 4th Egyptian Tank Division—at least one complete T-55 brigade—were still intact and unmolested in the central Sinai quadrilateral whose corner points were Jebel Libni, Bir el-Hassne, Bir Gifgafa, and Bir el-Thamada.

Moreover, the powerful Israeli divisional concentrations that had launched the ground war had been seriously weakened during the first day of the war. Already, *Ugdah* Tal's parachute brigade had been left behind in the Gaza Strip, and the elite 7th Armored Brigade had suffered heavy losses, particularly among its tank commanders. To the south, *Ugdah* Sharon had become, for all practical purposes, a slightly reinforced armored brigade overseen by a divisional headquarters. Moreover, *Ugdah* Sharon was advancing laboriously overland *away* from the main Egyptian concentrations in the extremely optimistic hope of overcoming, cutting off, or neutralizing the entire and quite powerful 6th Egyptian Mechanized Division, and perhaps Shazli Force as well. Of the three Israeli *ugdot*, only *Ugdah* Yoffe was intact.

In the next phase of the campaign, *Ugdah* Tal and *Ugdah* Yoffe—four armored brigades in all—were to advance from Bir Lahfan to take on the tail of the 4th Egyptian Tank Division and the entire 3rd Egyptian Infantry Division—plus, if the Egyptians chose to shift them northward, any or all the brigades of the 6th Egyptian Mechanized Division and Shazli Force. As far as Tal and Yoffe knew, the job ahead was formidable.

As things stood on the morning of Tuesday, June 6, *Zahal* was a long way from winning the war and the Sinai Field Army was a very long way from having suffered a decisive strategic defeat. However, in only twenty-four hours, it turned out that *Zahal* had psychologically defeated the one key player who could hand Israel one of the greatest military victories of the century.

Shortly after noon on June 6, three of Field Marshal Amer's senior staff officers got it through to him that, excepting the loss of the Egyptian Air Force, the events of the first day of the war had more or less coincided with the Kahir Plan and that the bulk of the Sinai Field Army was intact and virtually unmolested. Amer calmed down and moderated his original retreat order with a follow-up plan for the Sinai Field Army to fall back in orderly fashion, fighting as it went, to the western defensive line from Bir Gifgafa southward to Bir el-Thamada.

But by then it was too late; the Sinai Field Army was in a state of chaos from which it could not recover. Amer had sealed the fate of his entire army. By the time the follow-up order had been promulgated to the lowest-ranking Egyptian soldier in Sinai, the *will* of the Sinai Field Army had collapsed and the cohesion of even Egypt's undefeated divisions and brigades had evaporated. Before the afternoon was over, many of the Sinai Field Army's highest ranking commanders had literally abandoned their units, and many mid-ranking officers followed their example. Thus, the bulk of the Sinai Field Army, which might have stemmed the increasingly diluted Israeli tide, collapsed into a rabble of tens of thousands of individuals whose only purpose in life was saving themselves.

Before they quite knew what was happening, the Israeli armored *ugdot* fell forward into the vacuum created by the collapse of the Sinai Field Army. The test for Southern Command went from cracking the Egyptian defenses to racing the fleeing Egyptians to the Mitla Pass. For, according to *Zahal's* bedrock precept covering this very eventuality, "A War of Attrition," the Egyptian collapse heralded Southern Command's solemn duty to destroy as much of the Egyptian Army's fighting capability as it could in order to put off an inevitable next war for as long as possible. What ensued was one of history's most thrilling pursuit campaigns—and one of the briefest and most complete destructions of a large army by a small one in modern military annals.

29

Beginning in the early afternoon of June 6, the Tal and Yoffe *ugdot* jumped off west out of Bir Lahfan with their trusty but exhausted lead brigades still in the lead. Following the opening of the El Arish–Bir Lahfan road, Talik had ordered Shmulik Gonen's 7th Armored Brigade to get some rest, but it turned out that *Ugdah* Tal's second armored brigade, Colonel Men Aviram's, was experiencing ongoing difficulties extricating itself from the sandy sea south of the Jiradi Pass. Only limited quantities of fuel could be transported to Men's tanks and halftracks, so the process of reconstituting its two tank and one armored-infantry battalions at El Arish was going very slowly. In *Ugdah* Yoffe's zone, the Sela Armored Brigade had only gotten a little way along the Abu Agheila–Bir Lahfan road during the night when it had been ordered by General Yoffe to stand fast where it was. The brigade remained a short distance northwest of Abu Agheila throughout the morning and early afternoon of June 6 and was finally ordered to backtrack to Abu Agheila and then sweep the Abu Agheila–Jebel Libni road clear of whatever Egyptian units might be using it in either direction.

It turned out that Jebel Libni was pretty much abandoned by the time the Shadmi Armored Brigade's reconnaissance company approached it at around 1600 on June 6. Several parting shots were fired by a departing Egyptian armored rearguard, and the oncoming tank battalions of the 7th and Shadmi Armored brigades were waylaid here and there by other determined but small Egyptian armored rearguards charged with covering the Sinai Field Army's retreat to Bir Gifgafa. In all, the Egyptian rearguards lost thirty-two tanks and the 7th and Shadmi brigades lost a handful in a series of isolated, time-consuming clashes.

Southern Command's pursuit phase of the war with Egypt—chasing down the retreating Sinai Field Army and destroying it—officially began with a command meeting near Jebel Libni at 1820 on June 6. A helicopter deposited Brigadier General Shaike Gavish beside the *Ugdah* Tal mobile command post, and Shaike stepped right into a meeting with Generals Tal, Yoffe, and Sharon. Sharon himself had arrived by helicopter only a few minutes earlier. Shaike revealed the startling news that the entire Egyptian Sinai Field Army had been ordered to fall back from eastern Sinai, and then a novel plan of action was agreed to in a meeting of the minds that lasted only a few minutes.

The basis of Shaike's brainstorm was the realization that most of the as-yet-untouched components of the Sinai Field Army had a headstart in the mad dash that the Israelis were only about to begin, and that they could thus save themselves simply by beating the Israelis to the Suez Canal and crossing it. The Egyptians correctly assumed that the Israelis had no intention of crossing the canal. If the six armored brigades available to Southern Command simply chased the Egyptians in the classic style of the modern armored pursuit, they would win the war but would end up losing the opportunity to destroy Egypt's war-making potential. So, starting at first light on June 7, fast-moving armored spearheads from the two northern *ugdot* were to race the Egyptians to the passes fronting the Suez Canal. The Israeli armor was to get ahead of as many Egyptian tanks and other vehicles as they could, by any means possible, and establish blocking positions at places the fleeing Egyptians could not bypass. Even if it meant ignoring sitting ducks on the road, the fast-moving spearheads were to get in front of the main body of Egyptians—using the same roads the Egyptians were using at the same time the Egyptians were using them!—and *then* destroy everyone and everything they had passed.

On the Israeli left, *Ugdah* Sharon's one armored brigade would continue southward from Umm Katef to cut off Shazli Force and the 6th Egyptian Mechanized Division by establishing a blocking position at Nakhle. The independent Mendler Armored Brigade, which had spent the past two days putting on a show of force in the vicinity of Kuntilla, was operationally attached to Sharon's command.

Shifting their attention to the main show in the north, the generals decided that *Ugdah* Tal would advance at dawn to unseat the defensive positions that one reinforced brigade of the 3rd Egyptian Infantry Division had established a short distance west of Jebel Libni. *Ugdah* Tal was then to attack due east and overcome another brigade of the 3rd Egyptian Infantry Division at Bir el-Hamma, an auxiliary airfield roughly halfway between Jebel Libni and Bir Gifgafa. Next, *Ugdah* Tal was to advance on Bir Gifgafa to take on whatever forces it found occupying the 4th Egyptian Tank Division's base camp. Once Bir Gifgafa was in its hands, *Ugdah* Tal was to halt and await further orders.

While *Ugdah* Tal was driving west, *Ugdah* Yoffe was to proceed southwest from Jebel Libni to Bir el Hassne, which was in the 3rd Egyptian Infantry Division zone. Next, *Ugdah* Yoffe was to move as rapidly as possible to Bir el-Thamada and then split into two brigade columns. One brigade was to drive west to establish a blocking position at the eastern end of the Gidi Pass and the other was to drive southwest to establish a blocking position at the eastern end of the Mitla Pass.

In keeping with the original plan, the northernmost Sinai route, the El Arish–Kantara coastal highway, was to be probed as far as Romani by Southern Command's independent reconnaissance group, an AMX-13 battalion and a jeep-mounted 106mm recoilless rifle company commanded by Colonel Yisrael Granit.

Shaike also decided to launch the planned airborne assault on Sharm el-Sheikh and subsequent moves to occupy other Egyptian installations in the far south. Accordingly, he alerted the commander of the Sharm el-Sheikh Task Force, Colonel Aharon Davidi, to prepare to execute his strategic mission at dawn.

The final objective of all major Southern Command mobile units was to reach a line from Romani, on the coast, to Nakhle by way of the Mitla and Gidi passes—as quickly as possible, before an armistice was forced upon Israel by an international community that was all of a sudden urgently interested in a "Middle East settlement." There were no Israeli plans at that time to advance all the way to the Suez Canal. That decision was a strategic one, and the government had not yet made it. More important than reaching the canal or this or that line, however, was the *prime* objective of Southern Command's general pursuit—the complete destruction of the Sinai Field Army and thus an end to Egypt's ability to wage a war or even to credibly threaten Israel's sovereignty for years to come.

After Gavish and Sharon left, Talik and Yoffe got together to plan their attacks. Even though the two northern *ugdot* would be following diverging routes out of Jebel Libni, the two generals hoped to coordinate their advances—lest the Egyptians recover some of their lost composure and attempt to mass for an overwhelming counterattack against one *ugdah* or the other. As the two were putting the final touches on their arrangements, the Sela

Armored Brigade's vanguard pulled into Jebel Libni from the direction of Abu Agheila. Yoffe diverted this small tank force a short distance straight down the road branching south toward Bir el-Hassne with orders to prevent the Egyptians from launching a dawn counterattack in case they had second thoughts about relinquishing Jebel Libni.

Egyptian artillery located in the infantry-brigade blocking position out along the Bir el-Hamma road shelled the Israeli tank laagers and resupply points at long range during the night, but the Egyptian gunners were firing blind, and there was virtually no damage inflicted. While all the Israeli tanks, halftracks, and other vehicles were being refueled and rearmed, everyone who could got some sleep. There was no telling when there would be another opportunity.

30

Israeli intelligence had estimated before the war that the Egyptian garrison at Sharm el-Sheikh had been built up to two stoutly emplaced independent infantry battalions supported by artillery and antiaircraft batteries. Further, a number of Egyptian naval vessels, including a destroyer, had reportedly sailed through the Suez Canal to take up patrol stations within supporting range of the Straits of Tiran.

Southern Command planned accordingly. Three Israeli motor torpedo boats out of Eilat had been lurking in the Gulf of Aqaba north of the Straits of Tiran since long before the outbreak of the war, and these were assigned the task of bombarding the Egyptian garrison from the sea and then guarding against an Egyptian naval attack. The bombardment was to commence at 0430, June 7, per Shaike's decision of the previous evening. At 0500, the first lift of Israeli paratroopers was to be dropped by parachute directly on top of the airfield, and then, as many additional Israeli paratroopers as could be accommodated in each succeeding lift were to be flown as quickly as possible into the airhead by transport airplanes and helicopters.

The Sharm el-Sheikh Task Force was commanded by *Zahal's* Chief Paratroop Officer (the first ever appointed), Colonel Aharon Davidi. Davidi had been Arik Sharon's deputy commander before and during the Sinai Campaign and had succeeded Sharon as the 202nd Parachute Brigade commander in 1958. He had attended a senior officers' course in France and subsequently had overseen the organization of *Zahal's* two Reserve parachute brigades. Davidi's Sharm el-Sheikh Task Force consisted mainly of two parachute battalions, one each drawn from Colonel Raful Eitan's 202nd Parachute Brigade and Colonel Dani Matt's 31st Reserve Parachute Brigade.

At 0400, when there was just enough light in the sky, an Israeli reconnaissance plane overflew the Egyptian base whose reestablishment had precipitated so much trouble and so much bloodshed. One or two passes over the airfield and military camps revealed that the Egyptian garrison apparently had evacuated the place. The Israelis would not know for some time that the decision—taken by the garrison commander on his own authority—was less a matter of military necessity than a lack of water. It turned out that the U.N. troops who previously had been in possession of the base had disabled a small desalinization plant when they had departed, and the Egyptian garrison eventually had grown beyond the output of the local spring. As long as there was an army resupply system in Sinai, plenty of water was trucked in, but that came to an abrupt end on Monday, June 5. So, in addition to being ordered to fight to the last man—never a reassuring sign for the men at the receiving end—the Sharm el-Sheikh garrison commander simply could not give his troops enough water to sustain them. During the night of June 6–7, nearly the entire garrison of 1,600 soldiers and a few air force technicians piled aboard their vehicles and made off down the road leading to El Tur, on the Gulf of Suez.

The Israeli reconnaissance pilot reported that Sharm el-Sheikh appeared to have been abandoned. At 0430, after the three Israeli torpedo boats arrived and confirmed the report from their vantage point, one of the torpedo boats crept toward the beach and put a small landing party over the side. Neither the boat nor the handful of excited sailors was fired on. The sailors poked through the deserted defenses for a few minutes without finding a single soul, and then they boldly raised the blue-and-white Israeli national colors above an observation platform. By then, several Egyptian stragglers had appeared in the streets of the distant military camp. The IAF's aerial attack was due to commence shortly, so the Israeli sailors departed and made their way back to their boat to report.

In short order, news of the landing party's findings was flashed to higher headquarters. Colonel Davidi decided to forego an unnecessary combat jump. Though the keyed-up paratroopers in the first lift were openly disappointed, it was certainly Davidi's call. He also canceled the pre-drop shelling by the torpedo boats, and the preliminary air strike.

At 0515, while Israeli fighter-bombers patrolled threateningly overhead, a single IAF Noratlas transport circled over Sharm el-Sheikh airfield once and then set down firmly on the runway. In short order, the paratroopers inside the airplane fanned out to begin a systematic sweep through the airfield buildings. Within minutes, following a radio report, two more Noratlas transports landed and disgorged their passengers, who broadened the ring of control around the runway. These paratroopers ran into a lone platoon of

Egyptian soldiers that somehow had been left behind. The Egyptians put up a brief, meager resistance. Twenty of the defenders were killed and the rest surrendered after setting fire to the base's fuel-storage tanks. In all, eighty prisoners were rounded up while nearby Ras Narani was occupied by sailors from the motor torpedo boats, thus physically ending the blockade of Eilat.

During the afternoon, after Sharm el-Sheikh and its environs had been tightly secured, IAF transport helicopters lifted a detachment of paratroopers due east across the point of the Sinai Peninsula to El Tur, a little oil town on the banks of the Gulf of Suez. There, for all practical purposes, the Israeli troopers blockaded access to the Suez Canal. By dusk, the Israelis had also occupied Ras el-Durba, another oil town on the coast north of El Tur.

31

The various components of the main body of the Sinai Field Army had the choice of four main axes over which they could retreat toward the Suez Canal: the northern El Arish–Kantara highway, the "central" Jebel Libni–Bir Gifgafa–Ismailia road, or the more southerly roads through the Gidi and Mitla passes by way of Bir el-Thamada. By virtue of their starting deployments from Jebel Libni southward, the Egyptians could not use the coastal highway, which, west of El Arish, was inaccessible from the south. But on the morning of Wednesday, June 7, tanks, APCs, and every type of wheeled military vehicle imaginable were streaming eastward along the three other routes as the Tal and Yoffe *ugdot* opened their all-out race to Bir Gifgafa and the passes.

To help the Tal and Yoffe armored spearheads catch up with the fleeing Egyptians—all of whom were well ahead of the Israelis—the IAF launched a classic tactical-air holding action. Through the early morning, IAF jets— mainly Fougas, Ouragans, and Vautours—swept from north to south over the Mediterranean coast and turned east directly into the faces of the oncoming Egyptians. The Israeli jets bombed, rocketed, and strafed Egyptians tanks and other vehicles wherever they could find them, but mainly at points along the roads that could not easily be bypassed. The objective was to slow the traffic by blocking the roads, but not so much that the oncoming Israeli tanks could not later get through. It was a classic but ticklish use of tactical air power, and the IAF pilots achieved notable success. There were simply too many Egyptian vehicles to shoot up or blow up, but sometimes the mere appearance of an Israeli jet brought vehicles to a halt and sent scores or hundreds of Egyptians fleeing headlong into the desert, never to return.

There must have been some sort of crisis of confidence in *Ugdah* Yoffe. The Shadmi Armored Brigade had fought well and bravely through the night of

June 5–6 and then through the day of June 6. It took that long for the slightly stronger Sela Armored Brigade to catch up, what with delays and orders to block certain escape routes. But, after advancing up the road linking Abu Agheila with Jebel Libni, the vanguard of the Sela Armored Brigade had indeed caught up with the rest of *Ugdah* Yoffe late on June 6. It had even advanced to the fore along the Jebel Libni–Bir el-Hassne road preparatory to opening *Ugdah* Yoffe's drive toward the Gidi and Mitla passes to cut off several Egyptian divisions. One would have expected the fresh, intact, and unblooded Sela Armored Brigade to lead the Israeli armored division, but it was the battle-worn Shadmi Armored Brigade that Yoffe ordered to spring ahead beginning at 0800. Later that morning, for some reason, Yoffe relieved Colonel Sela of his command and turned the brigade over to its deputy commander.

Colonel Yiska Shadmi's battalions were refueled, the tanks had full ammunition racks, and the crews were as well rested as could be hoped. But the tank battalions, one of which had gone to war with only twenty-four tanks in service, had suffered both combat losses and equipment failures. The Shadmi Armored Brigade was considered the *Zahal* Reserve's best, but it was not as strong or as fresh as the Sela Armored Brigade. Still, its stalwart tank crews accepted the challenge with pride.

Advancing off the main road, mainly along a lateral track, the Shadmi Armored Brigade vanguard bulled its way toward Bir el-Hassne, shooting up several abandoned Egyptian military camps and a number of straggling vehicles as it went. There was no organized resistance, only encounters with stunned or demoralized Egyptians intent upon getting out of the way or surrendering.

As the Israeli tanks advanced farther from Jebel Libni, the track became increasingly congested. Everyone was heading in the same direction with roughly the same sense of urgency. If the Israelis ran up the back of an Egyptian tank, they destroyed it with gunfire. If they ran into a clot of soft vehicles, many of which were stalled or had been demolished by IAF jets, the Centurions usually just veered off the track and around the trucks, often firing bursts from their machine guns as they went. There was progress, but it was enragingly slow because abandoned Egyptian vehicles were everywhere and the Israeli tanks often had to wait their turn to press through one massive traffic jam after another. Though unmolested, hundreds of Egyptians riding in serviceable vehicles bolted into the desert on foot.

The Shadmi Armored Brigade's lead Centurion battalion—Lieutenant Colonel Fedele's—burst into Bir el-Hassne at about noon, destroying five 3rd Egyptian Infantry Division T-34s inside the base. Minutes later, as Yiska was entering the former Egyptian camp with *Ugdah* Yoffe's two 105mm SP battalions in tow, a lone T-34 charged the brigade commander's command halftrack. The T-34 was blown to bits at the last moment when two of the SPs fired their 105s straight at it. Moments later, the vanguard of Lieutenant Colonel Avraham Bar-Am's small Centurion battalion also arrived in Bir el-Hassne.

The Israeli tanks had undertaken a grueling run of nearly 30 kilometers, and it was best to refuel them. As that dangerous operation began, the Sela Armored Brigade vanguard arrived and assumed responsibility for guarding the camp and making prisoners of the hundreds of Egyptians who were clamoring to find a way out of the war. All that could be spared to guard the prisoners were two squads of armored infantrymen.

General Yoffe was impatient, but the *ugdah* chief of staff, Colonel Bren Adan, was even more so. Bren huffed and fumed for nearly an hour over the Shadmi Armored Brigade's glacial refueling operation. When he could bear no more, he stalked off to confer with Yoffe. The two agreed that the Israelis were losing ground in the race. Bren was to resume the chase with as many of Yiska's tanks as had been refueled. He told Yiska the plan, and Yiska passed the news to Lieutenant Colonel Avraham Bar-Am. At 1300, Bar-Am reported that he had gathered a mixed bag of twenty-eight Centurions from the various companies of his and Fedele's battalions. Good enough, Bren declared, and off they charged, pulling Yiska's command halftrack and Bren's jeep in their wake. The rest of the Shadmi Armored Brigade would follow when it had refueled, and then the Sela Armored Brigade would refuel and follow when it could.

Overseen by Yiska and prodded by Bren, Bar-Am's lead Centurion force raced along the main road and parallel tracks leading south to Bir el-Thamada. Initially, it was feared that the Centurions might be stopped by the thousands of mines the Egyptians had sown along the verges of the roadways, but when a Centurion inadvertently ran over two mines that did not detonate it was discovered that perhaps only one mine in twenty had been armed. Thereafter, the Israelis spent most of their time off the road, running around the Egyptian traffic jams. Several tanks were damaged by mines, but that was not enough to stop the main body from advancing 32 kilometers, all the way to Bir el-Thamada. Along the way, only a few Egyptian tanks were encountered, and only they received any attention. Bren kept insisting that forward progress was all that mattered; Fedele would be along soon, and he would pick up the stranded Centurions. Bar-Am's Centurions destroyed twelve Egyptian tanks along the way, but they also passed fifty-one T-34s, JS-3s, and SU-100s that had been destroyed by IAF warplanes.

Nine of Bar-Am's Centurions reached Bir el-Thamada at 1515. Bren and Yiska arrived moments later, and then three more Centurions joined up. As Bren huffed and fumed, Yiska argued in favor of searching the base for fuel—there had to be some!—topping off fuel tanks, and checking the roughly handled Centurions for critical wear and tear. Bren, whose command radio was telling him what was going on throughout Southern Command, peremptorily ordered Yiska to get Bar-Am on the road to the Mitla Pass, right away, with as many Centurions as there were. Yiska reluctantly agreed, but, by then, only five of the Israeli tanks, a dozen halftracks—including three that were carrying 120mm mortars—and a battery of four 105mm SPs possessed enough fuel to even risk the journey.

At Bren's relentless insistence, the small force of Centurions, halftracks, and SPs advanced out of the Bir el-Thamada camp. Moments later, Israeli armored infantrymen rooting through the camp found some fuel—three jerrycans. Yiska personally sloshed it into the empty tanks of four additional Centurions. As he did, Fedele radioed that he was approaching the north edge of the town. Right away, someone else told Yiska that hundreds of APCs and other Egyptian vehicles were approaching from the east. Yiska ordered Fedele to rake the Egyptians from the flank, and then he dispatched the Centurions he had just refueled to chase after Bar-Am.

Yiska, who was usually easygoing, hectored Bar-Am by radio every few minutes or so, ordering the younger officer to push his shabby little force all the harder. By 1630, Bar-Am and his small company had arrived at the Parker Memorial, 15 kilometers east of the eastern end of the Mitla Pass. By then, four of the Centurions and two or three of the halftracks had run out of fuel and were advancing at the ends of towing bars. Yiska ordered Bar-Am to set up a block there, but Bar-Am averred that the position was too exposed to defend with so small a force. Yiska told him to go find a better solution, and Bar-Am headed west, toward the pass.

An hour later, the Israelis hit a flat, open space within sight of the Mitla Pass. At that moment, a large Egyptian unit was passing through the junction formed by the confluence of the Bir el-Thamada and Nakhle roads—a kilometer to the west of the Israelis and only 2 kilometers east of the mouth of the pass. For reasons that have never been adequately explained—in all of Sinai, just two companies of the 6th Egyptian Mechanized Division were equipped with Centurion tanks—the Egyptian gunners held their fire. Fettered by the towed Centurions, Bar-Am's Israelis advanced gingerly across the open ground, on which they would otherwise have been sitting ducks. Then, with hundreds of Egyptians watching—including tank and antitank gunners—Bar-Am's Centurions, halftracks, and SPs cut at an oblique angle toward the mouth of the pass, labored up a slight rise, and took up more-or-less protected firing positions on a flat-topped hill directly overlooking the roadway. Even as the Israeli Centurions were going into position, three more ran out of fuel, and the two that remained had to go back, hook them up, and tow them behind the meager cover. All the while, scores of Egyptian vehicles, including tanks and assault guns, jostled for space between the road junction and the entrance to the pass.

As the Israeli armored infantrymen and tanks set up a 360-degree perimeter around the 105mm SPs and 120mm mortars, a large mass of Egyptian tanks and other vehicles from the 6th Egyptian Mechanized Division appeared at the road junction from the direction of Nakhle. It was time to block the pass.

The Israeli position was not entirely favorable to the Israeli gunners, and many of the Egyptian tanks were able to run through the Centurion fire and away up the pass. However, just as the effort seemed doomed, a pair of IAF Vautours appeared overhead and, on their own, swept in from west to east to lay bombs and napalm on the receding Egyptian tanks. An ammunition truck that was intermingled with the Egyptian tanks blew up with tremendous force in the confined pass, and a chain-reaction fire blew up yet more vehicles. It was a spectacular display of the effects of air power on ground targets. And the Mitla Pass was all but choked off.

As hundreds of Egyptians merely gawked, a pair of the Israeli Centurions crept down from their rise and *rearranged* some of the twisted, smoldering trucks in such a way as to channelize Egyptian vehicles approaching from the east into the direct fire of the Israeli tank guns. Within the half-hour, just as the sun was setting behind the high hills to the west, twenty T-55s and JS-3s arrived on the scene. The T-55s attacked Bar-Am's position, but all save one were destroyed or disabled.

Shortly, several more of Yiska's Centurions arrived. And then another battery of 105mm SPs reached Bar-Am's position with some fuel drums and other supplies. More armored infantrymen in halftracks also arrived. For the time being, the crisis had passed. No more Israelis got through to the Mitla Pass that night, and several running fights with Egyptian tanks that blundered into Bar-Am's block consumed much of the new fuel supply brought in by the Israeli SPs. Even sitting still, tanks consumed fuel, for the tank engines had to keep idling in order to operate the turrets.

By first light, only four of the Centurions had any fuel in their tanks, and just then twenty-eight T-55s appeared at the road junction to the east. The four Centurions gamely swept toward the T-55 battalion, but just as they were about to be overwhelmed, a pair of IAF Super Mystères streaked in and pasted the T-55s closest to the Centurions. The rest of the Egyptian tanks turned tail on a dime and scattered across the desert. After that, relays of IAF jets held hundreds of Egyptian vehicles at bay and burned scores of them as uncountable Egyptian soldiers took to the desert and hills on foot.

Back at Bir el-Thamada, Yiska prepared a convoy of halftracks chock full of jerrycans of fuel, which he sent forward with a covering force of Centurions. Shortly, General Yoffe dispatched the Sela Armored Brigade to relieve Bar-Am's force at the pass. In all, since leaving Bir el-Thamada, Bar-Am had lost one soldier killed and four wounded. The relief, by one battalion of the Sela Armored Brigade, was completed by 0830, and the Shadmi Armored Brigade was ordered to regroup at an abandoned Egyptian camp 24 kilometers north of the Mitla Pass.

In less than twenty-four hours, *Ugdah* Yoffe had advanced approximately 130 road kilometers from Jebel Libni to the Mitla Pass and had accounted for the direct destruction of scores and perhaps hundreds of 3rd and 6th Egyptian division and Shazli Force tanks and other military vehicles. Counting what it did to slow or stymie other Egyptian vehicles that were abandoned by their drivers and crews or destroyed by roving IAF strike aircraft, *Ugdah* Yoffe might have assisted in the loss of Egypt of many hundreds of tanks, APCs, and soft vehicles. Certainly, hundreds of Egyptian soldiers died at the hands of the Shadmi Armored Brigade during the twenty-four-hour race. However, for all that *Ugdah* Yoffe accomplished on June 7, it had had to spread itself too thin, and so the Gidi Pass remained open and thousands of Egyptians slipped through there with their equipment intact. Nevertheless, the performance of the Shadmi Armored Brigade Centurions was nothing short of epic.

32

The first serious rest the men of the 7th Armored Brigade's two battle-weary tank battalions received in the war was at Jebel Libni on the night of June 6–7. Artillery of the 3rd Egyptian Infantry Division fired on the base from a brigade-size blocking position a short distance to the west, but the rounds landed closer to the Shadmi Armored Brigade's area than to the 7th's. This gave Shmulik Gonen's Patton and Centurion crews a chance to sleep a bit. Meanwhile, working in relays, Shmulik's crews filled their tanks to brimming with fuel and ammunition. And the tanks that needed fixing were put back in the best running order possible under field conditions in a forward combat zone.

Also during the night of June 6–7, the headquarters and two somewhat reduced Patton companies from Colonel Uri Baron's Armored School Tank Battalion arrived at Jebel Libni. Talik held Baron's demi-battalion as a divisional reserve.

At first light, with plenty of tactical air support on station overhead, Talik ordered the 7th Armored Brigade to lead the attack through the Egyptian brigade position west of Jebel Libni and strike for the *ugdah*'s next intermediate objective, Bir el-Hamma. Colonel Men Aviram's untested armored brigade, which had closed up on Jebel Libni the previous evening, also moved up to the line of departure in order to swing into the Egyptian defenses on the south side of the road while the 7th Armored Brigade attacked on the north side.

The previous afternoon, Centurions from the Shadmi Armored Brigade had been stopped cold along what was now *Ugdah* Tal's axis of advance. A number of Egyptian tanks had fought stubbornly and bravely from hull-down positions in a wadi that could not be approached in any way except frontally. Selected to lead the frontal attack after Israeli jets tried to drive off the Egyptian tanks was Major Shamai Kaplan's Centurion company.

The jets hit the wadi, but they could not direct all their bombs, rockets, and cannon shells into the narrow defile. In short order, Shamai's company had to advance. There was still plenty of fight left in these particular Egyptian tank crews, and they were difficult to engage on terms that did not favor themselves. Nonetheless, the Israeli crews were more determined and the Israeli gunners were better marksmen. The advance of Shamai's Centurion company was painstaking, but the rewards were plentiful. In gun duels between single Centurions and single T-34s or SU-100s, the Israelis prevailed. At length, the surviving Egyptians fled. By then, the rest of the Egyptian brigade that had been blocking the Jebel Libni–Bir Gifgafa road had already fled toward Bir el-Hassne, in *Ugdah* Yoffe's zone.

Lieutenant Colonel Gabi Amir's entire Tank Battalion 82 led the way out of Jebel Libni and soon butted up against an Egyptian mechanized battalion whose defensive zone fronted Bir el-Hamma. Fearful of getting bogged down in another protracted gun duel, Gabi attacked straight through the Egyptian line, turned his battalion around, and fired on the Egyptians from their rear.

As the Centurions and a company of Israeli armored infantrymen were reversing to fire in the Egyptian front line, it was discovered that a hill overlooking the Egyptian main line was honeycombed with bunkers and pillboxes. While the main body of Tank Battalion 82 went for the main line, at ground level, one Centurion company and the halftracks charged up the hill. While the tanks blotted out the Egyptian fire, the armored infantrymen hurled grenades and fired their machine guns and personal weapons over the sides of their halftracks, and then they vaulted into the trenches to clear them and adjacent pillboxes and bunkers on foot. The battle for the hill was painstaking and extremely violent. It took the Israelis until just before noon to subdue the last of the brave defenders.

Next up on *Ugdah* Tal's agenda was a way station at Bir Rod Salim, 40 kilometers west of Jebel Libni. The *ugdah*'s mission was to block the escape of the main body of the 4th Egyptian Tank Division, which was known to be conducting an orderly and quite professional withdrawal toward Ismailia by way of its base camp at Bir Gifgafa. The Pattons of Major Chaim's Tank Battalion 77 spearheaded the initial phase of the drive, and the rest of Shmulik's and Men Aviram's armored brigades followed closely. There was a sharp little rearguard action at Bir Rod Salim when a handful of T-55s tried to stall Chaim's Pattons, but the Israeli tanks rolled right over them.

Following a brief pause, the 7th Armored Brigade turned the lead over to Men's brigade. Men placed his Super Sherman battalion in the vanguard and followed with his command group and AMX-13 and armored-infantry battalions. The next stop, hopefully, would be Bir Gigfafa. The 7th Armored Brigade stopped at Bir Rod Salim to refuel and replace expended ammunition; it was to follow Men at a more leisurely pace, mopping up stragglers and rearguards Men's brigade had been ordered to bypass for the sake of speed. The entire *ugdah* was to reform in front of Bir Gifgafa and immediately attack the sprawling base in the hope of catching the main body of the 4th Egyptian Tank Division at home.

The Aviram Armored Brigade's rush toward Bir Gifgafa was as dramatic and frustrating as the Shadmi Armored Brigade's concurrent drive toward Bir el-Thamada via Bir el-Hassne. The road was clogged with panicked and often leaderless Egyptians who preferred running away to fighting. It was a constant battle for space atop the narrow blacktop, and, like Yiska's tanks and halftracks, Men's often had to wait their turn while giant traffic jams unsnarled of their own accord, at their own speed. There were running duels with Egyptian tanks wherever they were encountered, but these were few and far between. Along the way, hundreds of Egyptian soldiers were seen fleeing into the desert on foot, and many of them had discarded their shoes to do so.

The vanguard of Israeli Super Shermans rolled up to the edge of the sprawling Bir Gifgafa encampment at 1530, having made surprisingly good time despite the many handicaps encountered along the way. There were too few of them to enter the main camp, which would have absorbed many times their number, so the crews contented themselves with reconnaissance and clearing excursions along the very edges of the base. When a handful of AMX-13s arrived, Men sent them and several halftracks full of armored infantrymen against a radar station on a hill overlooking the northeast side of the base. This was as much to deny the Egyptians a useful vantage point as to gain one. Meantime, while waiting for the 7th Armored Brigade and the Armor School Battalion to arrive, the main body of the Super Sherman battalion readied itself for the big sweep by advancing in stages toward a vital road junction north of the radar hill and west of the main Bir Gifgafa camp. At the same time, the main body of the AMX-13 battalion (commanded by Lieutenant Colonel "Ze'ev") and an armored-infantry company established a static blocking position just north of the crossroads.

While the Israeli tanks and armored infantrymen were developing their attack on the radar hill through the fire of a company of dug-in T-55s, four MiG-17s that had been launched from a base deep within Egypt streaked onto the scene and opened fire with their 20mm cannon. The brave Egyptian pilots went around several times, strafing the road leading to the radar hill on each pass and causing several Israeli casualties. A flight of four IAF Mystères was vectored to the scene, and they engaged the MiGs in a dogfight. For once, the MiG pilots got the best of the Israelis, and one of the Mystères was shot down before all four MiGs got away. Thereafter, Israeli ground-attack aircraft and fighter-bombers congregated over Bir Gifgafa. While delta-wing Mirage interceptors patrolled overhead, they worked over ground targets with bombs, rockets, and cannon. The radar hill fell after many of the defending T-55s were disabled from the air.

Talik and his staff arrived on the scene at 1700 and set up their mobile command post behind a small hill about 3 kilometers east of the main Egyptian encampment. Just as they did, a huge dust column was spotted moving out of the Wadi Ml'ez, a defile about 10 kilometers south of Bir Gifgafa along the road leading from Bir el-Hassne. At least one brigade of tanks and other vehicles could be seen moving toward the junction with the Jebel Libni–Ismailia road, but it was not clear if they were intent upon retreating toward the Suez Canal or attacking through Lieutenant Colonel Ze'ev's force at the road junction.

Rather than wait and see, Talik ordered Men to launch his Super Shermans into an immediate attack, directly against the exposed Egyptian right flank. If the Egyptians intended to attack Ze'ev's task force, the Super Shermans would blunt the effort. If the Egyptians turned toward the canal, then the Super Shermans had to cut them off before they could get through a defile about 10 kilometers west of Bir Gifgafa, for the defile was undoubtedly held in strength by an Egyptian blocking force.

As Men was issuing his orders to the Super Shermans—Ze'ev's task force was to remain in its blocking position—Shmulik arrived on the scene with Major Chaim's Tank Battalion 77 and Major Shamai Kaplan's Centurion company. Talik ordered Shmulik to leave the Centurions at the *ugdah* command post and advance with Chaim's Pattons straight into the attack to cut through the Egyptian road column at the Wadi Ml'ez, 12 or 13 kilometers south of Ze'ev's position above the crossroads.

It was not as easy for Men and Shmulik to organize the attack as it had been for Talik to order it. During the delay, the head of the Egyptian column turned obliquely to the left, off the Wadi Ml'ez road from Bir el-Thamada, and cut across country to pick up the Ismailia road on the west side of the Bir Gifgafa encampment. The Egyptians were bypassing Ze'ev's block and getting farther away from the Israeli tanks much more quickly than the Israelis had anticipated.

While Chaim's Pattons lit out across country toward the Wadi Ml'ez, Men's Super Shermans opened their attack, but not before many of the Egyptians had rushed beyond range of their guns. As the Super Shermans advanced, a large force of Egyptian tanks moved to protect their column's right flank, and these effectively blunted the Israeli armored onslaught. The Super Shermans were obliged to halt and duel the T-55s and SU-100s, which were manned by cool, competent crews.

Sometime later and far to the Israeli left, Shmulik and Major Chaim's Pattons infiltrated to within several kilometers of the Wadi Ml'ez, but they also were confronted by a large force of T-55s. The Israelis claimed a dozen T-55s and a score of APCs destroyed in a long-range duel, but the Patton attack petered out well short of the wadi.

Soon, while the main body of the Egyptian column steadily drew away from the fight, Men's Super Sherman crews began reporting fuel and ammunition shortages. Talik was left with no choice but to call off the attack. All the Israeli tanks—Shmulik's and Men's—were ordered to halt in place and engage the Egyptians at long range. Then Men's Super Shermans pulled out, one company at a time, to take on fresh fuel and ammunition. Darkness overtook the battle before the Israelis could complete their preparations to restart their attack. Gnashing his teeth to no avail, Talik ordered all his tank units to go into defensive laagers for the night.

Chaim's Pattons began an arduous withdrawal by a circuitous route. Along the way, two of the Pattons ran out of fuel. Befuddled by lack of sleep, Shmulik misconstrued an order from Talik to abandon the Pattons. He remained with them for long hours with the rest of the Patton battalion—until Talik finally made his point clear. The crews were evacuated and the two tanks were left behind, but it was many hours—after 0200—before the main body of Tank Battalion 77 slipped in behind Men's Super Sherman battalion to rearm and refuel. Tank Battalion 77 was therefore in no position to help beat back one of the Egyptian Army's most determined attacks of the war.

* * *

While the Israeli Pattons and Super Shermans went about their business after dark, the Egyptian column, which seemed to have no end, ground up from the south and disappeared to the west. After sunset, a small number of the T-55s that previously had simply shielded the right flank and rear of the passing road column pressed toward the blocking position held by Ze'ev's AMX-13 battalion and one armored-infantry company. Ze'ev's position did not appear to be in any serious danger, but Men, Talik, and, of course, Ze'ev naturally kept their weather eyes on the pushy T-55s while all the Pattons and Super Shermans that could continued to refuel and rearm.

It turned out that the interest of the T-55s in Ze'ev's blocking position was much more serious than the Israelis realized. There were still hundreds of 4th Egyptian Tank Division soldiers trapped in the camps on the west side of the road junction Ze'ev was holding, and the 4th Egyptian Tank Division's extremely competent commander, Major General Sidki el-Ghoul, was interested in opening a route through which they could join the rest of the division on the Ismailia road.

At 0300, June 8, sixty T-55s and an estimated battalion of motorized infantry whose preparations had not been observed by the Israelis launched a direct assault against Ze'ev's position. No one knew there was going to be an all-out attack until shots fired by a pair of AMX-13s set fire to a pair of trucks filled with Egyptian infantrymen that were attempting to sneak around the north side of the roadblock.

Moments later, shots fired by other AMX-13s at several low silhouettes approaching from the south were seen to bounce off the frontal glacis plates of T-55s. This was not a good sign. The 35-ton T-55s were much more heavily armored than the 14.5-ton AMX-13s, and the high-velocity 75mm AMX-13 main guns could not penetrate the T-55s' frontal armor at any but the closest ranges—less than 50 meters.

Ze'ev ordered his lone 120mm mortar to disperse any other soft vehicles that might be approaching the roadblock behind the T-55s, and a pair of 81mm mortars was put to work illuminating the space in front of the crossroads. Just as the 120mm mortar crewmen were breaking out their ready ammunition, a chance shot by a T-55 struck their halftrack. At the same moment, an engineer halftrack filled with explosives was also stuck by another Egyptian 100mm tank round. Exploding mortar ammunition and engineering explosives triggered a terrible run-away chain-reaction that destroyed two AMX-13s and killed twenty Israeli mortar crewmen, engineers, and tankers, and wounded many others.

At that point, while Talik gave Ze'ev the option of withdrawing a kilometer or two to the north, *Ugdah* Tal's two SP artillery battalions fired on the T-55s, blunting their attack. And one of the Super Sherman companies was dispatched to pitch into the flank of the T-55s that were attacking Ze'ev.

Ze'ev ordered his outnumbered and outclassed blocking force to withdraw, but just then one of the AMX-13s lit up one of the leading T-55s at a range of only 40 meters, and that restored Ze'ev's confidence. The order to hold in place was flashed across the battalion tactical net, and an intense battle at extremely close range ensued. When the Super Sherman company arrived on the scene, it destroyed five of the Egyptian first-line tanks before the Egyptians could react to its presence. In the same confusing minute, an Israeli jet buzzed the battlefield and, even though it did not fire, its sudden and unexpected appearance very likely unnerved many of the Egyptian tank crews.

Though the Egyptians vastly outnumbered the Israeli tanks and armored infantrymen holding the crossroads, it was dark and there was confusion. Even though they had initiated a night battle and had infrared sights aboard every one of their T-55s, the Egyptians did not like fighting in the dark. The attack by the Super Shermans and the appearance of the Israeli jet decisively unsettled the T-55 crews, and they withdrew 5 kilometers to the west to regroup. The Super Sherman company, followed by Major Shamai Kaplan's Centurion company, joined Ze'ev's task force at the crossroads, and then all the Israelis waited for the T-55s to return. But the attack was not renewed. A pair of IAF Vautours arrived overhead and illuminated the area around the crossroads with powerful parachute flares. The threat of air attack by these Vautours and relays of others that kept station through the rest of the night held the Egyptians beyond gun range. At first light, all the surviving T-55s and Egyptian motorized infantrymen were gone.

By dawn on Thursday, June 8, the main body of the 4th Egyptian Tank Division had safely traversed the defile west of Bir Gifgafa, winning the race to the Suez Canal. Moreover, the afternoon, evening, and early-morning tank battles initiated by the Egyptians delayed the Israeli refueling and field-repair operations. *Ugdah* Tal was therefore unable to commence its final pursuit at the crack of dawn, as Talik had hoped.

The Israelis held Bir Gifgafa when the shooting died down, so it can be argued that they won their battle with the excellent 4th Egyptian Tank Division. But the main body of the 4th Egyptian Tank Division had been able to escape a potentially fatal trap—right under the noses of an Israeli armored division—and that was also a significant victory.

33

On June 7, *Ugdah* Sharon's Zippori Armored Brigade set out from Umm Katef on a long overland drive to close the southern Sinai route and hopefully trap the 6th Egyptian Mechanized Division and Shazli Force east of Mitla Pass. Delayed by rough ground, a few minor running clashes, and several conflicting orders from on high, Sharon's tanks and armored infantry were unable to catch up with the withdrawing Egyptian brigade that had been holding Nakhle or to get into position to block the Shazli Force's egress from south-central Sinai via Nakhle. At dusk, Sharon finally had to stop in front of Jebel Karim, a lonely battalion position about 30 kilometers northeast of Nakhle.

The Zippori Armored Brigade spent the night on the verges of a minefield fronting Jebel Karim, preparing to launch a lightning dawn assault. All night long, the brigade reconnaissance company reported strange doings inside the Jebel Karim position, but it was only at dawn, June 8, that the Israelis learned how strange.

Sometime previous to *Ugdah* Sharon's arrival, the defenders had withdrawn. The Israelis had not arrived until after sunset on June 7, and they had been fooled by a tiny rearguard into believing the position was held in strength. There was nothing strange about that. The odd thing was the presence of a brigade's worth of *abandoned* Egyptian tanks and other vehicles in and around the Jebel Karim position. There were no Egyptian soldiers save a handful of stragglers, but there were eighteen JS-3s, thirty T-34s, a contingent of SU-100s, and even a company of Egyptian Army Centurions. But no crews.

It later developed that the tanks and other vehicles belonged to the 6th Egyptian Mechanized Division's 125th Mechanized Brigade. They had been abandoned the previous afternoon, after the brigade commander had received orders to withdraw his *troops* through the Mitla Pass. The addled brigadier had therefore abandoned the fighting vehicles at Jebel Karim. Later, he even abandoned his troops and tried to go around the blocked pass on foot. He had been captured and interrogated, and when the pieces of the puzzle were finally laid out, the Israelis were no longer mystified. But they remained incredulous.

Also at dawn on June 8, the Mendler Armored Brigade attacked into Kuntilla following an Israeli air strike. It appeared that the border post had been abandoned during the night, so the brigade was ordered to proceed toward Themed to drive out its garrison. Meantime, the Zippori Armored Brigade left Jebel Karim to cut the southern Sinai road at Nakhle. It was hoped that the Mendler Armored Brigade would be able to drive the main bodies of the 6th Egyptian Mechanized Division and the Shazli Force into the arms of the waiting Zippori Armored Brigade.

But it was not to be. The entire Shazli Force had slipped through Nakhle during the night, while *Ugdah* Sharon was waiting in front of Jebel Karim, and at least one mechanized brigade of the 6th Egyptian Mechanized Division had also withdrawn past Nakhle. However, an Egyptian mechanized brigade and detachments and battalions amounting to yet another brigade were still on the road between Kuntilla and Nakhle, between Mendler and Zippori. It was still possible to crush them in an Israeli nutcracker. And that is what happened.

At about 1030, the disorganized and demoralized rear elements of the 6th Egyptian Mechanized Division ran headlong into a blocking position established across the road at Nakhle only minutes earlier by Colonel Motke Zippori's Super Sherman battalion. As the Egyptians recoiled from this shock, Motke's Centurion battalion drove into their flank from the north.

Just ahead of the advancing Centurions, Israeli jets delivered one final strike that really caused the Egyptian tank force to come unglued. The majority of the Egyptian tanks raced ahead of the softer vehicles they had been protecting, but it is unclear if they intended to disperse the hull-down Israeli Super Shermans or if they were merely trying to save themselves by driving through the Israelis. It did not matter; the Israeli gunners picked them off. At the same time, Motke's armored-infantry battalion attacked the soft Egyptian vehicles, and machine gunners and riflemen aboard the Israeli halftracks shot up everything and everyone they could reach with their weapons. In short order, hundreds and hundreds of shoeless Egyptian soldiers were running in panic deep into the Sinai wasteland.

The Mendler Armored Brigade fought through a stubborn rearguard of

T-34s at Themed by 1400 with the help of IAF ground-attack aircraft and then it tried desperately to catch up with the rear of a much larger Egyptian force. But the Egyptians were racing flat out on a good road, and they could only be reached by IAF jets, which destroyed many vehicles and killed many soldiers. Mendler's tanks were still far to the rear when the Egyptians ran into the Zippori Armored Brigade at Nakhle.

It took from 1430 until after 1700 for the Zippori Armored Brigade to mop up the last pockets of resistance in front of Nakhle, and thereafter the Israelis counted over sixty abandoned, destroyed, or disabled Egyptian tanks, plus an estimated 400 assault guns, artillery tanks, APCs, trucks, and other vehicles on the road and in the sand fronting the Nakhle block and all the way on back to Themed, 50 kilometers to the east. Dozens of modern artillery pieces and several hundred undamaged or repairable vehicles were captured. Many of these, along with the 125th Egyptian Mechanized Brigade's abandoned Centurions, eventually passed into the *Zahal* inventory.

Late in the afternoon, after refueling and rearming, Motke's Centurion battalion raced northwest to assume control of the eastern end of the Mitla Pass from *Ugdah* Yoffe. Motke's Super Sherman and armored-infantry battalions were left to mop up along the road. And the Mendler Armored Brigade was ordered to northern Israel to take part in an attack against Syria.

Until the night of June 7–8, Defense Minister Moshe Dayan had been doing everything in his power to *prevent* Southern Command from reaching the banks of the Suez Canal. Certainly there were Israeli units that were capable of reaching the canal that night, but the far-thinking Israeli defense minister was convinced that a defensive line running from Romani, on the Mediterranean coast, through the Mitla and Gidi passes, and angling on down to the Gulf of Suez around El Tur would be easier to defend, if need be, than a line along the sea-level canal.

Moreover, it was Dayan's conviction that the appearance of Israelis on the canal would trigger a ceasefire imposed by the United Nations and backed by direct threats from the Soviet Union. Dayan did not desire a ceasefire— not one bit! Southern Command was doing a splendid job destroying the Egyptian Army, and, faithful to the precept, "A War of Attrition," Dayan did not desire the destruction to end for another day or two.

What Dayan could almost have counted on, however, was that his subordinates would not see the situation the same way. It was almost assured from the start of the Sinai pursuit phase that Israel's "wild young stallions" were going to decide on their own to strike for the symbolic and, to most, obvious final target, the Suez Canal. When this indeed occurred on June 8, Dayan did not raise an objection, and the old soldier in him—if not the canny world-class politician—no doubt reveled in the accomplishment.

The first Israeli force to head for the Suez Canal in earnest was Granit Force, the light force composed of one AMX-13 battalion and one reconnaissance jeep company. After driving along the coast highway all the way from El Arish without encountering any opposition on June 7, Colonel Yisrael Granit had been forced by higher authority to halt at Romani, 40 kilometers from Kantara and the canal. However, under orders apparently originating from or through Talik, Granit jumped off at dawn and once again sailed on up the isolated highway. Only a few hours to Granit's rear, and coming on fast all the way from Khan Yunis, were Colonel Raful Eitan, a battalion of the 202nd Parachute Brigade mounted in halftracks, and a company of Patton tanks from the 7th Armored Brigade's Tank Battalion 77.

The first opposition encountered by Granit Force along the coastal highway was at a narrow causeway across a salt-water marsh. The blocking force was composed of a small independent Egyptian commando battalion supported by two companies of T-55 tanks. The fight began when the T-55s opened fire on the by-then incautious Israelis from hull-down positions astride the causeway. Immediately, the Israeli AMX-13s deployed off the roadway and traded shots at long range with the T-55s. At this point, several Egyptian MiGs unexpectedly pounced on the Israelis, but a larger force of IAF jets came to the rescue and drove away the brave survivors of a defeated air force. Under air cover, Granit's recoilless-rifle jeeps veered off the south side of the highway and undertook a cautious and circuitous advance across soft, marshy ground toward the flanks of the Egyptian position. Once in position, the 106mm recoilless-rifle gunners in the jeeps fired antitank rounds at the T-55s. When the 35-ton T-55s tried to maneuver to counter the jeeps, several of them bogged down in the salt-water marsh and had to be abandoned. While the T-55s were busy with the Israeli jeeps, a number of the Israeli AMX-13s eased in around the north side of the Egyptian position. The Egyptians eventually pulled back in fear of succumbing to the developing pincers attack. By then, several of the Israeli jeeps had become mired in the marsh, and it took until 1000 to retrieve them and resume the advance.

As Granit Force came within only 20 kilometers of Kantara, it ran into another strong Egyptian blocking position. At that juncture, Raful arrived with one paratroop battalion mounted in halftracks and the company of Patton tanks. Since Raful was senior to Colonel Granit, he assumed command of the combined force. Without pausing to do more than learn about the Egyptian dispositions from Granit, Raful ordered the Patton company to attack straight up the middle.

The Egyptians were well led. They allowed the Pattons to drive straight through their position, but they blocked the road again and fired up the rear of the Israeli tanks with antitank missiles. Though several of the Pattons were struck by the missiles, none was disabled. The recoilless-rifle jeeps, which tried to follow the Pattons through the Egyptian block, were turned back by intense fire and a number of drivers and gunners were wounded. Next, while the Pattons tried to suppress the Egyptian fire from west of the block, the AMX-13s tried to outflank the block from the east by hooking into the powdery sand to the south. Several of the AMX-13s became stuck in the sand, and the remainder had to form defensive positions to protect the mired crews as they attempted to dig out. The only good news was that a substantial force of IAF fighter-bombers was on the way.

As Israeli jets went into action against the Egyptian blocking position at 1230, Raful attacked straight up the road with the last combat force at his command, the paratroop battalion. Almost before the two sides clashed, Raful himself was shot in the face, and he had to be evacuated by helicopter. Though Colonel Granit instantly resumed command, the paratroopers were shocked by the loss of their "untouchable" leader, and their attack faltered. Pitiless heavy air strikes fell on the Egyptians, but it was 1500 before another ground attack could be launched by the paratroopers. By then, most of the Egyptian tanks and APCs were smoldering wrecks, and many of the crewmen and other soldiers were dead or wounded—victims of the IAF.

Two more hours passed before the last of the foundered AMX-13s was dug out of loose sand south of the blocking position. There were ammunition and fuel shortages throughout the force, but higher headquarters were pressing Granit for results. He ordered his entire force to advance at top speed and, only an hour later, at around 1800, the Granit Force vanguard was a mere 7 kilometers from the outskirts of Kantara. At that point, without warning, a handful of T-55s struck paratroop-laden halftracks from the flank. After a brief moment of indecision, the halftracks counterattacked the powerful tanks. This stunning development caused the T-55s to falter. In that brief moment, the Israeli AMX-13s, Pattons, and recoilless-rifle jeeps rallied to cries for help and attacked the T-55s from their flanks. It took an hour to subdue the Egyptians, but then Granit Force resumed the race into Kantara and on to the banks of the Suez Canal, where it arrived at 2000. Granit Force was the first Israeli unit to reach the waterway.

Under orders from Southern Command, Colonel Granit left two paratroop companies and all the Pattons to scour deserted Kantara while he proceeded south along the canal at top speed with the remainder of his mobile strike force. His objective was the El Firdan Bridge, a railway span that swung on a pivot to allow ships to pass. Egyptian tanks and other vehicles had been using the bridge all day to cross the waterway. There was a powerful blocking force standing between Kantara and the bridge, so the much lighter Israeli force had to pull up in the dark.

After a tense night of watching many Egyptian tanks and other vehicles escape across the El Firdan Bridge, Colonel Granit called in a powerful dawn air strike and mounted an immediate ground attack in its wake. The Egyptian block that had caused Granit to halt during the night had been intentionally thinned out, and the remaining defenders collapsed as Granit's AMX-13s arrowed through on the way to the bridge. IAF fighter-bombers all but cleared a path for the AMX-13s, which, along with the paratroop company, took control of the eastern approach lanes. A short time later, Egyptian artillery opened up from the west bank of the canal, and in due course antiaircraft and antitank guns were also put into operation from across the waterway. The Israelis merely hunkered down and called in air support.

Though the flower of the Sinai Field Army—indeed, of the entire Egyptian Army—was in full retreat or lay in ruins from one end of Sinai to the other, there was still some fight left in Egypt's best and most professional tank force. On the morning of June 8, as *Ugdah* Tal stirred around Bir Gifgafa, 4th Egyptian Tank Division T-55s were establishing a formidable blocking position astride the last barrier along the central Sinai road.

After sun-up, the main bodies of the 7th and Amiram Armored brigades completed refueling operations that had been interrupted by the attack on Lieutenant Colonel Ze'ev's roadblock north and west of the Bir Gifgafa camps. Meanwhile, Ze'ev's AMX-13s and Major Shamai Kaplan's Centurion company were sent on a short leash to find out if the Egyptian T-55s were still in the area. As far as Ze'ev and Shamai could learn they were not, but as soon as they reported, Shamai severed the leash he was on and led his company into the hilly country west of Bir Gifgafa. The broken terrain cut off radio communications with the rear, and neither Shamai nor any of his tankers could be recalled by radio.

Shamai Kaplan was a man possessed. In a small army that tended to gossip endlessly about past infractions and humiliations, there was still whispering about his poor showing as a company commander during the first Tel Nukheila battle, in November 1964. Since then, Shamai had more than proven his value to the Armor Corps as an instructor, but the cloud yet remained over him. On the first day of the war, he had led a picture-perfect sweep through the Rafah North defensive zone, more than making up for his poor gunnery and imperfect knowledge of the Centurion tank in late 1964, and he had been painfully wounded in both hands doing so. On the second day, when the Tank Battalion 82 deputy commander had been killed, Shamai became the battalion's senior surviving major and had been offered the staff job. He had refused in order to remain at the head of his company. Shamai's wife was due to give birth within a day or so, and everyone wanted Shamai to be safe, to celebrate the birth of his new child. But Shamai had different desires. He wanted to expunge the blot on his record, and being the first Israeli to reach the Suez Canal would do just that, and more.

The eight Centurions that were left in Shamai's company ground steadily up the grade toward the Ismailia Pass. As the Israelis neared the crest, Shamai told his tank commanders that the whole company was to engage any blocking forces the retreating Egyptians might have set out. Minutes later, with the crest in sight, Shamai repeated the order.

As the Israeli tanks closed to within 100 meters of the crest, the first three cautiously spread out to take up the whole width of the road. They were in spear-point formation, with Shamai's tank ahead in the center. A moment later, Shamai, who was standing tall in his commander's cupola, called out the position of several T-55s he could see hunkered down between sand dunes on either side of the roadway.

The three lead Centurions lurched ahead and gained speed. Their guns barked as the gunners found the targets. Three T-55s were set alight without ever having fired a shot.

The Centurion commanders did not lose any time looking over the burning T-55s. With Shamai in the lead, they raced ahead.

Suddenly, one of the Centurion commanders radioed Shamai to say that his clutch had gone out, that the tank was undriveable. Shamai told him to drop out while he and the others searched ahead to see if there were any more Egyptians. Moments later, Shamai yelled over the radio to no one in particular, "We will be the first to the canal."

At that very moment, a 100mm antitank round fired by a T-55 that was in a hull-down position behind a dune, dead ahead and just off the road, struck the turret of the company commander's Centurion. The Egyptian round did not penetrate the turret, but a spray of shrapnel destroyed the .50-caliber cupola machine gun and killed Major Shamai Kaplan where he stood—killed him instantly. A second Egyptian gunner hit the third Centurion in line, killing the driver and causing the tank to run away from its startled crew.

Shamai's gunner took command and ordered everyone to withdraw behind the nearest dunes to the rear. The crew of the runaway bailed out of the turret while the tank, with the dead driver aboard, ran over a steep embankment. In short order, however, the Israelis spotted a half-dozen T-55s at ranges between 400 and 1,300 meters, and they advanced to covered firing positions to trade shots.

It was only when the company headquarters halftrack returned to Bir Gifgafa with Shamai Kaplan's body that Colonel Shmulik Gonen learned that Shamai's company was gone and that the Egyptians were holding the Ismailia Pass in strength. Shmulik reported the news to Talik, and the *ugdah* commander ordered Shmulik to launch an immediate attack with both of his tank battalions to clear the pass. As far as Talik knew at that moment, Bir Gifgafa was the end of the line for his *ugdah*; at last report, Defense Minister Dayan was saying that he had no intention of closing on the Suez Canal. But Talik felt compelled to rescue the rest of Shamai's company from what appeared to be a battle against overwhelming odds.

By the time all the remaining tanks of the 7th Armored Brigade reached Shamai's company, the six remaining Centurions, including Shamai's, had already fought through a position held by a company of ten T-55s. All the Egyptians tanks had been destroyed or disabled, but many others lay ahead, in nearly perfect defensive array. The lead Centurion company was stymied. Shmulik's arrival with the rest Tank Battalion 82 and all of Tank Battalion 77 was none too soon.

The road across the top of the Ismailia Pass was bounded on both sides by a sea of low sand dunes that appeared as waves as far as the eye could see. Each dune ran more or less at right angles to the road, which cut through them, and each dune was just high enough to protect the top of a T-55's turret. The Egyptians had cannily placed their T-55s between the dunes, in such a way so their long 100mm guns could bear to the east without exposing more of the tank than the front of the turret and the frontal glacis plate. Against less-well-trained gunners than those of the 7th Armored Brigade, it would have been a perfect, hermetic blocking position, although it seemed to lack eyes and ears in the form of supporting infantry.

While fresh Israeli gunners occupied the Egyptians for several minutes, Shmulik peered at the Egyptian defenses and formulated his plan. Borrowing from Shamai's initial, instinctive tactic, Shmulik ordered all the Centurions to advance in waves, directly up the road, three abreast. There was no way the Israeli tanks could reach the T-55s by merely sniping at them; a frontal attack was all there was to it. Next, Shmulik ordered Major Chaim to divide his slightly lighter (46-ton) Pattons into two groups and send them through the undulating sand sea that stretched away north and south of the roadway. While the Egyptians were focused on the Centurions, the Pattons would knock them out from the rear.

Shmulik's plan worked. Unfortunately, a reinforced T-55 battalion of the 4th Egyptian Tank Division was deployed along the Ismailia Pass to a depth exceeding 7 kilometers. As soon as Talik could arrange to get continuous on-call air support over the pass, the 7th Armored Brigade began making steady if painstaking progress, but it could not have done so without the bombs, rockets, napalm, and 30mm cannon fire of the Israeli jets. As it was, for the loss of only two more Israeli tanks, the 7th Armored Brigade destroyed a total of forty T-55s in a relentless six-hour battle. Only unsurpassingly accurate shooting by the tank gunners and pinpoint aerial attacks saw the 7th Armored Brigade through this most formidable of natural defensive barriers.

During that time, however, the rest of the 4th Egyptian Tank Division, and untold other Egyptian formations, slowly crossed the Suez Canal to Ismailia. Scores of IAF jets flew continuously over the canal, attacking everything in sight through a shockingly deep belt of antiaircraft fire. During the course of its relentless daylight attacks over the canal, the IAF lost three Ouragans and two Mystères to the intense and accurate ground fire.

Toward evening, the Egyptian rearguard atop the Ismailia Pass received its final warning that the canal crossings might be closed during the night by Israeli armor advancing toward Kantara along the coastal highway. With that, the T-55s that still lay ahead of the slowly grinding 7th Armored Brigade bolted from their protected positions between the dunes and were fried—literally fried—by napalm from circling IAF birds of prey.

Once free of resistance, the 7th Armored Brigade's two otherwise unfettered tank battalions were prevented from quickly following through all the way to the Suez Canal by the twisted wreckage of the Egyptian tanks destroyed by the IAF. Each T-55 that blocked the roadway had to be pushed aside by Centurions and Pattons as the rest of the Israeli tank column waited and Shmulik huffed and fumed. However, there was no opposition all the way to within 3 kilometers of the canal crossing opposite Ismailia, and then only four T-55s and a company of infantry stood in the way. The Israeli tanks overran this last roadblock with impatient indifference and surged ahead to arrive on the east bank of the canal at 0030 on Friday, June 9. On the far bank, Egyptians manning the crossing signaled with torches, apparently to let the newly arrived tanks know that the pontoon bridge at that point was still intact. If there was any impulse among the Israelis to cross the pontoon bridge, it was throttled from on high. The east bank of the canal was absolutely as far as *Zahal* was permitted to go.

At 0900 on Friday, June 9, a small force of tanks from *Ugdah* Tal's zone opposite Ismailia advanced north along the canal and linked up with Granit Force at the El Firdan Bridge. In *Ugdah* Tal's zone, then, a solid line along the Suez Canal from Ismailia to Kantara was in Israeli hands.

Ugdah Yoffe's Shadmi Armored Brigade was supposed to have gotten June 8 off. After being relieved at the Mitla Pass at 0830 by a battalion of the Sela Armored Brigade, Lieutenant Colonel Avraham Bar-Am's task force was to roll north to Bir Adama to rejoin Yiska Shadmi and the rest of his triumphant but weary brigade. There, the troops were to rest.

Earlier, Brigadier General Avraham Yoffe had been ordered by Shaike to form three armored task forces and dispatch them to occupy three key points along the Suez Canal. Yoffe was determined to give Yiska and his troops the day off, but, for reasons never fully explained, the as-yet unblooded rear Centurion battalion of the Sela Armored Brigade was simply unable to comply immediately with the *ugdah* commander's order. At 0600, in a state of complete frustration, Yoffe radioed Yiska and apologetically ordered him to drive to the canal. Yoffe's only stipulation was that Bar-Am and the crews that had been with him at the Mitla Pass be excused from the operation. Yoffe told Yiska to strike through the Gidi Pass to the Great Bitter Lake.

After much prodding from Yoffe, the Sela Armored Brigade Centurion battalion that had assumed control of the eastern end of the Mitla Pass left one company at Bar-Am's former position and pushed westward through the pass. The road was blocked almost every step of the way by charred Egyptian tanks and other vehicles, and there were even a few skirmishes with functioning Egyptian tanks whose crews still had some fight left in them. Progress was tedious along this axis, but the main body of this Centurion battalion eventually debouched at a spot overlooking the man-made portion of the canal between the Great Bitter Lake and the Gulf of Suez. There, the battalion developed a blocking position as proof against a feared Egyptian counterattack. Late that night, the Centurion battalion of *Ugdah* Sharon's Zippori Armored Brigade arrived at the eastern end of the Mitla Pass and set in there.

The Sela Armored Brigade's second Centurion battalion got a late start along an undeveloped camel track that ran from the mouth of the Mitla Pass southwest toward Ras Sudar, on the Gulf of Suez. It took until 1230 for it to get to the outskirts of Ras Sudar to link up with a paratroop company from the Sharm el-Sheikh Task Force that had landed nearby at dawn from helicopters. The tanks and paratroopers immediately attacked Ras Sudar, but it took several hours for them to overcome a determined stand by the Egyptian garrison. Approximately 100 Egyptians were captured and an unknown number escaped.

After fighting its way with the aid of air support through an unexpected Egyptian rearguard composed of about thirty T-55 tanks, the Shadmi Armored Brigade's ad hoc tank and armored-infantry task force reached the eastern end of the Gidi Pass at about noon. There, they cut the heavy flow of Egyptian traffic into the only escape route still left in the hands of the withering Sinai Field Army. The Egyptians on the scene were a disorganized rabble, and they barely resisted. Yiska established as powerful a defensive position as he could manage and then advanced westward into the pass with sixteen Centurions and a detachment of armored infantrymen. The Egyptian Air Force's last reserve attacked Yiska midway through the pass, but IAF interceptors chased the Egyptians away. From then on, Yiska had an aerial umbrella overhead at all times, and IAF jets worked ahead to destroy Egyptian tanks that might pose a threat or cause a delay. Withal, it was nearly dusk before Yiska's Centurions debouched from the Gidi Pass at Chalufa, which stood at the southern end of the Great Bitter Lake.

At 1900, when news reached General Yoffe that a ceasefire was about to be imposed, he ordered every tank in his *ugdah* that could still run to be standing on the canal by midnight. As a result, when the fighting finally ended, *Ugdah* Yoffe held all the important features between Chalufa, on the Great Bitter Lake, and Ras Sudar, on the Gulf of Suez. After the 7th Armored

Brigade reached the canal at 0030, June 9, *Zahal* controlled the entire east bank of the Suez Canal.

Of the estimated 1,000 tanks and assault guns the Egyptians had deployed in Sinai and Gaza by June 4, 1967, only about 100 escaped back across the Suez Canal. The Israelis captured over 300 intact and were eventually able to restore scores of others. *Zahal* admitted to the loss of only sixty-one of its tanks *permanently* destroyed. However, it is certain that several hundred Southern Command tanks suffered battle damage or were at least temporarily disabled during the course of the war. The Israelis also captured over 400 field guns and fifty intact or repairable JS-3 artillery tanks, and they captured over 10,000 miscellaneous military vehicles, many of which were in running order. As much of this as *Zahal* desired or needed, it kept.

According to President Nasser's own admission, over 5,000 Egyptian and Palestinian soldiers died in Gaza and Sinai, but other estimates put the number as high as 10,000 killed. The Israelis and Egyptians agree that approximately 5,000 Egyptian soldiers and 500 officers were taken prisoner. No one knows how many Egyptians succumbed to heat and thirst as they fled across the desert, but, here again, the Egyptians estimated that 5,000 of their men had gone missing.

Israel lost 383 of her sons killed in Sinai and Gaza, and nearly 1,000 wounded. Only three Israelis were captured by the Egyptians—all pilots shot down over Egypt.

The Sinai Campaign of 1967 was as complete a victory as any modern army has ever achieved. In it, Israel attained all of her strategic objectives, and *Zahal*—little Israel's little Third World army—forever changed the complexion of maneuver warfare. In years and wars to come, some of the best thinkers in the other world-class armies often stopped and pondered, "I wonder how the Israelis would do it."

Part V

Jerusalem

34

For Brigadier General Uzi Narkiss, the Israeli GOC, Central Command, the start of the war with Egypt on the morning of June 5, 1967, was one more exercise in frustration. Narkiss was one of Israel's leading heroes of the brave but futile fighting in 1948 to win and then retain control of the Old City of Jerusalem, but he had nothing better to do that morning than sit and watch and wait. If Jordan's young King Hussein did nothing more than threaten Israel in order to preserve his throne and his life, then Narkiss's Central Command had no role in the war. On the other hand, if the young ruler sent his highly rated army into battle against Israel, Narkiss had a dream and a hope of winning control of Old Jerusalem for the Jewish people. But, alas, he had few resources for doing the job.

For all the desire among Israelis to seize the holy Old City from the Jordanians and Palestinians who held it, the reality was that Jordan was seen as being little or no threat to Israel, and Central Command was assigned only a token force to prevent the Royal Jordanian Army from crossing the narrow coastal plain to the sea. At the outset of the massive strike against Egypt, Central Command consisted of the out-sized (eight-battalion) 16th "Jerusalem" Reserve Infantry Brigade, which was deployed in and around the Jewish western half of Jerusalem; an infantry brigade in the area opposite Latrun, a bastion overlooking the old Tel Aviv–Jerusalem highway; and an infantry brigade opposite Tulkarm and Kalkiliya, which were northwest of Jerusalem and garrisoned by Jordanian troops who, it was feared, might be sent to cut Israel in half at its narrowest point. Central Command's job was to watch and wait and see what the Jordanian monarch did to make good on his pledge to support Egypt's war with Israel.

It is unclear what King Hussein intended to do in the event of war. It is not likely that he thought the Israelis might start the war, and thus it is possible that Hussein never thought there would be a war. It is likely that the Jordanian monarch believed that President Nasser's intimidation tactics alone would render the Israelis malleable to Arab demands. And, if so, then Hussein's May 30 journey of obeisance to Cairo would be all that was needed to lift the pressure from the monarch's shoulders.

Still, it paid to be prepared. And it certainly paid for a Jordanian monarch to *look* prepared to go to war with Israel at a moment's notice.

To look the part he had acquired for himself in the May and June 1967 Middle East melodrama, Hussein moved the bulk of his little army into proximity with Israel's and allowed two Egyptian commando battalions and an Iraqi motorized-infantry brigade to settle into his vulnerable kingdom. The Iraqis took up a reserve position east of the Jordan River to await three more brigades of their countrymen, and the Egyptians moved into the fortress at Latrun, at the very edge of Jordan's border with Israel.

The Royal Jordanian Army itself consisted of 56,000 soldiers formed into nine infantry brigades, two armored brigades, and two independent tank battalions. All but two of the Jordanian brigades were deployed by June 4 on the West Bank, the Arab area west of the Jordan River that the Kingdom of Jordan had acquired from the Jewish and Arab Palestinians in 1948.

The focus of the bulk of the Jordanian deployments was Jerusalem, which would be the focus of all the attention the Israelis were expected to pay to the West Bank if there was a war. The orientation of most of the Jordanian units on the West Bank was defensive. However, if there was one area in which the king definitely desired to open an offensive, it was in Jerusalem. On June 2, he personally ordered an infantry battalion based northwest of Jerusalem to bolster the infantry brigade that regularly garrisoned the holy city, and he conducted a personal inspection of East Jerusalem on June 3. At that time, Hussein issued specific instructions to at least two senior officers that seem to belie his true intentions: He ordered the commander of the reinforced brigade on garrison duty in Jerusalem to prepare to storm Israeli West Jerusalem. It also appears that the Jordanian brigade at Latrun, west of Jerusalem, was ordered to pinch off the Jerusalem Corridor, which was West Jerusalem's only link with the rest of Israel. It is doubtful that Hussein intended to attempt to cut Israel in half with a drive to the sea, but it is almost a certainty that he intended to seize West Jerusalem and close the Jerusalem Corridor.

In the northern two-thirds of the West Bank, which the peoples of the Bible had named Samaria, the El Yarmouk Infantry Brigade was deployed in the northeast, just south of the Israeli town of Beit Shean. To the west of the El Yarmouk Brigade, in a wide area around the far-northern city of Jenin, the Khalid Ibn el-Walid Infantry Brigade was deployed to cover Samaria's northern shoulder. Counterclockwise from Jenin was the Princess Alia Infantry Brigade, which screened the towns of Tulkarm and Kalkiliya. Near the city of Nablus was the 12th Independent Tank Battalion. The El Hashimi Infantry Brigade, bolstered by two Egyptian commando battalions, was set to screen Jerusalem from Latrun northward to a point opposite the Israeli town of Petah Tikva. The complete King Talal Infantry Brigade and a battalion of the Imam Ali Infantry Brigade were in and around the Arab portion of Jerusalem. The remainder of the Imam Ali Infantry Brigade was holding the high ground along the northern side of the Jerusalem Corridor. In the southern one-third of the West Bank—Judea—the Hittin Infantry Brigade was scattered in several garrisons along the crest of the long central ridgeline from around Bethlehem through the city of Hebron to the border area south of Samua. The 10th Independent Tank Battalion was based around Hebron. The Jordanian West Bank reserve was the Royal Jordanian Army's two armored brigades. The 40th Armored Brigade, which was based west of the Damiya Bridge, was responsible for covering all of Samaria, and the 60th Armored Brigade, which was based along the road between Jericho and the Dead Sea, was responsible for covering Judea. The bulk of two Jordanian infantry brigades plus one Iraqi motorized-infantry brigade were east of the Jordan River. Jordan's Qadisiyeh Infantry Brigade was deployed defensively along the river opposite the Israeli town of Beit Shean only because an Israeli infantry brigade from the *Zahal* GHQ Reserve had been deployed west of the river just south of Beit Shean. The Iraqi 8th Motorized-Infantry Brigade was based in an area east of the Allenby Bridge, and the last of Jordan's nine infantry brigades was deployed around Amman.

All the Arab forces arrayed in Jordan—Jordanian, Iraqi, and Egyptian—were under the command of General Abdul Moneim Riadh, an Egyptian who had been appointed by President Nasser to oversee the newly created "United Arab Command." Riadh had arrived in Amman on June 1. Major General Mohammed Ahmed Salim, King Hussein's uncle, was commander of the Royal Jordanian Army's West Bank Force.

The Royal Jordanian Army was a kind of showpiece. The lineal descendent of the British Army's crack Arab Legion, it had been the creation of Lieutenant General Sir John Bagot Glubb, who had been its commander in chief until he had been driven from Jordan by nationalistic Jordanian officers in 1956. It was still a good and quite efficient army, but its primary function was to serve as a palace guard. Young Hussein was the grandson of Jordan's first king, Abdullah, a man who had gone to war with the Jews in 1948, had secretly signed a peace treaty with Israel in 1950, and had been murdered on the steps of Jerusalem's al-Aqsa mosque by fellow Arabs in July 1951. From Hussein's perspective, the Arab world was filled with enemies, and the maintenance of a crack *loyal* army was paramount.

Virtually the entire Royal Jordanian Army was composed of Bedouin volunteers from Jordan itself or Bedouin mercenaries recruited from clans in Syria, Iraq, and Saudi Arabia. These men had family ties with the Hashemite dynasty and were fiercely loyal to it. Very few Palestinians served in the Regular army, and they were rarely recruited outside the technical services. There had been a rather strong Palestinian National Guard of 10,000 nominally part-time West Bank soldiers before 1965, but the king had become skittish over its tendency to back demands for Palestinian rights in his Bedouin kingdom, so the force had been disbanded. There had been some talk, along the Palestinian rights issue, of conscripting Palestinians into the Jordanian Army, but little or no action had yet been taken in that direction. In point of fact, the large portion of the Jordanian Army that had been permanently based in the West Bank prior to May 1967 constituted an army of occupation in a territory that before 1948 was to have been the real heart of an Arab nation called Palestine.

The Jordanian Army was undergoing a major upgrade when it was called out to deploy in the West Bank during the first days of June 1967. The two armored brigades had recently been reequipped with nearly 270 fairly modern battle tanks—a mix of diesel-powered British Centurions armed with 20-pounder (83.4mm) cannon and gasoline-powered American M-47 Pattons armed with 90mm cannon. Also, the United States had provided about 250 modern M-113 APCs, which were far superior to *Zahal's* twenty-five-year-old M-3 halftracks. The Jordanian infantry was armed mainly with British .303-caliber bolt-action rifles of World War II vintage. Several artillery battalions had just been reequipped with American 155mm field guns, but the bulk of the Jordanian artillery branch still employed old British 25-pounder (104.25mm) field guns and 17-pounder (70.9mm) antitank guns.

The war found the Jordanians in the midst of switching from old British equipment to fairly modern or at least better-quality American equipment, but the transition was not complete. Moreover, the level of proficiency with the new weaponry and equipment was, on average, marginal.

The Royal Jordanian Air Force was not seen as a threat at all. Its entire striking power was represented in the form of twenty-four obsolete British-made Hawker Hunter jet fighter-bombers. There were five modern American-made F-104 Starfighters in Jordan at that time, along with a 100-man American training contingent, but none of the F-104s had as yet officially been turned over to Jordan. (The F-104s were flown by American pilots to Turkey as soon as the war started.)

It is impossible to gauge King Hussein's intentions with respect to how his army was to be employed. It was Hussein's widely *stated* intention to invade Israel at the outset of hostilities, but he had precious little on hand that seemed prepared to carry out the threat. All of Jordan's combat brigades in proximity to Israel were in decidedly defensive deployments, but that is not to say that they could not quickly go over to the offensive. The truth-teller seems to have been the positioning of Jordan's two armored brigades well back from the front, which strongly suggests that they were to be committed to cut off Israeli thrusts toward the Jordan River, and not in offensive operations toward the Mediterranean coast. However, if the armored brigades advanced toward the frontier in the absence of a direct Israeli provocation, then it would be safe to assume that Hussein did indeed intend to invade Israel.

On the evening of June 4, General Riadh, the Egyptian commander in chief, held a conference in Amman that was attended by all the top Jordanian military leaders. He asserted that there were not yet enough Arab forces in Jordan to conquer Israel, and he recommended that the Arabs wait until all four of the brigades promised by the Iraqis and three brigades promised by the Saudis had arrived. At the same time, Riadh urged King Hussein to ask Syria to deploy a number of its brigades in Samaria, more to defend against a possible Israeli invasion than to bolster the Arab force being mustered to invade Israel. Hussein did send the request, but it was never even answered.

The fear that Israel might invade Samaria *appeared* well founded. Though Central Command had only three infantry brigades to deploy against all of the West Bank from Kalkiliya south, Israel's Northern Command had the equivalent of two rather formidable *ugdot* built up in its area—north of Samaria and west of the Golan Heights. In Israeli eyes, the mobile northern *ugdot* were primarily proof against a Syrian thrust toward Haifa, on the Mediterranean, but, yes, it had occurred to the Israelis that the Northern Command *ugdah* deployed nearer to Samaria was in a good position to invade the Jordanian province. However, Israel had no intention of opening a second front while the main threat to her existence—Egypt's Sinai Field Army—was still intact and holding positions from which it could invade Israel.

The Israelis were so intent upon maintaining the status quo with respect to Jordan that, even as the first IAF fighter-bombers were striking their first targets in Egypt, Prime Minister Levi Eshkol arranged with United Nations intermediaries to tell King Hussein that *Zahal* would hold its fire against the Royal Jordanian Army if the Royal Jordanian Army would hold its fire against Israel. Within the hour, however, at 0850, Cairo informed King Hussein that Egypt was under attack. This put Hussein on notice that Egypt expected the mutual-defense pact that bound the two Arab nations to be honored. Next, in a direct communication at 0900, Cairo ordered General Riadh to open hostilities against central Israel. At 0930, King Hussein publicly went on record with a radio address to the nation announcing that "the hour of revenge has come."

But those were only words. Until or unless Hussein and his allies actually went to war on the central front, Israel was willing to accept all the verbal slaps the Jordanian king cared to issue.

35

Hussein ordered his armed forces to open a war they did not have to fight on the morning of June 5, 1967, as soon as he had completed his 0930 radio address to the nation. Jordanian 155mm field pieces located in western Samaria, opposite Israel's narrow waist, and in northern Samaria, opposite the Jezreel Valley and Beit Shean, opened fire at carefully preselected targets as far away as Israel's principal city, Tel Aviv. The bulk of the slow, methodical fire fell on Israeli military installations.

While Israeli attention was riveted on the fall of the artillery shells, tiny Egyptian commando raiding parties began working their way from Latrun toward Israel's international airport at Lod. It appears that the commandos were acting on orders from General Riadh, in Amman, and without the direct knowledge or approval of King Hussein or any senior Jordanian officers.

For the time being, the Israelis knew nothing about the Egyptian infiltrators and they were willing to forebear the Jordanian shelling in the belief that it was Hussein's way of showing other Arab leaders that he was a brother in "the struggle against Zionism." No Israeli leader expected Hussein to plunge his nation into a war. Unfortunately, when the Israeli guns remained silent, the Jordanians became bolder. At 1000, a volley of 155mm shells reached north into the Jezreel Valley and fell on and around the runway of the Ramat David air base, the IAF's largest installation north of Tel Aviv. Even if *Zahal* had no plans to go to war with Jordan, it did intend to push the Syrian Army back from the Golan Heights, and the air support that was to be provided out of Ramat David was vital to that attack and, indeed, to the defense of northern Israel.

The Israelis will not say what event or events caused them to decide to go to war against Jordan, but the worst thing the Jordanians did to Israel on the morning of June 5 was the shelling of Ramat David. Certainly, the Israelis had been thinking long and hard about a war with Jordan, but they did not issue their orders nor even complete final troop commitments until after Ramat David was struck, between 1000 and 1015. It was only then that the 10th "Harel" Armored-Infantry Brigade was transferred to Central Command from the GHQ Reserve, and responsibility for northern Samaria was transferred from Central Command to Northern Command.

The Harel Armored-Infantry Brigade was the only Israeli unit that even approximated a strategic reserve in central Israel. Its only purpose up until about 1030 on June 5 was to stand ready to cut off a thrust toward the Mediterranean by whatever force the Arabs launched out of northwestern Samaria or the Golan Heights. Until *Zahal* GHQ confirmed its attachment to Central Command at 1030, the Harel Armored-Infantry Brigade had no place in *Zahal*'s or Central Command's contingency plans regarding an Israeli invasion of the West Bank. And, realistically, there could have been no invasion of the West Bank without the Harel Brigade tanks and halftracks.

Likewise, the Northern Command armored *ugdah* commanded by Brigadier General Elad Peled was oriented entirely toward Syria until it was alerted at around 1030 on June 5 for a possible thrust to shut off the Jordanian artillery fire that was being directed at Ramat David. It is unclear if General Peled even had tactical maps of northern Samaria when the alert was issued.

The Jordanians acted first. From all appearances, the Jordanian plan was improvised, but it did stem from a sort of wish-fulfillment on the part of the Jordanian monarch. Though Hussein had done little to prepare his army for an offensive war against Israel, it is virtually certain that he did expect to emerge from the war in possession of at least West Jerusalem. Thus, while little was done elsewhere beyond harassing the Israelis north and west of Samaria, a real offensive plan was set in motion inside Jerusalem.

Following several hours of odd outbreaks of small-arms fire along and around the Green Line—the truce line between Jordanian East Jerusalem and Israeli West Jerusalem—Jordanian light 2-inch mortars suddenly came into play at 1115 against several Israeli border outposts manned by second-line troops from the Jerusalem Infantry Brigade. When the light mortars opened fire, the Israelis ratcheted up the violence by firing bazookas (2.76-inch rocket launchers) at Jordanian positions that had previously answered only with small arms. These escalating exchanges were typical; they had been flaring up with nauseating regularity ever since the truce lines had been drawn in 1949. For a change, however, there were no Israeli citizens to be mown down on the streets; everyone was indoors or, at least, well back from the truce line.

The mortar, bazooka, and small-arms duels along the Green Line gained in intensity. Then, at 1130, Jordanian 25-pounder light field guns opened fire on Kibbutz Ramat Rachel, the Israeli settlement that screened West Jerusalem from the south. At the same time, a mixed volley of mortar and artillery rounds fell on Mount Scopus, an Israeli enclave in the northern part of East Jerusalem. The Israelis responded to the Jordanian artillery fire with their own artillery, but the fire from the Jordanian 25-pounder batteries never abated.

While the artillery duels opened in and around Jerusalem, news arrived at Central Command Headquarters that the Royal Jordanian Air Force was attacking Israeli towns and several Israeli air bases in central Israel and that retaliatory flights of IAF fighter-bombers were being launched to take out the two-dozen jet warplanes under King Hussein's command. In all, sixteen Jordanian Hawker Hunters attacked Israeli air bases and villages around Netanya, Kfar Sirkin, and Kfar Saba. The Jordanians claimed to have destroyed four Israeli planes on the ground, but the Israelis admit to the loss of only one Noratlas transport. There were no lives lost.

What really was lost was the Royal Jordanian Air Force. Fourteen of the sixteen Hunters that took part in the attack returned safely at one time to either of Jordan's two air bases, and there the ground crews began the tedious task of refueling and rearming them. It would be two hours before the first Hunters could take to the air again, but the Israelis needed only about ten minutes to deny them the ability to do so.

Two flights of IAF Mirages—just eight planes in all—were pulled from the rotation against Egypt and their pilots were hurriedly briefed for strikes against the Jordanian air bases at Amman and Mafraq, the latter in northeastern Jordan. The Mirages arrived over their targets at 1215 and commenced low-level strafing runs against individual aircraft with their 30mm cannon. In the course of destroying the partially refueled Hunters, the Mirages also released a number of 1,200-pound concrete-busting bombs and thus disabled both runways. The only challenge was issued by a pair of Hunters that was late in returning from a mission over Israel. The two brave Jordanian pilots pitched into the Mirages over Mafraq, and one was shot down immediately. The second Hunter pilot was extremely good; he survived three firing passes at the dogfighting Mirages, which were a bit sluggish at low altitude, but then he and his airplane were blown to bits by a burst of 30mm cannon shells in the cockpit.

Eighteen of the Royal Jordanian Air Force's twenty-four Hawkers Hunters were destroyed in the one raid, and the remaining six were extensively damaged. The only pilot fatalities were the two shot down over Mafraq. The Mirages over Amman Airport also accounted for two parked helicopters and three parked light transports, of which one unfortunately belonged to the British air attache. In simultaneous action, a flight of four Mystères bombed the Royal Jordanian Air Force radar station at Mount Ajlun and caused extensive damage.

At 1330, after two hours of sporadic and inconclusive duels along Jerusalem's Green Line, the little war in Jerusalem finally boiled over. The event that finally forced Israel to act on a much grander scale began at noon with an order from King Hussein to Brigadier Ata Ali Haza'a, the commander of the Jerusalem-based King Talal Infantry Brigade. The monarch directed Haza'a to occupy the long, broad ridge in southern Jerusalem that incorporated Government House, formerly the residence of the British High Commissioner for the League of Nations Mandate in Palestine and lately the headquarters of the United Nations Truce Supervision Organization (UNTSO). The sprawling U.N. compound and the entire ridge upon which it sat presented a commanding view of the entire southern half of the city. Israelis, who had had little use for the British and now had little more than contempt for what they saw as being a pro-Arab United Nations, took great pleasure in calling the hill by its Biblical name, Jebel Mukaber—the Hill of Evil Counsel.

Interestingly, Radio Amman had announced the seizure of Jebel Mukaber at 1030, fully three hours before the Jordanian operation actually began. The Israelis had taken notice of the announcement, but the government had been unwilling to do anything to deflect the presumed blow in advance. In any case, for Jordanian troops to seize Jebel Mukaber was really throwing down the gauntlet; it was an act that would certainly evoke a hostile response from the Israelis. It was also an act that immediately confused and alarmed the Israeli military authorities, for the hill was in the south of the city, in the exact opposite direction of Mount Scopus, which is where the Israelis expected any Jordanian blow to fall. There were 120 lightly armed

Israelis on Mount Scopus, and many more as close to it as they could get. But there were only five Israeli soldiers in proximity to Government House. They were guarding Kibbutz Ramat Rachel, which had been evacuated days earlier.

The unit that Hussein specifically ordered Brigadier Haza'a to employ in the seizure of Government House was a battalion of the Iman Ali Infantry Brigade that had been brought into East Jerusalem on June 2. In fact, during his June 3 inspection tour of Jerusalem, the king had given Haza'a and the battalion commander, Major Badi Awad, direct orders to reconnoiter Jebel Mukaber and Government House from the Jordanian side of the truce line. This Major Awad had done, so, when the moment of truth was upon him, he was fully prepared to send two of his three small infantry companies up the hill.

The 150 Jordanian infantrymen climbed the hill by way of a motor road. They encountered most of the U.N. staff and a number of their dependents—about 100 souls in all—in a small wooded area just to the north of the main U.N. headquarters building. The civilians had taken shelter in the woods because several Jordanian artillery rounds that had been meant to pass over the hill toward targets in West Jerusalem had clipped several structures atop the hill.

While a handful of U.N. military officers and civilian officials complained bitterly to Major Awad and other officers about the incursion into the neutral zone, the Jordanian infantrymen set to digging in along the western and southern crests of the ridge. Several jeep-mounted 106mm recoilless rifles were driven up from East Jerusalem, and an artillery forward-observer team began spotting fire against targets that had hitherto been visible only on maps. The U.N. officials could do little to stop the Jordanians from occupying the woods and outlying buildings, but several of them manhandled a Jordanian machine gun out of Government House itself when the crew tried to set the weapon up in a second-floor window. The U.N. commander, Norwegian Air Force General Odd Bull, argued vehemently but to no avail with Major Awad.

In short order, the Jordanian artillery forward observer was directing fire from a 25-pounder battery against Kibbutz Ramat Rachel, to the south, and *Zahal's* Allenby Barracks, to the west. At the barracks, one of the Jerusalem Infantry Brigade's four second-line infantry battalions was just then mobilizing. The five-man squad at Ramat Rachel was forced to take cover, and the second-line infantry battalion had to evacuate the barracks after the battalion commander, a company commander, and several soldiers were wounded.

As soon as Jebel Mukaber was firmly under his control, Major Awad ordered his reserve company to advance against Ramat Rachel, and a platoon was sent forward to occupy the Israeli Ministry of Agriculture experimental farm in the neutral zone west of Government House. The five Israeli infantrymen holding the little kibbutz were allowed by higher authority to flee, but the Jordanian troops on their way to the experimental farm were stopped cold when the farm director's wife and an elderly auxiliary policemen fired an ancient Czech light machine gun at them. The Jordanian troops backtracked into a treeline bordering the farm and, before they could muster another attempt, two reinforced companies from the Jerusalem Infantry Brigade's Infantry Battalion 161 rushed up the hill to occupy the experimental farm in force. The remainder of Infantry Battalion 161 beat the Jordanian company into Ramat Rachel.

All along the truce line, Jordanian soldiers were firming up their positions while waiting to see what the Israelis were going to do about increasingly strident provocations, particularly the seizure of Jebel Mukaber. Most of the Jordanian troops and officers did not know very much about what was going on beyond their little nodes of hostility, but all the news that was reaching them was good. Radio Amman was reporting the death of the Israeli Air Force and uncontested penetrations by several Egyptian divisions into southern and south-central Israel. Across the way, where Israeli Reservists from the Jerusalem Infantry Brigade were trying to cope, there was not much more news to be had. Kol Yisrael, the Israeli national radio station, wasn't saying anything. However, Jordanians and Israelis alike were thinking, "Now is the time; now is the time to strike. Now is the time to correct the mistakes of 1948."

36

Uzi Narkiss had been dreaming about taking control of all of Jerusalem off and on for nearly two decades—ever since the relief force he had commanded in 1948 had broken into the Old City, had fought a bloody battle there, and then had been thrown out with heavy casualties. Jerusalem was an old wound Jerusalemite Narkiss never quite allowed to heal, and he often thought about what had gone wrong in 1948.

Now, however, since he had become one of his nation's senior military officers, Uzi Narkiss's plans were less sanguinary than his dreams. He only hoped he might have a chance to ease some of the pressures and many discomforts the 1948 truce had imposed upon his fellow Jerusalemites. In the week before June 5, 1967, all Narkiss thought he might be able to get out of the impending war was a band-aid here and a lifeline there—a snip, a cut, a stitch. However, it happened that the Jordanian occupation of Jebel Mukaber and Government House played more into Narkiss's decades-old dream than into the modest plan he had formulated.

It was Narkiss's plan that his first moves in Jerusalem—once the government authorized *any* moves—would be a breakthrough to the enclave on Mount Scopus, followed by some sort of pretext to get Israeli troops atop Jebel Mukaber. That way, Israelis would be in control of the dominating heights to the north and the south of the Old City, and from there they could extend their holdings along the curve of ridges and hills that further dominated the Old City from the east. Narkiss knew exactly how he was going to get a large force atop Mount Scopus—a direct assault to open a permanent route to the enclave—but he had no clear idea about how to get troops atop neutral Jebel Mukaber. Nevertheless, as early as 0930 on June 5, Narkiss ordered the commander of the Jerusalem Infantry Brigade to be prepared to seize both heights, and he made his first official requests to Chief of Staff Yitzhak Rabin at 1130 and 1150. Rabin said "No" both times, and a third request, this time to Deputy Chief of Staff Chaim Bar-Lev, was answered with a terse *"Nyet!"* However, Narkiss was not easily deterred; he kept telling the Jerusalem Infantry Brigade commander to be prepared to seize both objectives at a moment's notice.

In the end, Narkiss's dilemma with respect to Jebel Mukaber was resolved by the King of Jordan. When Major Badi Awad's infantry battalion appeared around formerly neutral Government House, Narkiss had all the pretext he could have craved.

The initial Israeli decision to respond to the Jordanian occupation of Government House was made on his own authority by Lieutenant Colonel Asher Driezin, the combative 34-year-old Regular in command of the Jerusalem Infantry Brigade's Infantry Battalion 161. Driezin was at the Allenby Barracks, due west of Government House, directing his own mortars against Jordanian positions. The moment he heard that Jordanian troops had attempted to occupy the Israeli experimental farm just to the west of Government House, he sent two companies of his battalion directly to the farm, and only then did he transmit news of his action to his brigade commander, Colonel Eliezer Amitai. By then, acting on *his* own authority, Amitai was already at work implementing a long-standing plan to counter a long-feared Jordanian occupation of Jebel Mukaber. The Jerusalem Infantry Brigade's single squadron of French Sherman tanks and the brigade reconnaissance company had been alerted to undertake a counterattack alongside Infantry Battalion 161.

As soon as Lieutenant Colonel Driezin finished speaking with Colonel Amitai, he, his runner, and a forward observer for the battalion's mortars sprinted out of the Allenby Barracks and ran all the way up the hill to the experimental farm. Without regard to the damage they might cause to the U.N. facility, Driezin ordered his battalion's 81mm and 60mm mortars to open fire on the Jordanian troops digging in along the treeline. At the same time, machine guns set up in the forwardmost Israeli positions succeeded in forcing the nearest Jordanians to pull back out of sight of the experimental farm.

Half the Jerusalem Infantry Brigade's French Sherman tanks and all its reconnaissance halftracks and jeeps were on the way. As soon as they arrived, the two companies of Infantry Battalion 161 that were already at the experimental farm were to join in coordinated attacks against two key positions atop Jebel Mukaber. The first was Antenna Hill, the highest point atop the ridge, on which the U.N. force had set up a radio antenna. The other was Government House itself. Once these positions were in Israeli hands, the attack was to continue on to Government House's east gate in order to sever the north-south Jerusalem-Bethlehem secondary road that passed right by. Then the Israelis were to turn south to attack out of the U.N. neutral zone and through a heavily defended portion of Jebel Mukaber known as the Sausage. Finally, once through the Sausage, the Israelis were to proceed partway down the ridge to occupy the Arab town of Sur Bahir and a Jordanian defensive zone that dominated Kibbutz Ramat Rachel.

By the time eleven of the Jerusalem Infantry Brigade's twenty-one French Sherman tanks and the brigade reconnaissance company reached the Allenby Barracks, Lieutenant Colonel Asher Driezin was at the experimental farm, and communications with the brigade headquarters were temporarily down. Neither of the company commanders knew what was expected of him, but they decided to advance abreast up a dirt lane that connected the barracks with the experimental farm. The tanks moved ahead in a column on the road itself, and the halftracks and reconnaissance jeeps drove through fields to the right of the roadway. As soon as the Israeli armored vehicles moved out of the Allenby compound, a Jordanian 25-pounder battery set up on Abu Tor, a high defended hill just to the northwest of Jebel Mukaber, opened a furious direct-fire barrage. A number of the Shermans were struck by artillery shells, and all were sprayed with shrapnel, but none were damaged.

The tanks, which arrived first, were met at the farm gate by Asher Driezin, who despite his rank was younger and less experienced than either of the Reserve company commanders. The tank commander, Major Aharon Kamara, an especially aggressive product of guerrilla action in the late 1940s against the British, was all for pitching straight into the Jordanians with all of his tanks. Driezin ordered him to deploy five of the Shermans in the trees to lay down a base of fire while three others advanced on Government House and Antenna Hill and the remaining three made straight for the east gate. Kamara agreed and went off to brief his tank crews. Driezin then went over to brief the reconnaissance company commander, Major Yosef Langotsky, who had just arrived.

Langotsky was more deliberate than Kamara, and even a bit too deliber-ate for Driezin. He asked the infantry battalion commander to draw a diagram in the dirt so as to avoid blind confrontations between separate Israeli forces attacking through the trees. Driezin was primed to go, and he yelled at Langotsky, "If you are not ready to go immediately, I will shoot you." With that, one of Langotsky's corporals butted in and said to Driezin, "Take it easy. If not, I'll cut your throat."

Only in *Zahal*! Langotsky remained calm, and he managed to calm Driezin, who knelt in the sand and drew the diagram. Basically, the tanks were to break down the UNTSO compound's west gate and deploy in the trees or attack Government House and Antenna Hill or straight through to the east gate. The halftracks were to follow the tanks through the west gate. While one section attacked Government House, the main body was to veer southward to attack the Sausage position down its long axis. On foot behind the halftracks, one of Driezin's infantry companies was to turn north to clear the woods in that direction.

Everyone was ready to go and Driezin was about to order the attack to commence when, a little before 1430, Colonel Amitai canceled the attack in a radio message from brigade headquarters. Five minutes earlier, General Odd Bull, the UNTSO chief, had requested a ceasefire, and the government had felt obliged to comply. The Israeli attack was called off. The Israeli tanks and halftracks tried to back down from their attack positions, but eight of the Shermans became mired in mud in the open. When the Jordanians peppered the tanks with small-arms fire, many Israelis returned the fire. The exposed tanks opened fire at Government House and Jordanian artillery positions on Abu Tor and farther to the east. For some reason, the Jordanian jeep-mounted 106mm recoilless rifles, which could have destroyed the exposed Shermans, never put in an appearance.

The Israelis occupying the experimental farm endured the Jordanian shelling and gunfire for an hour, until, at 1530, Central Command ordered it to complete the occupation of Jebel Mukaber. With eight of eleven tanks unable to advance out of the mud, Lieutenant Colonel Driezin opted for a scaled-down plan.

The three drivable French Shermans crashed through the west gate on cue, but the Israeli infantrymen were unable to cut their way through the barbed-wire fence and had to use the gate also. By the time they got there, the tanks and halftracks were well ahead and the Jordanians defending the gate had recovered. The Israeli company commander was shot dead, several of his men were wounded, and the infantry company took cover.

Asher Driezin was directing the approach of the Israelis on Government House from aboard Major Kamara's headquarters halftrack. He personally accounted for three recoillness-rifle jeeps with a .50-caliber machine gun, but shrapnel from the Jordanian 25-pounders on Abu Tor severed an artery in his right forearm. He stopped firing just long enough to allow a medic to apply a tourniquet and strap the arm to his waist.

By the time the halftracks and lead tanks were approaching Government House, the crews of the mired tanks had managed to tow several of them from the mud. These followed the lead elements into the U.N. compound, one by one, and joined the fighting wherever they were needed.

Two of the Shermans and the command halftrack bypassed Government House and rolled through the east gate. The view was breathtaking; everyone commented on it. Even the native Jerusalemites had never seen their city from that direction. After having his look, Driezin ordered the halftrack to return to Antenna Hill, which was by then in the possession of three Shermans. He expected to find Major Langotsky and the reconnaissance halftracks below Antenna Hill, ready to attack the Sausage, but only the three tanks were on the scene.

Langotsky and one of his halftrack platoons was at Government House, which took a little more time to secure than Driezin had anticipated. There were a few dozen Jordanians in and around the U.N. headquarters building, and it took considerable ingenuity to pry them out without killing any innocent U.N. personnel or dependents. Once the Jordanian soldiers had been overcome, it also took some haggling with General Bull to get him to stop protesting the violation of his neutral compound. In the end, though Bull insisted on being repatriated via Jordan, he and his staff were led down the west side of Jebel Mukaber to Israel.

Through the fighting for Antenna Hill, the east gate, and Government House—and despite over an hour's fair warning—Major Awad, the bulk of his battalion, and several recoilless rifles remained on the northern brow of Jebel Mukaber, from which Awad inexplicably expected the major Israeli attack to develop. Even after the Israeli tanks broke through the main gate, Awad and most of his soldiers stayed where they were, well away from the fighting. Awad did call in artillery fire from Abu Tor, but it hit his troops as well as the Israelis. When three Shermans attacked the left side of his static position, Awad radioed the King Talal Infantry Brigade headquarters and asked for permission to withdraw by way of the east gate. Brigadier Ali Ata Haza'a agreed, and Awad's force pulled out, leaving five dead and twenty-five wounded to the Israelis. Firing from the former Jordanian positions, the French Shermans blanketed Abu Tor.

Shortly after regrouping the main body of his battalion east of Government House, Major Awad asked Brigadier Haza'a to support a counterattack with an artillery barrage. Haza'a complied, and the 25-pounder battery on Abu Tor blanketed the entire summit of Jebel Mukaber. The Jordanian infantry then attacked through their own artillery fire and occupied an undefended salient on the northeast side of the U.N. compound. With that, the Jordanian 25-pounders turned their attention to West Jerusalem, using the King David Hotel as an aiming stake.

As soon as the Jordanian artillery was shifted away from Jebel Mukaber, a small force of Israeli infantrymen and tanks attacked Major Awad's little enclave. Once again, Awad and his soldiers left the field—this time for good. It was then 1550—only twenty minutes after the Israeli attack had begun.

In all, fifteen Jordanians were killed and over thirty were wounded and left to the Israelis. One Israeli died in the attack on Jebel Mukaber, and seven were wounded. Toward dusk, the U.N. colors were struck and an Israeli flag was raised over Government House. By then, Lieutenant Colonel Asher Driezin's makeshift task force of tanks, reconnaissance vehicles and troops, and infantrymen on foot had invaded Jordan.

The inexpert Jordanians had created a catastrophic dilemma for themselves by failing to place one commander over the Jerusalem sector's three separate infantry brigades. East Jerusalem itself was defended by Brigadier Ata Ali Haza'a's King Talal Infantry Brigade, but the adjacent area to the northwest came under the control of the Imam Ali Infantry Brigade, and the area just to the south came under the control of the Hittin Infantry Brigade. Later in the afternoon, the Imam Ali Infantry Brigade was placed under Brigadier Haza'a's command, which helped when the fighting spread to northern Jerusalem, but Haza'a was not put in charge of units on the southern edge of his sector.

The Hittin Infantry Brigade's headquarters was in the Judean city of Hebron, and nearly all the troops were spread out along the ridgeline from Bethlehem all the way to Samua. But two companies of the battalion that was headquartered in Bethlehem were actually in what the Israelis—but not the Jordanians—considered to be the southern environs of East Jerusalem. One of these companies, which had no direct communications link with the King Talal Infantry Brigade headquarters, was the one that was occupying the heavily defended portion of Jebel Mukaber known as the Sausage. This company had no part in the seizure or defense of the adjacent U.N. compound, and it is doubtful that its commander ever received news of what happened only a matter of yards to the north of his defensive zone.

Lieutenant Colonel Asher Driezin waited for nearly thirty minutes at the top of Antenna Hill for Israeli troops to emerge from the fog of war that had spread across the UNTSO compound. During that time, he assembled several Sherman tanks, the reconnaissance company jeep platoon, and a platoon from one of the infantry companies.

The Sausage had been built to prevent the Israelis from attacking into East Jerusalem from Ramat Rachel. Its complex of three trenchlines and numerous bunkers were oriented to the southwest. Relying upon standard *Zahal* breaching tactics, Driezin ordered the jeep platoon's twenty-four men to break down into three teams, one to seize each trenchline. While the tanks fired to force Jordanian heads down, one of the teams crept forward to breach a barbed-wire barrier. As soon as the wire was cut, all the recon troopers dashed across a stretch of open ground and on into the trenches, firing their Uzi submachine guns as they ran. Behind the recon teams, Driezin sent squads from his infantry company to mop up bypassed bunkers and pillboxes.

Only a third of the way through the Sausage, the recon squads began running out of hand grenades and bullets. There was no way to get a resupply from the rear, so they slung their Uzis and picked up Jordanian rifles, which were clumsier but just as lethal at close range. By then, 1630, most of the Jordanians had fled by way of the south end of the defensive zone.

Thirty Jordanians died in the Sausage, and only one Israeli was wounded. The Jordanian commander, a major, was one of the dozen or so wounded Jordanians captured in the Sausage. He could not understand why his countrymen had not counterattacked.

As soon as Driezin reported that his troops were in possession of the Sausage, Colonel Amitai, the Jerusalem Infantry Brigade commander, ordered him to proceed south to Sur Bahir and attack west into a Jordanian strongpoint known as the Bell, which directly overlooked Kibbutz Ramat Rachel. The wounded battalion commander replied that he had only a few dozen soldiers at his direct disposal and that they were nearly out of ammunition, Amitai told Driezin to find more men and that he would send up more bullets and hand grenades.

It took nearly two hours for the Israelis to reopen their attack. In that

time, Driezin spread six of the French Shermans and his entire Infantry
Battalion 161 across Jebel Mukaber and through the Sausage to deflect a
possible Jordanian counterattack. The attack on the Bell would be undertaken
by the Jerusalem Infantry Brigade's reconnaissance company and five of the
Sherman tanks.

It was not yet 1830 and thus still light out when the column of halftracks
and tanks proceeded down the Jerusalem–Bethlehem secondary road that
ran past the east side of the UNTSO compound and behind the Sausage.
The next settlement on the road was Sur Bahir, but the road twisted and
turned along the tops and around the edges of several steep hills. At the first
blind curve, the column was stopped by two stalled civilian automobiles that
blocked the narrow roadway. The occupants of the cars were merely fright-
ened civilians who were found hiding in a shallow cave. Without further
ado, the lead Sherman drove right over the cars, and crushed them flat. For
some reason, the second tank tried to go around, and it tipped over the edge
of the road. One of the crewmen was killed in the fall. Major Aharon Kamara
made the tough choice; he ordered the column to proceed without stopping
to see if the tank crewmen needed help. Too much time had been lost to
too many little incidents, and the column was now in a vulnerable position
on the open road.

It was almost dark when the lead tank reached Sur Bahir. The village was
full of anxious and scared civilians, but no soldiers were in evidence. The
Bell was to the west, across some fields on the far side of the built-up area.
The tanks turned right, off the secondary road, and advanced quickly along
the village's main street. Unbeknown to the men in the lead, the sixth Israeli
vehicle, a halftrack, broke down and blocked the narrow passage. Thus, only
two tanks and three halftracks were advancing in the dark toward the quite
formidable Bell.

When the Israelis reached the end of the village street—the lead tank crushed
a house that blocked its view of the Bell—Major Langotsky jumped down
from his halftrack and asked in a loud voice, "Where is everybody?" More
than half the column had failed to arrive, but there was no time to straighten
out the mess. Asher Driezin ordered Langotsky to get on with it, and this
time Langotsky was as eager as the battalion commander. A brief radio
message was flashed to the Infantry Battalion 161 rear command post, and
an array of recoilless rifles, machine guns, and tanks assembled in the Sausage

and by another infantry battalion that had fortified Ramat Rachel reached out toward the Jordanian trenchworks. Unfortunately, some of the fire from Ramat Rachel went astray in the dark, and the Israeli attackers had to dodge to avoid being struck by the friendly fire.

There was supposed to be a whole infantry company from the Hittin Infantry Brigade manning the six trenches and numerous pillboxes and bunkers that comprised the Bell position, and perhaps there was when the attack started. But, if so, fully half the Jordanians melted away into the night before the Israelis could catch up with them.

The only unobstructed route into the Bell was via an access lane that ran from Sur Bahir into the rear of the defensive position. The lead halftrack, with Major Langotsky and most of the recon troops aboard, drove along the lane, which was paralleled by a deep steel-reinforced granite trench. Langotsky ordered his driver to stop, and he and a few recon troopers entered the trench. They took a prisoner, who was led to the rear. Then, as he was leading his men deeper into the trench, Langotsky shot and killed two Jordanians.

When he heard the first shots fired, an impatient and mildly unnerved Asher Driezin ordered the drivers of the other two halftracks to follow his command group with their vehicles into the Jordanian position. He had no idea where Langotsky's team was, but he feared for the safety of his men.

Langotsky's team was making good progress in the dark, shooting up and grenading bunkers and pillboxes as it went. There was one close call when one of the Shermans far to the rear fired blindly and blew up a bunker moments before the recon men were about to enter it. A few minutes later, a Jordanian soldier shot and killed the recon company communications sergeant.

While the main body of the recon team worked around from the right, Driezin and his headquarters men entered the Bell from the left and worked toward them. Over their heads, a gunner in one of the halftracks pounded bullets into the trench just in front of the running men. At least a dozen Jordanians were killed by grenades, small arms, and the machine gun as Driezin's team worked through the trenchline. Soon, however, the sound of gunfire from the right grew loud enough to cause Asher Driezin to wonder when he was going to run into friends. In the nick of time, the two groups of Israelis stopped firing. In a few moments, they joined up, fortunately without mishap.

The Israelis climbed out of the trench to make way for the halftracks and tanks to fire at other Jordanian positions inside the Bell. Word arrived that a company of Israeli infantrymen was on the way up from Ramat Rachel, and that Driezin's force could return to Government House as soon as it arrived.

The Israeli officers and their men relaxed. Five dark shadows approaching along the trenchline appeared to be joining the group when there was a cry in Arabic, followed by bursts of gunfire. The men on either side of Asher Driezin were shot dead, and he was severely wounded by grenade fragments in the left hand and arm. Two other Israelis were shot and killed, and a lieutenant was shot in the eye. All five Jordanians were killed by a hand grenade that landed in their midst.

It was nearly midnight before the relief company could pick its way across thick belts of Israeli and Jordanian mines to take possession of the Bell. The wounded and dead Israelis were evacuated in the reconnaissance company halftracks, first to Government House and then to a hospital in West Jerusalem. Also, the crew of the Sherman tank that had gone off the road to Sur Bahir was eventually rescued.

By the late evening of June 5, most of southern Jerusalem was securely in Israeli hands.

37

Uzi Narkiss was a Jerusalemite. He had been born there in 1925, and had spent his early years there. The really important events of Narkiss's life, especially his life as a soldier, had been played out in the wondrous city of his birth. He was only thirteen years old when he began his military service as a courier for the old *Haganah*, and he joined the elite *Palmach* in 1941, when he was only sixteen. Young Narkiss was sent to a platoon leaders' course that included in his class Chaim Bar-Lev and Zvi Zur, two future chiefs of staff. In 1946, in the guerrilla war against the British, Narkiss and Bar-Lev blew up the Allenby Bridge across the Jordan River, and in 1948, at the ripe old age of twenty-three, he was made a sector commander of the four West Bank settlements known as the Etzion Bloc. After holding off Arab raiders there for six months (the Etzion Bloc was later overrun and many of its defenders were executed), Major Narkiss was posted as deputy commander of an infantry battalion, and he took part in fierce battles along what became the Jerusalem Corridor. On the night of May 18, 1948, Narkiss was put in command of two infantry companies and ordered by the Harel Brigade commander, Colonel Yitzhak Rabin, to capture and hold Mount Zion, at the southwest corner of the Old City. He was to leave one company and, with the other, penetrate to the Jewish Quarter to provide the beleaguered defenders with ammunition and other supplies. Narkiss's small force did capture Mount Zion, it did fight its way into the Old City by way of the Zion Gate, and it did bring ammunition to the besieged Jewish Quarter. But, after vicious fighting, Narkiss was obliged to withdraw, and the Jewish Quarter—indeed, the entire Old City—had to be surrendered. Narkiss later commanded a battalion in the Negev Desert, and after the war he directed *Zahal*'s first company-commanders' course. He commanded the Negev district brigade in the early 1950s and attended the *École de Guerre* from 1953 to 1955, following which he was named *Zahal*'s Director of Operations. He next served as deputy director of the Intelligence Branch and held that post during the 1956 war. After a three-year tour as military attache in Paris, Brigadier General Narkiss founded the National Defense College, which he headed until he was named GOC, Central Command, in 1965.

On the morning of June 5, as Brigadier General Uzi Narkiss undertook the first steps to secure the Jewish half of the city of his birth from a possible Arab invasion, several of his conversations with higher headquarters revolved around the 10th "Harel" Armored-Infantry Brigade. The unit, which had been held back as the GHQ strategic reserve in central Israel, was finally released to Central Command's direct authority at 1250. At 1300 Narkiss ordered the brigade's new commander, with whom he had met earlier in the day, to be ready to move upon command into Jerusalem from the brigade depots around Netaniya.

The Harel Armored-Infantry Brigade had been in the midst of being upgraded in recent months, and as late as late May it had been considered by senior *Zahal* officers to be a bit unsteady. When, in the course of events, the brigade was assigned to the GHQ Reserve and positioned in central Israel, it came time to appoint a new brigade commander. The man everyone agreed would be best for the job was Reserve Colonel Uri Ben-Ari, who had been a printing executive since leaving the Standing Army in 1957.

The former Berliner was 42 years old in 1967, and his once-jet-black hair was beginning to gray. But he stood as straight and tall as he ever had when he arrived in the Harel Armored-Infantry Brigade headquarters on June 1 to begin barking orders and generally drive everyone in the brigade to an exaggerated state of frenzy and preparation. The Harel Brigade, which had been *the* premier unit of the War of Independence, had fallen into disrepute at Umm Katef in the 1956 Sinai Campaign, and it had operated under a shadow ever since. Though it was the best-equipped brigade in central Israel when Ben-Ari took command, it was far from being the best trained.

Four days is not much time for turning a 3,500-man brigade around, but Ben-Ari did his very best. When the first shots were finally fired on the morning of June 5, it remained to be seen how well Ben-Ari's frenetic restoration program had taken hold.

Uzi Narkiss and Uri Ben-Ari were old comrades in arms. When Narkiss had been sent to break into the Old City on May 18, 1948, Ben-Ari had commanded the company that had seized and held Mount Zion. As the two old soldiers—they were both 42 years old—talked over the radio, they fell into a familiar cant, and in short order they reached an agreement as to how and where the Harel Armored-Infantry Brigade's two armored-infantry battalions and large tank battalion were to move toward the city.

The perceived danger at the time of the late-morning discussion was Mount Scopus. It was Narkiss's intention to use Ben-Ari's brigade to open and hold a corridor from West Jerusalem to the enclave, which was held by 120 lightly armed Israeli soldiers and border policemen. Narkiss told Ben-Ari to move the entire brigade from Netaniya through Ramle and on to West Jerusalem. Ben-Ari replied that there might be delays and breakdowns because every one of *Zahal*'s tank transporters was committed to Southern Command; the brigade's sixty French Shermans and twelve new Centurions would have to run all the way on their own tracks. Ben-Ari then asked if he could go straight into the attack as soon as his tanks arrived in Jerusalem. Narkiss told him that he had not yet received permission from the government to attack East Jerusalem. To be sure, Narkiss telephoned Minister of Defense Moshe Dayan, who told him that, if Mount Scopus was under attack, Ben-Ari could certainly go straight into the attack. Otherwise, he was to await orders.

Ben-Ari arrived in Ramle at 1405 and went straight to Central Command Headquarters. There, Uzi Narkiss told him that the attack on Government House was underway. "This," Narkiss confided, "is to be revenge for Forty-eight." By the time Ben-Ari left at 1430—there were many interruptions—the simple plan to open a corridor to Mount Scopus had been changed. Ben-Ari's brigade was to seize the long complex of ridges along the entire northeastern shoulder of the Jerusalem Corridor. Mount Scopus, which was an eastern extension of this line of hills, was to be seized in due course by another brigade that had just become available to Central Command.

If Ben-Ari's and the other fresh brigade succeeded in their missions, not only would Israel have widened the Jerusalem Corridor, it would have isolated the entire Jerusalem area from the north. According to standard military doctrine accepted the world around, the first step in seizing a city was isolating it from outside assistance. If the Harel Armored-Infantry Brigade could occupy the high hills at the eastern end of its zone of operations, then it would effectively dominate the strategically vital Ramallah–Jerusalem highway and thus deny the Jordanian Army access to the city from the north. Taken together with the seizure of Jebel Mukaber and other objectives to the south, it was clearly Narkiss's intention to isolate all of Jerusalem from the West Bank. In fact, once it was able to free up some fighter-bombers, the IAF would be sent out in force over the last main axis to Jerusalem, the east-west road from Jericho to Jerusalem. If that axis could be interdicted by air and the northern and southern hills seized, then East Jerusalem—and especially the Old City—could certainly be isolated, and might eventually be captured.

The factor that most influenced Narkiss's approval of using the Harel Armored-Infantry Brigade to implement the broader plan was the transfer in the late morning of the 55th Parachute Brigade from Southern Command to Central Command. Narkiss could use the paratroopers closer in to the city while Ben-Ari's tanks and armored infantrymen put into play the broad maneuver tactics Ben-Ari had fathered in the 1950s. The only problem was that armor was going to be used to attack a ridgeline from the bottom up. As Ben-Ari later put it, "If anyone had taught at the Command and Staff School that it was possible for an armored brigade from the plains to attack the Jerusalem positions . . . he'd have been thrown out."

As Ben-Ari climbed into his jeep outside of Central Command Head-quarters, word reached him that the headquarters group and lead elements of his brigade's tank battalion were just beginning to pass through Ramle. It was then 1430. The attack was to begin at 1700.

The Jordanians were far from passive during the long afternoon hours it took the Israelis to position their forces to begin the conquest of East Jerusalem. At 1430, just as Uri Ben-Ari was leaving his command post, Uzi Narkiss asked where the 60th Jordanian Armored Brigade was. It had been in reserve along the secondary road between Jericho and the Dead Sea, but if the Jordanians had any hope of holding Jerusalem, the 60th Jordanian Armored Brigade was it. Narkiss expected it to be on the move by then, but the latest aerial reconnaissance said it was not. The Israelis did not know at the time that the brigade had been alerted to move on Jerusalem and was awaiting an execute order.

Beginning at 1500, the Jordanians put *both* of their armored brigades in motion. The 60th Jordanian Armored Brigade was ordered to proceed to Jerusalem via the main road from Jericho, and the 40th Jordanian Armored Brigade was ordered to drive south and disperse east of Jericho. As soon as these two brigades started moving, small numbers of IAF warplanes were dispatched to slow or stop them with bombs, rockets, and cannon. The IAF also took on the 8th Iraqi Motorized-Infantry Brigade, whose tank battalion was spotted in the open as it moved toward the Damiya Bridge from well to the east of the Jordan River.

The gravest danger to Israeli plans and dreams was the advance of the 60th Jordanian Armored Brigade from Jericho toward Jerusalem. It was considered to be a crack unit, well trained and highly motivated, and it was the only Jordanian unit within reach of Jerusalem that could possibly stand up to Ben-Ari's Harel Armored-Infantry Brigade. If it could reach the Ramallah-Jerusalem highway before Ben-Ari's tanks, it might just upset Israel's best hope for achieving her chief emotional objective in the war. Therefore, though the 40th Jordanian and 8th Iraqi brigades received ample attention, the bulk of the limited IAF sorties over the West Bank that afternoon were aimed at destroying or at least disabling the 60th Jordanian Armored Brigade as it labored up the steep narrow ribbon of roadway that linked Jericho with Jerusalem.

At 1600, as the Harel Armored-Infantry Brigade was moving into final attack positions, Brigadier Ata Ali Haza'a, the King Talal Infantry Brigade commander, was given overall command of the Jerusalem sector. This placed the main body of the Imam Ali Infantry Brigade under Haza'a's authority and allowed Haza'a to undertake some necessary adjustments aimed at consolidating his force's grip on East Jerusalem and several key hills to the north and northwest. Haza'a immediately ordered one of the Imam Ali battalions to move to Tel el-Ful, the highest hill north of the city overlooking the Ramallah–Jerusalem highway. In anticipation of this unit's speedy move, Haza'a also ordered the battalion of his King Talal Infantry Brigade that was already holding Tel el-Ful to close up toward the Old City. These simultaneous moves would leave Tel el-Ful unguarded for a few hours, but Haza'a was convinced that the greatest immediate danger lay in an Israeli ground attack closer in to East Jerusalem—toward Mount Scopus, in fact.

Unintentionally, Haza'a withdrew one of the two Jordanian infantry battalions charged with defending the northern shoulder of the Jerusalem Corridor only an hour before the Harel Armored-Infantry Brigade was set to attack that very area. And not only was the Jordanian defense of the corridor disrupted at the critical juncture, the battalion that had been set in motion was spotted on the open road and butchered by IAF ground-attack aircraft and fighter-bombers. It never even reached Tel el-Ful, which was the Harel Armored-Infantry Brigade's intermediate objective.

The Jordanians were not passive during the two hours before the Harel Armored-Infantry Brigade launched its attack, but every move they made cost them far more dearly than they could afford. It is the price they paid for Israel's air supremacy.

38

The defeat of Captain Awad Saud Eid's company of Jordanian Patton tanks in front of the West Bank town of Tel Zahara turned out to be *the* decisive action of the battle for Jerusalem.

Once the four spearhead elements of Colonel Uri Ben-Ari's Harel Armored-Infantry Brigade were in position opposite the points at which they were to break into the northeastern shoulder of the Jerusalem Corridor, the biggest headache facing them was mines. Since 1948, uncounted thousands of mines had been sown by the Jordanians holding the line of defended villages and hilltop bastions, and there was no way for the Israelis to know where they all were. The mines severely complicated a plan that by its very ambition was complicated.

True to the tenets he had drawn up over a decade earlier, Ben-Ari had mixed and matched the various companies of his brigade to form three tank-infantry task forces. The largest was Lieutenant Colonel Zvi Dahav's Tank Battalion 95, which had swapped out two of its four large French Sherman companies in exchange for an armored-infantry company from each of the two armored-infantry battalions. Zvika Dahav's task force, which also included Tank Battalion 95's company of twelve Centurions, was to break into the Jordanian line at the farthest eastern point of the brigade zone; it would thus be the closest Israeli armored unit to Tel el-Ful and the strategically vital Ramallah–Jerusalem highway. If he could, Dahav was to end his attack with a push to close on Mount Scopus from the north.

To Dahav's left was Major Amnon Eshkol's Reconnaissance Company 41, which was the only unit in *Zahal* equipped with AML armored cars, a French-built light wheeled fighting vehicle mounting a 90mm main gun. Eshkol's company was to jump off beside Dahav's task force and proceed to the Ramallah–Jerusalem highway by a slightly different route.

Farther to the left was the armored-infantry task force built around Lieutenant Aharon Gal's Armored-Infantry Battalion 106. It was to jump off from Castel, on the main Tel Aviv–Jerusalem highway, and break into the Jordanian position 1.5 kilometers to the north, at Abdul Aziz Hill.

Well to the left of the rest of the brigade, the task force built around Lieutenant Colonel Yigal Ben-David's Armored-Infantry Battalion 104 was to jump off from Abu Ghosh, on the Tel Aviv–Jerusalem highway, and attack northeast toward Biddu by way of a feature known as Radar Hill. At Biddu, Ben-David's force was to set up a blocking position to prevent the Jordanian battalions stationed around Latrun from counterattacking the Harel Armored-Infantry Brigade from the rear.

Uri Ben-Ari established his brigade command post atop the high hill at Castel. As a young company commander, he had fought over these same hills in 1948. The terrain was rugged and the roads ranged from goat paths to dirt lanes to paved blacktop, but distances were short. Though all the task forces would need to travel farther because their routes did not run straight through, it was only about 15 kilometers from the farthest western break-in point to Tel el-Ful.

But the mines had everyone worried. Until they could be cleared in front of each of the break-in points, only the infantry could advance safely, and on foot at that. The tanks, halftracks, and armored cars could support the breaching operations only at a distance. Fortunately, a crack unit of engineers had been assigned to Ben-Ari's brigade. However, all their mine-clearing equipment, including bangalore torpedoes, had been turned in for use in Sinai. Consequently, these engineers had to clear paths through the minefields the low-tech way, by hand.

Beyond the problem of clearing the mines were time constraints. The 60th Jordanian Armored Brigade was on its way up from Jericho, and there was no doubt that it would be employed to counter the Harel Armored-Infantry Brigade's attack.

The Harel Armored-Infantry Brigade jumped off at 1700, precisely. French Sherman tanks attached to each of the three main task forces advanced north out of their covered jump-off positions and took up firing positions opposite the Jordanian-held hills that were to be assaulted first. The areas in which the attacks were to be made were well-known to the Israelis. The tank gunners had maps that clearly showed the position of every Jordanian bunker, pillbox, and trench, and these were the basis of the extremely accurate pinpoint shooting that opened the brigade assault. From around the brigade command post on Castel, the brigade's battalion of twelve 120mm mortars also struck the main Jordanian defenses. And two Fougas arrived to bomb and strafe Radar Hill.

On the far left, engineers working ahead of Lieutenant Colonel Yigal Ben-David's armored-infantry task force felt their way beneath intense tank, machine-gun, and small-arms fire into the 200-meter-wide minefield fronting Radar Hill's three defended knobs. It was painstaking work, and dangerous. Several engineers accidentally detonated mines and, though none were killed, well over a dozen of the brave men were maimed.

It took three hours, until nearly 2000, for the engineers to breach the minefield in front of Radar Hill. There was, however, no time to be certain that all the mines had been lifted out of the nominally cleared lanes. Lieutenant Colonel Ben-David gave the order to advance. He took a calculated risk by sending one of his Shermans forward ahead of the dismounted armored infantrymen, in the hope that it would detonate any anti-personnel mines that had been missed—and that it would avoid any remaining antitank mines. The risk bore fruit. Despite intense Jordanian machine-gun fire, the lead platoons of armored infantrymen followed the tank in its tread marks. Ben-David was a little less fortunate; his command halftrack ran over an antitank mine because its narrower footing did not precisely match that of the Sherman. Ben-David was unhurt, and he followed the tank on foot.

By the time the battalion commander caught up with his leading infantrymen, the first knob of Radar Hill had fallen. The Jordanians, who moments before had been putting up a wall of bullets, evaporated just before the Israelis closed on their pillboxes and covered trenchworks. The simultaneous final assault on an adjacent knob was delayed for several minutes because no one had thought to bring wire cutters. After the Israelis smashed through the wire with their rifles, the Jordanians deserted the second knob. One Israeli was killed and four were wounded.

As Ben-David was reforming his companies to resume the attack toward Radar Hill's third knob, several companies of the Jerusalem Infantry Brigade arrived on the scene. When their commander asked to be allowed to seize the third knob, Ben-David assented. Major Yaacov "Jackie" Even's company of the Jerusalem Infantry Brigade's so-called Academic Reserve—non-resident Hebrew University students—did the honors. The attack was flawless, and virtually uncontested. While Jackie led his student-soldiers far to the left to get around the main defenses, the Jordanians put out desultory fire, and then they ran for their lives.

In 1948, Captain Uri Ben-Ari's Harel Brigade infantry company had launched five costly attacks before it had been able to secure Radar Hill, and the feature had later been lost by another unit in equally costly fighting. In 1967, at a cost of one dead infantryman, four wounded infantrymen, and about fifteen injured engineers, Radar Hill, was again in Israeli hands.

The engineers advanced ahead of Ben-David's tanks, halftracks, and other vehicles, checking for mines along the dirt track to Biddu. Well short of the objective, the column was stopped cold by an eight-foot-deep antitank ditch. There was no earth-moving equipment in the column, so everyone who was not screening the worksite pitched in to toss rocks into the ditch. The job was completed around 0200 on June 6.

The Imam Ali Infantry Brigade company defending Biddu was ready; it had had all the time in the world to get ready. It was well-entrenched and, for once, ably led. The resistance was fierce, but the dismounted Israeli armored infantrymen fought their way to the top of the hill and fanned out through the Jordanian trenches. Twenty Jordanians and one Israeli were killed in the brief hand-to-hand struggle, and then the surviving Jordanians melted into the night. A French Sherman commander scanning the road into Biddu with his searchlight caught a 106mm recoilless-rifle jeep in the powerful beam. The tank gunner blew the jeep to bits. When the Israelis finally entered Biddu, the town was deserted. Before 0230, Lieutenant Colonel Yigal Ben-David ordered his tanks and armored infantrymen to defend the newly won hills and town against a possible counterattack from the direction of Latrun.

At 1700, and 8 kilometers to the east of Radar Hill, Lieutenant Colonel Aharon Gal decided to forego the tedious mine-clearance operation that had proceeded Ben-David's attack. Gal's company of eleven French Shermans jumped off straight into the 300-meter-deep minefield fronting Abdul Aziz Hill and simply advanced into the Jordanian fire while the dismounted armored infantrymen followed in the tread marks. Seven of Gal's Shermans were disabled by mines before the Israeli armored infantrymen could reach the hill and, in broad daylight, climb toward the Jordanian trenches. Many of the Jordanians, including all their officers, fled, but a dozen or so fought bravely to retain possession of the trenches. The commander of one of the

Israeli companies was killed, as was an Israeli sergeant. Eight Jordanians also died before the rest ran away.

As soon as the Jordanian infantrymen had withdrawn, Jordanian artillery struck the hill. It was directed by a forward-observer team on a hill only 100 meters north of Abdul Aziz Hill and was therefore quite accurate. Despite the fire, three French Shermans and several halftracks filled with armored infantrymen advanced over rough terrain and seized the observation post in a bloodless little foray. Gal's task force then deployed to defend the two newly liberated hills and await further orders.

To Gal's right, also at 1700, Major Amnon Eshkol's Reconnaissance Company 41 advanced north across the Green Line from the Israeli settlement at Mevasseret Yerushalayim. There was no opposition beyond several antitank barriers, which were bypassed by Eshkol's nimble AML armored cars and light jeeps. The reconnaissance company occupied the village of Beit Iksa without a fight and settled down to await further orders.

The easternmost Harel Armored-Infantry Brigade task force, which was built around Lieutenant Colonel Zvika Dahav's Tank Battalion 95, met no enemy opposition in its zone of action, but it was nearly extinguished in a struggle of another kind.

It is sometimes hard to remember that a map is a *representation* of a battlefield, and not the battlefield itself. The squiggles and lines the soldier sees on his map merely approximate the terrain he will encounter. In the case of Zvika Dahav's task force, the squiggle representing a goat trail that meandered along the sides of steep hills could not be printed any narrower than it was; it was the same width as the narrowest motor road. This Dahav's tank crews learned to their regret.

Dahav was absolutely correct in placing Tank Battalion 95's new and newly manned twelve-tank Centurion company at the head of the battalion file. The tall Centurions were the tanks with the best road clearance, and they were his most powerful tanks. Therefore, they had the best chance of getting across rough terrain *and* in winning a battle with any 60th Jordanian Armored Brigade Pattons they might encounter upon reaching the Ramallah–Jerusalem highway near the battalion objective, Tel el-Ful.

The problem with the Centurions was that they were both high *and* wide. Moreover, they were in the hands of newly selected drivers and commanders who were not used to navigating them across rough terrain.

The goat trail was a disappointment. It was exactly the same width as one Centurion track. Whether the other track was placed uphill or downhill of the goat trail, it had to be driven across a profusion of loose rocks and around a profusion of boulders. By 1830, within an hour of moving across the Green Line, every one of the Centurions had literally beached itself on boulders; many of the brand-new tanks wound up with both tracks pathetically churning in midair. The entire Centurion company was lost in broad daylight without a shot having been fired.

Dahav's twenty-six French Sherman tanks were built somewhat lower to the ground than the Centurions, but they were somewhat narrower and quite a bit more agile. Major Uri Berez's Sherman company was ordered to the head of the reduced battalion column, and it made slow but steady progress in the waning light. Meantime, Uri Ben-Ari caught up with Zvika Dahav to find out why Tank Battalion 95 was so long delayed in reaching its objectives. When the predicament was laid out for him, the brigade commander ordered the rear Sherman company to backtrack to the Tel Aviv–Jerusalem highway and move west to catch up with Lieutenant Colonel Aharon Gal's task force on Abdul Aziz Hill. It was then to drive by way of Biddu on adequate dirt roads to the town of Nebi Samwil.

While Ben-Ari drove back toward Castel—his jeep became stalled for hours in the flood of military traffic using the highway—Zvika Dahav moved forward on the goat trail. All his once-powerful task force had left was Major Berez's fourteen French Shermans and the two attached halftrack companies.

The Shermans were much better for navigating across the rough terrain than the Centurions had been, but, after it grew dark, Berez's own tank became hung up on a boulder, and Berez had to jump into the next Sherman in line. A short time later, at 2200, the pitch-dark trail was struck by the King Talal Infantry Brigade's entire 25-pounder artillery battalion. The Jordanians had no way to observe the fall of the artillery shells, so they adjusted their guns to the sound of bursting rounds. In the best of conditions, this is an inaccurate method. In these stony hills, where echoes abounded, it was a waste of time. Several more Shermans became hung up, but none of them nor any halftracks were disabled by the Jordanian artillery.

At 0200, June 6, seven Shermans reached the top of the ridge overlooking Nebi Samwil. Major Berez waited awhile for stragglers to close up, but no more tanks arrived; the other seven were all hung up along the goat track. The tanks assembled on the asphalt road that ran out of Nebi Samwil toward Jerusalem and formed a screen for the halftracks. Of these, only six arrived.

Berez was in favor of attacking Tel el-Ful with this small force, but Zvika Dahav decided to wait. The men were exhausted by their eight-hour ordeal (in which they had traveled only 2.4 kilometers in a straight line), and there was still a chance that more might get through. At 0300, Major Amnon Eshkol's Reconnaissance Company 41 arrived, and two more halftracks made it to the top of the hill. At that point, Lieutenant Colonel Dahav decided to drive to Tel el-Ful.

Eshkol's armored cars were placed at the head of the column and the small Israeli force accelerated straight down the asphalt road toward the Ramallah–Jerusalem highway. Along the way, Major Berez's lead Sherman drove straight off the road in the dark and landed in a ditch from which it could not be extricated. Berez climbed aboard yet another Sherman and the crew climbed aboard a halftrack. The column started up again—six French Shermans, six halftracks, and a platoon of AML armored cars against who-knew-how-many Jordanian Pattons.

Brigadier Sherif Zaid bin Shaker's 60th Jordanian Armored Brigade was still the pride of the Royal Jordanian Army when it received its orders to proceed from its cantonment near the Dead Sea to Jerusalem. Sherif Zaid and his staff had expected to be ordered south to link up with the Egyptian Army in Israel's Negev Desert, and it was disconcerting for them to receive orders to Jerusalem, of all places. But the brigade complied by putting the three Patton companies of Major Khalid Awad's 5th Jordanian Tank Battalion on the Jericho–Jerusalem highway at 1900. Awad's companies were under orders to bolster various elements of the King Talal and Imam Ali Infantry brigades.

The 60th Jordanian Armored Brigade had been absorbing Israeli air attacks for most of the afternoon, but Major Awad and his company commanders expected to be protected by darkness as their battalion advanced up the steep road from well below to well above sea level. Ordinarily, it would have been a short drive, only about 30 kilometers. As soon as it became dark, however, several Israeli jets dropped parachute flares over the highway and attacked the tanks in the stark, eerily moving light.

There were other vehicles on the highway, both civilian and military, and many of them had already been wrecked. Time and again, the 5th Jordanian Tank Battalion's Pattons and other vehicles had to stop while the lead tanks laboriously shoved aside smashed and burning wrecks. The advance slowed to something less than a crawl and left the entire column at the mercy of Israeli jets attacking at will in the bright flarelight.

The lead Jordanian tank company, commanded by Captain Awad Saud Eid, finally reached the road junction at Abu George, where it began the tedious process of refueling. There, Eid's company lost the first of its fourteen Pattons when a tread broke. Meantime, Major Awad and his small battalion command group drove straight through over a less cluttered road to Tel el-Ful. Shortly after Captain Eid's company left Abu George, Israeli jets torched three of the Pattons with napalm. Nevertheless, Eid's ten remaining Pattons joined Major Awad's command group at Tel el-Ful at 0500. Fourteen Pattons of Captain Dib Suliman's company were due to arrive a short time later.

Two more Shermans blundered into deep excavations in a quarry as they were entering the Christian Arab village of Tel Zahara, which was just a stone's throw from Tel el-Ful. By then, only seventy weary Israelis remained under Zvika Dahav's immediate command. They possessed a vital piece of high ground overlooking the vital highway from Ramallah to Jerusalem, but it remained to be seen if they could hold it—much less advance to their ultimate objective, Mount Scopus.

For the time being, Dahav opted to interdict the traffic along the highway with fire. He personally positioned each of the four tanks, the AMLs, and the halftracks in an arc along Tel Zahara's narrow crest. Within minutes, a short column of troop-laden trucks carrying a company of Jordanian infantry appeared from the north. The French Shermans set all the trucks on fire, but the sudden spate of shooting alerted the King Talal Infantry Brigade's 25-pounder battalion, and the Jordanian field guns started probing Tel Zahara. Despite the fall of the 25-pounder shells, which the Jordanians were again firing blindly, the Israeli Shermans managed to torch a small convoy of 106mm recoilless-rifle jeeps that tried to rush past. After that, the Jordanians stopped using the vital highway.

One of the Jordanian artillery batteries and the battalion fire-direction center were at Neve Yaacov, a former Jewish settlement less than 2 kilometers north of the Tel el-Ful crossroads. Machine guns guarding the battery were able to reach Tel Zahara with their fire, but return fire from Israeli machine guns forced the Jordanians off the crest of their hill. With that, for no known reason, the Jordanian artillery battalion commander ordered his headquarters and the 25-pounder battery to withdraw to the east. The Israelis on Tel Zahara spotted the movement, opened fire with mortars, and called for air support. Israeli jets were soon bombing and strafing the Jordanian artillery units on the open road. Within ninety minutes, the entire Jordanian column lay in ruins.

The lead platoon of Captain Awad Saud Eid's Patton company began its attack on Tel Zahara at about 0600. The three Pattons were spotted instantly by Major Amnon Eshkol, the commander of Reconnaissance Company 41, and he pointed them out to Major Uri Berez, the tank-company commander.

The Jordanians had all the advantages. Their tanks were on higher ground when they came into view, and the sun was at their backs—in the eyes of the Israeli gunners. Also, the Patton 90mm guns outranged the Sherman 75mm guns. Nevertheless, Major Berez ordered his gunners to fire at the lead Pattons.

Most of the Israeli shells merely bounced off the Pattons, but a few detonated without penetrating. The deputy commander of the Patton company was severely wounded, and the commander of another Patton was killed by machine-gun fire from Tel Zahara. However, three Israeli halftracks were blown up by the Pattons, and a 90mm round killed an Israeli tank commander. This tank had to withdraw, and then the firing mechanism on another Sherman's main gun broke. The two remaining Shermans fired and moved, fired and moved, but their 75mm high-velocity rounds had no effect on the three Jordanian Pattons. All three of the remaining Israeli halftracks were blown up. Several Israeli armored-infantrymen were killed and a dozen were wounded.

It does not get any grimmer than that. Captain Eid's company could have had Tel Zahara if it wanted it. But Eid lost his will; he became unnerved at the idea of fighting in a built-up area against a force of undetermined size. He ordered his Patton company to pull back while he thought things through.

As soon as the pressure lifted, the crew of the disabled Sherman advanced their tank to the brow of the hill; at least it could fire its two machine guns. All three Shermans were ready when six Jordanian Pattons appeared on the brow of Tel el-Ful. By then, Captain Dib Suliman's Patton company had arrived from Abu George. Captain Eid ordered his drivers to swing to the left to join up with Suliman's as-yet-unseen company for a final attack on Tel Zahara.

The Jordanian Pattons had been equipped with external long-range gasoline tanks. As Eid's tanks pivoted to match the course taken by Suliman's, the fuel tanks became exposed to the hitherto ineffectual Israeli machine-gun fire. By sheer luck, the commander of the disabled Sherman hit one of the external fuel tanks with bullets from his .50-caliber machine gun. A tracer round set the gasoline ablaze, and the Patton was engulfed in flames. Instantly, the panicked crew of a second Patton abandoned ship and scurried from the battlefield on foot. A moment after that, an Israeli jet destroyed Captain Eid's Patton with a direct bomb hit. Then the commander of Eid's second platoon was blown out of his Patton, also by a direct bomb hit.

The Jordanian tank company came unglued. Eid managed to climb aboard another Patton, but he led his six survivors away to the south rather than toward the vulnerable Israelis on Tel Zahara. Captain Suliman left a small rear-guard detachment and followed Eid with the main body of his company. Three more of Suliman's Pattons were destroyed by Israeli jets before they cleared Tel el-Ful.

Later in the day, around 1430, all the surviving Pattons from the 5th Jordanian Tank Battalion rendezvoused at a suburb several kilometers east of Tel el-Ful. After refueling, the force set out for Jericho. On the way, five more Pattons were destroyed by Israeli jets.

39

In a short war filled to overflowing with stirring events and superhuman sacrifices, the ordeal of Colonel Mordechai Gur's 55th Parachute Brigade would become the emotional touchstone.

The ordeal of the 55th Parachute Brigade began at noon on Monday, June 5, when someone at *Zahal* GHQ telephoned Brigadier General Uzi Narkiss to ask if he could use a battalion of paratroopers in Jerusalem. Narkiss replied that he could use a whole brigade. Ten minutes later, GHQ called to offer Narkiss a second parachute battalion, and five minutes after that, the entire 55th Parachute Brigade was turned over to Central Command.

How Colonel Mordechai Gur's Reserve parachute brigade would finally be used in the war had been a matter of intense debate at GHQ and Southern Command for most of the morning. In the original war plan, the brigade was to be dropped or landed at night at the El Arish airfield, behind Egyptian lines, but that plan had slowly begun to change almost as soon as the three Southern Command *ugdot* jumped off. Finally, a little before noon, one parachute battalion had been alerted for a "possible" move to Jerusalem in the event there was a full outbreak of war there. Shortly, the battalion was definitely ordered to Jerusalem and another battalion was put on alert for a possible move. By 1230, the war in the south appeared to be going so well that the entire brigade was definitely transferred to Central Command and alerted for the move to Jerusalem.

As soon as the official transfer was complete, Colonel Gur—"Motta"— was reached by telephone from Central Command Headquarters, in Ramle, and asked when his brigade would be ready for duty. Given the change in plans, Motta had to tell Central Command that none of his paratroopers could reach Jerusalem from Lod International Airport—usually a twenty-minute drive—before late in the evening. They had to unpack ammunition and weapons that had been prepared for the air drop, and then they had to rustle up some transportation, because the brigade had only a few jeeps to its name, and even they were packed away aboard large transport planes. Everyone at Central Command was impatient, but they understood Motta's predicament. They hastily factored the delay into their thinking. Motta volunteered to drive up to Ramle right away, but first he had to rent a civilian car to do so.

Motta reached Ramle at about 1300. Then and there, Uzi Narkiss gave him a terse, distracted briefing, taking time out from a hundred other chores and emergencies to do so. About all Motta learned was that his brigade was slated to seize several stoutly defended features along the inner arc of northern hills between the Green Line and Mount Scopus. With that, Gur left Ramle with a handful of his key officers to set up a headquarters in the city and begin reconnoitering the objectives from the Israeli side of the Green Line.

Narkiss and Motta next met at about 2000, when Narkiss arrived at the Knesset to attend Moshe Dayan's swearing-in ceremony as Minister of Defense. (Dayan was busy elsewhere and did not arrive.) By then, Narkiss knew that the Harel Armored-Infantry Brigade had seized Radar Hill and other objectives and was proceeding rather unevenly toward Tel el-Ful—the back door to Mount Scopus. Motta reported that the first busloads of his paratroopers had finally gotten underway from Lod at 1900, and that he expected at least two battalions to be assembled in West Jerusalem by 0200, June 6. Narkiss wanted to use the paratroopers—however many there were—to break into East Jerusalem directly toward Mount Scopus, where they would link up with Ben-Ari's wide left hook. On the way, several key Jordanian defensive positions and an East Jerusalem neighborhood or two would have to be secured, and that in turn would help clear the way for Ben-Ari's final drive into the city. It was therefore no big deal that the paratroopers would be arriving late; as things stood then, the spearhead of Ben-Ari's brigade was not expected to reach the Ramallah-Jerusalem highway until a little before dawn. In fact, the more Narkiss thought about it, the better he liked it. The lightly armed paratroopers were night-fighting experts, and the night could be used to their advantage. So, as far as Narkiss was concerned, an attack that would open between 0200 and 0300 was just about right.

At that point, Chief of Staff Yitzhak Rabin, who was also waiting for Dayan to appear, weighed in with advice that Narkiss postpone Motta's assault until 0800. By then, Rabin declared, he could guaranty ample air and artillery support. But Narkiss rebutted that air and artillery would just get in the way during the fast-moving house-to-house battle in which he thought the paratroopers would immediately become embroiled; there was simply no way to accurately control the fall of artillery shells and bombs under those circumstances. Giving in to the principle that the man on the scene makes his own plans, Rabin left the matter to Narkiss.

For his part, Motta simply went along with Narkiss. At 0140, he accompanied the general to the former's newly opened makeshift forward command post, nearly opposite a Jordanian-held feature known as Ammunition Hill. Narkiss and Motta climbed to the roof to look at Ammunition Hill in the glow of artillery shells and flares that were bursting far and wide across the city sky. Ammunition Hill would be the 55th Parachute Brigade's first and chief objective because it and a neighboring hill dominated both the direct route to Mount Scopus *and* a stretch of the Ramallah–Jerusalem highway that Ben-Ari's tanks and halftracks needed to traverse on their way to Mount Scopus. As the two commanders discussed details of the attack, a Jordanian 25-pounder shell burst on the roof's parapet. Neither of the commanders was hurt, but two paratroop officers were.

Motta Gur was 37 years old in 1967. Several years earlier, he had been the youngest of all *Zahal* brigade commanders. He had been born in the Old City of Jerusalem but had spent most of his childhood in Rehoveth. Motta had been involved in anti-British activities for the Jewish Underground from an early age. Though he should have been a scholar, he had become a fighter. At the outbreak of the War of Independence, young Gur was selected to train other young fighters, but he argued his way into a commando unit and fought the Egyptians in the Negev Desert. Captain Gur mustered out of full-time service after the war, but he spent protracted periods on active duty, between odd semesters at the Hebrew University. After earning his degree in 1954, he returned to *Zahal* full time and volunteered for Arik Sharon's Parachute Battalion 202. He was made a company commander and took part in many of the early paratroop raids. After recovering from a leg wound in early 1956, Motta was placed in command of a newly formed parachute battalion of the newly formed 202nd Parachute Brigade, and he fought bravely in that capacity at the Mitla Pass. In 1957, Lieutenant Colonel Gur attended a year-long course at the *École de Guerre,* and then he served on the General Staff. He was made a colonel in 1959, and commanded the Standing Army's 1st "Golani" Infantry Brigade. In late 1966, after several staff assignments, he was named commandant of *Zahal*'s Staff and Command College. His emergency war-time assignment was as commander of the 55th Reserve Parachute Brigade.

Facing Gur's brigade across the Green Line was the first-class 2nd Jordanian Infantry Battalion of Brigadier Ata Ali Hazza'a's King Talal Infantry Brigade. Though Hazza'a's personal control over the defense of Jerusalem had been considerably strengthened by the addition of the Imam Ali Infantry Brigade to his command, he still had to rely upon his own understrength battalions to withstand the expected Israeli assault toward Mount Scopus. Offsetting the King Talal Infantry Brigade's numerical weakness, the Jordanians possessed several extensively fortified defensive zones, each designed to withstand pro-tracted aerial and artillery bombardment and massive ground assaults.

Part of Hazza'a's 8th Jordanian Infantry Battalion was in the Old City itself, guarding the presumed ultimate Israeli objective against attack, and the rest of that battalion was spread out toward Abu Tor, in East Jerusalem's southern environs, across from Government House. A company of the 4th Jordanian Infantry Battalion was at Tel el-Ful, but it was under orders to move south toward East Jerusalem. That left the fortified area between the Green Line and Mount Scopus—Ammunition and Mivtar hills and the hilly American Colony and Sheikh Jarrah neighborhoods—in the hands of Major Mansaur Kreishan's 2nd Jordanian Infantry Battalion.

As it turned out, Kreishan's battalion not only sat astride the Wadi el-Joz, the direct route from West Jerusalem to Mount Scopus, its defensive positions atop Ammunition Hill dominated the last stretch of the Ramal-lah–Jerusalem highway leading past Mount Scopus. In Uzi Narkiss's view, this dominating position and the neighborhoods on either side of the Wadi el-Joz had to be seized, one way or another, before the isolated Mount Scopus garrison could be fully relieved. In other words, it was not enough merely to reinforce and resupply Mount Scopus; a permanent supply route had to be driven through and held. If Ben-Ari's tanks and armored infantrymen could do it from the north, then fine. But they were Narkiss's insurance policy. He was pinning his best hopes on Gur's paratroopers. If they could secure Ammunition Hill, then Ben-Ari's chances of success would be magnified. And even if Ben-Ari was stopped north of the city, the paratroopers themselves were expected to get through to Mount Scopus on their own. In any case, the main strength of the large Jerusalem Infantry Brigade could be employed in the northern attack if it was needed, or in other fruitful pursuits if the Harel and/or 55th brigades fought through to Mount Scopus.

Overall, Narkiss's thinking was sound. But there was a flaw in his planning, and that was his own impatience to complete the attack as soon as possible, at all costs.

Uzi Narkiss later explained that he did not feel that Colonel Eliezer Amitai's Jerusalem Infantry Brigade was up to the task of attacking, seizing, and holding Ammunition Hill, the Wadi el-Joz, the American Colony, and the Sheikh Jarrah district. But Amitai could never figure out why Narkiss thought such a thing. It is true that Narkiss had asked Amitai if he thought his troops could do the job, but all Amitai had said in reply was that it would be tough. However, that is when Narkiss assigned the mission to Motta Gur's much smaller and lightly armed 55th Parachute Brigade. Amitai was mystified; his brigade had drawn up specific plans to seize these objectives, and his troops had trained hard for the mission because it had been obvious for years that the outbreak of a war with Jordan would be accompanied by an Israeli attack to relieve Mount Scopus. The paratroopers had never trained to attack toward Mount Scopus from West Jerusalem; few if any paratroopers had ever even cast a military eye on a map of the area.

But Uzi Narkiss's mind was made up. The light parachute battalions would attack all the vital but unfamiliar waystations in the dark of night, without air or artillery support. Though this flew in the face of *Zahal*'s decade-long development of the indirect approach to battle—an approach that was already being executed toward the same ultimate objective by Ben-Ari's Harel Armored-Infantry Brigade—no one protested loudly enough to get Narkiss to think about his plan once again. Not even Yitzhak Rabin had argued against the unsupported direct assault at night; he had merely offered an alternative.

The route the 55th Parachute Brigade was to take to Mount Scopus was indeed the direct one. Using it played directly into the strength of the 2nd Jordanian Infantry Battalion. While Uzi Narkiss told Motta Gur to be prepared to swing to the right to begin moving toward the Old City, he also obliged Gur to put blinders on and attack straight ahead, through the Sheikh Jarrah district and across Ammunition Hill, directly toward Mount Scopus. It is true that *some* Israelis knew every last detail of the Jordanian defensive establishment, but most of that knowledge was offset by the decision to attack at night without air or artillery support. Thanks to Narkiss's decision, Gur could not finesse his way into East Jerusalem. The attack had to be blunt, and it was therefore inevitable that it would be costly.

Coincidentally, Gur and his brigade intelligence officer had been in Jerusalem on June 3, making a contingency plan to conduct a raid-in-force to rescue the Israeli garrison on Mount Scopus. Even then, no one actually expected the paratroopers to be employed in Jerusalem, but *Zahal* was trying to cover every eventuality. By sheer coincidence, Motta had decided to punch through to Mount Scopus by way of the Wadi el-Joz. However, though he had actually looked at the ground from the Israeli side, he and his troopers were not especially familiar with it—at least, not in military terms. If there was any way around Ammunition Hill, Motta did not know it or had not thought about it. This only heightened the bulldog attitude that prevailed when at last the orders had to be handed down. Everyone accepted the straightforward approach because all the movement and planning was so haphazard, so rushed. There was no time to stop and think.

At the last minute, the uncommitted half of the Jerusalem Infantry Brigade French Sherman squadron was attached to the 55th Parachute Brigade, and a number of halftracks and other weapons were also loaned to the paratroopers to make good some of the shortages resulting from the hurried departures from Lod Airport. Unfortunately, very few maps were forthcoming.

To help take the place of maps, the paratroop commanders, who arrived hours before their troopers, spoke with many residents of the city. All the talking was helpful, of course, but none of the people who rendered such aid had been in East Jerusalem for nearly two decades, and none had specific knowledge of the Jordanian defenses.

40

It took nearly until zero hour for the parachute battalions to prepare—as well as they could. The troopers were late in reaching Jerusalem because the traffic on the Tel Aviv–Jerusalem highway had forced the makeshift convoys of buses from Lod International Airport to proceed via a tortuously long alternate route over secondary roads. The men were tired and tense, but there was a sort of electricity running through the brigade. Everyone's mind was on the job at hand, but no one was without the hope that the Old City would be their final objective. It meant the world to them to be so close to fulfilling the national obsession.

The Jerusalem Infantry Brigade's ten uncommitted French Sherman tanks were hurriedly transferred to the control of the 55th Parachute Brigade and, as the bombardments back and forth over the Green Line intensified, everyone moved swiftly into place. Major Yosef Yaffe's Parachute Battalion 66 was faced with conducting a series of attacks to clear the Police Training School, Ammunition Hill, and the Sheikh Jarrah district. After these objectives had fallen, Yaffe's battalion was to attack through to Mount Scopus. To Yaffe's right, Major Uzi Eilam's Parachute Battalion 71 was poised to begin the attack through the American Colony and toward Mount Scopus by an alternate route. Eilam's battalion was also to contain the northwestern corner of the Old City. Lieutenant Colonel Yosef Fradkin's Parachute Battalion 28 was to follow Eilam's Parachute Battalion 71 across the Green Line, turn sharply to the right, and screen the twin moves to Mount Scopus alongside the Wadi el-Joz by seizing and holding a line directly overlooking the Old City's northern wall.

The entire area in front of the 55th Parachute Brigade was held by Major Mansaur Kreishan's very good 2nd Jordanian Infantry Battalion, a part of the King Talal Infantry Brigade. The Israeli brigade zone exactly coincided with Kreishan's zone.

*   *   *

Of the 500 men in Major Uzi Eilam's Parachute Battalion 71, only Eilam and his deputy had seen combat. All the other officers and men were too young to have served in 1956. Eilam was the only officer in the battalion who had lived in Jerusalem—for two years, while his wife was in medical school. He selected as the battalion's jump-off point a spot a little more than a kilometer from the northern wall of the Old City and about 800 meters south of Ammunition Hill. The immediate objective was a defended wall lining the west side of Nablus Road.

A Jordanian artillery observation post was directly opposite the point at which Eilam had chosen to break in. Moments before 0200, June 6, as the Israelis deployed to attack, the Jordanian artillery forward observer placed his battery's entire output on Eilam's battalion. Three Israelis were killed and a handful were wounded, but the Israelis opened their own attack in good order. Two powerful searchlights the paratroopers had hurriedly installed atop West Jerusalem's tallest structure were lit off right in the eyes of the defenders, and a volley of wire-guided antitank missiles was fired from truck-mounted launchers, also straight into the faces of the defenders. As the Jordanians aimed the bulk of their small-arms fire at the searchlights, the paratroopers closed on the Green Line and opened fire with their mortars, machine guns, and small arms, plus two Jerusalem Infantry Brigade French Shermans and three jeep-mounted 106mm recoilless rifles.

The first files of Parachute Battalion 71 moved across the Green Line at 0215. Bangalore torpedoes were shoved beneath the thick belts of barbed wire, and these touched off numerous mines as well as opening a breach in the wire barrier. One paratroop company attacked straight through the breach—right across no-man's land—and two others fanned out to engulf the Jordanian defensive sector a short distance up and down Nablus Road. At the last minute, as the Israelis were closing on the Jordanian-held wall at at least three points, the Jordanian artillery observer called fire from his battery of 25-pounder guns right down on his own position. In this way, he killed himself and the other members of his observer team, but no Israelis.

When Uzi Eilam radioed the news that he had reached Nablus Road, Motta shot back, "You deserve a kiss." Eilam ordered the handful of tanks, halftracks, and recoilless-rifle jeeps under his control to cross no-man's land, but the two Shermans had their tracks blown off by mines in the narrow passage.

From their foothold on Nablus Road, Parachute Battalion 71's three forward companies advanced swiftly into the American Colony district and began sweeping toward Mount Scopus by way of several streets and roads. The going was slow because scores of houses had to be cleared, but there was little opposition. The heavy fighting was in the battalion rear, where the fourth paratroop company was put to work expanding the breach along the defended wall fronting Nablus Road. A Jordanian infantry company was dug into deep, mutually supporting bunkers and pillboxes, and the Jordanian soldiers put up a tenacious resistance.

From 0200 until dawn, Eilam's forward companies cleared the battalion's sector of Nablus Road and the American Colony. Then one company penetrated into the Wadi el-Joz and advanced farther east, toward Mount Scopus. Meantime, the bulk of two of Eilam's companies turned south and cleared a large area in the direction of the northern wall of the Old City. By 0800, Eilam's battalion was firmly in control of the Wadi el-Joz and had hooked nearly to the rear entrance to the Rockefeller Museum, a ten-acre complex of buildings hard against the northeast corner of the Old City.

The hurried planning, the lack of maps, the do-or-die attitude that prevailed in the 55th Parachute Brigade by the time zero hour arrived—these factors made an utter disaster of Parachute Battalion 28's sweep toward the Old City in the wake of Parachute Battalion 71's attack through the Green Line.

Even before Lieutenant Colonel Yossi Fradkin's Parachute Battalion 28 jumped off at 0430, the battalion command group was struck by a volley of Jordanian 81mm mortar rounds that felled everyone except Fradkin and one other officer. One paratroop company was also severely mauled. As medics and volunteers rushed in to give aid to the wounded, a second volley detonated on top of them. Thirty-five paratroopers were killed or wounded.

Fradkin's battalion followed Eilam's and, according to plan, turned sharply to the right, toward the Old City. Several men were killed or wounded in the road, but one company cleared a portion of the Jordanian defenses along the Nablus Road wall, and the bulk of Fradkin's battalion passed through in safety.

The fatal error was made at the intersection of Nablus Road and East Jerusalem's main business thoroughfare, Salah ed-Din Street. Both angled to the south, toward the Old City, but one was defended in depth and the other was quite literally the path of least resistance. In the excitement of the moment, Fradkin and the commander of his battalion's lead company, neither of whom was familiar with Jerusalem, misread Fradkin's map in the eerie dawn glow, and they opted for the wrong street.

The only possible salvation arrived at the last moment, as Fradkin was committing himself to the gravest of errors. The deputy commander of the Jerusalem Infantry Brigade's French Sherman Squadron reached Parachute Battalion 71 with seven of his tanks, an unplanned bonus because the tanks had not been able to take part in the fighting on Ammunition Hill.

Even as the tanks entered the fray, Fradkin's lead company was engaged to the hilt by the self-reliant Bedouin soldiers of the 2nd Jordanian Infantry Battalion, who were able to improvise strongpoints in the buildings around their otherwise outflanked pillboxes and bunkers. The tanks unnerved some of the defenders, but others stood up well to the armored attack. Most of the Israeli tank commanders were wounded by fire from over their heads, and one tank commander was shot dead.

Despite the fierce resistance, the Israelis fought through to the American Consulate by 0600. A short distance past the consulate, Nablus Road was intersected at a sharp angle by Shmuel Hanevi Street. This thoroughfare ran from West Jerusalem to the Old City via an old crossing point known as the Mandelbaum Gate, which was on the west side of the American Consulate. Because of the Mandelbaum Gate, the intersection of Nablus Road and Shmuel Hanevi Street and an adjacent square comprised one of the most heavily defended points in the entire area. It cost the lead paratroop company dearly to cross the intersection and square, and it finally took direct fire by one of the Shermans to destroy the key strongpoint, which the Jordanians had set in at the end of a narrow blind alleyway. The lead paratroop company took so many additional casualties in this one fight that it was rendered ineffective. Even getting its wounded to safety cost the company more wounded.

The relief paratroop company resumed the attack, but it was stalled by yet another makeshift Jordanian strongpoint. A tank finally ran right over the position, crushing the men in it, but that exposed the Sherman to direct bazooka fire from the wall of the Old City, which was held by the King Talal Infantry Brigade's 8th Jordanian Infantry Battalion. With the Damascus Gate in view dead ahead, the tankers searched for the source of the fire. At length, the company commander fired blindly at the wall, and that drew another bazooka round. The commander of the second tank saw the backblast from the bazooka, and he fired at the source. There was no bazooka fire after that, but machine-gun fire from atop the wall wounded the company commander and a tank commander.

Coordination between the tanks and the paratroopers broke down. The paratroopers had never trained with tanks; they did not know that coordinating their actions with those of the Shermans was as easy as picking up an intercom telephone that every Israeli tank had strapped to its rear fender. The tankers had not been given the paratroopers' radio frequencies or call signs, or vice versa.

All the tanks formed a line facing the Damascus Gate and opened fire on pinpoint targets along the Old City's northern wall, which Jordanian infantrymen were defending like a castle of old. The lead company of Parachute Battalion 28 occupied the buildings directly behind the tanks, but they did not fire on the city wall. They even took over other buildings to the east and wound up staring straight at Herod's Gate, which was just to the west of the Rockefeller Museum.

For over an hour, the tanks fired at the Old City wall over and on either side of the Damascus Gate, but the paratroopers right behind them did not. Neither group of Israelis knew how to contact the other to coordinate their actions. No one thought of simply going forward or back to talk face-to-face. Finally, when Motta Gur radioed the commander of the tanks to find out how things were going, the captain said that his tanks were on the verge of exhausting their ammunition. As Motta started forward to confer with Lieutenant Colonel Fradkin, he ordered the tanks to withdraw to get resupplied.

Motta and Fradkin met at the Rockefeller Museum at 1100 on Tuesday, June 6, only thirty minutes after Fradkin's support company had secured the ten-acre complex. After congratulating Fradkin on reaching his objective, Motta ordered him to send a company back to clear Nablus Road. When Fradkin revealed that he had attacked by way of Nablus Road, Motta was stunned. When the brigade commander explained that Parachute Battalion 28 was supposed to have advanced by way of Salah ed-Din Street, Fradkin, a War of Independence veteran who had jumped into Mitla Pass in 1956, merely thought, "That's what happens in war."

To the north, dozens of other paratroopers were killed or wounded on Ammunition Hill—because of another simple error.

After receiving a handful of virtually useless maps, the officers of Major Yosef Yaffe's Parachute Battalion 66 cobbled together their tactical plans. It somehow became "common knowledge" that the main Jordanian defensive position in the battalion's zone was the Police Training School at the base of Ammunition Hill, and not Ammunition Hill itself. The real situation was known to key officers of the Jerusalem Infantry Brigade, but a liaison officer who had been assigned to help the paratroopers had no role in planning the Parachute Battalion 66 attack. As a result, Major Yaffe assigned three of his four companies to the Police Training School and, for the time being, none to Ammunition Hill. As far as Yaffe and his officers and men knew, the big battle would be in overcoming the Police Training School—at which Brigadier Ata Ali Hazza'a was rumored to have set up his brigade headquarters— followed by clearing operations across Ammunition Hill and the Sheikh Jarrah district. And then it would be on to Mount Scopus.

There were hardly any Jordanians in the Police Training School, which in 1951 had been converted for use as the local headquarters of the United Nations Relief and Works Administration (UNRWA). This small platoon of Bedouin soldiers was part of Captain Suliman Salayta's 2nd Company of the King Talal Infantry Brigade's 2nd Jordanian Infantry Battalion. The rest of the 2nd Company, and a 25-pounder battery, was on Ammunition Hill, manning a formidable complex of concrete-and-stone trenches and bunkers that had been based upon a rabbit's warren of ancient burial caves.

Beginning at 0200, the Parachute Battalion 66 mortars and a battery of Israeli 25-pounders opened fire on the no-man's land on both sides of the Green Line in front of the Police Training School. The object of the fire was to break up numerous barbed-wire barriers and set off as many mines as possible. Then, at a word from Major Yaffe, paratroopers equipped with bangalore torpedoes stole into no-man's land and blew back the barbed wire and set off mines along a narrow path in dead ground leading straight to the Police Training School. Immediately, as several Jerusalem Infantry Brigade French Shermans fired at the objective and Israeli 25-pounders blanketed Ammunition Hill, the lead paratroop company advanced into no-man's land and picked up a concrete-lined trench that curved from the front to the rear of the UNRWA complex.

The lead paratroop company built up a firing line on three sides of the three barracks buildings. The next company moved through the breach and set to work clearing several outguard bunkers on the edge of the school grounds. Though about half of the dozen to fifteen Jordanians deployed in the bunkers bolted up Ammunition Hill, the remainder stood and fought with hand grenades until they were all killed.

While the second paratroop company rooted through a total of thirty-four abandoned or captured bunkers, the third paratroop company assaulted directly toward the UNRWA administration building. Most of the remaining Jordanians made good their escape up Ammunition Hill, but one brave soldier stalled the Israeli attack by throwing down nearly three dozen hand grenades from the second floor.

The main body of Parachute Battalion 66 was still rooting carefully through the UNRWA complex when it started becoming light to the east, at about 0430. By then, several platoons of paratroopers had advanced to the base of Ammunition Hill, a rather unimpressive feature that nonetheless dominated the entire neighborhood across the way in West Jerusalem. About 800 meters north of Ammunition Hill, and dominating it, was Mivtar Hill, through which passed the Ramallah–Jerusalem highway and on which the paratroopers were now certain the Jordanians had based their main defensive zone.

Given everything he knew about the local situation and all of about five minutes to plan his battalion's ongoing sweep, Major Yaffe assigned two companies to clear Ammunition Hill and two companies to clear the Sheikh Jarrah neighborhood. After these objectives had been secured, it would be decided by whom and by what means Mount Scopus was to be relieved.

The main body of Parachute Battalion 66—two parachute-infantry companies, the support company, and the battalion headquarters—was going to finish clearing the Police Training School and would soon strike out into the Sheikh Jarrah neighborhood. Meantime, Captain David Rutenberg's paratroop company led the way out of the Police Training School toward the southwest corner of the ring of trenches at the base of Ammunition Hill. Behind Rutenberg's company, and moving around to the east side of the hill, was Captain Oved Yaacovi's company. One of Captain Salayta's platoons stood directly in the path of each Israeli company.

As soon as Yaacovi's company began taking fire from ahead, a pre-planned Israeli mortar barrage fell in on the Jordanian position. Captain Salayta responded with an artillery barrage, sent one squad to reinforce the platoon at the point of contact, and ordered two other squads to counterattack Yaacovi's paratroopers. In addition, though Salayta did not know it, most of the men who had earlier escaped from the Police Training School were manning bunkers and trenches in the area.

Within moments, two of Yaacovi's officers were shot to death and two of the three paratroop platoons faltered. The third Israeli platoon penetrated into the complex of trenches and began climbing the hill by what appeared to be the path of least resistance. Unfortunately, this also intermixed Israelis with Jordanians, and that called for an extra level of caution that further slowed the main body of Yaacovi's company. In fact, it virtually assured a hand-to-hand, toe-to-toe battle for Ammunition Hill, from bottom to top and front to back.

On the west side of the hill, out of sight and out of touch, Rutenberg's company also faced an early disaster. Jordanian 81mm mortars caught the company in motion in front of the hill, killing two men. Then, in the first surge against the Jordanian bunkers and trenches, six more Israelis were killed and many more were wounded.

The Israelis on both sides of the hill fought like tigers, but the Jordanians were up to it. Each side won its share and lost its share in a series of heart-rending little battles waged entirely between individuals or, at most, Israeli fire teams against Jordanians squads. True to the heritage of the paratroopers, most of the Israeli losses were among officers and NCOs. In fact, when Yaacovi's company finally ran out of steam on the northeast slope of the hill, seventeen of the eighty men who had started the attack were dead, and forty-two had sustained wounds ranging from light to grave. Nevertheless, Yaacovi's company had penetrated to within 15 meters of Captain Salayta's command bunker on the northeast brow of the hill.

With the Israelis so close—he had no idea that Yaacovi's company had run out of steam—Captain Salayta led a stirring counterattack that resulted in many Jordanian losses but left the Israelis stunned and immobile. It also sprang Salayta from his doomed command bunker and gave him the run of what little remained of the Jordanian holdings on Ammunition Hill.

The cavalry arrived just as Yaacovi's company was about to roll over. Sent back from the Sheikh Jarrah district in response to cries for help, Captain Gavriel Magal's paratroop company arrowed straight into the fight along one of the captured trenches. It was about to pass through Yaacovi's exhausted unit when Captain Salayta called his own artillery straight down on his command bunker. The barrage caught the new arrivals bunched up along one short stretch of the narrow trench and wounded many of them.

The desperate fight continued. The survivors of Yaacovi's and Magal's companies became hopelessly intermingled as they struggled ahead against fierce Jordanian resistance. On the far side of the hill, nearing the crest, Rutenberg's company also lost its cohesion and attacked over and around the hill in several ad hoc groupings.

Two Sherman tanks from the Jerusalem Infantry Brigade laboriously climbed the hill, and one of them was instrumental in destroying a stubbornly held bunker that was barring the way for everyone. However, as the Israelis passed that bunker, they came under intense long-range fire from Mivtar Hill.

The desperate hand-to-hand killing continued. Captain Salayta, of all the Jordanian infantry officers in Jerusalem, shared the risk of death with his men until, finally, there were not enough men left alive to hold the hill. Of the ninety Bedouin soldiers in the 2nd Company at the start of the battle, only a badly wounded Captain Suliman Salayta and three others left Ammunition Hill on their own feet. They reached Mivtar Hill, but all the others died—including several who fought on even after Captain Salayta left.

By 0715, three badly mauled Israeli paratroop companies were virtually in possession of Ammunition Hill, and Parachute Battalion 66's fourth infantry company was in possession of the Sheikh Jarrah neighborhood, from Ammunition Hill to the edge of the Wadi el-Joz.

After spending the entire night trapped in traffic on the Tel Aviv–Jerusalem highway, the Harel Armored-Infantry Brigade's Colonel Uri Ben-Ari was finally rescued by an Alouette scout helicopter dispatched all the way from Sinai for just that purpose. He arrived at Nebi Samwil a little before 0800 to conduct a commanders' meeting, just as the lead elements of Lieutenant Colonel Aharon Gal's two tank and two armored-infantry companies were arriving from Abdul Aziz Hill by way of Biddu. By then, the tiny group of survivors of Lieutenant Colonel Zvika Dahav's drive to the Ramallah–Jerusalem highway were atop Tel Zahara, awaiting relief.

After ordering Gal's task force on to Tel Zahara, Ben-Ari flew there to confer with Zvika Dahav. When Gal's force arrived, Ben-Ari ordered it to seize Tel el-Ful.

Gal's force of French Shermans and halftracks, plus several AML armored cars, crossed the deserted highway at 0830 and mounted Tel el-Ful. On the way to the crest, the lead AMLs and Shermans were challenged by several Jordanian Patton tanks that were serving as a rearguard for the withdrawing 5th Jordanian Tank Battalion. Two of the AMLs were destroyed and several crewmen were killed, but the Shermans rallied and destroyed two of the Pattons, which were by then running from the hill. Counting those two, the Israelis found eight destroyed or abandoned Pattons on Tel el-Ful.

When Ben-Ari radioed Central Command Headquarters with the good news that his brigade was in possession of Tel el-Ful, he was ordered to attack down the Ramallah–Jerusalem highway to clear the roadside village of Shu'afat and seize Mivtar and French hills. Ben-Ari gave Aharon Gal every available tank and three armored-infantry companies and ordered him to move swiftly to all the objectives. In the meantime, Zvika Dahav's reduced task force dug in on Tel el-Ful to guard the highway against a feared Jordanian push from the direction of Ramallah.

Gal's force, with Ben-Ari along in one of the halftracks, made swift work of Shu'afat, which was in the hands of the northernmost company the King Talal Infantry Brigade's 4th Jordanian Infantry Battalion. The main body of Gal's tanks and halftracks merely arrowed along the highway through the village, firing their cannons and machine guns as they passed. The rear Israeli armored-infantry company dropped out of Gal's column and had the town firmly in hand by 1000.

After passing through Shu'afat, four Shermans led by Gal and four halftracks, including Ben-Ari's, surged ahead of the main body. These vehicles and a command jeep were just entering a steep cut that carried the highway through the center of Mivtar Hill when the main body of the 4th Jordanian Infantry Battalion opened fire from directly overhead. The jeep was blown off the roadway by an antitank gun and its four occupants were killed. Gal allowed the tanks to fire only their machine guns. Mount Scopus was in a direct line from the highway, and Gal feared hitting it if the main-gun rounds went over Mivtar Hill. As the Shermans and halftracks advanced deeper into the road cut, many Jordanians turned their fire from Ammunition Hill, which was 800 meters away to the south, to fire down on the highway.

There were two Jerusalem Infantry Brigade French Shermans to the south of Mivtar Hill. They had fought on Ammunition Hill. Though nearly out of fuel and ammunition, they were the only means by which the light Israeli forces in northern Jerusalem might beat back a feared counterattack from the north by the Jordanian Pattons.

When news was passed to the tank commanders by paratroopers on the roof of a nearby building that four tanks were approaching from the cut through Mivtar Hill, the two tankers jumped to the conclusion that the

Jordanian counterattack was underway. They backed their tanks into a small street that opened onto the main highway and waited to ambush the approaching armor force.

Gal's tiny spearhead force dashed all the way through the Mivtar Hill road cut without further loss and eased to the left to turn up the road to Mount Scopus. Just as Gal's lead Sherman made the turn, the two Jerusalem Infantry Brigade Shermans dashed out from the side street and fired from a range of 300 meters.

Before the matter could be straightened out, four IAF Mystères streaked in to strafe the tanks on the highway. Gal's lead Sherman was knocked out by a pair of direct hits—one from a Jerusalem Infantry Brigade Sherman ahead and one from a Jordanian antitank gun on Mivtar Hill. The Mystères destroyed a second Sherman and torched two halftracks, killing most of the armored-infantrymen riding in them. Aharon Gal was painfully wounded in the back when his tank was also hit by cannon fire, and Uri Ben-Ari was struck painfully in the elbow by a stone that ricocheted up from the street.

The survivors pulled off the road into a built-up area and, there, Ben-Ari screamed epithets into his radio until, by way of his brigade rear command post, the friendly hounds were finally called off. Within fifteen minutes, most of the rest of Gal's task force had fought through the road cut, and Gal used every vehicle to attack Mivtar Hill from the rear. Gal's Shermans surged to the top of the hill by way of an access road, and the halftracks followed. Working from the top down, the dismounted armored infantrymen cleared the defenders out of a 360-degree defensive zone that should have been able to withstand any attack. Later, while assembling captured Jordanian equipment, the Israelis found thirty-seven Jordanian antitank guns. A follow-up attack against nearby French Hill was anticlimactic; the Israelis found the defensive positions abandoned.

The first Israelis to reach Mount Scopus from the outside were not paratroopers, tankers, or armored infantrymen. They were Minister of Defense Moshe Dayan; Brigadier General Uzi Narkiss; Brigadier General Ezer Weizman; and the *Zahal* Operations Officer, Brigadier General Rechavam Ze'evi. Dayan, Weizman, and Ze'evi happened to be visiting Narkiss's forward command post in the city when news arrived that the road to Mount Scopus was open. They all jumped into Narkiss's jeep, which Narkiss himself drove to the top of the former enclave. The four were as surprised as anyone that they were the first to arrive. While two companies of Major Yosef Yaffe's battered

Parachute Battalion 66 hiked up the mountain road and bolstered the defensive perimeter, the Israeli generals ate a hot lunch served by the garrison commander's cook, and then they returned to Narkiss's headquarters, from which Dayan, Weizman, and Ze'evi flew back to Tel Aviv.

While viewing the city of Jerusalem from Mount Scopus, Uzi Narkiss had briefed Dayan on his plan to take possession of the Old City. Dayan had listened with great interest, but he had also had to rein Narkiss in. Because of enormous international implications, the government had not yet decided what it should do about the Old City. Dayan advised Narkiss to go on securing the high ground around it but to hold his men back from assaulting the Old City itself.

41

The afternoon fighting on Tuesday, June 6, kicked off in Jerusalem with an attack by Lieutenant Colonel Michael Peikas's Infantry Battalion 163 against Abu Tor, the hill-top defensive zone dominating the south side of the Old City. Opposing the Israelis, a reinforced company of the 8th Jordanian Infantry Battalion was holding a series of interconnected emplacements based around four stoutly built blockhouses on a large knob and a defensive sector on another, smaller, knob.

For some reason, Peikas chose to attack all four of the Jordanian block-houses frontally, at the same time. When one of his company commanders suggested a flank attack that could roll up the Jordanian blockhouses from end to end, along their blind sides, Peikas declined on the grounds that the opposition would be light and the frontal attack would take less time.

The attack started poorly at 1500. One of the Israeli assault companies was pasted by some of the last Jordanian 25-pounder shells to be fired in the battle of Jerusalem. Three soldiers were killed in the shelling, and twenty were wounded. Even worse, the company was stopped cold for several minutes, and thus Peikas's intricate plan, which relied upon split-second coordination between companies, came unglued at the outset. Rather than being attacked simultaneously by all four assault companies, the Jordanian blockhouses were attacked in a piecemeal fashion that allowed the defenders to concentrate on just one threat at a time. Moreover, Major Jackie Even's Academic Reserve company, which was on the flank closest to the Old City, was victimized by Jordanian sharpshooters who were able to reach Abu Tor from Mount Zion, at the Old City's southwest corner.

Jackie's company blasted through a barbed-wire-covered wall fronting its objective, and Jackie led the way through the breach. When he paused in an abandoned house to allow others to catch up, however, he found that only his radioman, his runner, and three riflemen had followed. When

Jackie's runner went back to find out why no one else had come forward, he learned that the next twelve men in a row had been shot by the snipers on Mount Zion. Jackie and three of his men—the fourth fell into a hole and broke his leg—attacked the company objective on their own. After seizing a house across from the objective, Jackie was shot in the left shoulder and hand by one of the sharpshooters on Mount Zion. Despite his injuries, he led his team into the company objective, which they found deserted.

By the time Jackie Even reached his objective, the company that had been hit by the Jordanian artillery barrage had reached its. With an assist from Jackie's fire team, it assaulted through the blockhouse without loss. The third Israeli company also reached its objective at this time, and it launched a successful attack. However, four Jordanians counterattacked the third company. Two were shot dead and two sought refuge in a trench in which Lieutenant Colonel Michael Peikas had ensconced himself and several staff officers to watch the attack. One of the Jordanians wounded Peikas in the back before he was stabbed to death by the battalion intelligence officer, and the last Jordanian was shot to death. Michael Peikas succumbed to his wound moments before the battalion surgeon reached the trench. In the time it took for the doctor to arrive, Infantry Battalion 163's fourth company overran the blockhouse in its zone.

There remained a small, somewhat isolated knob to be overwhelmed, and the fourth company set out to do that. The company commander called for support from the Jerusalem Infantry Brigade's 120mm mortar battalion, but either the infantry jumped off too soon or the mortars fired too late. In the event, forty Israeli infantrymen were killed or wounded by Israeli mortar fire after the knob had been seized without opposition. It was all several infantry officers could do to get the mortars turned off before the entire company was wiped out.

It took all afternoon for all the Jordanian defenders of Abu Tor to be pried or rooted out of the immediate neighborhood. While many Jordanian soldiers cut and ran—some who were captured were disguised in women's clothing—a number of them fought on. In many cases, they laid low until the Israelis had passed and then attacked from the rear. Eventually, the resistance petered out. At dusk on Tuesday, the badly mauled Infantry Battalion 163 turned Abu Tor over to a second-line infantry battalion and limped from the scene.

Abu Tor cost seventeen killed and fifty-four wounded, but its downfall completed the seizure of the high ground south of the Old City begun the previous afternoon by Lieutenant Colonel Asher Driezin's reinforced Infantry Battalion 161.

A simple wrong turn on an unfamiliar city street had brought immense pain and suffering to the 55th Parachute Brigade's Parachute Battalion 28 during the night, and that should have been instructive as to the special nature of combat in a built-up area. Unfortunately it was not. Two more wrong turns, also involving 55th Parachute Brigade operations in Jerusalem, caused immense additional pain and suffering before Tuesday was out.

In the second case, which began at about 1100, three busloads of paratroopers on loan from Colonel Dani Matt's 31st Parachute Brigade, arrived in Jerusalem at just about the time the Rockefeller Museum was being cleared by Parachute Battalion 71. The lead bus took a wrong turn in the vicinity of the Old City, and soldiers from the 8th Jordanian Infantry Battalion who were manning the city wall opened fire. The bus drivers panicked, and so did many of the paratroopers in the buses. In moments, the open area in front of the city wall was littered with dead and wounded paratroopers, and within the next minute, many would-be rescuers from Parachute Battalion 71 and the 55th Parachute Brigade headquarters were also killed or wounded. It took hours to bring in all the dead and wounded, and even for the uninjured survivors to inch their way to safety.

In a totally unrelated action later in the day, a misdirected column of tanks ran into a particularly nasty situation in the city. This disaster was precipitated by the quite reasonable desire on the part of the Israeli commanders to extend their holdings all the way around the strategic high ground overlooking the Old City. In the zone of the 55th Parachute Brigade, this meant an attack to clear the Augusta Victoria Ridge and the Mount of Olives, which were on a southeastward extension of the complex of hills and ridges that included Mount Scopus. By taking the Augusta Victoria Ridge and the Mount of Olives, the paratroopers would be assured a clear view of the Old City and, by the way, would control an equally clear view of the Dead Sea and the main road from Jericho.

The Israelis were in control of Jerusalem, there was no doubt about it. Though there were still many organized Jordanian combat units in the city, the sense of urgency that had pervaded the fighting during the first twenty-four hours of the war had dissipated by the middle of the afternoon of June 6. There was a sense, at the highest levels in any case, that any objective that Central Command, GHQ, or the government wanted to reach in and around Jerusalem could be had almost for the asking. The last best hope the Jordanians had for salvaging a position in the area had dissipated when the 60th Jordanian Armored Brigade had failed to get most of its Pattons through by way of Jericho.

Still, the Israelis were uneasy because the Old City remained in Arab hands—and their own government had withheld permission to attack. Unless the Old City ended up in Israeli hands, all the death and suffering would have been for nothing. Given little else to do to ease the tension, the Israeli commanders decided to take control of all the high ground—to at least make the Old City an Arab enclave in a Jewish city.

There were delays. Motta wanted to get the Augusta Victoria attack underway as soon as possible, but he did not want to send his paratroopers into another battle without adequate support. Therefore, he agreed to wait for two tank units to join Parachute Battalion 71 at the Rockefeller Museum, where he had set up his brigade forward command post before noon. One group of tanks was composed of the Jerusalem Infantry Brigade Shermans that had withdrawn to the Police Training School before noon, after shooting up the Old City's northern wall around the Damascus Gate in support of Parachute Battalion 28. Unfortunately, the resupply trucks that were to link up with these Shermans became intermingled with a much larger supply column bound for Motta's paratroopers, and the tanks and ammunition trucks failed to find one another until nearly 1700.

Another company of Shermans, this one from Tank Battalion 95 of the Harel Armored-Infantry Brigade, also reached the rendezvous at the Rockefeller Museum late. In fact, only four of the company's Shermans had arrived by dusk.

The attack, scheduled to take place in afternoon daylight, finally began in the evening gloom. The Jerusalem Infantry Brigade Shermans were to jump off first, and the Tank Battalion 95 Shermans were to follow. Behind them, the main body of Major Uzi Eilam's Parachute Battalion 71 was to climb the Augusta Victoria Ridge by means of a good road and, behind Eilam, Lieutenant Colonel Yossi Fradkin's Parachute Battalion 28 was to clear the northern Kidron Valley between the Old City and the ridge. The attack force of tanks and paratroopers was to clear the Mount of Olives after taking the Augusta Victoria Ridge.

Long before the attack jumped off, the commander of the Mount Scopus garrison, who had been observing Jordanian troop movements for days, radioed Central Command Headquarters with vital news: There were no Jordanians holding the Augusta Victoria Ridge. The attack that was about to take place need never have been launched. Somehow or other, this fact was never communicated to Motta.

The Jerusalem Infantry Brigade Shermans finally jumped off in full darkness. Instantly, the company commander was faced with the choice of five roads that converged on a square between the Rockefeller Museum and the Old City's northeast corner. He needed to make the sharpest left turn he could—almost a U-turn—but he missed it and went down the road that led south *through*—rather than across—the Kidron Valley. This road was exposed to direct fire from the Old City's east wall.

The Jordanians had not yet noticed the Israeli movement when the tank-company commander realized his error because the road dropped away into the Kidron Valley instead of rising toward the Augusta Victoria Ridge. The commander radioed Motta and told him he was on the wrong road. Motta told the tank commander to turn on his lights so they both could see where the tanks were. The tank's dimmed running lights had been shot out during the day, so the commander turned on his coaxial searchlight. Motta had no trouble seeing it, and neither did Jordanian bazookamen and machine gunners along the eastern city wall. The Jordanians had been waiting tensely all day for an Israeli attempt to breach one of the Old City's seven gates and now they thought the moment had arrived. They opened fire on the tanks and a small convoy of paratroop reconnaissance jeeps that had also taken the wrong turn.

The result was an unmitigated disaster. The tank-company commander was temporarily blinded by a wound over his eye, and his terrorized radioman contrived to direct the tank in such a way as to run off a bridge. Within moments, the entire tank column was lit up by fire from the Old City, and a tank that had not even left the Rockefeller Museum yet became a beacon when its rolled-up camouflage netting was set on fire by a tracer round.

The real damage was sustained by the reconnaissance paratroopers in the open jeeps. They were just blown off the road. Two tanks tried to rescue the wounded paratroopers, but one of the Shermans was disabled by a bazooka rocket and at least one of the reconnaissance troopers it had rescued was killed.

All the Israelis who could see the Old City wall overlooking the misdirected column fired on the Jordanians who were firing on the tanks and jeeps.

In relatively little time, the sheer volume of the Israeli fire subdued the Jordanian fire. The tanks and two of five jeeps withdrew, but it was 0200 before a group of reconnaissance paratroopers could crawl down the road to bring in their dead and wounded. Less than a dozen tankers were injured, and none was killed, but the paratroop reconnaissance company lost five killed and fourteen wounded.

The attack on the Augusta Victoria Ridge was postponed until daylight.

The misdirected Israeli night movement was the last straw for Brigadier Ata Ali Hazza'a. He thought his soldiers had defeated an attempt by the Israelis to break into the Old City by way of the Lions Gate—the shortest route to the Temple Mount—but he knew that it was just a matter of time before the Israelis would be back in force.

From Hazza'a's perspective, the thirty-hour stretch between noon on June 5 to the evening of June 6 had been the worst time of his life. The only ray of hope had come at the end, when the apparent Israeli attack along the Kidron Valley was repulsed. In the interim, Jordanian soldiers under Hazza'a's command had lost control of Jebel Mukaber and Government House; a battalion of his own King Talal Infantry Brigade had been forced out of Shu'afat and off Mivtar and French hills; and a second battalion of his brigade had been all but obliterated in the defense of Ammunition Hill, the Nablus Road, and the American Colony and Sheikh Jarrah districts. By the evening of June 6, also, the commander of the King Talal Infantry Brigade's artillery battalion had reported that not one of his unit's 25-pounder field guns was still in service. And nearly an entire battalion of Jordanian tanks seconded to Hazza'a's command had been destroyed or turned out of the city. In all his years as a soldier—going back to 1938, when he had enlisted in the Arab Legion as a private—Hazza'a had not had a worse day.

There was even an element of personal humiliation thrown in. Hazza'a had begun the day at his makeshift forward command post in the Wadi el-Joz, and from there he had personally witnessed portions of the rout of his two northern battalions, the 2nd and 4th Jordanian Infantry battalions. During the afternoon, he had been forced to leave his command post, because it was surrounded by Israelis, and to sneak into the Old City. This he had done with the commander and just forty survivors of the 2nd Jordanian Infantry Battalion.

Ata Ali Hazza'a did the best he could with what he had. The commander of the 8th Jordanian Infantry Battalion reported that he had just one antitank gun in the entire Old City, a tripod-mounted 106mm recoilless rifle that had been manhandled up to the city wall overlooking the Rockefeller Museum. Except for a few bazookas and mortars, there were no large weapons in the Old City. To guard the seven gates into the Old City, Hazza'a had the commander of the 8th Jordanian Infantry Battalion form seven picked units of forty soldiers apiece led by officers that Hazza'a personally selected for the job. Everyone else who could bear arms was to man the walls facing the Israelis or stand ready to rush to the defense of a gate that was being attacked. At noon, Hazza'a ordered the 8th Jordanian Infantry Battalion to abandon all its positions south of the Old City—except for Abu Tor—and to concentrate within the ancient walls.

At 1700, long after the Old City had been all but totally surrounded, Major Badi Awad, whose battalion of the Imam Ali Infantry Brigade had seized and then lost Government House on June 5, reported that the remnants of his unit had reformed in an eastern suburb. By then, it was too late for Awad's men to reach the Old City, so Hazza'a ordered the battalion to withdraw toward Jericho after dark. A short time later, the commander of a fresh 60th Jordanian Armored Brigade Patton company radioed Hazza'a with news that he and his Pattons had gotten through to Bethany, directly behind the Mount of Olives. Hazza'a ordered the tanks to link up with Major Awad's battalion and withdraw back to Jericho. It was too late to do anything about stopping the Israelis, and there was no point in adding to the ledger of needless brave deaths.

Toward dusk, the Jordanian West Bank commander, Major General Mohammed Ahmed Salim, authorized the evacuation of all Jordanian military units from the vicinity of Jerusalem. By then, there were precious few Jordanian soldiers who could respond. The survivors of the two Imam Ali Infantry Brigade battalions that had been defeated and dispersed by tne IAF or during the Harel Armored-Infantry Brigade's break-in northwest of the city responded and got on the road to Jericho, and so did the dispersed elements of the King Talal Infantry Brigade's 2nd and 4th Jordanian Infantry battalions, which had been defeated between Shu'afat and Nablus Road.

In the end, at most, 600 Jordanian soldiers and several dozen uniformed policemen gathered inside the Old City. But their decision to stay was for nothing. Even the repulse of the Israeli tanks in the Kidron Valley was for nothing.

Israelis facing the Old City's three northern gates fired at the Jordanians manning the city walls all evening and into night, and the Jordanians fired back without let-up. Neither side inflicted many casualties on the other, but the Jordanians were being worn down by the sheer hopelessness of their situation. They were trapped, and the Israelis were not; their numbers were finite, and the Israelis were free to bring up as many reinforcements as they wanted to. At 0130 on June 7, Arabic-speaking Israelis began broadcasting surrender pleas over loudspeakers, and that added to the funk into which the Jordanian soldiers and policemen had been sinking all day.

Finally, at 0230, Brigadier Hazza'a had enough. He consulted with the governor of the city, and the two agreed that it was time for the soldiers to escape if they could. Word went out to the troops that anyone who wanted to could leave. Most did, by way of the Dung Gate, a portal in the Old City's southern wall that the Israelis might intentionally have left unguarded for just this purpose. Brigadier Ata Ali Hazza'a left at 0300 with his intelligence officer; his bodyguard; his driver; and Major Mansaur Kreishan, the commander of the 2nd Jordanian Infantry Battalion. They were bound for Jericho—on foot.

Scores of Jordanian soldiers changed into civilian clothing and tried to blend into the civilian population, but about 140 policemen and soldiers opted to remain at their posts inside the Old City.

42

Jerusalem must be made whole again. So it was no accident—no accident at all—that the 55th Parachute and Jerusalem Infantry brigades controlled all the high ground overlooking the Old City. Though the war had started with no official decision to take the Old City by storm, Israeli political leaders and military commanders had come to share one paramount desire the moment King Hussein had unleashed his artillery against the Jewish half of the divided city: The Old City must be taken. If the Israelis were going to try to capture the Old City, the first requirement was that they control the high ground all the way around the Old City.

Perversely, Moshe Dayan, of all people, had been the restraining influence from the start. In his bones, the defense minister felt that the Arabs in the Old City would simply "hang out white flags" once the high ground was in Israeli hands and they realized they were cut off from the rest of the Arab world. In reality, Dayan feared the high casualties a house-by-house battle would certainly entail. His was a fear all Israeli commanders shared. Since 1948, *Zahal* had done everything in its power to avoid city fighting. Doing so was a matter of doctrine.

But the Old City of Jerusalem? No. The Old City was different. The Old City was worth any price.

The pressure began mounting from the outset of the war. The unbelievably swift collapse of the Egyptian Army in Sinai and the world community's mounting concern over the safety of the holy sites in Jerusalem were pointing toward the early imposition of a United Nations–mandated ceasefire. And the exigencies of Israeli domestic politics were coming to the fore. Chiefly, the religious parties in the ruling Labor coalition were pressing for an immediate direct assault on the Old City, but there was mounting fear in other quarters that the Moslem Arabs would never relinquish the Dome of the Rock and the al-Aqsa Mosque without engulfing the entire region in a *jihad*, a holy war—the Armageddon. The leaders of the religious parties, without whom Labor could not rule, demanded a coup de main to the uncertainty of an Arab surrender. So, though Dayan the soldier protested to the end, the politicians took the decision on the evening of Tuesday, June 6. At an emergency Cabinet meeting at 0500 on Wednesday, June 7, the government issued Dayan his marching orders. Dayan readily agreed for, by then, the Israeli brigades in Jerusalem had victory within their grasp.

By the time the Cabinet's prime directive to seize the Old City came down to Central Command Headquarters early on the morning of June 7, Brigadier General Uzi Narkiss knew in his heart that the prize of a hundred generations would be his. The battle was going well in Jerusalem; better than anyone had dared dream. The northern city had been sealed from outside help by the Harel Armored-Infantry Brigade, and the Jerusalem Infantry Brigade had achieved all its objectives to the south. Closer in to the Old City, the 55th Parachute Brigade was preparing to clear the Augusta Victoria Ridge and the Mount of Olives, the last of the high ground overlooking the Old City from the northeast and east. Casualties were running extremely high in Motta's brigade, but the paratroopers were ready to assault the Old City if orders came down to them. Once the entire ridge running from Mount Scopus, in the northeast, to the Mount of Olives, in the southeast, was in Israeli hands, East Jerusalem and the Old City would be sealed from Jordan by a line of dominant Israeli-held hill barriers.

Brigadier General Chaim Bar-Lev, the Israeli deputy chief of staff, arrived in Jerusalem at 0700, June 7, to personally oversee the capture of the Old City. Chief among Bar-Lev's concerns was that none of the holy shrines of Islam or Christendom—not to mention Judaism—be damaged in the course of what the world would certainly call a "Jewish" assault. Bar-Lev checked in at the Central Command forward command post. He spoke with the Central Command operations officer, and then he went to the Rockefeller Museum to confer with Motta Gur.

By the time Bar-Lev reached the Rockefeller Museum, Motta was gone. Beginning at 0830, while the deputy chief of staff was flying to Jerusalem from Tel Aviv, two companies each from Major Yosef Yaffe's Parachute Battalion 66 and Major Uzi Eilam's Parachute Battalion 71 captured the Augusta Victoria Ridge and the Mount of Olives in an all-but-bloodless assault. On the latter, the paratroopers had captured the Intercontinental

Hotel, to which Motta had displaced his command group to take advantage of the sweeping vista it afforded of the Old City. Though Motta still had not yet received official word when he left the museum that his brigade was to seize the Old City, the rumor mill had provided ample warning. He was already issuing orders by radio by the time his command jeep topped the Mount of Olives.

In a way, the view from the Mount of Olives was depressing. The modernistic white Intercontinental Hotel had been built upon the ancient Jewish cemetery that stretched all the way down the slope and across the Kidron Valley to the walls of the Old City fronting the Golden Gate. This was no ordinary cemetery, either. For over a thousand years, the bones of pious Jews had been interred there so that their owners could be among the first to rise up and enter the Holy of Holies when God descended to the Valley of Jehoshaphat on the Day of Judgment. The Arabs defiled the portion of the cemetery directly beneath the sprawling grounds of the opulent hotel, and they had vandalized all the rest of the hallowed ground by removing monuments and headstones for use as common building materials. The desecration aside, the view from the mountain was inspiring, even mesmerizing. Directly in front of Motta was the Temple Mount—Harun el-Sherif to Moslems. There, burning in the morning sun that rose steadily in the uncannily clear Jerusalem sky behind Motta's back, was the blue-tiled, golden-domed Mosque of Omar, the Dome of the Rock. From here, the Prophet Mohammed had ascended to heaven. (Indeed, it was from the Mount of Olives, on which Motta stood, that Christ had ascended to heaven.) Even earlier, Abraham had built his tabernacle there and had prepared to sacrifice his only son, Isaac, to the One God. Just to the left of the golden dome was the delicate-columned beauty of al-Aqsa Mosque. And tucked away unseen behind both Moslem shrines was Motta's moral objective, the 2,000-year-old gray-white limestone wall that had once been the western containment of the Second Temple of the Jews. This was the Wailing Wall, a shrine to which all Jews had been denied access since that fateful day in 1948 when the last Israeli had been forcibly evicted from the Old City.

On a day—any day—the view from the Mount of Olives will inspire any Jew, Christian, or Moslem who knows a shred about this ancient and marvelous city. On this day, June 7, 1967, Mordechai Gur was enraptured. "It was difficult," he later admitted, "to move [my] eyes away from the breathtaking vision."

By the time Motta did succeed in pulling his eyes from the unprecedented view, the 55th Parachute Brigade's attack on the Old City was under-way. Based on orders that had been promulgated by Motta to his battalion commanders by radio, Major Uzi Eilam's Parachute Battalion 71 was being diverted from the barely completed brigade assault on the Augusta Victoria Ridge; it was to secure the Lions (or St. Stephen's) Gate, the only access through the east wall of the Old City and the quickest route to the Temple Mount. Once through the Lions Gate, Eilam's paratroopers were to rush by way of the Temple Mount directly to the Wailing Wall. During that time, Lieutenant Colonel Yossi Fradkin's Parachute Battalion 28 was also improvis-ing an assault against the Lions Gate from its reserve position at the Rockefel-ler Museum. To block a hypothetical but reasonably anticipated Jordanian armored counterattack to rescue the holy shrines, the parachute brigade's reconnaissance troop and a company of Harel Armored-Infantry Brigade Shermans were ordered down the Jericho Road to the town of Abu Dis, the best blocking position east of the city. Parachute Battalion 66 was to remain atop the Augusta Victoria Ridge and Mount Scopus, also to guard against a Jordanian counterattack from the direction of Jericho.

The race was on as soon as Motta's orders had been issued. Everyone wanted to be the first Israeli into the Old City, the first Jew to liberate the Wailing Wall.

Before the 55th Parachute Brigade even entered combat in Jerusalem, Cap-tain Yoram Zamush, the brigade's only pious company commander, had inveighed a promise from Motta that he, Zamush, would be the first man into the Old City. As it happened, Zamush's company was the rear unit of Parachute Battalion 71 during the attack against the Augusta Victoria Ridge, so it was easiest to turn it around to lead the rest of the battalion toward the Old City. Major Uzi Eilam, the battalion commander, attached two halftracks to Zamush's company and ordered Zamush to attack from the Palace Hotel, directly toward the Lions Gate, and then move on to the Temple Mount and down to the Wailing Wall.

Zamush was exultant. He scrambled aboard the nearest halftrack with as many of his men as could clamber up after him. Then, with the rest of his troopers jogging behind on foot, he directed the driver toward the objective.

While Parachute Battalion 71 turned itself around, the Israelis bom-barded the Old City to the full extent allowed by the Cabinet. The 55th Parachute Brigade was authorized to support itself by firing no more than ten mortar rounds into the Moslem Quarter, the northeast corner of the Old City, which was well away from any of the holy shrines. For twenty minutes, while the ad hoc brigade assault was developing, the mortars were fired, one carefully aimed round at a time.

After leaving cover behind the Palace Hotel, the lead halftrack, with Captain Zamush aboard, turned right up the gentle slope that ran from the hotel to the Lions Gate. There was a cemetery on either side—Jewish to the left and Moslem to the right. Several Jordanian riflemen—they might have been policemen—had staked out the road between the cemeteries, but their fire was desultory and inaccurate. Inured to far worse opposition, Zamush and his troopers ignored the fire and rolled and jogged forward. Ahead was the Lions Gate, which was closed and apparently barred.

In Christian lore, the gate is named St. Stephen's, after the first Christian martyr, who was stoned to death nearby. Jews and Arabs call it the Lions Gate because a pair of carved stone lions face one another from either side of the portal. They had been carved there at the order of the great Turkish emperor, Suliman the Magnificent, when he built the gate in 1538. He had dreamed that he would be eaten by lions if he did not rebuild the city walls following his epic siege.

As Zamush waited, a Harel Armored-Infantry Brigade Sherman moved to the end of the roadway and fired a 75mm round at the wooden gate. The stone arch crumbled and the left door fell off its hinges. A second 75mm round set an abandoned bus afire in the roadway.

At 0945, Zamush's halftrack ground forward and nearly reached the gate, but it stopped momentarily when the company commander decided to share the honor with his footborne subordinates, who were still panting up the hill. The pause cost Yoram Zamush his place in history, for, in that brief interval, Motta's command halftrack squeezed through the portal and Motta, his driver, and several members of the brigade forward command group apparently became the first Jews to enter the Old City in nearly two decades. A moment later, Zamush's halftrack crashed through the right half of the gate and entered the Via Dolorosa. The last halftrack followed, and the rest of Zamush's company streamed through the gate behind it on foot.

There was immediate—but spotty—resistance. As a squad of Zamush's company veered left to set up a security screen, the brigade headquarters combat platoon entered the Lions Gate and turned right to sweep several Arab snipers from rooftops and a minaret overlooking that side of an open square. One Israeli soldier was killed in the duel, and six were wounded, but the Arabs were overrun or had melted away in the few minutes it took the bulk of Parachute Battalion 71 to catch up and begin scouring the entire area dead ahead and to the right of the Lions Gate.

At virtually the same moment Motta and Zamush were entering the Old City via the Lions Gate, a company of the Jerusalem Infantry Brigade's Infantry Battalion 163 was doing the same thing via the Dung Gate. It has never been determined which unit actually arrived first.

Infantry Battalion 163 was tried and true. It had taken Abu Tor the day before, and had lost its commander doing so. For June 7, the battalion, now under Lieutenant Colonel Yosef Brosh, was to secure Mount Zion, the hill at the southwest corner of the Old City on which King David's Tomb had been erected.

There was nothing in Brosh's orders to give him leave to enter the Old City, but one of his company commanders, Captain Eli Kedar, had reason to appeal to Brosh's sense of history. Kedar and all of his six brothers and sisters had been born in the Jewish Quarter of the Old City. He had been fifteen years old in 1948, and his family had been the last Jewish family in Jerusalem to be arrested by the Jordanians after the Old City fell. According to Kedar, who had been imprisoned for nine months following the fall of the Old City, he had been the last member of his family—the very last Jew—to leave the Jewish Quarter. Naturally, he wanted to be the very first to return.

So, during a reconnaissance tour of the approaches to Mount Zion, Lieutenant Colonel Brosh informed Eli Kedar that Kedar's company would be given the honor of leading Infantry Battalion 163 back to Mount Zion. Kedar was exultant. He radioed his men to get ready to jump off. Then, as soon as he rejoined the company, Kedar led the assault.

The Jordanians resisted briefly with ineffective recoilless-rifle fire, and Mount Zion fell in short order as the Jordanian defenders retreated in disarray. Without stopping, Eli Kedar led his men straight to the Dung Gate, at the eastern end of the Old City's south wall. The two vast metal doors of the Dung Gate were closed, but a smaller hatchway in one of them stood open. Without pausing, Eli Kedar stepped through. The last Jew to leave the Old City in 1948 believes he became the first Jew to reenter the Old City in 1967.

There was no one about, and many of the buildings were draped with white flags. About fifty of Kedar's men followed their captain into the ancient city and fanned out to secure the area around the Dung Gate. A few scattered

Jordanians fired on the Israelis, who returned the fire. There were casualties on both sides.

When Kedar reported his position, Lieutenant Colonel Brosh ordered Kedar's company to secure the Wailing Wall. But Eli Kedar had other priorities. He told Brosh that he wanted to be the first Jew to reenter the Jewish Quarter because, after all, he had been the last to leave. Brosh relented.

Kedar turned the Dung Gate over to another company of Infantry Battalion 163 and proceeded to his personal objective. While en route, however, he met a company of paratroopers on its way to secure the Jaffa Gate, in the center of the Old City's west wall. With that, Kedar left his company in the care of his deputy and raced to his father's home in the German Colony of West Jerusalem. Father and son returned to join the stream of soldiers and civilians that was by then pouring through the narrow streets toward the Wailing Wall.

Immediately after entering the Old City by way of the Lions Gate, the main body of Captain Yoram Zamush's company of Parachute Battalion 71 turned left just inside the Lions Gate and breached the Asbat Gate, which led up to the Temple Mount. There was no opposition. A Jordanian Army field kitchen steamed and bubbled away, but there was no one to be seen.

On reaching the top of the deserted holy mount, Motta sealed the moment with a radio message to Central Command Headquarters: "Temple Mount is in our hands. Temple Mount is ours. Temple Mount is ours." Uzi Narkiss replied with great emotion evident in his voice, "Message received. Great show. Great show."

With that, Motta climbed down from his command halftrack to the flat, flagstoned summit. Before he could act or speak, Yoram Zamush appeared. The two stared at one another for a few seconds, but no words came. Silently, they embraced.

The word that the Temple Mount was in Jewish hands spread through West Jerusalem like wildfire. Moments after reaching the Holy Mount, Zamush sent soldiers to fetch two venerable rabbis from their homes. One had vowed to remain inside his house from the moment he had been driven from the Old City in 1948 until the Wailing Wall was once again in Jewish hands, and indeed he had until Zamush's soldiers arrived to relieve him of his hermetic existence.

But the Wailing Wall was not yet quite in Jewish hands. While several of Zamush's paratroopers chased four Arab civilians who made a dash into the Mosque of Omar, Zamush joined Major Moshe Stempel, the parachute brigade deputy commander, in a search for a route down to the base of the Western Wall. Dropping paratroopers along the way to mark the path, Zamush and Stempel meandered hither and yon until they encountered an ancient Arab. When they asked the man if he knew the way, he answered in Hebrew that he would take them. Then he pulled a huge key from the folds of his clothing and opened the Mughrabi Gate, whose stone stairs led straight down from the Temple Mount to the base of the last vestige of the containment wall that Herod the Great had had built around his splendid temple in 20 B.C.

Getting to the base of the wall cost some lives. As Zamush and Stempel led the way, a truck towing an antitank gun pulled up across from the stairway and a handful of Jordanian soldiers jumped down and opened fire on the Israelis. When the paratroopers returned the fire, the Jordanians all dived beneath the truck. The gas tank blew up and all the Jordanians were killed.

Stempel and several paratroopers stayed behind on the stairs to guard the vulnerable route, but Zamush and three of his men continued down. The houses had been built so close to the Wailing Wall that the four Jews had virtually no room to stand and look at it.

Zamush had been there before, as a child. He had last seen the Wall, had last touched the ancient limestone blocks when he was four years old. He thought of his father, a German Jew who had escaped from his native land in 1936. And he thought of the Wall and remembered that the temple it had surrounded had been destroyed by the Roman Emperor Titus in A.D. 74. As Zamush looked around, he saw, freshly lettered on a building—in Hebrew!—the benediction, "If I forget thee, O Jerusalem." He could not imagine who had written it, or when, for clearly he, Yoram Zamush, was the first Israeli to stand in that spot in nearly two decades.

There were two Arab men loitering near the Wall. Zamush left them in the care of two of his soldiers and reclimbed the stairs with the last of his men. He rejoined Major Stempel, who in the meantime had himself been joined by Eli Landau, an Israeli journalist.

Yoram Zamush had one more appointment to keep, one more promise to fulfill. Shortly after the 55th Parachute Brigade had begun staging into West Jerusalem on the first day of the war, Zamush had been entertained briefly by a civilian couple and had boasted—prematurely, but accurately, as it turned out—that the paratroopers would retake the Old City. On hearing that, the husband had gone into another room to fetch an Israeli flag. He explained that it had been made by his mother and had flown over the Old City during the final days of the siege of 1948. He had asked Yoram Zamush to return it to its rightful place at the first opportunity.

And so, mindful that the moment was as fervently nationalistic as it was religious, Zamush improvised a color guard of ten of his men. With Major Moshe Stempel and Eli Landau looking on, he affixed that historical flag of modern Israel to a fence above the north side of the Wall and unfurled it in the clear Jerusalem breeze.

Finally, Yoram Zamush—the 55th Parachute Brigade's only pious officer—descended to the alleyway beside the Wall once again and donned his *tefillin*, the leather-bound cases containing holy scripture that observant Jews wrap around their forearms and drape from their foreheads when they recite their morning prayers. Then, along with five or six of his similarly observant subordinates, Zamush stood peaceably before God and became the first Jew in nearly twenty years to intone the ancient prayers in the shadow of the Wall.

While Parachute Battalion 71 and the 55th Parachute Brigade command group secured the Wall, the Temple Mount, and the immediate neighborhood, Lieutenant Colonel Yossi Fradkin's Parachute Battalion 28 was hard at work securing other gates and opening other routes to the Wall. Working its way along the north half of the east wall from the Rockefeller Museum, part of Fradkin's battalion attempted to enter the Old City and join Parachute Battalion 71 by way of the Lions Gate. Unfortunately, near the southern end of the Moslem cemetery was an open square that was outposted by several clever and determined Jordanian Army machine-gun teams. Several paratroopers were killed in the open by the first volley of Jordanian fire, but the others kept moving forward. It was not known that Parachute Battalion 71 had already reached the Wall, so the pressure was really on. Besides, there was brass in the crowd. Brigadier General Chaim Bar-Lev, the deputy chief of staff, had caught up with the forward elements of Parachute Battalion 28, and so had Uzi Narkiss. Indeed, so had Brigadier General Shlomo Goren, *Zahal*'s chief rabbi. Though Narkiss was vocal in his orders to exert caution, the paratroopers could not be restrained. But neither could they get across the fire-swept square.

Uzi Narkiss had been there before. During the War of Independence, he had personally led the last best effort to relieve the Old City in 1948. He had been unable to accomplish his mission back then. He had come close, but not close enough. There was no way Uzi Narkiss was going to leave the Old City to the Arabs again. Not even if it meant his life. Without further ado, the general rallied several bazooka teams to his side and personally led them back to a small hill near the Rockefeller Museum. From there, the bazookas were able to dominate the Jordanian positions. In time, a bazooka team managed to destroy one of the machine guns. At least one other machine gun and several snipers armed with rifles still had the square zeroed in, but by then several members of Parachute Battalion 28 had safely crossed the square. The cautious trickle turned into a reckless flood. Somewhere along the line, the last Jordanian machine gun and all the snipers were overrun—or slunk away.

As soon as Lieutenant Colonel Yossi Fradkin found Motta on the Temple Mount, he was ordered to secure the Damascus Gate by sweeping around two sides of the Moslem Quarter. There was a rumor afoot that Prime Minister Levi Eshkol was due to arrive soon and that he planned to enter the Old City by way of the Damascus Gate. Fradkin reformed his battalion and sped off to carry out his new assignment. He never reached the Wailing Wall; as soon as he and his men had secured the Damascus Gate, Parachute Battalion 28 was ordered to head north to take part in storming the Golan Heights.

Within fifteen minutes after Yoram Zamush donned his *tefillin* and began praying, the narrow alley fronting the Wailing Wall became filled with important personages—Moshe Dayan, Yitzhak Rabin, Chaim Bar-Lev, Uzi Narkiss, Motta Gur, and others.

Along with the Torah—the scroll of the Law—Rabbi Shlomo Goren had brought a *shofar*, a ram's horn that is blown to mark special religious festivals and celebrations. As the rabbi was lifting the ram's horn to his lips, Major Uzi Eilam, the commander of Parachute Battalion 71, spoke up: "Rabbi, give me the *shofar*. I'm a trumpet player. I can do it." And he did. Beautifully. Lustily. *Teh-KEEEEE-yeh*, the shofar bleated.

As the full breathy notes reverberated up and out along the narrow stone passage—as Yoram Zamush and all the other men of the hour looked on and listened—the bespectacled, white-bearded rabbi, whose olive-green uniform was fittingly decorated by a set of silver paratrooper wings, faced the Wall, shifted the Torah higher on his chest, and uttered in a proud, strong voice, "I, General Shlomo Goren, chief rabbi of the Israeli Defense Force, have come to this place never to leave it again."

Part VI

The West Bank

43

In the very beginning of her confrontation with the Hashemite Kingdom of Jordan, Israel's response to King Hussein's provocations and violent assertions were entirely defensive: open a route to the Mount Scopus enclave, end the threat represented by the Jordanian occupation of Jebel Mukaber, go after the artillery that was hitting the Ramat David air base and the coastal cities, widen the Jerusalem Corridor. But then Israel gave in to her dreams. If these limited defensive objectives could be achieved—if all the headaches and heartaches of the past two decades could be mitigated—then what was there to prevent Israel from going the whole route and simply seizing all of Samaria and Judea—taking a little extra to repay all the heartache and suffering?

And that is what happened. Once the limited defensive objectives fell, there was no stopping the steamroller. Jordan went on the ropes early, and Israel gleefully punched her deaf, dumb, and blind. As the Jordanian monarch had said himself, "The hour of revenge has come."

There was a seeming simultaneity to the multiple Israeli attacks into the West Bank that obscures the improvised nature of the entire offensive effort. Dreams aside, *Zahal* was in no way prepared to conquer half of Jordan. What made doing so thinkable—not to mention possible—was training; the commanders of the brigades to whom the responsibility fell were professionals who had been selected and trained precisely because *Zahal* wanted to be ready to jump off into the unknown—literally to change the course of history—at a moment's notice.

Counting the break-in by Colonel Uri Ben-Ari's Harel Armored-Infantry Brigade, four Israeli brigades, all operating more or less independently, broke into the West Bank during the afternoon and evening of Monday, June 5, 1967.

* * *

At 2000, fully three hours after the Harel Armored-Infantry Brigade's tanks had advanced out of covered positions opposite Radar and Abdul Aziz hills, the French Sherman company from Colonel Moshe Yotvat's 4th Infantry Brigade attacked the Jordanian infantry battalion holding the defensive sector at Latrun. The objective was an extremely important military target, but this attack was also another of the emotional legacies of the War of Independence, another bit of unfinished business. In 1948, wave upon wave of Jewish fighters—most of them survivors of Nazi death camps newly arrived in the Promised Land—had been smashed in the vain effort to win the Latrun position. As a result of the futile battles nineteen years earlier, Jerusalem had been choked off from the rest of Israel and the Old City had been lost.

The Arab Legion soldiers of 1948 had fought well and bravely, and even Israel's most ardent nationalists admitted down through the years that, in the end, they deserved to hold their position. But that was then. In 1967, Latrun was another old wound that needed to be healed, another old blot that needed to be expunged.

The 4th Infantry Brigade's main concern was protecting Lod International Airport, which by Israeli standards was more or less in the neighborhood of Latrun. It was a simple matter, once the Jordanians began showing their cards a few days before the shooting started, to reposition the 4th Infantry Brigade to counter a potential Jordanian thrust from Latrun toward Lod and Tel Aviv. And, once the final decision was made to attack Jordan at several points on the afternoon of June 5, it was even simpler for the 4th Infantry Brigade staff to develop an offensive plan.

Colonel Yotvat reported to Central Command Headquarters as early as 0930 that his brigade was ready to attack Latrun, but Uzi Narkiss's repeated attempts to win permission to launch the attack were rebuffed by GHQ. The government was not yet prepared to become embroiled in the conquest of the West Bank. Even as late as 1550, as the battle for Jebel Mukaber was nearing a conclusion, GHQ refused Narkiss permission to attack Latrun. When the order to attack came down shortly before 2000, it took the 4th Infantry Brigade only a few minutes to execute it.

In 1948, the Jews had tried to take Latrun frontally, and that had not worked at all. Later, several brigades, including the one from which the 4th Infantry Brigade was descended, had been used in a last-ditch effort to surround Latrun and cut it off from the rest of Jordan in the last days before the imposition of a truce. That had only partially worked. In the end, the hilltop monastery, the police fortress, and several villages remained in Jordanian hands, but the unfinished business of 1948 had left the place in somewhat exposed circumstances.

Facing the 4th Infantry Brigade was the southernmost battalion of the Jordanian El Hashimi Infantry Brigade and the two Egyptian commando battalions. The Egyptian units, which numbered only 120 men apiece, had broken themselves down into small groups and had begun infiltrating into Israel late in the morning. Though the commandos themselves were of some concern once their presence inside Israel was discerned, they had no impact on Colonel Yotvat's plan to take Latrun. In fact, by not being there, they made Yotvat's plan easier to implement.

The 4th Infantry Brigade's breaching operation was initially concerned with getting through the extensive Jordanian minefields. This the brigade accomplished by using the indirect approach, which carried its tanks into Jordan in a roundabout sweep that encountered no opposition at the outset. The break-in route, in fact, ended at the Old Jerusalem Highway, which the Jordanian positions dominated and which had been the point of the bloody fighting in 1948.

By the time the Jordanian infantry battalion holding Latrun itself knew that there were Israelis in its rear, it was too late to stop the flood. The French Sherman company was followed closely by a motorized infantry battalion that cut the old highway at a feature known as Bab el-Wad (Gate to the Valley). The tanks continued from northeast to southwest to attack the old Latrun police fortress, and the remainder of the brigade followed them in trucks and jeeps as quickly as possible, fighting as it went. All of the key positions—the police fortress, the monastery, and villages located on commanding hilltops—fell in a series of brief but often bitter little fights.

In a matter of two hours, the entire Latrun salient was in Israeli hands and the survivors of its former Jordanian garrison were on the run. The 4th Infantry Brigade's attack was a perfect complement to the Harel Armored-Infantry Brigade's attack in the adjacent sector. When all its objectives had been secured, the brigade dug in on the spot to await orders.

44

What had yet to become the strategic invasion of the West Bank began at 1700 on June 5. It was undertaken by one of the two armored brigades attached to *Ugdah* Peled, and it was the responsibility of Brigadier General Dado Elazar's Northern Command. Initially, the attack was aimed merely at neutralizing the Jordanian 155mm artillery fire that was striking Ramat David air base and numerous Israeli villages and towns within range of Jordanian Samaria.

Ugdah Peled's planning started from scratch. Absorbed for days in preparing to counter an all-out invasion of northern Israel from out of Syria, the bulk of *Ugdah* Peled was given somewhat under five hours to figure out how to invade Samaria—and to do it. It was not until noon on June 5 that Brigadier General Elad Peled himself was called in from a patrol along the Syrian frontier to oversee the planning.

Ugdah Peled's immediate objective was obvious to anyone who could read a map: Jenin. Though the city stood on the Jordanian side of the line, it was geographically at the southern terminus of Israel's Jezreel Valley. The Jordanian 155mm artillery that was endangering and frightening so many Israelis was based nearby, and that certainly was *Ugdah* Peled's chief objective.

At the outset, Peled and his staff faced two problems. The chief one was reorienting and moving the bulk of the *ugdah* a significant distance, and the other was figuring out how and where to break into Samaria. The latter concern was driven by the topology around Jenin. The city sat atop a major road junction in a little valley that was dominated by hills to the north, the west, and the south. The best way into the valley was from the southeast, but that would entail a wide encirclement from the northeast that might in turn be cut off by a counterattack either from the city itself or by the Jordanian infantry brigade based farther to the east.

To assist in offsetting a potential counterattack, the motorized Gavish Infantry Brigade, which was screening Beit Shean, opposite the Jordan River, was set in motion at 1600 on June 5 as a means of tying down the Jordanian El Yarmouk Infantry Brigade in the northeastern corner of Samaria. Under the direct control of *Zahal* GHQ, the Gavish Infantry Brigade crossed into the West Bank hard against the Jordan River and advanced about 16 kilometers before digging in for the night. In the first hour of this diversionary advance, only a few shots were exchanged at long range because the El Yarmouk Infantry Brigade opted to protect the strategic Damiya Bridge across the Jordan by remaining in its static defensive positions—exactly what the Israelis intended.

At the same time the Jordanians in northeastern Samaria were being forced to keep an eye on the Gavish Infantry Brigade, the Jordanian Princess Alia Infantry Brigade was also obliged to sit still in western Samaria because Central Command's Shaham Infantry Brigade made threatening moves from across the frontier. The Shaham Infantry Brigade only needed to look busy to get the attention and thus hold in place the Jordanians across the way.

While the Jordanians reacted and fretted well to the east and southwest of Jenin, two columns of Super Sherman tanks and armored infantrymen from Lieutenant Colonel Moshe Bar-Kochva's armored brigade crossed into Samaria nearer the key city at 1700. The right-hand column, which was composed of a Super Sherman battalion bolstered by one armored-infantry company, was assigned another more-or-less diversionary role. It crossed into Samaria from near the Israeli Arab town of Umm el-Fahm and overran a small border post held by a platoon of the Khalid Ibn el-Walid Infantry Brigade. From there, the Israeli column proceeded without opposition southeastward toward Ya'bad, the largest village in the area. At nightfall, this column was still 6.5 kilometers from Ya'bad, but it stopped and the tanks and armored infantrymen established a temporary defensive laager. This movement obliged the commander of the Khalid Ibn el-Walid Infantry Brigade, who was headquartered in Jenin, to tie down one of his infantry battalions to the west of the main event.

The main event was the Israeli penetration toward Jenin by the Bar-Kochva Armored Brigade's main body—a battalion of Super Shermans; most of the armored-infantry battalion; and the brigade headquarters and support units, including a reconnaissance battalion equipped with jeeps and AMX-13s. This force, which was led by the reconnaissance and Super Sherman battalions, crossed the frontier near the Israeli town of Megiddo and crashed right over a Jordanian border post. The platoon of Jordanian soldiers defending the post was stunned and shocked by the sudden onset of the attack and thus did not fire a shot until the Israeli tanks were gone and the armored-infantry halftracks were rolling through the breach. The brief pitched battle between the Jordanians and a platoon of Israeli armored infantrymen had not quite ended in the latter's favor when Jordanian 155mm artillery rounds began probing the area. By then, the Israeli AMX-13s and Super Shermans had climbed onto a decent road that exited the area, and most of the armored-infantry halftracks were right behind them.

Next on the Israeli hit list were the villages of Yamun and Kfar Dan, northwest of Jenin. The Israeli column split into two tank-infantry task forces and entered both villages simultaneously at 1930. The villages were outposted, but nearly all the Jordanian soldiers retreated and only a few shots were fired. (These and other withdrawals were actually consistent with the Jordanian defensive plan; these tiny squad and platoon garrisons from the 20th Jordanian Infantry Battalion were supposed to come together far to the rear and deliver a counterattack as soon as the Israelis were committed to one axis of advance or another.) In Yamun, the by-then merely putative objective of the Israeli attack was achieved when an entire battery of 155mm field guns fell into Israeli hands intact.

The Israeli column reformed at dusk and continued to the southeast, apparently toward the gap in the hills around Jenin. In short order, as daylight failed altogether, the Israeli spearhead crossed the Jenin–Nablus highway, the black-topped two-lane road that actually ran on to Jerusalem by way of Ramallah, and from there all the way to the Judean city of Hebron.

The first Jordanian tank the Israeli column encountered was a Patton from the 12th Jordanian Independent Tank Battalion. It was one of a company of fourteen Pattons that had been sent to bolster the Khalid Ibn el-Walid Infantry Battalion. But this one had been set afire minutes earlier by a roving IAF fighter-bomber as the Patton company raced to Jenin from its base at Nablus.

So far, so good. But *Zahal*'s easy break-ins in the far north—three of them so far—were destined to come a cropper. The Jordanians had been caught looking the other way in all three cases, and the attention of their commanders was fully occupied with events in Jerusalem. By the time the Israelis broke into northern Samaria, the regional strategic reserve, the 40th Jordanian Armored Brigade, had already been put in motion from around the Damiya Bridge toward Jericho, and it was under attack from the air.

Also, the 8th Iraqi Motorized-Infantry Brigade, which might otherwise have been rushed to northern Samaria, had been gutted by Israeli air attacks throughout the afternoon. There was no help on the way from Syria, either; Jordan's erstwhile Arab brothers in Damascus had not even responded to Egyptian General Riadh's plea that a brigade or two to be dispatched to Jordan.

Israeli feints, voluntary misdirection of forces, and brotherly disinterest aside, King Hussein's army had defeated itself in northern Samaria several *years* before the 1967 war.

The vision British Lieutenant General Sir John Bagot Glubb had had for the defense of the West Bank during his tenure as the Royal Jordanian Army's chief of staff had been based upon drawing the Israelis deep into the rugged hill country and defeating them in detail as they drove along the vulnerable narrow roads that snaked through the region. Glubb's plan had been maintained after his ouster by Jordanian officers in 1956, but it had been scrapped in 1962 to accommodate the massive expansion of the Jordanian National Guard. Under the new plan, which was still quite promising, a static defense along the frontier and in the West Bank's principal cities by many newly created National Guard battalions was to be combined with a fluid defense in the hill country by the brigades of the Royal Jordanian Army.

Under the latter plan, six National Guard battalions would have been deployed around Jenin, and twelve others would have been based at Nablus. In addition, a stiffener of two Royal Jordanian Army infantry brigades would have been based in northern Samaria as a regional reserve, and other infantry and even armored brigades could have been sent across from eastern Jordan, where they would have been deployed as a strategic reserve. However, the entire Jordanian National Guard had been disbanded in 1965 because King Hussein perceived it as being a threat to his existence, and the rather mediocre Jordanian military leaders of the day had not reinstituted the Glubb plan, which was still realistic in 1967. As a result, when war seemed imminent, the Royal Jordanian Army wastefully deployed the bulk of its limited combat power in Samaria at the periphery. Thus, if the Israelis broke through, the hilly terrain of the interior would be left without a viable defense.

On top of everything else, the independent, self-contained Jordanian infantry brigades had no mechanism whereby they could assist one another in the defense or combine their power in the attack. All lines of authority on the West Bank passed through the West Bank Force commander, Major

General Mohammed Ahmed Salim, who was much more King Hussein's uncle than a useful military thinker. Several of the officers over Salim's head were competent, but their authority had been circumscribed by the injection at the last minute of Egyptian General Abdul Moneim Riadh into the West Bank formula. Riadh had already sent the Jordanian Army reeling toward disaster by undertaking such unauthorized ventures as setting the crack Patton-equipped 40th Jordanian Armored Brigade in motion toward Jericho, away from Samaria—not to mention along an exposed roadway beneath the aggressive and uncontested IAF aerial umbrella. It would have been better for Jordan if there had been no one in charge.

It is true that the Jordanian units manning the peripheral defenses were considered first-rate. Moreover, the few Patton tanks they had at their disposal outclassed the Super Shermans the Israelis committed initially. And it is also true that the Israelis were not initially as disposed to conquering Samaria as to neutralizing it, which meant that they had to attack directly into the Jordanian defensive zones. But it remains that the Jordanian dispositions in Samaria were based upon incompetent military thinking.

The Bar-Kochva Armored Brigade's right-hand column, which had entered Jordan opposite Umm el-Fahm at 1700, pressed on toward the town of Ya'bad after stopping in the open for several hours. Presumably, the halt was to allow the Jordanians to counter the threat with troops they might otherwise have sent to defend Jenin against the brigade's main body. If that is so, then the Israeli plan succeeded a little too well.

There was a tough fight for several hours at a fortified hill, but the Israelis eventually triumphed. Ya'bad itself was occupied at dawn on June 7, and cleared of the last Jordanian soldiers. Thereafter, the column picked up the Jenin–Nablus highway and rolled back toward Jenin a short distance until it ran into an entirely unexpected defensive zone around the good-sized town of Arraba, which was about 10 kilometers southwest of Jenin. The Israeli Super Shermans advanced until they provoked a spirited response from well-entrenched Jordanian infantry and antitank guns supported by a company of Pattons from the 12th Jordanian Independent Tank Battalion. Three frontal attacks failed before the wounded Super Sherman battalion backed off. There was no help for miles around, and no way for the Super Shermans to outflank the entrenched Pattons and antitank guns from the narrow, hemmed-in roadway. So, the Israelis just halted in place and tried to think of a solution.

* * *

After conducting a rather slow, cautious advance in the dark southeastward from Yamun, the head of the main body of the Bar-Kochva Armored Brigade nosed into the town of Birkin at 0200 on June 6. There, the brigade established a base camp and then Lieutenant Colonel Bar-Kochva ordered his tanks to advance westward into the Dotan Valley, which was just across the hills immediately to the south of Jenin. It was Bar-Kochva's intention to attack Jenin from the south rather than along the obvious route from the southeast, which the Jordanians probably had defended in depth.

Unbeknown to Bar-Kochva, the Jordanians had also defended his "unexpected" line of approach with considerable skill and in considerable depth. Jordanian antitank guns and the thirteen Pattons of the 12th Jordanian Independent Tank Battalion were deployed in three overlapping lines on the heights south of the city. They could reach as far as 3 kilometers into the flat Dotan Valley. This the Israeli Super Sherman crews learned to their dismay when, at 0300, they unwittingly attacked straight into the Jordanian guns without any preparatory fires whatsoever. Very quickly, Jordanian Pattons firing down from the cover of hillside olive groves broke up the Israeli attack. A second, also unsupported, attempt by the Israelis to drive forward—this time only to rescue injured tank crewmen and pull several disabled Super Shermans to the rear—was also beaten back with even greater losses.

Bar-Kochva dreamed up a ruse. At 0430, just as the early dawn light began infiltrating the battlefield, the Israeli tanks began pulling back in such a way as to give the impression that they were withdrawing for good—and without retrieving the large number of damaged Super Shermans that littered the valley floor. Sensing victory, the Jordanian Patton company pursued the broken and fleeing Israeli tanks.

As the Pattons swept past the abandoned Super Shermans, Israeli tank gunners who were lying doggo opened fire. They thus accomplished in the open, in broad daylight, and at very short range what they had been unable to accomplish in the dark against hull-down Pattons at much longer ranges. Eight of the Pattons—which were all fitted out with vulnerable external gasoline tanks—were knocked out in the first encounter, but the remaining Jordanian tank crews rallied and continued the pursuit of the slowly withdrawing Israeli main body. Shortly, *all* of the Pattons were destroyed or disabled. At that point, there seemed to be precious little that could effectively stop the Bar-Kochva Armored Brigade from reaching Jenin from the Dotan Valley.

The Jordanian infantrymen and antitank gunners manning the hills south of Jenin fought long, hard, and well. When the Israelis returned to the attack after destroying the Patton company, the Jordanian guns threw them back. At length, several local attacks succeeded, but several others failed. It was not until around 0700 that the Israelis had finally chipped away at the Jordanian defenses sufficiently to break all the way through them. The Super Shermans then charged directly toward Jenin while the armored infantry stopped to mop up the outer defenses.

By the time the Bar-Kochva Armored Brigade broke through from the Dotan Valley, *Ugdah* Peled's motorized Avnon Infantry Brigade had arrived in the area along the road Bar-Kochva's main body had opened previously. It attacked into Jenin by way of the easier southeast axis just as Bar-Kochva's Super Shermans began their final approach from the south.

In a classic Israeli assault on a built-up area, the tanks swept up and down the streets of the city several times, firing their guns while the infantrymen conducted a careful house-to-house clearing operation. The only serious opposition was encountered when the Israelis approached a former British police fortress, but it fell when several Super Shermans opened fire with their 105mm main guns at point-blank range. Lieutenant Colonel Moshe Bar-Kochva, who was wounded in the battle for the police fortress, declared Jenin secure at 0730.

Just as the garrison of the Jenin police fortress was surrendering, word arrived from the Bar-Kochva Armored Brigade reconnaissance commander that at least one battalion of the 40th Jordanian Armored Brigade—an estimated sixty Patton tanks—was rapidly approaching the city from the southeast.

The Jordanian Pattons seen moving toward Jenin from the southeast came on so quickly that the Israeli reconnaissance jeeps and AMX-13s were trapped in the Dotan Valley town of Kabatiya, where a secondary road branched off toward the town of Tubas. The Jordanians, who were advancing up the secondary road from the direction of Tubas, managed to surround the Israeli reconnaissance force, but not to overwhelm it, before the bulk of the Pattons kept driving toward Jenin.

The Israelis were faced with a complex set of problems. Though Jenin had been declared secure, there were still large pockets of resistance to be overcome throughout the town. Also, Bar-Kochva's Super Shermans were running low on fuel and ammunition. There was some solace in that the

Jordanians had all but abandoned the hedgehog that had been holding up Bar-Kochva's second column of Super Shermans and armored infantry at Arraba, on the main Jenin–Nablus highway 10 kilometers southwest of Jenin. However, though this welcome reinforcement would be arriving soon, the second Israeli Super Shermans battalion was also suffering from a lack of fuel and ammunition.

To keep the Jordanian tanks off balance and unable to exploit their swift and surprising advance, Bar-Kochva ordered an immediate counterattack toward Kabatiya by the depleted Super Sherman battalion that was already in Jenin. This attack succeeded in its prime mission—stopping the Jordanians, who moved from the road to the hills in good order. But the Israeli counterattack did not break through the Jordanian Pattons to relieve the trapped reconnaissance elements, and it did not cause serious harm to the Jordanian tank battalion. It did succeed in nearly destroying itself before the guns of the Jordanian Pattons, which accounted for seventeen Super Shermans and thirteen other Israeli vehicles destroyed or disabled.

As the stunned Super Sherman battalion withdrew from directly in front of the halted but intact Jordanian Patton battalion, Bar-Kochva was able to arrange a covering barrage by the bulk of the *Ugdah* Peled artillery battalion, which had followed the Avnon Infantry Brigade down from the frontier. The artillery did not cause the Jordanians much damage or loss, but it made them cautious and allowed Bar-Kochva's Super Shermans to reform. Also, Bar-Kochva's column from Arraba managed to reach the main body of the brigade at this time.

Israeli problems were mounting. Not only had one of Bar-Kochva's Super Sherman battalions been gutted, ammunition and fuel supplies were down to critical levels. There was plenty of fuel and ammunition available, but there was no time to load it into the Super Shermans. Moreover, Jordanian stragglers still holding out in Jenin must have received word of the 40th Jordanian Armored Brigade's approach, because they chose this critical juncture to try to drive the Avnon Infantry Brigade from the city. And the Bar-Kochva Armored Brigade reconnaissance elements trapped behind Jordanian lines were screaming for help.

Bar-Kochva tried one more counterattack, but it was beaten back by the perfectly situated and coolly led Pattons after advancing only a short way toward Kabatiya. It was all the Israeli artillery could do to contain the Jordanian Pattons as they surged after the departing Super Shermans.

* * *

The Kabatiya crossroads, in the Dotan Valley, was well worth fighting over. Not only were there Israeli troops trapped near the road junction, the strategic access to Samaria was at stake.

A direct-line link between Jenin and Nablus was made impossible because two sprawling mountains lay between the two cities. The major highway between Jenin and Nablus meandered far to the west of the direct line, at the base of the two great massifs. On the eastern side of the mountains was a less developed but equally important secondary road that meandered between the two cities by way of the town of Tubas.

Ugdah Peled's planners had foreseen the need to secure the vital Tubas Loop Road, as it was known, and Elad Peled had dispatched his third brigade—the Ram Armored Brigade—to pass well to the east of Jenin on the morning of June 6. Unbelievably, the Ram Armored Brigade cut onto the Tubas Loop Road south of Kabatiya *after* the Jordanian Patton battalion at Kabatiya had passed the spot. That is, the Israelis and Jordanians had contrived to place themselves back-to-back on the same road, and they were advancing in opposite directions.

To accomplish this feat, the Jordanian Pattons had begun their long drive up a secondary road from near the Damiya Bridge during the night of June 5. In fact, during the late evening of June 5, the entire 40th Jordanian Armored Brigade had retraced its steps all the way from Jericho to the Damiya Bridge before breaking apart to proceed to various places throughout Samaria.

Before the Jordanian Pattons bound for Jenin reached Kabatiya, the Ram Armored Brigade ran into other 40th Jordanian Armored Brigade Pattons north of Tubas, and it became engaged to the hilt. Even if the Israelis had wanted to use the Ram Armored Brigade to relieve Kabatiya from the southeast, the Ram Armored Brigade was fighting an isolated battle of its own.

For once, the Jordanian Army had everything going for it.

The IAF decided the contest south of Jenin. It took until the late afternoon for Elad Peled to convince the IAF mission planners to pull ground-attack aircraft from other sectors, but, finally, a strike force of Fougas and Ouragans arrived over the Dotan Valley. These warplanes accomplished from the air what the Bar-Kochva Super Shermans had been unable to accomplish from the ground—they got behind the hull-down Jordanian Pattons and held them at bay with bombs, rockets, and cannon.

Using the respite afforded by the more-or-less continuous air strikes, Israeli tanks and armored infantry crept forward on the open valley floor to salvage whatever human lives and fighting vehicles they could. The operation was well underway when the Jordanians caught on, and Pattons on the heights threw most of the Israelis back with accurate long-range fire. Nevertheless, an Israeli Super Sherman company passed around the Jordanian eastern flank and drove a wedge to the beleaguered reconnaissance force, which scuttled to safety.

The air attack continued into the night, giving the Israelis a further respite for refueling and resupplying the surviving Super Shermans and other vehicles. A night attack was contemplated, but the Israeli tank crewmen needed some time off to sleep, and ordnance crews were promising that they could restore a significant number of damaged Super Shermans if they were given more time. So it was decided to wait until dawn to launch a vigorous all-out attack to clear Kabatiya and secure the vital crossroads.

45

Beginning at the extreme southwestern point of contact along Samaria's frontier with Israel, Colonel Moshe Yotvat's motorized 4th Infantry Brigade expanded its newly won holdings around Latrun in the pre-dawn hours of Tuesday, June 6. Yotvat's brigade advanced in several directions from Latrun in order to overwhelm several outlying fortified positions and to climb to the top of the strategically important Ramallah Ridge.

The only serious opposition encountered in the 4th Infantry Brigade's zone of action came in the late morning, when a battalion of the Jordanian El Hashimi Infantry Brigade stood its ground northeast of Latrun around the junction of the Old Jerusalem Highway and the Ramallah road. While the Israeli main body fought the stubborn defenders face-to-face, the 4th Infantry Brigade reconnaissance company bypassed the action and struck out down the Ramallah road. In due course, the reconnaissance troops captured the Kalandiya airport, and that rendered the Jordanian blocking position untenable. After the main Jordanian force in front of the 4th Infantry Brigade's main body evaporated, an Israeli motorized infantry battalion and the brigade's French Sherman company sprang nearly all the way to Ramallah, a city of 50,000 about 16 kilometers due north of Jerusalem's Old City.

After the major fighting had ended along the Ramallah road, many Jordanian soldiers and even some Egyptian commandos returned to the hills overlooking the artery and peppered passing convoys with small-arms fire. This forced the 4th Infantry Brigade to dispatch a large infantry force to hunt down all the snipers, a job that was only nearing completion two days later.

By the time the lead task force of the 4th Infantry Brigade reached the outskirts of Ramallah in the late afternoon, Colonel Uri Ben-Ari was approaching the city from the direction of Jerusalem with three armored-infantry companies, a French Sherman company, and his brigade reconnaissance company. Ben-Ari was placed in command of the entire operation at 1700.

The Harel Armored-Infantry Brigade tanks stormed into the city from the south at 1830, firing into many buildings as they crisscrossed the city's main streets. After the citizens and defenders of the city had been subjected to this treatment for about 45 minutes, until dusk, the Israelis left the town. The Harel Armored-Infantry Brigade task force set up a blocking position on the main highway south of the city, and the reinforced battalion of the 4th Infantry Brigade did the same to the north. The citizens of Ramallah were so cowed by the Israelis shoot-'em-up entry that they remained fearfully quiet all night.

North of Latrun, *Zahal*'s Shaham Infantry Brigade crossed into Jordan after demonstrating its intentions for a day in order to tie down the Jordanian Princess Alia Infantry Brigade. The poorly led Jordanian brigade had had a day to prepare for the expected Israeli attack, but apparently it had done nothing; opposition to the Israeli direct frontal attack was meager and scattered. By 1400, the Israelis had captured Kalkiliya and a battery of Jordanian 155mm field guns. This move placed an Israeli force inside Jordan, on a good road, and with no Jordanian forces between it and Nablus, which was about 30 kilometers to the west. By 1700, one tank-reinforced battalion of the Shaham Infantry Brigade had advanced halfway to Nablus aboard a motley array of commandeered civilian vehicles.

In the far northeastern corner of Samaria, hard against the Jordan River, the diversionary attack by the motorized Gavish Infantry Brigade had tied down the entire Jordanian El Yarmouk Infantry Brigade along the river, and the Jordanians even committed part of a Patton battalion from the 40th Jordanian Armored Brigade. This tank force was eventually sent west to try to save Nablus, but its temporary diversion to contain the Gavish Infantry Brigade proved to be crucial.

After guarding the upper Galilee against a threatened Syrian attack on June 5, the main body of *Ugdah* Peled's Ram Armored Brigade had to travel 75 kilometers on its own tracks to open yet another breach into Samaria. Leaving its Super Sherman battalion behind to serve as a mobile force in upper Galilee, the main body of the Ram Armored Brigade attacked into Jordan at 0430 on June 6 from the vicinity of Mount Gilboa, about 15 kilometers northeast of Jenin. Once across the frontier, Colonel Uri Ram's force advanced along a rough country track leading in the direction of the Tubas Loop Road. As it turned out, the timing of Ram's unopposed thrust was just right to carry the head of the brigade column onto the Tubas Loop Road after a battalion of the 40th Jordanian Armored Brigade had passed by on its way to Jenin.

Well short of Tubas, at a little wooded roadside feature known as Deir Abu Daif, a platoon of Jordanian infantrymen supported by several antitank guns had developed a creditable road block. The men in the Israeli spearhead of reconnaissance halftracks and AMX-13 tanks did not realize there was a defensive position until the Jordanian antitank guns opened fire.

Uri Ram was unable to see what he was up against. While Israeli tanks and armored infantrymen worked toward the Jordanian flank, Ram ordered in an airstrike and deployed his 105mm SP artillery battalion against the Jordanian block. When the air and artillery support began, the tanks and armored infantrymen pitched into the Jordanian position and overwhelmed the defenders. The Israeli attack continued up the steep slope and engulfed two small hill villages, which were briefly defended.

As the main body of the Ram Armored Brigade resumed its advance at 1015, the lead reconnaissance element observed at a distance that a force of Jordanian Pattons was moving into the roadside village of Kufeir. The lay of the land obliged Ram's Centurion battalion to deploy for the attack on Kufeir without cover. Two Jordanian Patton companies were by then in possession of excellent hull-down defensive positions, from which they were able to fire on the more powerful but entirely exposed Centurions. The brigade reconnaissance company commander was killed and several reconnaissance vehicles and three Centurions were damaged or disabled as they slowed down to approach a barrier of concrete dragon's teeth fronting Kufeir. With that, the Israelis withdrew around a bend in the road to map out a better, safer course of action.

In the hope of repeating his earlier success, Ram again called in close air support. There was an hours-long delay, and when the IAF jets arrived they had little or no effect upon the Jordanian Pattons. By the time the Israeli Centurions had tested the defenses—and were turned back yet again—it was dark. Ram decided to wait at least a few hours to rest his men and refuel his tanks. Also, he wanted to see how things might go on the political front, for by then it appeared that the Royal Jordanian Army might be about to withdraw from the West Bank.

With the single exception of the armored struggle south of Jenin, *all* the news reaching King Hussein on Tuesday, June 6, was grim. The monarch's bad day started at 0530, when it finally dawned on him and his advisors and generals that the Syrians definitely were not going to send help and that the promised Iraqi and Saudi brigades, some of which were already in Jordan, were never going to reach the West Bank in time to save it.

The Egyptian general in charge of the so-called United Arab Command in Jordan, Abdul Moneim Riadh, offered the king no solace. Between 0530 and 0545, he told Hussein that the only choices that lay open were asking the United Nations to arrange a ceasefire with Israel or saving the Royal Jordanian Army by withdrawing it east of the Jordan River. To delay a decision, Hussein placed a direct phone call to Egypt's President Nasser, and the two massaged one another by cooking up the paranoid scenario that Israel was being directly supported from the air by British and American warplanes.

A little after noon, General Riadh spoke with the Egyptian Minister for War, Field Marshal Abdel Hakim Amer, who agreed that the Jordanians should retreat behind the Jordan River. When Riadh passed Amer's advice to Hussein, the king briefly convinced himself that his Arab brothers were plotting against him, but he came to his senses by 1400, when he finally realized that Egypt and Jordan were facing a matched set of epic defeats.

Hussein held out until 2200 on June 6, and then he ordered Riadh to authorize the withdrawal of all Jordanian military units to the east bank of the Jordan River. This order was broadcast to all Jordanian units in Judea and Samaria, and several immediately started packing it in.

Complicating matters immensely was a 2230 United Nations call for a ceasefire. Grasping at straws, Hussein reasoned that if the Israelis accepted the U.N.-mandated ceasefire, the war would stop with all units safe where they were. That would mean that most of the West Bank would be in Jordanian hands and most of the Royal Jordanian Army would be saved. Of course, the Israelis had no intention of accepting a ceasefire while so many Jordanian and Egyptian (and Syrian) brigades remained intact.

Even a Jordanian commander confounded the U.N. effort. Brigadier Rakan Inad el-Jazi, the aggressive and resourceful commander of the 40th Jordanian Armored Brigade, ordered all his troops to ignore the ceasefire order and to at least undertake a fighting withdrawal toward Nablus.

Perhaps Brigadier el-Jazi's example instilled the king with some new hope, or maybe the monarch's own ambivalence temporarily won out. In the event, General Riadh was ordered to countermand the withdrawal order. Many Jordanian units received the countermanding order in time to prevent their withdrawal, but others were already on the move, and these faced a desperate quandary as to which way to go—back to their old positions or on to the Jordan River, for the Israelis were still aggressively on the prowl and it was not easy for the Jordanians to move in any direction. In some cases— Jerusalem, for example—the countermanding order was never received.

Compounding the whole mess, Hussein issued a well-meaning communique to the army at 0150 on June 7. He simply told all his soldiers to stand fast. That would have been sufficient, but at 0230 the king went on the air again. This time, he told his soldiers to honor the U.N. ceasefire call—if they saw that the Israelis were honoring it. In the face of that extraordinary qualifier, each Jordanian commander was left to decide for himself if he and his men were still at war.

46

On Wednesday, June 7, nearly the entire Royal Jordanian Army West Bank Force withdrew, retreated, or collapsed. The only serious fighting that day was in *Ugdah* Peled's zone.

The Old City of Jerusalem fell on Wednesday, and that freed up two battalions of the Jerusalem Infantry Brigade to begin the work of occupying all of Judea. At 1500, a Jerusalem Infantry Brigade task force drove into Bethlehem, which had been abandoned at noon by the Jordanian Hittin Infantry Brigade. The Hittin Infantry Brigade and the 10th Jordanian Independent Tank Battalion had also abandoned Hebron at noon. Israelis entering Hebron found twenty-five Jordanian Centurion tanks that had been abandoned in perfect running order by their crews. Thereafter, the Jerusalem Infantry Brigade task force and its supporting tanks split into three parts and spread out across the length and breadth of Judea. There were no organized Jordanian units encountered anywhere in Judea on June 7, and no resistance.

At dawn on June 7, the task force of Colonel Uri Ben-Ari's Harel Armored-Infantry Brigade that had shot up Ramallah and then withdrawn the previous evening returned to occupy the city. Ben-Ari next organized the bulk of his brigade into two powerful tank-infantry task forces, which were dispatched along parallel routes toward the Jordan Valley. As the southern column descended into the valley on the main Jerusalem-Jericho highway, it found twenty 60th Jordanian Armored Brigade Pattons that had been abandoned by their crews after becoming mired in deep mud.

The southern Harel column was fired on late in the afternoon from the edge of Jericho. The Jordanian fire was returned at long range by Israeli AML armored cars, and then air support was requested. By the time the IAF jets showed up, the northern Harel column had arrived.

After several of his men mockingly sounded trumpets they had looted in Ramallah, Ben-Ari set up a neat pincers attack. The two Israeli tank columns closed around ancient Jericho while IAF jets screamed in low overhead. Finally, one column of tanks raced into the city and shot the place up on the run. After the Shermans had made several passes that appeared to quell the ardor of Jericho's defenders, the rest of the tanks and the armored infantry entered the city. At 1930, Ben-Ari reported to Central Command Headquarters that Jericho was firmly in his hands.

Though it was dark and he and his men were exhausted, the irrepressible Uri Ben-Ari advanced with the main body of his brigade toward the Allenby Bridge. Though admonished to remain well clear of the span, Ben-Ari sent his armored cars across it and the nearby Abdullah Bridge. When GHQ found out, the armored cars were ordered to withdraw and Ben-Ari's engineers were peremptorily ordered to blow both bridges, and a third one, into the river. Ben-Ari howled with indignation, but he obeyed. GHQ had Ben-Ari pegged; he had every intention of slipping his entire brigade across the Jordan River and striking for Amman.

Starting at the northern outskirts of Ramallah at dawn, the lead battalion of the motorized 4th Infantry Brigade headed north on the main highway to Nablus. There was no opposition all the way to the objective even though the highway twisted through and between several features that would have made ideal chokepoints. One reason for the lack of opposition might have been the preemptive nature of the air support at the 4th Infantry Brigade's disposal. As a matter of course, relays of Israeli jets simply bombed and strafed any likely looking ambush site before the truck-borne infantry quite reached it.

Most of the rest of the 4th Infantry Brigade advanced up the highway from Latrun, rolled through Ramallah, and advanced to the northwest by secondary roads to search for Jordanian holdouts in the hinterland between Ramallah, Nablus, and Kalkiliya. These somewhat diffused motorized infantry task forces also were supported by an aggressive aerial umbrella that shot up potential hazards without having to be asked. By the end of the day, most of the principal towns and villages in the densely settled region had been visited if not thoroughly checked.

On June 6, a nominally motorized infantry battalion of the Shaham Infantry Brigade had occupied Kalkiliya and advanced from there to within 16 kilometers of Nablus. This force, including a company of French Shermans, resumed its slow advance in commandeered civilian vehicles at dawn on June 7. Only a few soldiers of the Jordanian Princess Alia Infantry Brigade had remained in the area to contest the advance with desultory long-range fire, and so the Israeli column reached the Tubas Loop Road shortly after noon. There, a few kilometers south of Nablus, it waited for other Israeli units to arrive.

Another battalion of the Shaham Infantry Brigade, also riding in commandeered Israeli civilian vehicles and supported by several French Shermans, crossed the frontier at dawn to occupy Tulkarm. A small number of riflemen who initially opposed this advance surrendered when the Israelis closed in on their positions. It turned out that the prisoners were local Palestinian civilians who had taken up arms after the local garrison had fled into the night. Leaving a company to check through the town, the Israeli force advanced westward on country roads and eventually reached the Jenin–Nablus highway. There, it linked up with an armored column from *Ugdah* Peled.

In northern Samaria, matters might have gone as easily for the Bar-Kochva and Ram armored brigades had it not been for Brigadier Rakan Inad el-Jazi, the commander of the 40th Jordanian Armored Brigade. Alone among Jordanian commanders in the wake of King Hussein's confusing and defeatist broadcasts during the night, El-Jazi was determined to stay the course. His proud and powerful brigade, which would have been a credit to any army in the world, had suffered losses on June 5 and 6, but it was relatively intact, and it was on the verge in some places of turning the Israelis back.

In *Ugdah* Peled's western zone, the Ram Armored Brigade had been stopped cold for most of June 6 on the Tubas Loop Road in front of Kufeir. There, two companies of the 40th Jordanian Armored Brigade occupied superior positions that utterly dominated the restricted roadway.

After attempting to bull through twice, Uri Ram had drawn in his horns and bided his time. Centurions damaged during the day were repaired, all the brigade's vehicles were refueled, and the troops were given time to eat and rest. Ram reckoned that the Jordanians around the bend in the road were doing the same, and that was the basis of his unorthodox plan.

At 0100 on June 7, Ram's SP artillery opened fire on the Jordanian front line. Then, as the Israeli Centurions advanced down the road and blew up concrete tetrahedrons with direct fire from their 105mm main guns, the SPs isolated the battlefield by shifting their fires toward the Jordanian rear.

As Uri Ram had hoped, the Jordanian tank crews were sleeping. Many of the surprised and sleepy Jordanians bolted from the area, so the opposition was ragged and inconsistent. The Israeli charge up the road penetrated into the Jordanian hedgehog. The defenses unraveled, but not enough to allow the Israelis all the way into Kufeir.

As the fighting raged at point-blank ranges, Ram authorized his Centurion crews to flash their running lights, headlights, and searchlights—the former for recognition and the latter for qualifying targets. The Israelis ground forward into Kufeir, and the surviving Pattons retreated to the next big town, Akaba, which by then was held by the remainder of their battalion.

Ram waited restlessly until 0415 before he began advancing his Centurions toward Akaba. This allowed him to call in air support. The jets arrived overhead at the crack of dawn and drove the Jordanian Pattons out of the objective. As the jets picked off the Pattons streaming down toward Tubas, the Israeli column advanced apace, stung but not stopped by small packets of withdrawing Jordanian infantrymen from the Khalid Ibn el-Walid Infantry Brigade who had gotten mixed in among the Jordanian tanks. Three hours after jumping off, the Ram Armored Brigade spearhead reached Tubas, which the last of the retreating Jordanians had cleared only moments earlier.

The road between Kufeir and Tubas was littered with Jordanian Pattons from both the 40th Jordanian Armored Brigade and the 12th Jordanian Independent Tank Battalion. Sixteen of thirty-five Pattons located by the Israelis had been destroyed or disabled by direct fire from Israeli Centurions, and nineteen had been hit from the air.

After checking through Tubas, a small part of the Ram Armored Brigade continued south toward Nablus, but the bulk of the Centurion battalion, the entire armored-infantry battalion, and a reconnaissance element turned off toward the Jordan Valley to pursue the fleeing Jordanian Pattons toward the Damiya Bridge. By 0930, the bridge was within sight, but the brigade deputy commander was ordered to halt some distance away to allow civilian refugees free access to the crossing. By then, only five of the Jordanian Pattons the Israelis had been chasing were left in running order, and these crossed the river.

Uri Ram remained on the Tubas Loop Road for a dash into Nablus at the head of one Centurion company and the main body of the brigade reconnaissance battalion. This small task force began its final approach at 0930, well ahead of the other Israeli units converging on the city.

A few kilometers north of Nablus, the Tubas Loop Road entered a long, narrow defile, which Jordanians reportedly were defending in considerable strength. It took an hour for a reconnaissance element to penetrate all the way through the defile and report back that prisoners in its possession claimed the route had never been defended. With that, the Centurion company raced forward, bypassed the reconnaissance force, and ran up the city's main street at 1030.

The Ram Armored Brigade Centurion company was the first Israeli unit to enter Nablus, a prosperous city of 80,000. The populace inferred from the direction of their approach and strange clothing that the Israelis were Iraqis, and hundreds stormed into the streets to welcome them. There was considerable embarrassment among the revelers when the truth became known, and then Israeli tank commanders fired a few machine-gun bursts overhead to scatter the civilians back to their homes. Meager resistance ensued, but it was easily overcome.

After 1100, Ram's AMX-13 reconnaissance company encountered twenty-five Jordanian Pattons while it was sweeping the area east of Nablus. The Pattons attacked as soon as they were discovered, but the Israeli light tanks quickly went into hull-down positions and air support was called. Employing bombs, rockets, napalm, cannon fire, and just plain terror, the Israeli jets turned the Jordanian charge into an utter rout. At least fifteen of the Pattons were destroyed from the air. As the surviving Pattons turned tail, the AMX-13s were able to destroy or disable all of them with pinpoint fire from their 75mm high-velocity main guns. Once again, the key to this remarkable Israeli victory was the use by the Jordanians of unarmored external gasoline tanks strapped to the rear decks of their Pattons.

Before dawn on June 8, Uri Ram was ordered to rush his entire brigade north to Israel's Huleh Valley. Though mechanics reported that the brigade's abused tanks and halftracks were on the verge of facing massive mechanical breakdowns, the brigade was slated to take part in the invasion of the Golan Heights.

Following a 15-minute artillery barrage and 30-minute air bombardment at first light on June 7, the Bar-Kochva Armored Brigade opened what its commander hoped would be the final battle for Kabatiya. At 0445, the Israeli Super Shermans broke from cover and advanced across the open valley floor all the way to the Kabatiya crossroads. There were no Jordanian Pattons to be found; there was no sign of life. *Zahal's* toughest test and only near defeat of the war had ended.

The Bar-Kochva Armored Brigade reformed in Kabatiya and split into two roughly equivalent columns. One column struck off down the main highway toward Nablus and the other, with Moshe Bar-Kochva along, struck off down the Tubas Loop Road.

From Kufeir southward, the Tubas Loop Road was littered with burned-out Jordanian Pattons and other military vehicles. Otherwise, the road was deserted. Bar-Kochva turned off down the Damiya Bridge road and arrived within sight of the Jordan River at 1000. There, the Ram Armored Brigade's main body was already monitoring the heavy flow of refugees crossing the bridge.

The second of Bar-Kochva's columns made rapid progress along the Jenin–Nablus highway until just before 0800. Then, as it was nosing through a narrow defile toward the village of Silat Edh Dhahr, it was ambushed by a company of Jordanian infantrymen holding an old British police fortress overlooking the highway. As the Israeli column edged forward, several Pattons from the 12th Jordanian Tank Battalion opened fire. Two of the Super Shermans were damaged at close range, and the rest withdrew.

Though the Jordanians held the better position, they packed up and retreated in the direction of Sebastiya. There, they again stopped the Israeli armored column. IAF jets were called in, and they destroyed or disabled all of the Jordanian Pattons. Then the Israeli Super Shermans probed forward and the Israeli armored infantry moved against the police fortress, whose garrison was overwhelmed in a sharp fight.

While the Israeli task force regrouped around Sebastiya, Israeli reconnaissance elements probing ahead toward Nablus came upon fifteen Pattons that had been abandoned on the roadway by their crews. It turned out that most of them had simply run out of fuel. It also turned out that this was the last company of the 12th Jordanian Independent Tank Battalion. In less than forty-eight hours, in a series of widely dispersed battles, this battalion lost every one of its approximately sixty Patton tanks.

The Israeli task force arrived in the northern outskirts of Nablus shortly after noon. Later, it linked up with other Israeli units that arrived from several other directions during the course of the day.

By late Wednesday afternoon, the fighting in Samaria had all but ended. At noon, King Hussein had explicitly ordered all Royal Jordanian Army units still in the West Bank to withdraw across the Jordan River. These units did their best to comply. At 2000 on June 7, the king accepted a U.N.-sponsored ceasefire.

While thousands of Jordanian soldiers crossed safely into eastern Jordan, they brought precious few of their weapons and little of their equipment. For example, the 40th Jordanian Armored Brigade evacuated only five of the nearly 100 Patton tanks charged to its rolls. Even the more lightly engaged 60th Jordanian Armored Brigade salvaged only a few companies of its Pattons. Over fifty undamaged Jordanian Pattons and Centurions were left to the Israelis because they ran out of fuel, became bogged down in deep mud, or were simply abandoned by their crews.

On Thursday, June 8, the Israelis fanned out to occupy the entire West Bank. That was a job that would actually take days and weeks to accomplish fully, but for the time being a show of force was sufficient to quell any nascent desires on the part of the citizenry to resist. For the most part, Jordanian soldiers were allowed to cross the Jordan River. In fact, only about 500 military prisoners were reluctantly taken into custody.

The Royal Jordanian Army left behind an estimated 150 of its estimated 200 155mm and 25-pounder field guns and 17-pounder and 106mm antitank guns and nearly 200 of its estimated 270 tanks. Hundreds of vehicles and tons of ammunition and supplies were also captured, and so were thousands of personal weapons.

The reasons for the Royal Jordanian Army's utter defeat in less than two full days of combat did not lie in the bravery or inclinations of its soldiers but in the incompetence of its commanders. It is difficult to find even one thing that the Jordanian monarch or his commanders—especially Egypt's General Riadh—did not bungle. Only two of Jordan's generals—Brigadier Ata Ali Hazza'a and Brigadier Rakan Inad el-Jazi—turned in creditable performances. And only one other brigade commander, the Khalid Ibn el-Walid Infantry Brigade's Lieutenant Colonel Awad Mohammed el-Khalidi, deserves praise.

Israel's victory in its unexpected war against Jordan was an enduring testament to good training. The entire West Bank campaign, which looks fairly seamless in retrospect, was entirely improvised in all its phases. Moreover, it would have resulted in far more Israeli casualties but for the relentless ground-support campaign waged by the IAF.

As it was, Israel lost 302 of her sons killed in the brief war with Jordan (195 in Jerusalem alone), and 1,453 wounded (1,131 in Jerusalem). Jordan lost an estimated 6,000 soldiers killed, missing, or deserted.

Part VII

The Golan Heights

47

Though for two decades the Syrians had been loudly threatening to invade Israel, the Israelis knew they had little to fear in that regard. Even after the influx of Soviet advisors and weapons began, Israelis in the know remained confident that Syria would not back its words with deeds. Of course, as a matter of prudence, a sound defensive policy was established with regard to a possible Arab multi-national invasion of northern Israel via Syria. And, once the long-standing defensive plans had been reaffirmed, Northern Command was directed to oversee planning for a possible invasion (or counterinvasion) aimed at permanently pushing the volatile "crazies" in Syria back from the Golan Plateau. *Zahal's* view was quite cold-blooded in this regard; in order to satisfy the applicable bedrock precepts, the Syrian Army would have to be destroyed and Syria's ability to dominate northern Israel from the protected heights would have to be terminated. If no other good came of the entire 1967 war, these objectives—at least—were to be achieved.

If there was one place along Israel's entire frontier with four hostile neighbors that could provide a true test of *Zahal's* prowess and vision, it was the 60-kilometer stretch along the edge of the Golan Plateau. Between 1948 and 1967, successive Syrian regimes, all unutterably opposed to the existence of the Jewish state, packed the short, narrow region facing northeastern Israel with all manner of defensive works, artillery emplacements, and troop positions. By the beginning of June 1967, the Syrian Army had arrayed the bulk of 100,000 Regular, Reserve, and National Guard troops in successive lines of defensive works so densely built that they were for all practical purposes continuous to a depth of nearly 15 kilometers. Also, the Syrian Army had sited at least 265 medium- and heavy-caliber field pieces, heavy mortars, heavy-rocket launchers, and even permanently emplaced obsolete tanks along the Golan Plateau within range of many northern Israeli villages, towns, and cities. These artillery weapons were capable of firing 10 tons of shells and rockets per minute.

The test *Zahal* faced, once the government of Israel firmly decided to seize the Golan Plateau, was launching a frontal attack directly up a sheer 120- to 1,000-meter-high escarpment in the face of truly awesome firepower. To do so, Israeli combat units in the north could not use any of the tactics and ploys that had been developed against larger but more thinly spread Egyptian combat formations. In terms of numbers and deployment, *all* the advantages appeared to reside with the defenders.

On the Golan, not only were the Syrian defenses far deeper than any encountered by *Zahal* in the Gaza Strip or Sinai, they were also permanent, had been built up over many years on all the very best ground, and they were manned by June 5 in immensely greater strength than any comparable sector of the Egyptian front line. Of equal importance to Brigadier General Dado Elazar and his Northern Command planners, there was absolutely no way *around* the Syrian defenses—no indirect approach to exploit. The Syrian line was continuous and firmly anchored at each end on impregnable geographical features. To the north was the sprawling, permanently snow-capped 3,000-meter-high Hermon massif, and to the south was both the Kinneret and the Yarmouk River. Moreover, there were only a few winding roads that Israeli armor or motorized infantry could take to the top.

On paper, the Syrian Army of June 5, 1967, appeared quite a bit stronger than the Royal Jordanian Army on the same date. Its 60,000 Regulars and 40,000 Reservists and National Guardsmen were formed into six infantry brigades, two tank brigades, and two mechanized-infantry brigades. At least seven National Guard battalions were also available. Supporting the infantry, tank, and mechanized-infantry brigades was a huge artillery establishment amounting to as many as 1,200 field guns, heavy mortars, multiple heavy-rocket launchers, and antiaircraft and antitank guns. The Syrian Army boasted 550 tanks and assault guns, of which most were Soviet T-34s, T-54s, and SU-100s. There were also as many as 500 APCs of various types and vintages. Going into the war, the Soviet-equipped Syrian Air Force had at its disposal as many as 136 first-line fighter-bombers.

The Syrian Army brigades were grouped in a curious manner. After the Reserves had been called up, there were twelve field brigades available to defend the Golan Heights. These included five of Syria's six Regular infantry brigades and four of six Reserve infantry brigades. Of the latter, none was at full authorized strength. Both Syrian tank brigades also were deployed on or near the Golan Plateau, but only one of the two mechanized-infantry brigades.

The Golan-based brigades were divided into three "brigade groups" that had the appearance of standard divisions—very much like *Zahal ugdot*, in fact. However, the brigade groups were merely administrative shells whose headquarters only handled non-combat tasks such as supply. There was no means by which a brigade group's nominal commander could maneuver the various components of his brigade group in a harmonious offensive manner, or even in the defensive. Also, coordination between brigade groups was rudimentary. These arrangements and the Syrian Army's overall lack of operational finesse—*Zahal*'s forte—tended to underscore the defensive nature of Syria's role in the war. Though plans existed in Damascus for an invasion of Israel, the Syrian Army did not actually possess the means or the knowhow for coming down from the Golan Plateau in strength or in concert.

From south to north, the three Syrian brigade groups were the 35th (three Regular infantry brigades and the mechanized-infantry brigade), the 12th (one tank brigade, one Regular infantry brigade, and two Reserve infantry brigades), and the 42nd (one tank brigade, one Regular infantry brigade, and two Reserve infantry brigades). The 35th Brigade Group, in the south, was spread out from the Yarmouk River, up behind the Kinneret, and as far north as about the center of the Golan Plateau overlooking the Jordan River and Israel's Huleh Valley. (Two brigades from this group, including the mechanized-infantry brigade, were well to the rear, as part of the area reserve.) Two infantry brigades (one Regular and one Reserve) of the 12th Brigade Group were rather more densely packed along the edge of northern Golan Plateau, and the 12th Brigade Group's other two brigades (including a tank brigade) were in the area reserve. The 42nd Brigade Group was concentrated well back from the front along the highway linking Damascus with the Golan city of Kuneitra. Intermixed with the front-line brigade groups, the 12th and 35th, were seven National Guard battalions.

Rebuilt along the Soviet pattern, the Syrian brigades looked reasonably formidable on paper. The Regular infantry brigades comprised three motorized infantry battalions, a tank battalion (T-34s or SU-100s), and an antitank battalion. The mechanized-infantry brigades comprised two infantry battalions mounted in APCs and a tank battalion (T-54s and SU-100s), plus supports. And the tank brigades each fielded two tank battalions (T-54s and

SU-100s) and one infantry battalion mounted in APCs. Each of the Reserve infantry brigades was composed of three understrength infantry battalions and minimum supporting arms; they would have been useless in a war of movement.

Underlying the raw statistics of military power in Syria, however, was the usual problem involved in assessing all Arab armies of the period; though strong on paper, the Syrian Army was weak in reality. The vast majority of the 100,000 soldiers under arms on June 5, 1967, were conscripts whose training was marginal and whose duties and outlook had little to do with conventional warfare against an external enemy. The Syrian Army had a formidable array of equipment at its disposal, but even the latest Soviet tanks, APCS, artillery pieces, airplanes, and other weapons were indifferently maintained. At any given moment, as many as one-third of all Syrian military vehicles and weapons systems were less than ready for action by virtue of poor maintenance or lack of spare parts. Training, which had been improving steadily since the arrival of Soviet advisors in 1966, was well below Israeli, Jordanian, or even Egyptian standards. The Syrian Army was not very good, even by Third World standards.

Morale was not high in the Syrian armed forces, either. The army was a coup army—more a means for seizing or maintaining power than a serious threat to any of Syria's neighbors. The armed forces was the vehicle by which the regime in Damascus held Syria's multi-ethnic population of warring factions in check, but it was hardly employed as a means for molding a non-fractious society. The precarious fortunes of the latest of Syria's many ruling juntas and strongmen were in many ways enhanced by the ability of the junta to use the armed forces to prevent ethnic factions from coalescing; units composed in the main from members of one ethnic group were often garrisoned in such a way as to hold hostage the homeland of another ethnic group.

For all its shortcomings, the Syrian Army appeared quite capable of defending the ideal natural position afforded it by the geography of its frontier with Israel. But there was little possibility that the Syrian Army could be employed to carry out the government's promised invasion of northern Israel.

48

It is doubtful the Syrians had any real intention of invading northern Israel, but they did have an ambitious plan they had been showing their Arab brothers for some time. The plan was dubbed Operation Nazzar (Victory), and it was as fanciful as it appeared ambitious. In it, a division-sized task force was to descend from the high ground at the southern end of the Kinneret and sweep through Kibbutz Degania and on around the lakeshore into the Israeli city of Tiberias. At the same time, one brigade was to make a diversionary push in the far north, toward Kibbutz Dan. By the end of the first day of fighting, after other Syrian mobile forces became active in the center, the Syrian Army was to be in possession of the city of Sfad, in the high hills on the western side of the Jordan River.

The Syrian regime had no intention of launching such an offensive—unless Israel was by then on her knees as a result of the efforts of other Arab armies. The main function of the Syrian Army was keeping an uneasy peace within Syria; there was no way the junta in Damascus was going to risk the status quo with a potentially disastrous invasion of its powerful and aroused neighbor.

In truth, the Syrians *might* have done something substantive to support their allies, but the Damascus regime had come to feel insulted and left out during the final days of the slide to war. Its putative allies had done little to include it in the planning, or even to keep it informed. The Syrians had not been forewarned of King Hussein's trip to Cairo on May 30, nor even that President Nasser had seen fit to make peace with Hussein. Overall, Syria had been left out of the planning. It says much about why the proud Syrians ignored Egyptian pleas to open a second front and Jordanian pleas to send help.

On the other hand, short of sending its forces into battle against Israel or even coming to the aid of Jordan in its hour of need, the Syrians had to do *something* to at least appear to support the war it had worked so hard and so long to foment. This the Syrians appreciated, but they did not do what was expected of them. Enemies and putative allies alike expected the powerful Syrian artillery establishment based on the Golan Plateau to pulverize Israeli villages and towns within its reach, but there was absolutely none of that throughout the first day of the war. Israelis described the northern region as being "ominously silent."

All the action between Syria and Israel on June 5 was between their air forces. In the early afternoon, after the bulk of the Egyptian and Royal Jordanian air forces had been destroyed on the ground and there were IAF attack aircraft available, a large part of the Syrian Air Force was also destroyed on the ground. IAF Mirages and Mystères closed Syria's five military air bases and destroyed thirty-two (of thirty-six) MiG-21s, nineteen (of an estimated one hundred) MiG-15s and MiG-17s, two (of six) Il-28 bombers, and two (of fourteen) light helicopters. Israeli Mirages also shot down four MiG-17s. The IAF lost only one Mystère. (In separate attacks in western Iraq, the IAF destroyed nine MiG-21s, five Hawker Hunters, one Tu-16, and five Il-14s.)

During the night, the Syrians opened a path through their own minefield overlooking the B'not Yaacov (Daughters of Jacob) Bridge across the Jordan. It is possible that this was the unauthorized work of an overly ambitious local commander to facilitate Operation Nazzar's central attack scheme. The central attack never began, but the northern diversionary attack in the vicinity of Tel Dan did—late and halfheartedly.

Far from committing the entire infantry brigade that was to have gone into the offensive in the extreme north, the Syrians hedged on their own plan by scheduling just one infantry battalion and two weak tank companies to undertake what amounted to a probe. The 243rd Syrian Infantry Battalion of the 11th Syrian Infantry Brigade and two small companies (a dozen T-34s in all) from the 2nd Syrian National Guard Tank Battalion were to have jumped off at 0545 on June 6. Their objectives—the settlements of Kibbutz Dan, Dafna, and Shaar Yishuv—were to be reached from Tel Hamra, one of the many fortified hills on the Syrian side of the line.

Following a one-hour delay, during which an artillery bombardment fully alerted the Israelis, the reinforced 243rd Syrian Infantry Battalion attacked. Aided by artillery support and a small contingent of soldiers, it was the locals who stopped the three-prong attack in its tracks. At 0720, several

Israeli warplanes entered the fray and all but gutted the Syrian force with cannon, bombs, and rockets. At 0815, the 11th Syrian Infantry Brigade commander ordered the hapless attackers to withdraw. What should have been a fairly simple exercise turned into a rout. When the shooting finally subsided, six smashed and smoldering Syrian tanks and 200 dead Syrian soldiers lay upon the battlefield. Syrian prisoners explained that their officers had not actually shared the dangers with their men.

After the failure of the 11th Syrian Infantry Brigade to overrun the three northern settlements, the Syrians restricted their warlike efforts to artillery barrages on targets they had been attacking in similar manner for nearly two decades. The locals were inured to the fire, and few casualties resulted from it. This fire went on for the balance of June 6 and on through June 7 and June 8. Casualties on the Israeli side were negligible, but life in far northern Israel came to a complete standstill as everyone crowded into shelters to await the outcome. Israeli artillery responded in kind, and vast destruction was caused on both sides of the frontier.

On June 7, the IAF opened a remorseless air offensive aimed at destroying Syrian bunkers and trenchlines and killing or seriously jarring the defenders. The lattermost objective might have been achieved, but few Syrians were killed and few of their virtually impregnable emplacements were destroyed or even seriously damaged.

Artillery exchanges and aerial bombardment aside, the relatively quiescent nature of the war along the Syrian front gave Northern Command plenty of time to attend to business in Samaria and to plan its invasion of the Golan Plateau. With Dado Elazar away most of the time directing the fighting in northern Samaria, the planning fell to Northern Command's deputy commander, Brigadier General Dan Laner, a blooded Reserve general who was a member of a kibbutz located not too far from Syria.

Laner's job of planning would have been easier if the new Israeli national-unity government had been able to make up its mind about how to handle Syria. There was enormous pressure from one of the larger Labor parties to open a war with Syria. This came about because that wing of the coalition was under pressure from the kibbutz movement, among whose members was the principal bloc of northerners under the Syrian guns. There was considerable sentiment in the Cabinet for action against Syria, but it was tempered by the voice of Moshe Dayan. It was the defense minister's sad duty to urge a delay pending the outcome of fighting in Sinai and Jordan.

Though Dayan had been born on the shore of the Kinneret and had done much to throw the Syrians back from the area in 1948, he had to acknowledge that there were not enough Israeli brigades remaining in the far north to repel a serious Syrian attack—much less undertake an invasion of Syria. Without massive reinforcements from other fronts, Dayan averred, the passionately desired invasion of the Golan Plateau had no chance of coming off.

The arguments and pressure continued through Wednesday, but Dayan still could not see his way clear to weakening other fronts. Finally, on the morning of Thursday, June 8, the moment seemed to have arrived. Dayan ordered Dado, who was in Samaria, to prepare to attack up the escarpment in order to destroy the Syrian forces holding the high ground. A short time later, at the next Cabinet meeting, Dayan asked Prime Minister Eshkol for permission to attack Syria. The prime minister agreed without his characteristic hesitation. He seemed relieved to have been asked.

By then, the United Nations and the world community were pressuring Israel to accept a general ceasefire. Dayan told Dado to move fast and win early. To help, he restored *Ugdah* Peled to Northern Command, added several units from Central Command, and even ordered an armored brigade to be transported post haste from Sinai. With the help of Dan Laner and a superb staff, Dado did what was expected of an Israeli general in command of troops in a war—he planned on the fly and prepared to fling himself and his men into action.

For all the urgency proclaimed throughout the government, Dayan decided to delay the attack until Friday, June 9. Dado and his planners needed the extra time.

Because of the Kinneret, the area of operations—and the Israeli plans and dispositions—had to be divided into two fairly separate and separated segments, one in the south and one in the north. By virtue of the initial proximity and positions of the southern force, a vastly altered *Ugdah* Peled became responsible for the southern zone of operations. In addition to the main body of the Ram Armored Brigade and the entire Avnon Infantry Brigade, Brigadier General Elad Peled was given the headquarters and two battalions of Colonel Motta Gur's 55th Parachute Brigade, which had been rushed north shortly after taking the Old City. Also, at the last minute, a battalion of Colonel Dani Matt's 31st Parachute Brigade appeared from the Sinai front, and it was attached to *Ugdah* Peled as an independent task force. For the time being, *Ugdah* Peled—which had no large armored contingent—

was to screen the area around the southern shore of the Kinneret, but its ultimate objective would be the seizure of the southern Golan Plateau.

For political as well as sound strategic reasons, the main attack had to be made in the central and/or northern Golan, between Mount Hermon and the northern Kinneret. To accomplish the mission, a new *ugdah* was created under the leadership of Brigadier General Dan Laner. It consisted of the halftrack-mounted 1st "Golani" Infantry Brigade; the Ram Armored Brigade's Super Sherman battalion; the Gavish Infantry Brigade; the Shehed Armored-Infantry Brigade; and the Mendler Armored Brigade, which had been rushed north on June 7 from the Sinai front.

There was no way for *Zahal* to attempt a truly indirect approach on the northern Golan Plateau; the continuous Syrian defenses were anchored on two unbreachable natural obstacles, Mount Hermon in the north and the Kinneret in the south. The only way in was by means of several axes that climbed the Golan's one-in-eight slope. The only advantage the Israeli planners had was that they could attempt their breach at a time and, within a half-dozen viable options, at a place of their own choosing.

By far, the most suitable route into the central and northern Golan Plateau for large mechanized forces was the approach from the B'not Yaacov Bridge. It climbed a graded roadway and continued along the excellent, wide military road to Kuneitra via Naffach. This approach, however, was a little too obvious for the Israelis, and it was fraught with other problems.

The chief difficulty with the easy approach was that an attack in the center, directly toward Kuneitra from the B'not Yaacov Bridge, would likely oblige the Syrians to react resolutely at the outset in distant defense of their capital. Damascus was only about 60 kilometers from Kuneitra along an excellent highway. It would eventually be necessary for the Israelis to capture Kuneitra, but it was best not to alarm the Syrians unduly at the outset. Until Kuneitra and the Damascus highway were directly threatened, the Syrian strategic reserve—the 42nd Syrian Brigade Group—would be obliged to remain in place out along the Damascus highway, far from the actual battle.

The Syrians also had committed one infantry, two tank, and one mechanized-infantry brigades to an area reserve in front of Kuneitra. These mobile units posed the most serious threat to Israeli hopes, for an early and determined counterattack by them could throw Israeli breaching units from the edge of the escarpment before the breaches could be exploited. To keep the Syrian area reserve in suspense as to where the main blow was going to fall,

Northern Command decided to launch a total of *five* attacks up the escarpment north of the B'not Yaacov Bridge. All the attacks would be reasonably powerful, but four of them were aimed initially at achieving only limited objectives. All four of the minor breaches were designed to look like they *might* be the real thing, and indeed one or more of them could be massively exploited if the main attack failed.

The Israelis hoped that launching so many secondary attacks at once would paralyze the decision-making capabilities of the Syrian high command—to sow confusion and hesitation. Hopefully, the Syrians would not be able to recognize Northern Command's main effort or true intentions until after Israeli forces had already fought decisively into the Syrian rear at all or at least at several of the breaches. By then, it would be too late for the Syrians to react in strength and concert.

Finally, as part of its general policy of confusing the enemy, Northern Command also wanted to pin down the 35th Syrian Brigade Group's 19th Syrian Infantry Brigade in the far south. To accomplish this, *Ugdah* Peled was to threaten the relatively flat and open southern Golan Plateau but not to attack it until the main breach had been accomplished in the north.

The Syrians felt that an Israeli attack of some sort would certainly take place opposite Kibbutz Dan in order to provide relief for it and the other vulnerable settlements in the far north. But this approach did not seem to be suitable for the main Israeli breach because it would take the Israeli maneuver elements directly into a restricted and massively fortified defensive zone. It was inconceivable to the Syrians that the Israelis could advance a large mechanized force upon the narrow, boulder-strewn road that ran up the escarpment opposite Kibbutz Dan. And, without armor, the Israelis would never open a major advance toward Kuneitra and the Damascus highway.

Of course, the main Israeli attack was indeed to be launched from the vicinity of Kibbutz Dan. There, the Israelis intended to defy common wisdom, Syrian logic, and even gravity by advancing one armored brigade and one mechanized infantry brigade by way of a route up the escarpment that appeared to be completely inadequate for supporting a frontal breaching operation by armored vehicles.

This main northern attack was to take place in two unrelated parts, against two entirely divergent strategic objectives. In the farthest northern region of the Golan, three Golani Infantry Brigade task forces were to launch attacks to seize the defended high ground overlooking Kibbutz Dan and several nearby Israeli settlements. At the outset, the infantrymen were to attack from Givat Chaim to secure both sides of the Dafna stream, which marked the frontier and one bank of which was already in Israeli hands. Next, in seamless extensions of the opening move, two Golani columns were to advance to capture Tel Fakhr. This force was then to seize the Baniyas springs, only 1.5 kilometers inside Syria. Meantime, a second Golani infantry battalion was to storm Tel Azzaziyat, the major height that dominated the Israeli settlements. In later phases of these attacks, the Golani Infantry Brigade was to secure other local hills and features and generally take firm control of its far-northern sector. However, doing so was not expected to be easy or come without cost. The Golani Infantry Brigade's entire zone of action, which was extremely shallow, was densely built over with Syrian defensive emplacements and densely manned by the 11th Syrian Infantry Brigade and several Syrian National Guard battalions.

Just to the south of the Golani Infantry Brigade's zone, the Mendler Armored Brigade was to seize the town of Qala, the defensive keystone in the far-northern Golan and a good jumping-off point for an indirect attack on Kuneitra. The brigade's plan was highly complex in that it made use of the indirect approach in an extremely narrow and restricted area. The armored column would initially face a large portion of the dug-in 11th Syrian Infantry Brigade and several Syrian National Guard battalions. It might even be counterattacked by the 12th Syrian Brigade Group's potentially formidable reserve, the 89th Syrian Reserve Infantry Brigade and the 44th Syrian Tank Brigade.

The Israeli plan was still taking on solid characteristics when, at 1720 on the evening of June 8, the Syrian government announced that it was joining Egypt and Jordan in accepting the United Nations ceasefire resolution. There was a virtually audible collective intake of breath throughout northern Israel, but the Northern Command planners and Minister of Defense Dayan carried on as if they had not heard the news. Dayan called Dado and told him to begin the offensive at 0700 the next morning.

49

The IAF had nothing else to do on the morning of Friday, June 9, 1967—all of Israel's other warlike neighbors had been beaten—so a huge continuous air assault against the Syrian Golan defenses began at dawn. Many napalm and conventional high-explosive bombs were laid on targets with pinpoint accuracy, and even the French concrete-busting bombs that had lain waste to Arab runways throughout the region were dropped on Syrian bunkers. It appeared from the air that the attack was sowing a carnage, but in fact most of even the heaviest bombs were unable to penetrate or seriously damage the extremely stout Syrian bunkers. Even napalm was wasted because the Syrians had cannily installed gutters on their bunkers, and these carried the burning mixture away from the occupants. Many of the defenders were certainly deprived of their hearing, or even their senses—and all were to some extent traumatized—but not much material damage was done.

The continuous air and artillery attacks were designed to keep the Syrians indoors with their heads down while Israeli engineers bravely cleared paths through minefields at all the breaching points. The Syrian artillery was never quite subdued by the tons of explosives Israeli airplanes and artillery delivered, and a decent proportion of the Syrian fire was placed on the engineers. (Fortunately for the engineers and the Northern Command plan, most of the Syrian artillery fire continued to be directed at Israeli settlements, towns, and cities ranging well into the interior of northern Israel).

Worse than the artillery fire and some direct small-arms exchanges, however, were the mines themselves. The Israelis had maintained their minefields over the years, and it was relatively easy for the Israeli engineers to clear lanes on their side of the frontier. But the Syrians had been sowing their mines indiscriminately for two decades, and there were mines on top of mines on their side of the line. Even worse, the Syrians had made no effort over the years to pick up the hundreds upon hundreds of mines that had been displaced by heavy rains each winter. In some places and along many natural watersheds, the mines were piled up in mounds that could not be dismantled without facing certain sudden death.

Two factors prevented the Israeli mine-clearing operation from bogging down forever. Along the route from the B'not Yaacov bridge, the Syrians themselves had cleared lanes through their own minefields, and everywhere else the Israelis found that their Syrian counterparts had been quite lax in keeping their minefields intact. Where it was easy to sow mines, there were plenty of them. Where it was difficult—in rocky ground or in areas that could be observed from the Israeli side of the frontier—the coverage tended to be spotty.

As it was, it took the engineers many long hours to complete their job at all the crossing points—hours longer than the Northern Command master plan had anticipated. But, until the minefields had been breached, the Israeli assault forces could not advance even to their final staging areas.

Shortly after 0900, the intense artillery exchanges abated and finally tapered off. The exhausted and emotionally drained engineers, who were almost done by then, put on a burst of energy, and the lead assault units were told to advance from cover to their lines of departure. By 1000, there were so many Israelis in sight of the frontier that the sixteen Syrian artillery battalions on the plateau reopened their defensive fires with great intensity. As earlier, however, the vast majority of the Syrian shells sailed right over the battlefield and landed in and around Israeli settlements far to the rear. Soviet advisors working with the Syrians tried to get the Syrian fire redirected, but only a few batteries were relaid.

The Israeli attack in the north finally got started at 1000. In the lead out of Kibbutz Givat Chaim and Kfar Szold was the Mendler Armored Brigade's Super Sherman battalion, which was under the command of Lieutenant Colonel Arieh Keren, a 39-year-old Auschwitz survivor known as "Biro." Intermingled with Biro's tank companies was the brigade's armored-infantry battalion, and to the rear was the Centurion battalion. Once engineer bulldozers had removed boulders from the edge of the narrow roadway that wound up into Syria, Biro would lead the armored attack to Kuneitra by an extremely circuitous route.

As eight bulldozers moved to the head of the Mendler Armored Brigade column, Syrian heavy mortars reached out toward the crowded roadway. One 120mm round scored a direct hit on one of the armored-infantry battalion command halftracks, killing the unit's deputy commander and four others. An instant later, another 120mm round killed everyone aboard a medical halftrack.

By then, it was too late to disperse the vehicles off the crowded roadway. The bulldozers were inching forward, so Colonel Avraham Mendler—"Albert"—ordered Biro to follow them at their best pace. Then Albert's command halftrack and Biro's command tank advanced across the frontier. The objectives were almost straight up the escarpment, the bulldozers were advancing at a snail's pace, and the Syrian mortars were generally on target. The advance was hellish.

Up the steep hill and just on the far side of the frontier was the Syrian patrol road, which was adequate for tanks and halftracks. It led directly to Biro's first objectives, Gur al-Askar, Na'amush, and Ukda. All three of the tiny villages were modestly fortified, but beyond Ukda the Syrians had installed a major defensive zone between Sir Adib and Qala, of which the latter controlled access to the vital Kuneitra road. To avoid the defenses at and behind Sir Adib and to bring the Israeli tanks and halftracks in behind the even deeper defensive zone between Sir Adib and Qala, Albert planned to leave the patrol road with the main body of his brigade between Na'amush and Ukda and turn north. A blocking force would be left to hold Ukda and screen the brigade rear while Albert's main body advanced across country to the TAPline Road (an access road running beside the Trans-Arabian Pipeline) and, from it, on into Zaoura. From Zaoura, via Jebel el-Mis (due east of Sir Adib), the Israelis could advance by narrow mountain tracks so as to avoid the heavily defended area between Sir Adib and Qala and thus take the latter from its undefended rear.

By the time the armored force had scaled the heights, the lead formation had been intentionally altered. The vanguard tank in the column was that of Lieutenant "Nati," the lead company's commander. Biro's command tank was the fifth behind Nati's, and right behind it were two jeeps occupied by an eight-man all-volunteer reconnaissance detachment commanded by Major Raphael Mokady, the brigade reconnaissance commander. It was Mokady's job to locate the difficult-to-find turnoff from the Syrian patrol road. It would have made more sense to place the reconnaissance jeeps at the head of the column, but Albert had ordered tanks to take the lead because, as he put it, it would have been "suicide" for the jeeps to lead the way into Syria.

The lead platoon of Super Shermans, plus Nati's and Biro's tanks, darted past the bulldozers as soon as they topped the steep rise, and they and

Mokady's jeeps turned out toward Gur al-Askar. Time was of the essence, so Nati's tanks simply traversed their turrets to the left and fired on the Syrian positions as they passed. At Na'amush, Nati's second platoon stopped in front of the defenses and opened fire. Then the rest of the lead Super Sherman company ran through the place and shot it up.

The plan started coming unglued at Na'amush. The lead was to have been handed over to Captain "Ilan's" Super Sherman company, but Ilan's tanks were delayed on the way up the heights when several of them ran or slid off the twisting roadway and became hung up on boulders. In fact, the entire brigade column was stalled except for Biro, Nati's company, and Major Mokady's two reconnaissance jeeps. However, Nati thought nothing of Ilan's delay; things like that happened all the time. He radioed Biro and asked for permission to proceed to the turnoff. Biro readily assented, and Nati stormed forward.

As soon as Nati's company passed beyond Na'amush, Syrians manning a larger and stronger position in Ukda opened fire. Nati knew the brigade plan, but he was not actually part of it, and he was not thinking about it. He reacted to the fire from Ukda by attacking the place—right past the turnoff.

The axis was narrow and hemmed in, so Nati's company advanced on Ukda in column formation. When Major Mokady reached what he thought was the turnoff, he ordered his driver to stop. Riding in Mokady's jeep was the scout who was responsible for finding the turnoff. Mokady thought they were there, but the scout disagreed. Ahead, Nati kept advancing toward Ukda. Biro was brought into the conversation by radio, but he deferred to the scout and Mokady, who kept arguing. All the while, Syrians in the area were firing at everyone from close range. Finally, Nati said that he needed to overrun Ukda before anyone could safely turn off the patrol road. Biro agreed and ordered Nati to stream past Ukda by way of the patrol road, firing into the town as he went. This was a well-rehearsed *Zahal* tactic.

Nati passed Biro's order to his tank commanders, the drivers revved up, and the lead Super Sherman company surged forward, all guns blazing. The fire from Ukda was suppressed, but the lead tanks ran into heavy fire from an even stronger defensive position beyond Ukda. The hitherto unseen position was packed with hull-down tanks and emplaced antitank guns.

Biro had been looking at his map too long. The position beyond Ukda was Sir Adib, which the Israelis had meant to avoid. But Biro thought it was Zaoura, from which a large area of the Syrian defensive sector could be dominated. In fact, Zaoura was about 6 kilometers to the north.

Biro ordered Nati to go after the hull-down Syrian tanks and he requested that artillery be placed on "Zaoura." The artillery fire-direction officer claimed the guns were already hitting Zaoura, but Biro said that he could see no shells falling on Nati's objective. The artillery officer asked Biro to recheck his map, and it was then that Biro realized his error. But, by then, Nati's company was fully engaged and could not safely withdraw. Biro had no choice but to secure Sir Adib with as many tanks as he could bring forward.

Fearing that the Super Shermans might become broached on boulders, Biro ordered Nati to stay on the road, no matter what. This kept Nati's tanks in a column formation. Nevertheless, from the roadway, the Super Shermans destroyed a number of Syrian tanks and antitank guns before passing beyond the large town and its defenses. While their gunners did most of the damage, Biro and all the other tank commanders fired their personal weapons and tossed hand grenades at Syrian soldiers manning a roadside trench. On the way through, however, one tank commander was seriously wounded, and Biro's face was cut by shell splinters. Nati was yelling into his radio for help, and Biro was, too, but the only help that arrived was the two scout jeeps.

Dead ahead of the Super Shermans was Qala, the area's defensive keystone. Biro knew he was in the wrong place, but until then Nati did not. But, even when Nati realized where he was, there was still no turning back. The Syrian gunners along Qala's elevated defensive line had Sir Adib zeroed in, so a withdrawal by the Israelis would have been suicidal. Biro and Nati quickly agreed that it was safer to advance on Qala. As always, speed was of the essence. As Biro's gunner hit two Syrian antiaircraft guns on the Qala heights, Biro and Nati were on the command net, mapping out a plan. But, before the Israeli Super Shermans could move forward again, Biro was hit in the face by at least two machine-gun bullets that nearly severed his jaw and tore a hole in his throat.

As a teenager, at Auschwitz, Biro Keren had survived the worst terror the world has ever had to offer. He was a survivor and a fighter; nothing could stop him as long as he drew breath. Though the lower portion of his face was dangling by a thread of muscle, he climbed into the turret of his command tank and motioned for the gunner to bind his wounds. Then he motioned his battalion signals officer to give him a writing tablet. With the lieutenant doing the talking, Biro requested that all available artillery be placed on the Qala ridge and that Captain Ilan's tank company hurry forward to deliver an attack on the left side of Nati's. He also asked Albert to arrange for air support, which Albert got straight to work lining up. Biro was still writing orders and requests when the loss of blood caused him to pass out. With that, the command tank returned to Sir Adib and the signals officer passed command of the Super Sherman battalion to Major Raphael Mokady. Mokady traded places with Biro, who was by then able to climb aboard Mokady's jeep for the drive to the brigade aid station, back down the heights.

Before he left, Biro wrote a note to Mokady in which he asked the major to turn command of the battalion over to Nati, who was a trained tank officer whereas Mokady was not. Mokady gladly agreed, but by then Nati's tank had been hit and its radio had been knocked out. Without further ado, assuming Nati had been hurt or killed, Mokady ordered Biro's tank back to the firing line. He would oversee Biro's battalion until a senior tank officer with a working radio turned up.

Raphael Mokady, a 39-year-old lecturer at Haifa Technical Institute, was a brave officer, and a blooded veteran of the War of Independence and the Sinai Campaign. But he had only recently been transferred from the infantry to the Mendler Armored Brigade and was therefore adrift in a tank unit. His first instinct was to withdraw Nati's company from in front of Qala and try to lead the battalion to the rear of the town via Zaoura, as planned. From his position approaching Nati's company from the rear, it must have seemed to Mokady that the Syrian position was impregnable. By then, three hours had passed since the battalion had jumped off from Kfar Szold. It felt to everyone as if time was draining away.

Mokady ordered all the tanks to pull left toward a side track that would take them to the TAPline Road, but it also carried them out in front of two hitherto silent Syrian antitank localities. One of the first antitank rounds fired from the new positions hit Mokady's Super Sherman and caused the engine to seize. Though the tank was filled with acrid smoke, Mokady ordered the gunner to return the enemy fire. The first round blew up an antitank gun, but the battalion signals officer, who was acting as loader, did not know how to eject the empty shell casing. Neither did Major Mokady, so he stood tall in the turret and cranked back the charging handle of the .50-caliber machine gun. The major was hit straightaway by a bullet in the chest. He had a few moments left and he used them to blindly broadcast a plea for Nati to take over the battalion. And then Raphael Mokady tumbled out of the turret hatchway and fell dead on the rear deck of the tank. The battalion signals officer then stood up in the turret to fire the heavy machine gun. After firing only a few bursts, he, too, was shot to death. A moment later, the driver restarted the engine and backed into some dead ground, where he and the gunner abandoned the tank altogether and ran to the rear.

Eventually, Nati managed to repair the damaged radio in his tank. As soon as he plugged in his earphones, he heard the brigade deputy commander's orders to take command of the Super Sherman battalion. The deputy had been listening in on the battalion net when Major Mokady had been shot, and he had been repeating Mokady's last order to Nati ever since.

Nati sprang to action. He radioed the other company commanders to tell them he was in command, and then he explained the situation to Albert, who had just reached Sir Adib after a long delay getting up the mountain road from Kfar Szold. Albert already knew a little; he had met Biro's jeep on the road. Albert told Nati to carry on in front of Qala with the entire Super Sherman battalion, whose two rear companies had finally topped the escarpment. Albert added that he realized it was impossible for Nati's company to withdraw without incurring massive losses. However, Albert was going to take the armored-infantry and Centurion battalions around by the original route and, as planned, attack Qala via its blind northern approach. If Nati could break through, fine; if not, Albert would relieve pressure with his attack.

By the time the dust settled, Nati had twenty-one Super Shermans under his command. Several of the battalion's tanks had been sidelined due to mechanical problems in Sinai, and the rest had been stranded or damaged by mines or boulders on their way up the heights. Biro's command tank, of course, was out of action. Nati's own tank could take part in the fight, but Nati had to move to another Super Sherman because the radio in the first one kept going out.

For the time being, while Albert raced around by the long way, Nati was content to stand off and snipe at the Syrian positions in Qala. All the Super Shermans had brand new 105mm guns aboard, and new, freshly zeroed sights. They were able to hit the Syrian antitank guns with ease from 400 to 600 meters, and this they did with stunning accuracy and pleasing results. Nati's new gunner even bagged two or three T-34s that the Syrians foolishly moved into the open in a vain attempt to outflank the Super Sherman battalion.

Albert's force did find the right track between Na'amush and Ukda, and it did cross over to the TAPline Road, heading north. However, its progress was glacial. It was only at about 1500 that the lead Centurion neared the top of the first stage of the side road that climbed the steep hill leading to Zaoura. This tank was disabled by a hidden antitank gun and blocked the road. Fortunately, a tank commander farther back in the column located a side track, and the front portion of the Centurion battalion was able to backtrack onto it. In time, several other passable tracks were located. Though the battalion's cohesiveness was destroyed, the Centurions climbed upward by any route their crews could find on their own.

Zaoura was covered by a defensive locality below the village and another one above, on the crest of the hill. Ad hoc groups of Centurions attacked the lower one as they arrived. As IAF jets suppressed Syrian antitank guns dug in higher up, the Centurions closed to point-blank range and stormed the lower antitank locality and the village, all at once. From there, while the jets delivered pinpoint strikes until the last minute, the Centurions surrounded the upper defenses and shot them up until the Syrian defenders died, surrendered, or fled. All opposition had ceased at Zaoura by 1600.

Albert immediately organized a blocking force of one Centurion company and two armored-infantry companies. Then he ordered the two remaining Centurion companies and the one armored-infantry company to make haste toward Qala by a barely adequate supply road. As before, progress was glacial.

About the time the rest of the brigade was closing on Zaoura, Lieutenant Nati finally got tired of the stand-off battle in front of Qala. By then, also, he had learned enough about the Syrian dispositions to see a possible way in. Qala was on the far side of a steep-sided canyon from Sir Adib, and there was a powerful antitank locality in the middle of the canyon. To the north of the antitank locality was a secondary crest that stretched in a northward curve all the way across the canyon from Sir Adib to Jebel el-Mis, which was due north of Qala on the approach from Zaoura. During the stand-off battle, Captain Ilan's company had edged most of the way across the secondary crest. After a while, it occurred to Nati that Ilan might just as well cross all the way to Jebel el-Mis, which was on Albert's route from Zaoura to Qala anyway.

Ilan's company fought its way across the secondary crest and came to rest in a partially covered position from which it could support Nati's and Lieutenant "Eppi's" companies if they attacked Qala head-on. Nati decided to attack down through the Syrian antitank locality in the canyon and then straight up toward the Qala fortified hill, which was the brigade objective.

He arranged for artillery support. Just as Nati started to register the artillery, a bullet creased his scalp, and his blood short-circuited the radio. Nati had not even felt the round course through his helmet. Before Nati even raised his head, an antitank round fired from Qala disabled his tank.

After climbing aboard yet another tank, Nati sent Eppi's company across the secondary crest to take over the covering position from Ilan's. When Eppi's tanks were in position, Nati ordered what was left of his own company and Ilan's to attack through the antitank locality and on up into Qala. From its position beside Jebel el-Mis, Eppi's company would be able to provide direct support to the others.

Between immobile tanks that could still fire and Eppi's whole company, only ten of Nati's twenty-one Super Shermans opened the two-pronged advance into the canyon. Ilan's tank was hit and set afire, but Ilan and his loader scrambled out despite their wounds. The other three members of Ilan's crew were trapped because the turret was blocking their hatches. Ilan, whose scrotum had been opened by a shell splinter, scrambled back into the turret and, despite intense flames, straightened the turret and thus allowed the crewmen to escape. Now wounded *and* burned, Ilan scrambled into a wrecked Syrian Army truck.

Nati and the remaining Super Sherman crews drove on at all costs, stopping for nothing less than a disabling direct hit. The Super Shermans ran right up to the Syrian roadblock on the road from Sir Adib, and there one of the tank commanders, Sergeant "Vardi," was blinded by shell splinters. Incredibly, as Nati calmly radioed directions, Vardi guided his driver through the Syrian tank obstacles. On the far side, Nati stood guard while Vardi wiped congealed blood from his eyes to restore his sight. Both tanks lurched forward.

Two more Super Shermans were disabled on their way through the Syrian antitank locality, leaving seven. The commander of one of the seven was shot in the head on the way up the slope in front of Qala. At the top of the slope, another Super Sherman was knocked out—as it was learned later, by a T-34 concealed in a house—and yet another dropped out without making it to the top of the hill. That left Nati with five runners. Eppi's tank was set afire as it tried to bypass the Super Sherman that had been hit at the top of the slope. The next tank, which passed around Eppi's, raced toward the edge of town, but it was stopped by a direct hit only yards from its objective. Seven of fifteen crewmen in the three disabled Super Shermans were dead, and all the rest were wounded.

Three Super Shermans made it into Qala. One was commanded by Nati and another was commanded by Sergeant Vardi. Nati could hear the other two commanders on his radio, but they could not hear him. He had to use flags and hand signals to direct the attack toward the center of town. He signaled Vardi to turn left in the hope of finding the Syrian tank or antitank gun that had knocked out the three Super Shermans at the top of the hill. Vardi's tank had just made the turn up a side street when it was struck from the rear by an RPG. The crew got out, but the tank was left burning.

Fortunately, Nati was able to pinpoint the source of the deadly fire. Both Super Shermans fired armor-piercing rounds through the walls of the house, and the hidden T-34 blew up. When Nati looked around, he was dismayed to see that four T-34s and two SU-100s were entering the village square from the east.

Nati hid the two remaining Super Shermans in deep shadows on a side street and asked Albert for immediate air support. The brigade commander replied in a moment that there were no jets on station. Nati said he needed them, right away. Albert said he would try again. (There were scores of IAF jets over the Golan, but the forward air controllers were overwhelmed with support requests and the system just unraveled.) Meantime, Vardi rounded up all the ambulatory wounded and armed them with hand grenades and whatever rifles and pistols they could salvage from the disabled tanks. It appeared that Nati's "battalion" was going to make a last stand inside Qala.

Albert radioed Nati: There were no jets available, but Albert's force was closing on Qala from the direction of Zaoura. To Nati's next demand for air support, Albert replied firmly, "Hold on and wait patiently."

It was nearing 1800, and it would be dark soon. Nati was sure that the Syrian tanks on the east side of Qala were waiting for nightfall to advance and kill him and his men.

Minutes before dusk—the sun was nearly gone—several IAF jets appeared overhead. They circled over Qala, but Nati had no way to speak with the pilots, and they would not attack unless they could determine whose tanks were whose. The Syrian tanks had been inching slowly toward Nati's little stronghold, but they stopped when the jets whined in. At the last minute before the light failed, someone found a smoke grenade. Nati marked his position and prayed that the pilots would be able to figure things out for themselves.

The jets roared in and made a dummy pass. This unnerved the Syrian tank crews, who turned and raced away. That was all the jet pilots needed. With the distance between friend and foe opening rapidly, the IAF fighter-bombers roared in again. Nati ordered his gunner and the other to fire, and they blew up a pair of T-34s with direct hits.

Albert radioed moments later that he was entering Qala from the north. In order to avoid an intramural fight in the dark, the brigade intelligence officer advanced through the town in Albert's command halftrack. He linked up with Nati, and then the Centurion and armored-infantry companies advanced into Qala to secure the place.

By the time it stopped inside Qala, the Mendler Armored Brigade had cleared, bypassed, or overrun an 8-kilometer-wide slice of the Syrian Golan defenses to a depth of nearly 8 kilometers. The northern road to Kuneitra lay open, and Syrian forces of north Qala—the better part of the reinforced 11th Syrian Infantry Brigade—were cut off from outside supports. More important, successive waves of Israeli ground-combat units had free access to the plateau.

North of Qala, the Golani Infantry Brigade had had a rough afternoon fight, but it was achieving another notable success. And there were successes to the south as well.

50

Colonel Yona Efrat's Golani Infantry Brigade was ready to jump off into the attack at 0745, but it had to wait for over two hours in its covered positions near Kiryat Shmona for the engineers to complete their work. When the brigade's assault units were ordered to advance to their line of departure at 1000, they were fired on by Syrian artillery all the way.

There was a further delay. All the Golani assault units had to use the same narrow, boulder-impinged roadway as the tanks and halftracks of the Mendler Armored Brigade. In fact, the Golani vehicles had to follow Mendler's tanks and halftracks. So, when several Super Shermans in Biro's second company (Ilan's) went off the road and blocked access, the Golani attack had to be delayed yet again. It was not until after 1400 that the last Mendler Armored Brigade vehicles had been cleared from the roadway and the first Golani vehicles were ordered to begin climbing.

As soon as the order to advance was given, five of the Golani Infantry Brigade's French Sherman tanks raced to the top of Givat Chaim, the Israeli outpost closest to the access road. The tanks deployed to provide covering fire for the initial advance to Tel Azziziyat, which straddled the border only 1 kilometer to the north. Along this segment of the frontier, Tel Azziziyat was the key, but the vital objective in this extremely confined zone of action was Tel Fakhr, a hill complex nearly 5 kilometers from the top of the road whose *base* was 300 meters higher than the Israeli line of departure.

Upon reaching the top of the road, the Golani infantry battalion commanded by Lieutenant Colonel "Benny" was to turn sharply to the north to attack Tel Azziziyat and, from there, advance northward to secure such features as Tel Hamra and Tel Nukheila. At the same time, a second half-track-mounted infantry battalion commanded by Lieutenant Colonel Moshe Klein was to pass through Gur al-Askar and, from there, turn north to begin its climbing approach on Tel Fakhr. Once Tel Fakhr was secure, Klein's battalion was to go on to other nearby objectives. Finally, at the outer edge of the Golani zone, the brigade reconnaissance troop was to screen the edge of the battlefield and advance behind the Tel Fakhr position from the south and southeast while the main infantry attack went in from the northwest and north. The two mounted infantry battalions each were provided with several French Shermans and promised ample air support. The third Golani infantry battalion was the brigade reserve and would thus mount the escarpment last.

Every hill and virtually every fold in the earth on the Syrian side of the line was honeycombed with concrete bunkers and pillboxes tied together by concrete-lined fighting and communications trenches. It was not so much that there were hundreds and perhaps a few thousand Syrian infantrymen and gunners in the area—there were—as how deeply and securely those Syrians were emplaced in the continuous fortifications. The area had a civilian population that intensively cultivated the terraced fields and low places, but the main crop, as one shocked Israeli later put it, was gun emplacements, which sprouted everywhere.

There also were mines planted everywhere. In very little time, though their drivers tried hard to remain on the twisting, narrow tracks, many of the fighting vehicles were stopped by mines or because they simply ran off the roads and paths. All of the French Shermans were disabled or marooned, and most of the infantrymen were eventually forced to travel on their feet. Syrian fire also accounted for many of the vehicle losses, not to mention a rising toll of human casualties.

It took ninety minutes from the order to advance before there were enough Golani troops at the base of Tel Fakhr to risk an attack. Israeli jets and artillery had been working over the objective for, by then, over ten hours, but all that tonnage hardly seemed to have made a dent.

In all, fewer than 200 Israeli infantrymen from Lieutenant Colonel Moshe Klein's battalion arrived to undertake the planned simultaneous assaults on Tel Fakhr's two knobs. Except for the sprinkling of professionals whose job it was to prepare them for decades of Reserve service, nearly all the Israelis—junior officers, junior NCOs, and private alike—were conscripts aged 18 to 22. They were young and eager, but they were also raw. For all that, they considered themselves elite. To a man, they were ready to uphold the honor of their brigade.

The few halftracks that had made it to the northern base of Tel Fakhr had to abandon the effort to climb the steep, rock-strewn slopes. It was a miracle they got as far as they did. Ahead were mines, barbed wire, and impassable, boulder-strewn ravines. If ever there was a job for infantry on foot, Tel Fakhr was it. Nevertheless, the company bound for the left-hand knob tried to push ahead in its remaining halftracks. All seven of the aged troop carriers were knocked out in a matter of minutes. Among the dead was the Israeli company commander, who had been directing the brave but futile mechanized attack while standing in plain view in the rear of the lead halftrack. About the same time, the commander of the battalion's reserve company was also shot to death. And, with that, the Israeli battalion lost its internal cohesion—though not its ability to fight. Not by a long shot. When the halftracks were stopped cold in front of the Syrian wire, two young Israeli soldiers vaulted to the ground and made themselves into bridges. They intentionally fell across the barbed wire so that their comrades could cross safely without touching off mines with their feet.

The diverging lines of attack on the two knobs were so steep that they could not be covered adequately at close range by machine guns. Mortars and artillery were registered on both knobs of the objective, and back along the rear slope, but Klein's reduced companies of infantrymen would have to undertake the fruitful killing at arm's length.

The young soldiers crawled from their cover and fell back on their training. Under the watchful eyes and heated commands of their NCOs, they wriggled upward along any little furrows and wrinkles that provided cover. On the right-hand knob, the first concrete-lined Syrian trench was only 150 meters from the base of the hill. It was filled with Syrians, but they had their problems, too, for in order to fire down on Israelis they had to expose their heads and upper torsos to Israeli marksmen who had been set in below.

The first Israelis to reach the lower Syrian trench were seven young infantrymen led by their company commander, Major Alex Krinsky, a 31-year-old Rumanian-born survivor of the Holocaust. The rest of the men in Krinsky's company had been delayed or shot, or had given up trying.

It is an ancient military truth that, when it's time to go, you go with what you have. Major Alex Krinsky had seven brave men beside him—and he went. In the middle of his last lunge into the Syrian trench, Krinsky was shot dead by a brave Syrian soldier who at least had stood his ground.

The young Israeli soldiers who had accompanied Krinsky so far faltered.

But there was a shout from behind, and Lieutenant Colonel Moshe Klein, the battalion commander, suddenly appeared on the scene. Klein's halftrack had been blown up beneath him several kilometers to the rear, but he had raced ahead on foot, followed by a few headquarters men who were able to keep up. Klein yelled and leaped toward the trench, but he was shot dead in his tracks. The battalion deputy commander was right behind Klein. When he surged to the fore, he was shot in the neck, and it was all a medic could do to save his life and get him evacuated. The battalion's artillery forward observer leaped into the Syrian trench right behind Klein and the deputy, as much to save himself from the hail of Syrian bullets from above as to lay claim to the enemy position. The young artillery officer had only just regained his senses when he heard a sound and swung around to see what had caused it. Four Syrian soldiers were charging right at him. The artillery observer brought his Uzi to his hip and simply sprayed 9mm bullets. All four Syrians were bowled over, and none others appeared.

The Israelis had their lodgement, but only three men were still in shape to hold it; all the others were dead, dying, or incapacitated. In the nick of time, however, the brigade reconnaissance troop arrived from its long left hook around Tel Fakhr. It stopped just behind and below the fragile lodgement. After dismounting from their halftracks and jeeps, these and other welcome reinforcements climbed to the captured trench. Immediately, junior officers and sergeants led ad hoc squads—anyone—around the Syrian trenchline in both directions. Shortly, three reconnaissance halftracks were driven up to the captured trenchline to help clear a still-larger section.

When Colonel Yona Efrat heard that Moshe Klein was dead, he ordered his reserve battalion to attack Tel Fakhr frontally from the south and then left his deputy to direct the battle from afar (a few hundred meters) while he ran forward to take charge at the point of contact. By the time Efrat reached the rear of the hill, behind Klein's battalion, thirty-seven Israelis had been killed, and eighty-two had been wounded. The brigade commander did what he could to restore the battalion, but by then the advance along the trenchline was running pretty well under the guidance and prodding of lieutenants and sergeants. Withal, a major effort to reach Tel Fakhr's twin summits would have to be made by the Golani Infantry Brigade's fresh and intact reserve battalion from the south side of the Syrian defensive zone.

The attack from south of the hill kicked off at 1625, met serious opposition, and all but bogged down. It was deeply surprising to the Israelis that the Syrians held on until sunset. But after that, the defenders melted away. The fire from above died out, and soon only a sniper or two remained active.

In the morning, Golani troops sweeping the abandoned hill complex located approximately five dozen Syrian corpses on Tel Fakhr, and they took twenty prisoners.

Tel Azziziyat was a feature the local Israeli farmers had come to call The Monster. It was an ugly dark-gray basaltic pile, honeycombed with fighting positions. The hill's eastern face was supposed to have been in Israel, but Syria had simply taken it over and fortified it right after the 1948 ceasefire.

Taking Tel Azziziyat and an outlying position on Burj Babil was the job of Lieutenant Colonel Benny's battalion of the Golani Infantry Brigade. Though Benny's troops were supposed to assault Burj Babil before Moshe Klein's battalion attacked Tel Fakhr, the extra time it had taken Klein's halftracks to move up the escarpment had delayed Benny's assault to the point that it began later than Klein's. As in the case of Tel Fakhr, the extra hours of air and artillery bombardment hardly counted.

The assault on Burj Babil differed in one important aspect from the attack on Tel Fakhr. At the latter, the Syrians stood and fought bravely. At Burj Babil, Benny's approach caused the Syrian officers to bolt from the scene, and most of their men followed them across to Tel Azziziyat. Though only one Israeli halftrack—Lieutenant Colonel Benny's—actually completed the assault, Benny and his crew found only five meek and dazed Syrian soldiers in possession of the extensive defenses.

Tel Azziziyat was another strange one. As Benny's companies regrouped for the assault, the Syrian commander appeared on the road with his deputy, who was carrying a white flag. The Syrian offered to surrender his garrison, but, as Benny was getting ready to respond, Syrian soldiers on the tel registered their disapproval by opening fire on the little peace delegation.

Benny's battalion moved directly into the attack and fought a long uphill battle through the rest of the afternoon. The Syrians clung stubbornly to their positions even after large portions of the tel had been overrun. They had to be pried out, face to face and hand to hand. Nevertheless, after sunset, the fighting tapered off because the Syrian survivors withdrew. They left fifty of their comrades dead on the hill.

At Notera, south of the Mendler Armored Brigade zone, Israeli engineers cleared a path through Israeli and Syrian minefields. Then, late in the afternoon, an AMX-13 reconnaissance company from the Ram Armored Brigade accompanied a motorized battalion of the Gavish Infantry Brigade up the road toward Rawye. This attack was late jumping off and slow moving, but the prodigious use of air support finally helped the leading elements break through two Syrian defensive locales with the loss of only three AMX-13s to antitank fire. The Syrian main line was narrowly breached and Rawye was occupied a little before sunset.

Several kilometers south of Notera, another little track climbed the heights by way of Darbashiyeh. This back route was given to another motorized battalion of the Gavish Infantry Brigade and a platoon of Ram Armored Brigade AMX-13s. Once again, the mine-clearing operation took longer than expected, and here the Syrian defenses were resolutely manned by a reinforced company of the 132nd Syrian Reserve Infantry Brigade. Aggressive use of air support finally broke the back of the defenses, but by nightfall the Israeli column was only able to reach Darbashiyeh, which was only two-thirds the way to the summit.

In the southern portion of the 132nd Syrian Reserve Infantry Brigade zone, yet another side track led up the escarpment. At the top, this axis opened out to the southeast, toward Dardara, which was well back of the Syrian defenses, on the main Kuneitra road from the B'not Yaacov Bridge. One armored-infantry battalion and two French Sherman companies of the Shehed Armored-Infantry Brigade were tasked with driving toward Dardara by this route. The Syrians had not seen fit to defend this route up the escarpment, and the Israeli engineers had no trouble clearing it. The tank-and-infantry force easily penetrated the Syrian defenses—actually it went around and between several static defensive localities—and drove all the way to Dardara on a good, motorable road. The assault on Dardara itself began at 0930. By 1120, the town was in Israeli hands. In a little over an hour more, a detachment of the Dardara task force also occupied Tel Hillal, which dominated a long stretch of the Kuneitra road. Amazing to the Israelis was the fact that the Syrian brigades guarding Kuneitra or in reserve behind Kuneitra made no effort to drive out the Dardara (or any other Israeli) task force. Later still, in the hour before sunset, Israeli patrols from Dardara closed off several supply roads that ran through the area and cleared Syrian defensive positions atop the heights from east to west. There was hardly any opposition.

After dark, all the Israeli forces north of the Kuneitra road—elements of five brigades—consolidated their positions atop and within the many objectives that they had seized during the day. Tanks and other vehicles were refueled, repaired, and salvaged, and ammunition and other supplies were brought forward to make good all the expenditures of the day. Where necessary, combat units were reorganized or realigned.

Finally, beginning at midnight, a battalion of Colonel Motta Gur's 55th Parachute Brigade supported by a Super Sherman company from the Ram Armored Brigade advanced behind a rolling air and artillery bombardment toward Jelabina, a small town about halfway between the B'not Yaacov Bridge and Rawye. The garrison from the 132nd Syrian Reserve Infantry Brigade put up a spirited fight for the town, but it was driven out with heavy losses by 0430.

On the first day of the war with Syria, Israeli forces secured all of their major objectives and most of their lesser ones, albeit with heavy losses in some cases. At no time did a Syrian unit even attempt to aid a neighboring position. This was because each and every Syrians defensive unit had a fixed zone to man, and all had been forbidden in advance to leave their positions. By the time the Syrian high command got a handle on Israeli intentions—*if* it ever did—the Israelis held all the best ground or were in position to seize all the best ground. The continuous Syrian defensive belt in the far north had been overwhelmed, and the Syrian defenses in the center, north of the Kuneitra road, had been breached and even bypassed. Moreover, as hoped, the five separate Israeli breaching operations did indeed confuse the Syrian command to the point that no one in high authority could decide where to commit the mobile reserves.

At nightfall, there were plenty of intact Syrian units left manning sound, formidable fortified positions throughout the Golan, right up to the edge of the escarpment. But the Syrian main line of defense had been decisively breached and Israeli mobile forces stood in the rear of every major forward Syrian defensive sector in the northern half of the Golan Plateau.

By the end of the fighting on June 9, the Syrian Army had for practical purposes been defeated and the northern Golan defensive zone had been made untenable. For June 10 and beyond, it simply would be a matter of how far the Israelis wanted to or could advance before a ceasefire was imposed from the outside—and how many more Israelis and Syrians needed to die before the war ended.

51

In the far north, the dazed and bleeding Golani Infantry Brigade spent the night of June 9–10 in defensive positions, waiting for a counterattack that never came. The Syrian Regulars and National Guardsmen manning adjacent positions within the tightly choked battle arena fired their personal weapons at the Israelis all night, and Syrian artillery located north and east of the Banias springs did the same. Early on Saturday morning, June 10, as the Golani battalions were preparing to take important new ground, the Bar-Kochva Armored Brigade completed its move to the northern Golan from the West Bank. The Golani Infantry Brigade's dawn attack was postponed until Lieutenant Colonel Moshe Bar-Kochva's two Super Sherman battalions and one armored-infantry battalion could climb the escarpment and get into jump-off positions beside Tel Azziziyat. Thereafter, the two battle-worn brigades teamed up to launch powerful attacks out of Tel Azziziyat and Tel Fakhr against the stout Syrian defenses in the tightly packed neighborhood. Tel Hamra fell quickly in the wake of a rugged fight, but elsewhere the Syrians engaged in resolute resistance. It took until after 1000 for the Israeli tank-infantry teams to fight their way into the town of Banias and the ancient subterranean caves that housed the vital springs. From Banias, the Bar-Kochva Super Shermans launched an immediate uphill assault toward Ein Fit, and this objective fell in short order after yet another hard little fight.

After regrouping on all their newly won objectives, the Golani and Bar-Kochva tank-infantry teams once again moved into the attack on more-level ground suitable for long-reaching follow-on attacks. Zaoura, through which the Mendler Armored Brigade had passed the previous late afternoon, was scoured, and the main tank-infantry thrust next advanced on the town of Massada. As the Israelis were approaching this objective at 1100, huge explosions rocked that area of the Golan Plateau, and huge pillars of black smoke were seen rising over several prominent Syrian-held hills and towns.

No one could imagine what the Syrians had up their sleeves, but the advance on Massada and nearby objectives continued at a cautious pace until the Israelis encountered huge craters that had been blown in the surface of the roads. Switching to country lanes and tracks, the tank-infantry task forces proceeded at a cautious rate. They rolled into Massada in the early afternoon without encountering any Syrian defenders. The few wounded stragglers who were found in the town said that the defenders had withdrawn after blowing up their bunkers.

Israelis cautiously combed through Massada and nearby defense localities. Indeed, all the prepared defenses had been blown up and abandoned. As these and other task forces consolidated Israel's hold on the northern Golan, a special task force composed of one of the Bar-Kochva Super Sherman battalions and two companies of the Golani Infantry Brigade was formed to race up a twisting mountain track to claim one of the strategically useful peaks of Mount Hermon. Late in the afternoon, these soldiers planted the Israeli flag on the snow-clad peak while enjoying a stunning view of the entire Golan Plateau and much of the Damascus Plain.

The entire Mendler Armored Brigade concentrated in and around Qala after midnight and prepared to attack in the direction of Kuneitra at dawn. The armored brigade's first objective was the crossroads town of Vasit, which was nearly 8 kilometers south of Qala along a reasonably good road. Few Syrians were encountered between Qala and Vasit, but the latter was defended by T-54 tanks and mechanized infantrymen from the 12th Syrian Brigade Group's 44th Syrian Tank Brigade. After scouts had probed the defenses to learn what the brigade was up against, Colonel Albert Mendler ordered his Centurions and Super Shermans to stand off while IAF fighter-bombers reduced the Syrian fortifications. A well-executed flank attack by Mendler's tanks and armored infantrymen kicked over the defenses in a brief face-to-face fight.

The Mendler Armored Brigade was next to turn east toward Kuneitra and launch an attack via Mansoura in tandem with another Israeli force that was coming along the parallel main road from the B'not Yaacov Brigade. The Syrians had defended the entire length of the Vasit–Mansoura road in depth. Progress was maddeningly slow against endless pockets of resistance, each built around several dug-in tanks or towed antitank guns protected by a handful of infantrymen. Each and every little defensive team had to be engaged and wiped out or driven away.

At 0845, while Albert's troops were struggling mightily against a seemingly inexhaustible supply of Syrian soldiers and T-54s, Radio Damascus suddenly announced that the city of Kuneitra had fallen after a valiant and costly struggle. The Israelis who heard or heard about the Syrian announcement were baffled and mystified, for Kuneitra was at best hours away from even being directly attacked on the ground.

The Mendler Armored Brigade ran into a formidable final defensive line just outside of Mansoura. Air and artillery was again skillfully employed to soften the defenses, and then the final attack was launched. When the Israelis reached the Syrian defenses, they found that all the defenders had fled moments earlier. The area was littered with weapons and gear, including a large number of antitank guns and about a dozen serviceable T-54s, T-34s, and SU-100s.

While elements of the brigade scoured Mansoura for stragglers, the main body opened a race with retreating Syrians toward Kuneitra. When word had come down from on high that Syria appeared ready to accept a U.N. ceasefire, all Israeli assault units were urged to reach for the very best final defensive features in their zones of action. Though the Syrians had abandoned Mansoura, they were dug in back along the road to Kuneitra. The going remained slow against determined rearguards.

To the south of Albert's zone, the town of Rawye had been occupied the previous afternoon by a motorized battalion of the Gavish Infantry Brigade and a Ram Armored Brigade AMX-13 company. During the night, the Ram Armored Brigade armored-infantry battalion and the main body of the brigade's Super Sherman battalion also moved up to Rawye. At dawn, following closely behind a rolling artillery barrage and pinpoint air strikes, the Ram armored-infantry battalion and Super Shermans attacked uphill toward the top of the escarpment along a narrow supply road. After a bloody fight through successive Syrian defensive lines the Israelis finally topped the escarpment at 1000. After regrouping, they moved along the road to Vasit by way of Kanaba.

At Kanaba, the Ram Armored Brigade Super Shermans deployed to deliver what they thought would be an attack against determined defenders holding a strong defensive locality. Following another air attack, the Israeli tanks rolled forward—right into a vacuum. At Kanaba, as at a growing list of other Golan settlements and features, the defenders had left at the last minute after abandoning many of their weapons and other equipment. Here as elsewhere, stragglers claimed that the officers had left first and the soldiers had followed.

As the Ram Armored Brigade tanks and armored infantrymen were scouring Kanaba, news arrived that the Mendler Armored Brigade had overcome the Vasit defenses, only 6 kilometers to the east. As a result, the force in Kanaba was redirected toward Naffach, which was 13 kilometers south of Kanaba along a good road. A short time later, when the Ram Armored Brigade vanguard tanks encountered strong opposition at the roadside village of Koasset, Brigadier General Dan Laner ordered Colonel Uri Ram to bypass it and undertake a hasty dash into Naffach by any means he chose. Ram's reconnaissance AMX-13s found a track to the TAPline Road, and the advance proceeded at a good speed. However, as Ram's spearhead of tanks came within sight of Tel Shiban, it again ran into Syrian fire—this time from fifteen T-54s deployed on the hill. Once again, Ram sent his AMX-13s to find a detour. As soon as they did, the entire force of Israeli tanks and halftracks bypassed the blocking position.

All the detouring kept the Ram Armored Brigade main body from reaching Naffach until 1430. There, as elsewhere in the central and northern Golan, a powerful ground assault in the wake of an overwhelming pounding by air and artillery fell into defensive positions that had been abandoned by the defenders. Prisoners reported that the main body of defenders had withdrawn in good order two hours earlier.

From Naffach, Uri Ram dispatched his AMX-13s along the main road to Kuneitra to link up with the Mendler Armored Brigade when it arrived from Vasit. Meantime, detachments of Ram's Super Shermans and armored infantrymen established a series of blocking positions at villages, crossroads, and several features in the region around Naffach. Most of these positions faced back toward the edge of the escarpment and were set out to trap Syrians retreating from that direction. Others were set to hold back a possible Syrian counterattack.

South of the Ram Armored Brigade zone, a motorized battalion of the Gavish Infantry Brigade and a platoon of Ram Armored Brigade AMX-13s had captured Darbashiyeh the previous evening. This task force jumped off at dawn to fight the rest of the way to the top of the escarpment. This was achieved at 1100 against fierce opposition, and the tanks and truck-borne infantry turned out on the unimproved supply road leading southeast toward

Naffach. Though only lightly contested, the going was extremely slow for the trucks. This column did not reach Naffach until shortly after the town had been taken by the main body of the Ram Armored Brigade.

Also attacking out of Darbashiyeh that Saturday morning was the reorganized 10th "Harel" Armored-Infantry Brigade, which had arrived in the *Ugdah* Laner zone after dark on June 9 and reached Darbashiyeh at around midnight. The brigade was to have sat in Darbashiyeh as the Northern Command reserve, but, with a ceasefire deadline looming, it became necessary for Dado Elazar to order the brigade to undertake an urgent overland mission across most of the Golan Plateau.

As soon as the Gavish Infantry Brigade troops and Ram Armored Brigade AMX-13s had cleared the road to the top of the escarpment and made way, Ben-Ari's French Shermans and halftracks struck out overland toward the TAPline Road. There, they turned southeast in the direction of Boutmiyeh. Their final objective was the vital southern Golan crossroads town of Rafid, which guarded a viable invasion route from the Damascus Plain into the southeastern Golan Plateau. (The Israelis had not yet captured all the terrain they wanted, but they were already thinking about how to defend it.) Once it reached the TAPline Road, the Harel Armored-Infantry Brigade passed rapidly and smoothly from the northern Golan scene.

At dawn on June 10, two other Israeli task forces were situated south of Darbashiyeh. A battalion of the 55th Parachute Brigade and a company of Ram Armored Brigade Super Shermans had secured Jelabina in a lightning attack between midnight and 0430. Farther south, about half of the Shehed Armored-Infantry Brigade had seized Dardara, Tel Hillal, and other objectives the previous morning and afternoon. Overnight, both forces were ordered to drive for the TAPline Road beginning at dawn and to link up on it as soon as possible. Both attacks began on schedule, and both forces reached the TAPline Road at about 1000. In the course of extending their holdings laterally along the excellent roadway, they did link up. Next, the two forces were ordered to mount coordinated drives to roll up from north to south the Syrian forward defenses facing out over Israel's Huleh Valley.

The paratroopers, who were mounted in borrowed halftracks, and their supporting Super Shermans stuck to the TAPline Road, but the Shehed Armored-Infantry Brigade French Shermans and halftracks descended partway down the escarpment again and delivered their attack along a supply road that ran right through the Syrian main line.

At the outset, the attack along the supply road was determinedly opposed in considerable strength by well-emplaced elements of the 132nd Syrian Reserve Infantry Brigade. The Shehed task force was grinding forward slowly but steadily when, at 1100, the opposition suddenly slackened. It soon became apparent that fewer and fewer Syrians were standing in the way. At 1300, the Israeli tanks and armored infantrymen arrived within sight of the Customs House, an obvious defensive keypoint right beside the graded road that wound up the escarpment from the B'not Yaacov Bridge. This position, which was a former British fort built on the site of an ancient caravansary, had been defended in considerable strength throughout nineteen years of hostility. There were determined Syrians holding the Customs House, to be sure, but not many of them. At 1400, the Shehed task force launched a classic attack on a defended position—behind plenty of air and artillery support—but they could have saved themselves the trouble. The ground assault punched right through a thin outer shell of opposition. Here, as everywhere on the Golan that early afternoon, prisoners stated that the main body of defenders had withdrawn hours earlier.

When news reached the reinforced paratroop battalion, on the TAPline Road, that the Customs House was in Israeli hands, this force, and a company of Shehed Armored-Infantry Brigade French Shermans, advanced up the main road toward Naffach. By previous arrangement, the paratroopers and the tank company halted 3 kilometers west of Naffach and established another strong blocking position. After 1500, when a patrol of Ram Armored Brigade Super Shermans out of Naffach made contact, patrols composed of French Shermans, Super Shermans, and halftrack-mounted paratroopers fanned out to check and clear a web of supply roads running from Naffach southward clear to the Yarmouk River, on the Jordanian frontier.

Likewise, after dropping off two armored-infantry companies to guard the B'not Yaacov Bridge and the Customs House, the remainder of the Shehed Armored-Infantry Brigade task force began the tedious but necessary task of clearing the abandoned front-line positions of the 8th Syrian Infantry Brigade and exploring Syrian supply roads along the escarpment as far as the northern shore of the Kinneret. By 1800, several patrols had advanced down the Syrian eastern shore of the Kinneret and on into Israeli territory. These patrols found only a few stragglers, abandoned positions, and discarded equipment.

Ugdah Peled's Saturday attack into the southern Golan Plateau was as unsettling and strange as *Ugdah* Laner's in the north. It had been Dado Elazar's intention to send *Ugdah* Peled into the southern Golan during the night on June 9–10, but the Cabinet had withheld permission until 1130 on Saturday, June 10. Then, because of routine operational delays, *Ugdah* Peled's multi-brigade attack did not jump off until 1300. As the largely ad hoc *ugdah* fanned out in its area of operations, it encountered no opposition. None.

Leaping and driving forward madly throughout the afternoon, *Ugdah* Peled occupied virtually every choice piece of defensive real estate in the southern Golan. In many cases, in compliance with orders from on high, the unopposed Israeli forces voluntarily halted on good ground when they were perfectly free to advance at will deeper into Syria. By day's end, *Ugdah* Peled was firmly in control of the southern Golan as far as the Yarmouk River and Ruqqud Stream in the south and the defensible edge of the Damascus Plain in the east.

In the northern Golan, all roads ended in Kuneitra. After securing Mansoura late in the morning, the Mendler Armored Brigade spent the early afternoon advancing against diminishing opposition across good tank country northwest of the Golan's principal city. At 1430, only some thirty hours after opening its attack up the escarpment, the Mendler Armored Brigade Super Sherman battalion entered the city of 30,000 and found it utterly abandoned by its military garrison and entire populace alike. The brigade's main body set in to defend the Golan Plateau against a possible counterattack from along the Damascus highway while a large task force set off by interior roads to link up with the Harel Armored-Infantry Brigade in Boutmiyeh, a mission that was completed late in the day.

By nightfall on Saturday, June 10, 1967, Israeli forces were in firm possession of the entire Golan Plateau. The Israelis occupied excellent defensive positions facing south into Jordan, east toward the Damascus Plain, and northwest into Lebanon. At 1830, underscoring *Zahal*'s physical possession of the Golan, Syria officially accepted the United Nations truce proposal. Israel, which had everything it wanted, agreed a short time later to adhere to the U.N. ceasefire call. During the night, the fighting died away to nothing.

It turned out that the mysterious and then-inexplicable 0845 Radio Damascus announcement that Kuneitra had fallen after a bloody fight was the Syrian regime's way of throwing in the towel without actually admitting it. In a week that had seen two other Arab armies defeated and nearly destroyed by

Israel's lightning attacks, the Syrian regime was satisfied that it was putting into effect a convincing ploy that would both save its face and save the bulk of its army. The Syrian Army, of course, was less a field army designed to make war with Syria's external enemies as it was a tool of repression designed to make war with Syria's fragmented and mutually hostile minorities.

Unlike their Egyptian and Jordanian cousins, however, the average Syrian soldier had an abundance of fighting spirit that, properly channeled, might actually have led to a long and bitter war and, thence, to the Syrian Army's utter destruction. Right up until the middle of the afternoon of June 10, many *well-led* Syrian soldiers who were called upon to do so put up a fierce and spirited defense of their positions. Given that the war in the north was as good as lost the moment the Israelis won through at Qala and Tel Fakhr, it became the objective of the Syrian regime to save as much of its army of repression as it could.

During the night of June 9–10, the entire 42nd Syrian Brigade Group was swiftly and efficiently withdrawn from its strategic-reserve positions along the Kuneitra–Damascus highway. As it turned out, the Syrian regime had been willing to commit these four brigades to intimidating Israel, but not to a bloody and destructive defense of the Golan Plateau. During Saturday morning, three of the area-reserve brigades were withdrawn from in front of Kuneitra; only a portion of the 44th Syrian Tank Brigade advanced along the Mansoura–Kuneitra axis to slow the Mendler Armored Brigade before it could cut the egress from the Golan front via Kuneitra. Other elements of the 44th Syrian Tank Brigade advanced along the roads to Vasit and Naffach to prevent the Israelis from reaching Kuneitra too early from the west, but they apparently did not seriously engage Israeli forces before they, too, were finally withdrawn. The 35th Syrian Brigade Group's 8th and 19th Syrian Infantry brigades also withdrew from the central and southern Golan in good order and more or less intact. On the other hand, the 11th Syrian Infantry Brigade, the 132nd Syrian Reserve Infantry Brigade, and as many as seven Syrian National Guard tank and infantry battalions were destroyed or nearly destroyed in the northern Golan.

By admitting to the loss of Kuneitra following a purely fanciful defiant last battle (and doing so six hours before the city fell without a battle at all), the Syrian strongmen implied to the Arab world outside Syria that they had gone down fighting, and they signaled to the subject populations inside Syria that they had done their duty against the hated Zionist occupiers.

*   *   *

Syria admitted the loss of 145 soldiers killed and 1,650 wounded on the Golan, but reports from other sources support much higher figures—an estimated 2,500 killed and 5,000 wounded, plus 591 prisoners. (All the prisoners were later traded for the one Israeli pilot who survived a bailout over Syria.) Given the size of Syria's actual commitment to the war with Israel and the length of the fight, equipment losses were staggering: As many as 185 of 265 Syrian artillery pieces and over half of 200 antiaircraft guns were destroyed or captured; approximately eighty tanks were destroyed and forty were captured; thousands of personal weapons, mortars, and machine guns were captured; and so forth. Thanks to its timely retreat, the Syrian Army was far from destroyed, but its ability to fight was severely degraded.

Israel lost 127 soldiers and airmen killed and as many as 600 wounded in the thirty-hour battle for the Golan Heights. Two civilians were killed and sixteen were wounded in Syrian bombardments during the six days of the war.

By mounting its dangerous and unprecedented multiple armored attacks up the impossibly steep Golan escarpment, Israel gained an important strategic foothold—gateways to Damascus and southern Lebanon, and a position outflanking eastern Jordan. She also ensured the flow of water from two of the Jordan River's three main sources. Also, *Zahal* lifted the nineteen-year siege the Syrians had imposed upon seventeen Israeli towns and settlements situated in the immediate shadow of the Golan escarpment.

Epilogue

Within a week of Israel's acceptance of all the United Nations ceasefire resolutions, nearly every one of the 200,000 *Zahal* Reservists called up for the May–June emergency had been demobilized. Within a month, nose-to-tail supply flights by huge Soviet cargo planes had made good the losses of and in fact upgraded the Egyptian Army. On July 1, 1967, Egyptian forces on the west bank of the Suez Canal opened fire on Israeli forces occupying the cast bank. This marked the beginning of the three-year-long War of Attrition, in which hundreds of Israelis and possibly thousands of Egyptians died. On October 6, 1973, Egypt and Syria attacked Israel simultaneously across the Suez Canal and frontally against the Golan Plateau. Israel won the 1973 war and, with Egypt at least, embarked on the long process of making a peace. In 1982, Israel and Syria again fought a brief and largely unheralded war in southern Lebanon, and they remain bitter enemies today. Jordan, which has not fought a war with Israel since June 1967, remains the domain of King Hussein. To date (mid 1992), the Palestinians are yet under Israeli occupation on the West Bank and in Gaza, but there is finally some movement toward peaceful dialogue.

Zahal, whose finest hour by far was the 1967 war, is more powerful than ever, truly a force to be reckoned with. Many of the leading figures of 1967 went on to bigger and better things. Dado Elazar became chief of staff after Chaim Bar-Lev, who followed Yitzhak Rabin. Rabin was briefly the prime minister and later served as minister of defense. Motta Gur and Raful Eitan also became chiefs of staff. Arik Sharon commanded an *ugdah* in Sinai during the Yom Kippur War and has served in the cabinets of a number of Likud coalition governments, as has Raful.

By now, all or nearly all of the youngest warriors of 1967 have left the Standing Army and have even retired from the Reserves. They have been replaced by younger men, some not even born in 1967. But their legacy lives on—oh, my, how it lives on! In modern times, there has never been a bigger surprise than the one *Zahal* sprang on its Arab enemies—or on the military pundits of the world—in 1967, and *Zahal* has worked especially hard each and every day since to do and be even more than Israel and the world have come to expect of it. It was resting on old laurels in October 1973, and it nearly lost the one war it could not afford to lose. But it has been powerful and vigilant ever since. And though its goals have sometimes become enslaved to hateful political intentions, its ultimate purpose remains unaltered and untarnished: As long as any of Israel's neighbors remain implacably hostile to the survival of the Jewish state, then *Zahal* remains Israel's first, last, and best instrument of survival.

1967 Order of Battle

ISRAEL DEFENSE FORCE

Minister of Defense	Moshe Dayan
Chief of Staff	MajGen Yitzhak Rabin
Deputy Chief of Staff	BriGen Chaim Bar-Lev
General Staff Branch	BriGen Ezer Weizman
Operations	BriGen Rechavam Ze'evi
Intelligence	BriGen Aharon Ya'ariv
Manpower	BriGen Shmuel Eyal
Quartermaster	BriGen Matityahu Peled
Air Force	BriGen Mordechai Hod
Navy	BriGen Shlomo Erel

GHQ RESERVE

10th Armored-Infantry Bde[1]   Col Uri Ben-Ari
  1 French Sherman Bn
  2 Armored-Infantry Bns
  1 Centurion Company

Gavish Infantry Brigade[2]   Col Yehuda Gavish
  3 Motorized Infantry Bns

---

[1] Attached to Central Command on 6/5 for duty against Jordan.
[2] Deployed around Beit Shean.

427

+   4 Infantry Bdes

            SOUTHERN COMMAND   BriGen Yeshayahu Gavish

Granit Force   Col Yisrael Granit
    1 AMX-13 Bn
    1 106mm Jeep Rcn Company

Sharm el-Sheikh Task Force   Col Aharon Davidi
    2 Parachute Bns

El Arish Task Force   Col Mordechai Gur
    55th Parachute Bde[3]
    3 Parachute Bns

Gaza Task Force
    Reshef Armored-Infantry Bde   Col Yehuda Reshef
    2 Armored-Infantry Bns
    1 AMX-13 Bn
—   halftracks (*to 202nd Bde*)

Southern Sinai Diversion Force
    Mendler Armored Bde   Col Avraham Mendler
    1 Super Sherman Bn
    1 Centurion Bn
    1 Armored-Infantry Bn

            TAL Armored Division   BriGen Yisrael Tal

2 SP Artillery Bns

Baron Force   Col Uri Baron
    Armor School Patton Bn
    1 AMX-13 Rcn Company

_____

[3]Transferred to Central Command on 6/5.

7th Armored Bde   Col Shmuel Gonen
   1 Patton Bn
   1 Centurion Bn
   1 Armored-Infantry Bn
− 1 Patton Company (*to 202nd Bde*)

202nd Parachute Bde   Col Rafael Eitan
   2 Parachute Bns
− 1 Parachute Bn (*to Sharm Force*)
+ 1 Patton Company (*from 7th Bde*)
+ halftracks (*from Reshef Bde*)

Aviram Armored Bde   Col Menachem Aviram
   1 Super Sherman Bn
   1 AMX-13 Bn
   1 Armored-Infantry Bn

      YOFFE Armored Division   BriGen Avraham Yoffe

Shadmi Armored Bde   Col Issachar Shadmi
   2 Centurion Bns
   1 Armored-Infantry Bn

Sela Armored Bde   Col Elchanen Sela
   2 Centurion Bns
   1 Armored-Infantry Bn

     SHARON Armored-Infantry Division   BriGen Ariel Sharon

   1 AMX-13 Rcn Bn
   1 Engineer Bn
   6 Artillery Bns

Zippori Armored Bde   Col Mordechai Zippori
   1 Centurion Bn
   1 Super Sherman Bn
   1 Armored-Infantry Bn

Adam Infantry Bde   Col Yekutiel Adam
    3 Infantry Bns

31st Parachute Bde   Col Dani Matt
    2 Parachute Bns
—   1 Parachute Bn (to *Sharm Force*)

CENTRAL COMMAND   BriGen Uzi Narkiss

+ 55th Parachute Bde[4]
+ 10th Armored-Infantry Bde[5]

Jerusalem

16th Infantry Bde   Col Eliezer Amitai
    4 Infantry Bns[6]
    1 French Sherman Squadron

West Bank

4th Infantry Bde[7]   Col Moshe Yotvat
    3 Motorized Infantry Bns
Shaham Infantry Bde[8]   Col Ze'ev Shaham
    3 Motorized Infantry Bns
+   1 French Sherman Squadron

NORTHERN COMMAND   BriGen David Elazar

Deputy   BriGen Dan Laner

---

[4]Transferred from Southern Command on 6/5.
[5]Transferred from GHQ Reserve on 6/5.
[6]The 16th Brigade also included 4 second-line infantry battalions.
[7]Deployed opposite Latrun.
[8]Deployed opposite Kalkilya.

1st Mechanized-Infantry Bde	Col Yona Efrat
3 Mechanized-Infantry Bns	
Shehed Armored-Infantry Bde	Col Emmanuel Shehed
1 French Sherman Bn	
2 Armored-Infantry Bns	

+ 55th Parachute Bde[9]
+ Mendler Armored Bde[10]
+ Gavish Infantry Bde[11]
+ 1 Bn of 31st Parachute Bde[12]
+ 10th Armored-Infantry Bde[13]

PELED Armored Division[14]	BriGen Elad Peled
Bar-Kochva Armored Bde	LtCol Moshe Bar-Kochva
2 Super Sherman Bns	
1 Armored-Infantry Bn	
1 Jeep/AMX-13 Rcn Bn	
Ram Armored Bde	Col Uri Ram
1 Centurion Bn	
1 Super Sherman Bn	
1 Armored-Infantry Bn	
1 AMX-13 Rcn Bn	
Avnon Infantry Bde	Col Aharon Avnon
3 Motorized Infantry Bns	

---

[9] Transferred from Jerusalem on 6/7 for duty in Syria.

[10] Transferred from Sinai on 6/7 for duty in Syria.

[11] Transferred from West Bank on 6/8 for duty in Syria.

[12] Transferred from Sinai on 6/8 for duty in Syria.

[13] Transferred from West Bank on 6/9 for duty in Syria.

[14] On 6/5; vastly altered on 6/8 and 6/9.

EGYPTIAN ARMED FORCES

Minister of War	Field Marshal Abdel Hakim Amer
United Arab Command	Gen Ali Amer
Armed Forces Chief of Staff	LtGen Anwar al-Khadi
Air Force	Gen Mohammed Sidki Mahmoud
Navy	Adm Soliman Ezzat
Sinai Front Field Commander	Gen Abdel Mohsen Mortagui

SINAI FIELD ARMY	LtGen Salah ed-Din Mohsen
2nd Infantry Division	MajGen Sadi Naguib
3rd Infantry Division	MajGen Osman Nasser
4th Tank Division	MajGen Sidki el-Ghoul
6th Mechanized Division	MajGen Abdel Kader Hassan
7th Infantry Division	MajGen Abdel Aziz Soliman
20th PLA Infantry Division	MajGen Mohammed Abdel Moneim Hussein
Shazli Armored Task Force	MajGen Saad el-Shazli
Sharm el-Sheikh Force	Brig. Mohammed Abdel Moneim Khalil

JORDANIAN FRONT

United Arab Command   Gen Abdul Moneim Riadh[1]
    8th Iraqi Motorized-
Infantry Bde
+   1 Palestinian Infantry Bn
    33rd Egyptian Commando Bn
    53rd Egyptian Commando Bn

---

[1] Egyptian Army.

JORDANIAN ARMED FORCES

Commander in Chief	Field Marshal Habis el-Majali
Deputy Commander in Chief	Gen Sherif Nasir bin Jamil
Chief of Staff	MajGen Amer Khammash
Air Force	Gen Mufadi Abdul Musleh

West Bank Force   MajGen Mohammed Ahmed Salim

El Hashimi Infantry Bde[2]	Col Kamal el-Taher
El Yarmouk Infantry Bde[3]	Col Mufadi Abdul Musleh
Hittin Infantry Bde[4]	Brig. Bahjet Muhaisin
Imam Ali Infantry Bde[5]	Brig. Ahmed Shihadeh
Khalid Ibn el-Walid Infantry Bde[6]	LtCol Awad Mohammed el-Khalidi
King Talal Infantry Bde[7]	Brig. Ata Ali Hazza'a
Princess Alia Infantry Bde[8]	Brig. Turki Baarah
Qadisiyeh Infantry Bde[9]	Brig. Qasim el-Maayteh
40th Armored Bde[10]	Brig. Rakan Inad el-Jazi
60th Armored Bde[11]	Brig. Sherif Zaid bin Shaker
10th Independent Tank Bn[12]	
12th Independent Tank Bn[13]	

(+ 1 Infantry Bde near Amman)

---

[2] Deployed in Latrun salient and northward with HQ in Ramallah.

[3] Deployed in northeast Samaria.

[4] Deployed in Judea with HQ in Hebron.

[5] 2 Bns and HQ deployed northwest of Jerusalem, and 1 Bn deployed in Jerusalem.

[6] Deployed in northwestern Samaria with HQ in Jenin.

[7] Deployed in Jerusalem.

[8] Deployed in western Samaria with HQ in Nablus.

[9] Deployed east of Jordan River opposite Beit Shean.

[10] Deployed around Damiya Bridge.

[11] Deployed southeast of Jericho.

[12] Deployed around Hebron.

[13] Deployed around Nablus.

SYRIAN ARMED FORCES

Minister of Defense	LtGen Hafez al-Assad
Army Chief of Staff	MajGen Ahmed Souedani
Air Force	LtGen Hafez al-Assad

FIELD ARMY   MajGen Ahmed Souedani

Northern Golan

12th Brigade Group   Col Ahmed Amir
   11th Infantry Bde
   44th Tank Bde
   89th Reserve Infantry Bde
   132nd Reserve Infantry Bde

Southern Golan

35th Brigade Group   BriGen Said Tayan
   8th Infantry Bde
   17th Mechanized Infantry Bde
   19th Infantry Bde
   32nd Infantry Bde

Damascus Highway

42nd Brigade Group   BriGen Abdul Razzak Dardari
   14th Tank Bde
   25th Infantry Bde
   50th Reserve Infantry Bde
   60th Reserve Infantry Bde

(+ 1 Infantry Bde near Latakia, 1 Infantry Bde near Homs, and
   1 Mechanized-Infantry Bde near Damascus)

Bibliography

BOOKS

Allon, Yigal. *The Making of Israel's Army*. New York: Universe Books, 1971.

———. *Shield of David: The Story of Israel's Armed Forces*. New York: Random House, 1970.

Associated Press. *Lightning Out of Israel: The Six-Day War in the Middle East*. New York: Associated Press, 1967.

Barker, A. J. *Six Day War*. New York: Ballantine Books, 1974.

Bell, J. Bowyer. *The Long War: Israel and Arabs Since 1946*. Englewood Cliffs, New Jersey: Prentice-Hall, 1946.

Byford-Jones, W. *The Lightning War*. Indianapolis: Bobbs-Merrill Company, 1967.

Churchill, Randolph S., and Winston S. Churchill. *The Six Day War*. Boston: Houghton Mifflin Company, 1967.

Dayan, Moshe. *Moshe Dayan: The Story of My Life*. New York: William Morrow, 1976.

Donovan, Robert J. *Israel's Fight for Survival*. New York: New American Library, 1967.

Dupuy, Trevor N. *Elusive Victory: The Arab-Israeli Wars, 1947–1974*. New York: Harper & Row, 1978.

Generals of Israel (various editors). Tel Aviv: Hadar Publishing House, 1968.

Gruber, Ruth. *Israel on the Seventh Day*. New York: Hill and Wang, 1968

Gur, Mordechai. *The Battle for Jerusalem*. New York: Popular Library, 1974.

Heikal, Mohammed. *The Cairo Documents*. New York: Doubleday, 1973.

435

Herzog, Chaim. *The Arab-Israeli Wars*. New York: Random House, 1982.

Hunnicutt, R. P. *Sherman: A History of the American Medium Tank*. Novato, California: Presidio Press, 1978.

Hussein, King of Jordan. *My "War" With Israel*. New York: William Morrow, 1969.

Irving, Clifford. *The Battle of Jerusalem: The Six-Day War of June, 1967*. New York: Macmillan, 1970.

Jackson, Robert. *The Israeli Air Force Story*. London: Tom Stacey Ltd., 1970.

Kimche, David, and Dan Bawley. *The Sandstorm: The Arab-Israeli War of June 1967*. New York: Stein & Day, 1968.

Laquer, Walter. *The Road to Jerusalem: The Origins of the Arab-Israeli Conflict, 1967*. New York: Macmillan, 1968.

Larteguy, Jean. *The Walls of Israel*. New York: M. Evans and Company, 1969.

Luttwak, Edward, and Dan Horowitz. *The Israeli Army*. New York: Harper & Row, 1975.

Macksey, Kenneth. *The Guinness Book of Tank Facts and Feats*. Enfield, UK: Guinness Superlatives Ltd., 1980.

————. *Tank Versus Tank: The Illustrated Story of Armored Battlefield Conflict in the Twentieth Century*. Topsfield, Massachusetts: Salem House Publishers, 1988.

MacLeish, Roderick. *The Sun Stood Still: Perspectives on the Arab-Israeli Conflict*. New York: Atheneum, 1967.

Marshall, S. L. A. *Swift Sword: The Historical Record of Israel's Victory, June 1967*. New York: American Heritage Publishing, 1967.

Moskin, J. Robert. *Among Lions: The Battle for Jerusalem, June 5–7, 1967*. New York: Random House, 1982.

Neff, Donald. *Warriors For Jerusalem: The Six Days That Changed the Middle East*. New York: Linden Press, 1984.

Nutting, Anthony. *Nasser*. New York: E. P. Dutton, 1972.

O'Ballance, Edgar. *The Third Arab-Israeli War*. Hamden, Connecticut: Archon Books, 1972.

Peres, Shimon. *David's Sling: The Arming of Israel*. New York: Random House, 1971.

Rabin, Yitzhak. *The Rabin Memoirs*. Boston: Little Brown, 1979.

Rabinovich, Abraham. *The Battle for Jerusalem, June 5–7, 1967*. Philadelphia: Jewish Publications Society, 1972.

Rolbant, Samuel. *The Israeli Soldier: Profile of an Army*. London: Thomas Yoseloff Ltd., 1970.

Rothenberg, Gunther E. *The Anatomy of the Israeli Army*. New York: Hippocrene, 1979.

Rubenstein, Murray and Richard Goldman. *Shield of David: An Illustrated History of the Israeli Air Force*. Englewood Cliffs, New Jersey: Prentice-Hall, 1978.

Safran, Nadav. *War to War: The Arab-Israeli Confrontation, 1948–1967*. New York: Pegasus, 1969.

Schiff, Ze'ev. *A History of the Israeli Army: 1874 to the Present*. New York: Macmillan, 1985.

Stevenson, William. *Strike Zion!* New York: Bantam Books, 1967.

Teveth, Shabtai. *The Tanks of Tammuz*. London: Weidenfeld & Nicholson, 1969.

Weizman, Ezer. *On Eagles' Wings*. New York: Macmillan, 1976.

Wylie, J. C. *Military Strategy: A General Theory of Power Control*. Annapolis: Naval Institute Press, 1989.

Young, Peter. *The Israeli Campaign, 1967*. London: William Kimber, 1967.

PERIODICALS

Blanchard, Allan E. "The 6-Day War," *Army*, August 1967.

Ganz, A. Harding. "Abu Ageila," *Armor*, July–August 1974.

Heiman, Leo. "Infantry in the Middle East, Part One," *Infantry*, January–February 1968.

———. "Infantry in the Middle East, Part Two," *Infantry*, March–April 1968.

Kotsch, W. J. "The Six-Day War of 1967," *U.S. Naval Institute Proceedings*, June 1968.

Liddell Hart, B. H. "Strategy of a War," *Military Review*, November 1968.

Menzel, Sewall H. "Zahal Blitzkrieg," *Armor*, November–December 1968.

O'Brien, Philip. "The Six-Day War of 1967," *U.S. Naval Institute Proceedings*, September 1968.

Shoemaker, R. L. "The Arab-Israeli War," *Military Review*, August 1968.

Wallach, Dr. J. L. "The Israeli Armoured Corps," *Armor*, May–June, 1968.

Weller, Jac. "Lessons from the Six-Day War," *Military Review*, November 1971.

SPECIAL STUDIES

Day, Robert L. "The Arab-Israeli Conflict of June 1967: A Limited War," U.S. Army War College, 1973.

Farris, Karl. "Growth and Change in the Israeli Defense Forces Through Six Wars," U.S. Army War College, 1987.

McGruder, Beverly L. "A Study of Israeli Decisionmaking," U.S. Army War College, 1973.

Index